The UN Convention on the Rights of Persons with Disabilities

International Studies in Human Rights

Volume 100

The UN Convention on the Rights of Persons with Disabilities

European and Scandinavian Perspectives

Edited by
Oddný Mjöll Arnardóttir and Gerard Quinn

MARTINUS
NIJHOFF
PUBLISHERS

LEIDEN • BOSTON
2009

This book is printed on acid-free paper.

Library of Congress Cataloging-in-Publication Data

The UN Convention on the Rights of Persons with Disabilities : European and Scandinavian perspectives / edited by Oddny Mjoll Arnardottir and Gerard Quinn.
p. cm. — (International studies in human rights ; v. 100)
Includes index.
ISBN 978-90-04-16971-5 (hardback : alk. paper)
1. People with disabilities—Legal status, laws, etc.—Europe. 2. Convention on the Rights of Persons with Disabilities and Optional Protocol (2007) 3. People with disabilities—Civil rights—Europe. 4. People with disabilities—Government policy—Europe. 5. Human rights—Europe. I. Oddný Mjöll Arnardóttir. II. Quinn, G. (Gerard) III. Title: United Nations Convention on the Rights of Persons with Disabilities.
KJC3490.U53 2009
341.4'85—dc22

2008054032

ISSN 0924-4751
ISBN 978 90 04 16971 5

PRINTED IN THE NETHERLANDS

Contents

Preface

The United Nations Convention on the Rights of Persons with Disabilities came into force on May 3, 2008, the same year that we celebrate the 60th anniversary of the Universal Declaration of Human Rights (UDHR).

The UDHR makes no direct reference to persons with disabilities. Yet the UDHR's famous first article sums up the Convention succinctly:

> All human beings are born free and equal in dignity and rights. They are endowed with reason and conscience and should act towards one another in a spirit of brotherhood.

For all too long people with disabilities have been denied the promise of the UDHR. Laws, both international and domestic, and societal attitudes, have too often treated people with disabilities as objects, recipients of care and charity, rather than as the autonomous rights holders that they are.

The Convention changes the status of people with disabilities in international human rights law. It is a strong convention that recognizes that equality, dignity, autonomy, independence, accessibility and inclusion are the keys to ensuring that people with disabilities are able to fully realize equal citizenship in the world.

Yet the Convention will be of little benefit if the rights in it are not made real in, as Eleanor Roosevelt put it in relation to the UDHR: *small places, close to home – so close and so small that they cannot be seen on any maps of the world.* That is where the individual rights of citizens are given effect.

There can be little doubt that to realize these rights we must understand the Convention both in the legal sense and also in the context of the societies, cultures, legal systems and economies of the States that will be bound by the Convention.

This book, *The UN Convention on the Rights of Persons with Disabilities: European and Scandinavian Perspectives*, is a remarkable first step in building that understanding. The noted scholars and activists that have contributed papers, some of whom were active in the drafting of the Convention, bring a scholarly and practical approach to analyzing the Convention and providing advice on how it might best be implemented. It is to be hoped that this work will lead the way for other similar analyses of the Convention in the context of all regions of the world.

The International Coordinating Committee of National Human Rights Institutions, which I have the honour of chairing, brings together more than 60 accredited human rights institutions with mandates to protect and promote human rights. National Institutions participated actively in the work of the UN committee that drafted the Convention. In the years to come I know that they will be eagerly involved in its implementation.

On behalf of the National Institutions and all the many others around the world interested in making the Convention a reality, I congratulate the editors of this volume, Gerard Quinn and Oddný Mjöll Arnardóttir, and the authors of the individual papers, for their significant contributions to this important topic.

Jennifer Lynch Q.C.
Chair of the International Co-ordinating Committee
of National Human Rights Institutions
and
Chief Commissioner,
Canadian Human Rights Commission

Acknowledgments

This book contains a collection of articles originally presented at the conference 'The Human Rights of Persons with Disabilities: From Social Policy to Equal Rights', which was held at Reykjavík University in September 2007. It represents the culmination of a project conceived by the editors at the 'Nordic Symposium on Human Rights', which was hosted by Professor Martin Scheinin at Åbo Akademi, Finland, in 2006.

The project would not have been realised without the input of the many individuals and organisations that actively contributed to it. We are grateful for their support. The conference was hosted by Reykjavík University and the Icelandic Human Rights Centre and organised in cooperation with the Organisation of Disabled in Iceland and the National Federation for People with Learning Disabilities in Iceland. We would like to thank these organisations and their representatives for all their hard work and commitment to the project. In particular we would like to acknowledge the earnest support of Þórður S. Gunnarsson, Dean of Reykjavík University School of Law, and Guðrún D. Guðmundsdóttir, Director of the Icelandic Human Rights Centre. Thanks are also due to the Icelandic Ministry of Social Affairs and the main sponsor of the conference, the European Commission, which provided funding through the 2007 European Year of Equal Opportunities for All.

Special thanks are due to the Irish Human Rights Commission which chairs the European Group of National Human Rights Institutions and its President, Dr. Maurice Manning, for its and his strong support and encouragement at European level. We would also like to thank Jennifer Lynch who is chair of the Canadian Human Rights Commission and who also acts as chair of the International Coordinating Committee of National Human Rights Institutions for her preface and more importantly for the key role she – and her colleague Harvey Goldberg – is playing in ensuring that national human rights institutions worldwide play a constructive role in making the Convention a reality.

We would also like to thank Professor William P. Alford, Vice Dean of Harvard Law School and Chair of the Harvard Project on Disability, who provided facilities at Harvard to enable us to finish the project, and Professor Paula Escarameia, member of the International Commission of Jurists and Professor Richard Nunan of the College of Charleston, who in their personal capacities provided useful comments on parts of the work contained in this volume.

Last but not least we would like to thank the authors of articles as well as the other participants at the conference for their extremely valuable contributions to the work.

Reykjavík/Galway, October 2008
Oddný Mjöll Arnardóttir and Gerard Quinn

Introduction

Gerard Quinn and Oddný Mjöll Arnardóttir

This timely collection draws together a range of European and Scandinavian perspectives on the newly adopted United Nations Convention on the Rights of Persons with Disabilities (CRPD).[1] This Convention came into force on the 3rd of May 2008. At the time of writing it is well on its way to becoming one of the most ratified human rights conventions in the UN system. It is accompanied by an Optional Protocol that enables individual and collective complaints to be lodged with the new treaty monitoring body – the United Nations Committee on the Rights of Persons with Disabilities – which is set to be voted into existence by a Conference of States Parties in November 2008.

Europe in general has been much to the forefront of disability law reform in the past decade. The European Union (EU) Action Plan (2008–2009)[2] and the Council of Europe's Disability Action Plan (2006–2015)[3] have put in place an almost unstoppable dynamic of reform. The implementation of the Convention now figures prominently on the annual agenda of the EU Ministers responsible for disability and the EU Disability High Level Group (senior civil servants responsible for the disability sector across the EU) is also engaged in the process of reflecting on implementation. And the Scandinavian experience in reshaping its social model to support independent living and in ensuring adequate community support to hasten de-instutionalisation is worthy of study in its own right.

The EU – through its Presidency as well as through the European Commission – played an extremely important role during the negotiations of the Convention. Indeed, it should not be forgot that the Council of Europe also maintained a

---

[1] Convention on the Rights of Persons with Disabilities, GA Res. 61/106 (2007).

[2] 'Situation of Disabled People in the European Union: the European Action Plan 2008–2009' Communication from the Commission to the Council, the European Parliament, the European Economic and Social Committee and the Committee of the Regions, COM 738 final, 26 November 2007.

[3] 'The Council of Europe Action Plan to Promote the Rights and Full Participation of People with Disabilities in Society: Improving the Quality of Life of People with Disabilities in Europe 2006–2015', Recommendation of the Committee of Ministers, Rec (2006)5.

presence throughout the negotiations in New York. The fact that the European Commission has signed the Convention (on the basis of Article 13 of the Treaty of Amsterdam on non-discrimination as well as on the basis of Article 95 which deals with market harmonisation)[4] and is set to ratify it on behalf of the Institutions of the EU (as distinct from its constituent Member States) is an epoch making moment of huge constitutional significance in Europe. Its ratification by the Commission has a significance that goes far beyond the fact that it should help sustain and drive the European reform momentum in the disability field. In fact, it will be the first United Nations human rights convention to be ratified by the Commission and the precedent that this represents could very well lay the groundwork for future developments in the broader human rights field.

It is probably fair to say that, in the absence of a strong US presence from the outset (a fact that was universally regretted by the Global disability rights community), European ideas played a predominant role in shaping key parts of the Convention. What is equally interesting is that the dynamic of reform in Europe is itself now about to be reinforced by the Convention. Indeed, the Committee of Ministers of the Council of Europe recently debated whether to draft a new European convention on legal capacity issues in part because of Article 12 of the CRPD. And the CRPD has already been cited in briefs and arguments before both the European Court of Justice as well as the European Court of Human Rights. This form of normative osmosis is to be welcomed and demonstrates the transformative potential of international law at its best.

As might be expected, the European context of the Convention figures prominently in this collection. In her chapter Anna Lawson places the CRPD in a specifically European context and expands on how it might help refresh the European disability agenda. And in her chapter Lisa Waddington traces the connections and potential disconnects between the CRPD and EU law – always with a view to the ultimate reform and development of EU law. And in his chapter Judge Davíð Þór Björgvinsson of the European Court of Human Rights provides a panoramic overview on how the Strasbourg Court has dealt with disability thus far. Recent rulings that deepen the Court's understandings of discrimination as well as reach the issue of legal capacity are to be warmly welcomed. The interaction of the future jurisprudence of the European Court of Justice with the European Court of Human Rights (as well as the European Committee on Social Rights) on the issue of disability looks promising.

---

4 The legal bases for EC adhesion are set out in the European Commission proposal to Council to enable ratification: see, Proposal for a Council Decision on the signing, on behalf of the European Community, of the United Nations Convention on the Rights of Persons with Disabilities and its Optional Protocol, COM (2007) 77, final, 27 February, 2007.

It should be emphasised at the outset that the Convention does not purport to create new law. It seeks merely to clarify the applicability of existing human rights law in the specific context of disability. This means that those States that do not ratify are still bound by general human rights treaties as they apply to disability. Indeed, it is certainly plausible that treaty monitoring bodies as well as courts (especially the European Court of Justice and the European Court of Human Rights as well as the European Committee on Social Rights under the Revised European Social Charter) will increasingly draw on the CRPD as a tool in interpreting more general human rights obligations in the specific context of disability.

The papers contained in this volume comprise the bulk of presentations made at a pathbreaking conference on the new Convention held in Iceland and hosted by the Reykjavik University School of Law and the Icelandic Human Rights Centre in September 2007. Although wide ranging and worthy of serious study in their own right, there are nevertheless several cross cutting themes that connect them and provide useful insights into the nature of the Convention and what one might realistically expect from it.

The first cross-cutting theme has to do with the triumph of ideas that the Convention represents. It both reflects – and helps to clarify as well as accelerate – the shift from a traditional framework of reference on disability (often referred to as the 'medical model') to one based more explicitly on securing the rule of law and human rights for persons with disabilities. This paradigm shift has been informed by developments in disability studies, as discussed by Rannveig Traustadóttir in her chapter. It has been going on around the world for at least a decade. It is as if the Convention has crystallized this trend and so signals a shift from viewing persons with disabilities as 'objects' to be managed to 'subjects' with equal rights under the law.

The importance of this paradigm shift cannot be overemphasized. Indeed, it is remarkable that it has taken so long. One might have thought that the inherently 'universal' character of existing international human rights instruments would have been sufficient to secure the rights of persons with disabilities. In his chapter, Gerard Quinn, points out that the omission of any reference to persons with disabilities in most human rights treaties in fact is a symptom of a much deeper form of 'invisibility' – an invisibility that primarily exists within culture as well as within the 'normal' political process. It is as if the 'normal' default setting in the public policy apparatus of most countries is that disability costs, that the costs need to be contained and that separate welfare supports that reinforce social stereotypes of passivity and dependence can perform the job and cabin the costs. Reversing this policy default to one that insists that considerations of justice and human rights should be primary will be a considerable challenge. He suggests that the Convention will be ultimately judged by whether it can help internalise this new framework of reference within States. The Convention is not merely intended to be invoked to challenge particular pieces of legislation and policy that offend the rights of persons with disabilities that are produced by a political process that ignores their rights. It will ultimately be judged on whether it can change the process itself to the point that disability is seen primarily as an issue of justice.

A second cross-cutting theme in many of the chapters has to do with the much vaunted (but little understood) 'interdependency and indivisibility' thesis between civil and political rights on the one hand and economic, social and cultural rights on the other. In truth, all persons (whether disabled or not) depend on social supports at least at some point in their lives (especially when young or at the onset of old age) to make freedom and choice a reality. This underlying reality is simply more obvious in the case of persons with disabilities (though not for all of them). If one sought tangible proof of the interconnectedness of both sets of rights then disability is the obvious example. It is plainly not enough to enact anti-discrimination laws to break down arbitrary barriers. It is also necessary to assist people in getting past those barriers. The deeper paradox – one that obtains for all persons – is that personal freedom ultimately relies on social solidarity. In her chapter Ida Elisabeth Koch deals with the indivisibility thesis in the context of disability. There are many lessons here for other groups. And in his chapter Colm O'Cinneide explains the limits of existing international law (which tends to hermetically seal issues of formal justice from more substantive conceptions of justice) and how, by successfully integrating both sets of rights and focusing them on disability, the CRPD may point the way ahead in other fields.

Disability also brings out other interesting verities about economic, social and cultural rights. The political economy of freedom and choice depends on having the right kinds of supports in place at the right time and with the right result. Of course, one of the drawbacks of the classical 'medical model' of disability was not so much the complete absence of social supports but the reality that they were used to place people 'not on a pedestal but in a cage'.[5] The interesting thing about the shift to the rights-based framework of reference is that it reveals how these social supports were misapplied in the past to compound the social isolation of persons with disabilities. And it is also interesting because it reminds us that these rights ultimately subserve a higher purpose which is not merely to maintain people in dignity but also to prime them for a life of choice, participation and active citizenship in the community. Among other things, viewing social and economic rights thus (as freedom enablers rather than static supports)

[5] This phrase was famously uttered by Justice William Brennan when deriding paternalism toward women in *Frontiero v. Richardson*, 411 US 677 (1973). It could just as easily have been said of paternalism towards persons with disabilities.

provides a different vantage point on cost-benefit debates over social supports. It primes one to factor into the overall equation some sense of the value of the net contribution of persons with disabilities as active agents in their own right in the economy as well as in society. And, most importantly in the context of disability, it weighs heavily against separate, segregated programmes for persons with disabilities which have tended in the past to reinforce social assumptions of passivity and incapacity. To put this point negatively, this means dismantling social supports (such as institutions) that have only served to isolate and deny choice. To put this point more positively, it means a wholly new attitude to services (including community supports) to enable a genuinely independent life based on choice and preferences as well as participation and social inclusion.

A third cross-cutting theme is the concept of equality and non-discrimination that animates the Convention. It is noteworthy that the primary purpose of the Convention is stated in Article 1 to be 'to promote, protect and ensure the full and equal enjoyment of all human rights' for persons with disabilities. The drafters had a number of threshold choices at the outset. The first option was to draft a bald non-discrimination text. Such a text – as suggested in at least one State 'non-paper' – could have been short (perhaps two or three Articles) with a general prohibition against discrimination. Such a text could have been adopted fairly rapidly as most States respond favourably to the non-discrimination ideal and indeed many of the more advanced jurisdictions in the disability field have expressly adopted a non-discrimination approach. However, such a text would have lacked the specificity needed in complex areas like education to be a real driver of change. The second option was to follow the model of the Convention on the Rights of the Child (CRC) which takes great care to tailor the general human rights (both sets) to the particular situation of children. That would have had the merit of teasing out exactly where the obstacles to the equal enjoyment of these rights lay for persons with disabilities and to tailor all the rights accordingly. However, virtually no State had an appetite for this approach which would probably have taken much longer to bring to a successful conclusion. The end result is a curious hybrid between a simple non-discrimination approach and an approach that applies an informed understanding of non-discrimination to tailor a wide variety of substantive rights to the realities of persons with disabilitites (again, including both sets of rights). One reason this worked as well as it did had a lot to do with the fact that civil society groups were present throughout the negotiations and indeed played a decisive role on occasion in ensuring against a tendency to mechanically apply the non-discrimination principle to the various rights.

But the equality/non-discrimination approach is not without its own conceptual challenges. One dilemma has to do with the slippery Aristotelian notion of equality – treating equals equally and unequally unequally – as applied in the specific context of disability. The essence of the anti-discrimination tool is that it is unacceptable to treat certain individuals or groups less favourably than others in circumstances where they are similarly situated. Indeed, most of the rights are said to be secured 'on an equal basis with others.' Of course, the main conceptual problem in the disability context is that persons with disabilities are not always similarly situated with others. Through often exaggerated through stereotypes, the difference of disability can be real. However, this difference can be used – especially by courts – in two very different ways. Used negatively, it might be said that the differences are sufficient to justify existing exclusionary arrangements (to the point of even requiring them). Thus the 'natural difference' of disability might be invoked to explain/justify differential treatment. For example, some Governments might be tempted to argue that because of the significance of the 'difference' of intellectual disability, institutions are not only defendable also required to secure their equal rights. Used positively, it could be said that the difference of disability requires political authorities to respond affirmatively and in a way that underpins equal citizenship. It remains to be seen how the incoming Committee on the Rights of Persons with Disabilities will handle this conundrum. Suffice it to say, that vigilance will be required to ensure that it is not used negatively in order to rationalise any ongoing process of exclusion or segregation.

Another conundrum that attends the non-discrimination idea as applied in the context of disability has to do with the necessity for some positive action measures. Traditional non-discrimination law (including the Convention) gives a permission for 'positive action' but does not require it. Yet accommodating the difference of disability should mean more than merely abstaining from discrimination. Indeed, it is precisely because of these differences – and in order to respond affirmatively – that most comparative non-discrimination law in the context of disability takes one extra vital step in requiring 'reasonable accommodation' to the circumstances of the persons with a disability. This is not 'positive action' in the classic sense. The obligation of 'reasonable accommodation' is in fact one of the defining features of American and EU anti-discrimination law in the disability context and is indeed now a core feature of the new United Nations Convention on the Rights of Persons with Disabilities.

Even though 'reasonable accommodation is not part of 'positive action' it does lead to affirmative steps which can have very substantive and redistributive effects. For example the famous 1999 decision of the US Supreme Court in *Olmstead v. L.C. & E.W*[6] (declaring inappropriate institutionalisation to be a form of discrimination and thus mandating de-institutionalistion) might be cited as an example. This is especially so given that the would-be discriminator is often obliged to take the extra step of providing 'reasonable accommodation' in the

[6] 527 U.S. 581 (1999).

disability context. However, great care is needed when characterising 'reasonable accommodation'. It is obvious that it has some re-distributive effects. That is why it engenders a debate about whether it lies properly within the non-discrimination model or whether it (unwarrantably) extends it to embrace redistributive effects. Indeed, it is precisely because it can have such re-distributive effect that it was temporarily resisted by the EU Presidency during the climactic Working Group session in January 2004. The text of Article 2 as it now stands does however draw a direct link between a failure to provide 'reasonable accommodation' and non-discrimination. A violation of the former leads inevitably to a finding of a violation of the latter.

However, one should not draw too much out of this. This is not – as hoped by many and feared by some – an indirect way of rendering economic, social and cultural rights judicially enforceable. It is not a substitute for a separate debate about the enforceability of such rights. And in any event, Article 4.2 of the Convention must always be borne in mind to the effect that the more programmatic obligations contained in the Convention are to be achieved progressively. Granted, it will be difficult at times to distinguish between those elements of the Convention that are programmatic and those that are immediately achievable. The main point however, is that since the non-discrimination window onto social rights deals primarily with the justification/s of relativities between individuals or groups with respect to social rights it does not deal directly with the substance of those rights. The addition of an obligation of 'reasonable accommodation' does not alter that reality. In her chapter Brynhildur Flóvenz takes a closer look at the symmetry between civil and political rights and social and economic rights in the context of disability. And in her chapter Oddný Mjöll Arnardóttir sets out the various conceptual approaches to equality which frame some of the interpretive choices that the European courts as well as the incoming Committee on the Rights of Persons with Disabilities will face. This is useful especially when thinking about how formal and substantive conceptions of equality can be successfully married to ensure the objects of the Convention succeed.

A fourth cross-cutting theme has to do with implementation and monitoring – or the need to translate the majestic generalities of the Convention into hard domestic law and practice. Those who present during the negotiations were constantly reminded by States of the 'failures' of the existing system of international monitoring. Traditional international monitoring mechanisms had generally led to a paper mountain of unread State reports and the process placed considerable burdens on lesser developed countries which meant that they fell further behind in their reporting obligations. But perhaps the biggest failure of all was that these traditional monitoring mechanisms had failed to ignite a reform process. The transmission belt that should obtain between international obligations on the one hand and the dynamics of domestic reform on the other were not put in place. Various innovative proposals were put on the table to reverse this well-known deficiency and to make sure that the disability Convention was different. At the end of the day the drafters did opt to retain a fairly traditional treaty monitoring body (Committee on the Rights of Persons with Disabilities).

However, conscious of the need to embed a reform process, the drafters also took care to lay down and animate a matrix for domestic reform and a dialectic between the international and the domestic level. For example, the States Parties will be obliged to have a domestic 'focal point' within Government for implementation and Governments are obliged to consult actively with representative organizations of persons with disabilities (Articles 33.1 and 4.3). Furthermore, the States Parties are obliged to put in place an independent national monitoring mechanism (essentially a human rights commission or similar body or mix of bodies) to 'promote, protect and monitor' the implementation of the Convention (Article 33.2). Likewise this independent mechanism must actively consult with civil society. So the CRPD is innovative in this regard. Much will now depend on how this matrix of change can be animated. It probably calls on civil society groups not merely to deepen their knowledge of international law but to also develop their political entrepreneurship skills to interact constructively with Governments.

It is of course true that different legal cultures have different ways for ratifying international conventions. Some will not ratify until reasonably sure that their existing laws and practices pass muster. Others ratify rapidly and catch up later if some form of adjudication is made to the effect that their laws and practices run foul of international law. The CRPD does not of course purport to alter the reality of legal diversity – nor could it. It does, however, require State Parties to adopt appropriate laws, to repeal inconsistent laws and to effectively mainstream disability (Article 4). It is hard to see this happening in the absence of an ongoing domestic review process. In other words the Convention should be the occasion that triggers such an ongoing review process – one that must be done in active consultation with civil society. Furthermore, customary international law is to the effect that States that sign but which have not yet ratified conventions are nevertheless obliged not to do anything that would frustrate the objects and purpose of a convention. It is hard to see this happening (i.e., avoiding even an inadvertent violation of the Convention) without such an ongoing domestic review process in place. And indeed, it is one of the stated objects of international treaty monitoring that it would engender domestic debate about reform. All in all, it is hard to see how a State that ratifies but then fails to put in place some form of review process could be said to be acting in a manner consistent with its obligations. In their chapter and in addition to identifying the space the CRPD occupies under international law, Michael Stein and Janet Lord assess the Convention as a 'national action trigger'. This is quite crucial lest the CRPD remains just an ornament in the international ether. In his chapter Judge Holger Kallehauge takes stock of the different legal traditions around the world and how the implementation of the CRPD may nevertheless be successfully embedded in different legal orders. This too is important since it is possible to see the Convention come alive by respecting legal diversity. And in her chapter Ragnhildur Helgadóttir sets out how Scandinavian courts have wrestled with the domestic status of international treaties and speculates on how (whether?) the CRPD might be successfully invoked before domestic courts. This is another vital part of the jigsaw as it engages domestic courts (subject always to their jurisdiction) in the overall process of change.

A fifth cross-cutting theme has to do with the vexed issue of reservations. The changes and the reform process demanded by this Convention are in some instances profound and some States might be tempted to deflect some core obligations through the use of reservations and 'interpretive declarations' that may have the same effect. The Convention does in fact allow for reservations so long as they are not 'incompatible with its object and purpose' (Article 46.1). Leaving to one aside the question as to what criteria the Committee on the Rights of Persons with Disabilities should/could use in adjudicating whether a reservation went beyond the 'compatibility' test, international law does not yet appear to support the proposition that treaty monitoring bodies have this power and, even if so, what the legal effects of a finding of 'incompatibility' might be. The International Law Commission (ILC) has suggested that the various UN human rights treaties be amended to confer such a jurisdiction but this is unlikely in the immediate future. The ILC has yet to publish a long-awaited Study on the issue of reservations to human rights treaties. This is not merely an academic issue but is actually quite central to the CRPD since there are already many reservations and interpretive declarations. Perhaps a much broader point is that this problem of public international law is now a problem for the global disability community – and it must come forward with its own considered view on issues like reservations.

Finally, it must be remarked that Europe has responsibilities beyond its borders. The vast majority of persons with disabilities (perhaps as many as 500 million) live in developing countries. Law reform on its own will not necessarily enhance their status. It should be recalled that Article 32.1(a) of the CRPD on international cooperation, requires, *inter alia*, that the States parties (also the European Union) should effectively proof their development aid programmes from a disability perspective. If and when the Commission ratifies on behalf of the EU it is hoped and expected that that EU development aid programme – which is the single largest programme in the world – would do its part in ensuring that the Convention becomes an effective trigger for change where it is needed most.

The disability rights agenda has finally arrived at the global level. Europe has innovated in the past and is now set to accelerate the process of change. It is gives great hope to see both pan-European Institutions, the Council of Europe and the European Union – actively engaged. Perhaps disability is a good case study in how both organizations – working in a complementary manner – can together make a real difference in the lives of European citizens with disabilities as well as further afield.

Part I

From Social Policy to the Human Rights Law of the 21st Century

Disability Studies, the Social Model and Legal Developments

Rannveig Traustadóttir

1 *Introduction*

Disabled people and their allies worldwide have organized over the past few decades to challenge the discrimination and exclusion of disabled people from mainstream society. In particular, they have challenged the over-medicalized, pathological and individualist accounts of disability and the disabled people's movement has focused attention on social oppression and environmental barriers.[1] The politics of the disability rights movement has its roots in a family of social explanations of disability which have been developed by disability studies scholars and activists. This new social-contextual understanding of disability, most commonly referred to as "the social model," has created a new vision of disability and has influenced policy making at local and international levels. This re-conceptualization of disability shifts the focus from the individual to the environment and draws attention to the social barriers disabled people face in their everyday lives. Disability studies scholars have been instrumental in developing this new understanding of disability which has provided a foundation for legal development worldwide, including the adoption of the UN Convention on the Rights of Persons with Disabilities (CRPD).[2]

This chapter examines the roots of the personal experience, political activism and academic thought that has influenced the creation of "the social model." Although the social-contextual understanding of disability has many common characteristics worldwide, this new approach to disability has been expressed

---

1 Barnes, C., Oliver, M. and Barton, L. (eds.) (2002). *Disability Studies Today.* Cambridge: Polity Press; Barton, L. (ed.) (2001). *Disability, Politics and the Struggle for Change.* London: David Fulton; Campbell, J. and Oliver, M. (1996). *Disability Politics: Understanding Our Past, Changing Our Future.* London: Routledge; Hahn, H. (2002). Academic Debates and Political Advocacy: The US Disability Movement. In C. Barnes, M. Oliver, and L. Barton (eds.), *Disability Studies Today* (pp. 162–189). Cambridge: Polity Press.

2 Convention on the Rights of Persons with Disabilities, GA Res. 61/106 (2007).

and conceptualized in various ways in different countries, depending on the historical, social, cultural and academic contexts. In Britain the social model of disability has provided a materialist and structural analysis of the social barriers and exclusion experienced by disabled people.[3] In the Nordic countries a relational understanding of disability has been the most common,[4] and in North America the new conceptualization of disability has often been framed in terms of a minority group approach and civil rights.[5] In many countries the principles of normalization[6] and social role valorization[7] have also been influential and inspired the major reform of the last century, often referred to as the deinstitutionalization movement. Below is an account of the historical development and contexts leading to the formulation of the new social understanding of disability which has influenced policies and legal initiatives across the world.

2 *Disability Studies – Rethinking Disability*

Disability studies is a new scholarly discipline currently being developed in many countries with increasing numbers of disability studies courses, programs, scholarly journals, academic associations, conferences and researchers that focus their work on issues of disability.[8] Disability studies has developed in response to the increasing interest in the general area of disability and its perceived "prob-

---

[3] Barnes, Oliver, and Barton, *supra* note 1; Oliver, M. (1996). *Understanding Disability: From Theory to Practice.* Basingstoke: Macmillan; Thomas, C. (1999). *Female Forms: Experiencing and Understanding Disability.* Buckingham: Open University Press.

[4] Gustavsson, A., Tøssebro, J. and Traustadóttir, R. (2005). Introduction: Approaches and Perspectives in Nordic Disability Research. In A. Gustavsson, J. Sandvin, R. Traustadóttir and J. Tøssebro (eds.), *Resistance, Reflection and Change: Nordic Disability Research* (pp. 23–44). Lund: Studentlitteratur.

[5] Albrecht, G.L. (2002). American Pragmatism, Sociology and the Development of Disability Studies. In C. Barnes, M. Oliver and L. Barton, (eds.), *Disability Studies Today* (pp. 18–37). Cambridge: Polity Press

[6] Bank-Mikkelsen, N.E. (1969). A Metropolitan Area in Denmark: Copenhagen. In R. Kugel and W. Wolfensberger (eds.) *Changing Patterns in Residential Services for the Mentally Retarded* (pp. 227–254). Washington, DC: President's Committee on Mental Retardation; Grünewald, K. (1969). A Rural County in Sweden. In Kugel and Wolfensberger (eds.), *ibid.*, (pp. 255–287); Nirje, B. (1969). The Normalization Principle and Its Human Management Implications. In Krugel and Wolfensberger (eds.), *ibid.*, (pp. 179–195).

[7] Wolfensberger, W. (1985). Social Role Valorization: A New Insight, and a New Term for Normalization. *Australian Association for the Mentally Retarded Journal,* 9(1), 4–10.

[8] Albrecht, *supra* note 5; Barnes, Oliver and Barton, *supra*, note 1; Davis, L. (ed.) (2006). *The Disability Studies Reader* (2nd edition). New York: Routledge; Goodley, D. and Van Hove, G. (eds.) (2005). *Another Disability Studies Reader? People with Learning Difficulties and a Disabling*

lem" in today's societies. This is accompanied by a growing academic interest in explaining the place and meaning of disability in society and activist emphasis on empowerment, inclusion, normality and the politics of difference.[9]

In this context it is important to ask: What is new about disability studies? Clearly it is not new to study disability because "disability" has been the focus of scholarly inquiry for a long time. What is new is *how* disability is being studied and the approach taken within disability studies; an approach that is critical of the traditional ways of understanding disability and taken for granted knowledge about disabled people. For example, disability is traditionally understood as a problem, an abnormality and a personal tragedy. It has primarily been studied from a medical or clinical point of view where it has been as seen as the problem of the individual who needs to be cured, rehabilitated, fixed, taught, changed and trained to become as "normal" as possible. Prior to the 1980s the academic interest in disability was almost solely confined to individualistic, bio-medical explanations. With the development of disability studies in the 1980s and 1990s a new approach to disability was developed. Instead of taking the medical individual and pathological understanding for granted disability studies explored how this understanding of disability came about historically and how it has been socially created and culturally produced by social arrangements, through interaction, in literature, popular culture and the media.[10] Rather than viewing disability as an individual problem, disability studies focuses attention on the social, cultural, economic and political aspects of disability, and examines how environmental barriers, social attitudes and cultural images create and re-recreate disability. In an historical context this is, indeed, a new way of approaching disability.

As a new academic field disability studies has its origins in Britain and North America. Although disabled people's political activism can be traced back to the 19th century it was not until the1960s and 1970s that they began to organize

World. Antwerpen: Garant; Johnstone, D. (2001). *An Introduction to Disability Studies* (2nd edition). London: David Fulton.

[9] Bell, C. (2006). Introducing White Disability Studies: A Modest Proposal. In L. Davis (ed.), *The Disability Studies Reader* (2nd edition) (pp. 275–282). New York: Routledge; Grue, L. and Heiberg, A. (2006). Notes on the History of Normality: Reflections on the Work of Quetelet and Galton. *Scandinavian Journal of Disability Research*, 8(4), 232–246; Snyder, S.L., Bruggemann, B., Thomson, R.G. (eds.) (2002). *Disability Studies: Enabling the Humanities.* New York: Modern Language Association; Mitchell, D.T. and Snyder, S.L. (eds.) (1999). *The Body and Physical Difference: Discourses of Disability.* Ann Arbor: The University of Michigan Press.

[10] Snyder, Bruggemann and Thomson, *ibid.*; Davis, *supra* note 8; Shakespeare, T. (ed.) (1998). *The Disability Reader: Social Science Perspectives.* London: Cassell; Snyder, S.L. and Mitchell, D.T. (2006). *Cultural Locations of Disability.* Chicago: University of Chicago Press.

collectively.[11] Inspired by the political and social turmoil of that period disabled people protested against their incarceration in residential institutions and nursing homes, against poverty, exclusion and the discrimination they encountered. Early examples include the Independent Living Movement in North America, the Swedish Self Advocacy Movement and the Union of Physically Impaired Against Segregation (UPIAS) in Britain.[12]

From the outset, disability studies have also been closely related to the disability rights movement and disabled people's demands for citizenship rights and participation in every aspect of social life. Although non-disabled academics have taken part in developing disability studies, disabled scholars have provided the important leadership. In addition to being informed by the disabled people's movement, disability studies have also been inspired by new theoretical developments, in particular in the social sciences but also in the humanities. Led by feminist scholars in the 1960s, critical scholarship demanded that theories and research accounted for *all* human diversity, not just the white, middle-class, non-disabled, heterosexual, Western males who constituted the vast majority of academics in the 1960s and whose interests and viewpoints dominated research and knowledge production of the time. Women, disabled people, lesbians, gay men, and ethnic minority groups demanded that the academia also accounted for their lives and experiences.

In the larger academic landscape, disability studies belongs to a group of new interdisciplinary fields of study such as women's, gender and feminist studies, lesbian and gay studies, queer studies, African American studies, and other similar disciplines. What these interdisciplinary fields have in common is that they all emerged from social movements aimed at ending oppression, marginalization and social exclusion. Due to the connection to liberation movements there has often been a dynamic interaction between scholarship and activism with an emphasis on research that is empowering and liberating; is *for* people, not merely *about* them. Another characteristic shared by these disciplines is a critique of dominant theories and understandings that has constructed marginalized groups in negative ways. Examples of this is how disabled people have been portrayed as sick and deviant and their lives as a personal tragedy, how homosexuality has been presented as a crime, sin or sickness, black people as primitive and stupid,

---

11 Campbell and Oliver, *supra* note 1; Longmore, P.L. and Umansky, L. (eds.) (2001). *The New Disability History: American Perspectives*. New York: New York University Press.

12 Campbell and Oliver, *supra* note 1; DeJong, G. (1981). The Movement for Independent Living: Origins, Ideology and Implications for Disability Research. In A. Brechin, P. Liddiard and J. Swain (eds.), *Handicap in a Social World*. Sevenoaks: Hodder and Stoughton, in association with the Open University; William, P. and Shoultz, B. (1982). *We Can Speak for Ourselves: Self-Advocacy by Mentally Handicapped People*. London: Souvenir Press.

women as irrational and so on. Taken for granted notions of "normal" have also been opposed and new approaches to understand human diversity have been introduced. Within this scholarship key concept such as "gender" and "disability" have been challenged and re-defined.[13] These interdisciplinary fields also share an interest in the exploration of the connections between the social and biological. For example, the "gender" (social-cultural) and "sex" (biological) debate in feminist scholarship[14] and the controversy of the distinction between (social-cultural) "disability" and (biological) "impairment" in the British social model of disability.[15] In disability studies, "disability" is often treated in similar way as gender, sexuality and ethnicity, where disability is understood as socially constructed rather than a biological condition. Thus, the major characteristic of disability studies is the emphasis on a social and cultural understanding of disability and the economic and political aspects of exclusion and discrimination.

Disability studies has developed as an important new scholarly field. At the same time, however, it is in some ways more than an just academic field of study. It emerged from social movement of disabled people and has close links to disabled people's groups and to social and political action. Within disability studies there is an emphasis on emancipatory, collaborative, inclusive and participatory research where the power relations between the researcher and the researched is more equal than in traditional research relations.[16] Disability studies attempts to be accessible and engaged, but at the same time it must be independent from everyday politics and interests, retaining its academic freedom and commitment to knowledge and truth.

---

[13] Briadotti, R. (2002). The Uses and Abuses of the Sex/Gender Distinction in European Feminist Practices. In G. Griffin and R. Briadotti (eds.), *Thinking Differently: A Reader in European Women's studies* (pp. 285–307). London: Zed Books; Thomas, *supra* note 3; Traustadóttir, R. and Kristiansen, K. (eds.) (2004). *Gender and Disability Research in the Nordic Countries*. Lund: Studentlitteratur.

[14] Briadotti, *ibid.*; Butler, J. (1999). *Gender Trouble: Feminism and the Subversion of Identity*. New York: Routledge.

[15] Shakespeare, T. (2006). *Disability Rights and Wrongs*. London: Routledge; Thomas, *supra* note 3.

[16] Mercer, G. (2002). Emancipatory Disability Research. In C. Barnes, M. Oliver, and L. Barton (eds.), *Disability Studies Today* (pp. 228–249). Cambridge: Polity Press; Oliver, M. (1992). Changing the Social Relations of Research Production. *Disability, Handicap & Society*, 7(2), 101–114; Traustadóttir, R. (2001). Research with Others: Reflections on Representation, Difference and Othering. *Scandinavian Journal of Disability Research*, 3(2), 9–28; Walmsley, J. and Johnson, K. (2003). *Inclusive Research with People with Learning Disabilities: Past, Present and Futures*. London: Jessica Kingsley.

3 *What is Disability?*

The meaning of "disability" is currently one of the more controversial issues in disability studies and related fields. During the last couple of decades the disabled people's movements and disability scholars have challenged the taken for granted understanding of disability and struggled to re-define the meaning of being disabled. This has resulted in a number of approaches challenging the classical medical, biological, individualized model of disability.[17] What unifies the new approaches is a rejection of ways that focus solely on the individual's impairment and an assertion that social processes and cultural meanings greatly influence disabled people's lives and opportunities. This understanding shifts the attention from the individual and the impairment to the environment and the impact of cultural, social and environmental barriers.

Some authors, for example Oliver, claim there are two main approaches to understand disability.[18] One being an understanding that is based on an individual bio-medical view and the other an approach based on a social, structural and contextual understanding. Although this is an oversimplification and does not do justice to the complexity of disability it provides an understanding of the differences in these two approaches and highlights the new social understanding of disability. Thus, inspired by Oliver and Shakespeare, below is an outline of some of the characteristics of these two different views of disability.[19]

Individual or Medical Model	Social Contextual Model
• Focus on the impairment and the individual	• Focus on the social context and environment
• Emphasis on clinical and medical diagnosis	• Emphasis on the relationship between the individual and society
• Emphasis on individual deficits	• Emphasis on social barriers
• Views the person as the problem that needs to be fixed or cured	• Views discrimination, exclusion and prejudice as the problem
• Medical, psychological and rehabilitative services are the answers	• Ending discrimination, segregation and removing barriers is the answer

[17] Grue, L. (2004) *Funksjonshemmet er bare et ord (Disability is Just a Word)*. Oslo: Abstract forlag; Gustavsson, A. and Zakrzewska-Manterys, E. (eds.) (1997). *Social Definitions of Disability*. Warsaw: Zac; Kasnitz, D. and Shuttleworth, R. (2003). A Sociocultural Model of Impairment – Disability. Conference paper. *Disability Studies: Theory, Policy and Practice*, 4–6 September Lancaster University, UK; Thomas, C. (2007). *Sociologies of Disability and Illness: Contested Ideas in Disability Studies and Medical Sociology*. Hampshire: Palgrave Macmillan.

[18] Oliver, M. (2004). The Social Model in Action: If I had a Hammer. In C. Barnes and G. Mercer (eds.), *Implementing the Social Model of Disability: Theory and Research* (pp. 18–31). Leeds: The Disability Press.

[19] Oliver, *ibid.*; Shakespeare, *supra* note 15.

4 *Social Models of Disability*

In his book *Disability Rights and Wrongs*, Tom Shakespeare argues that there is not one social model but a "family of social-contextual approaches"[20] to disability. Below is an outline of three of these social approaches; the British social model of disability, the Nordic relational approach and the North American minority group understanding.

4.1 *The British Social Model of Disability*

The best known of the social approaches is the British social model of disability, originating in the 1970s in the British disabled people's movement.[21] An important characteristic of this model is that it distinguishes between *impairment* (the biological) and *disability* (the social). It is not the individual's impairment which causes disability, but rather that disability is caused by the environment which restricts people with impairments by placing social barriers in their way and otherwise oppressing them.[22] Thus, the British social model firmly places the cause of the problem faced by disabled people in the surrounding society. Michael Oliver, who has been influential in conceptualizing the British social model, describes it in the following way:

> In the broadest sense, the social model of disability is about nothing more complicated than a clear focus on the economic, environmental and cultural barriers encountered by people who are viewed by others as having some form of impairment – whether physical, mental or intellectual. The barriers disabled people encounter include inaccessible education systems, working environments, inadequate disability benefits, discriminatory health and social support services, inaccessible transport, houses and public buildings and amenities, and the devaluing of disabled people through negative images in the media – films and television, and newspapers.[23]

The benefit of the British social model is that it directs attention away from the individuals' mental or physical deficits to the way society includes or excludes them. It has its origins in materialist ideas about disability and society.[24] In the 1980s the social model of disability gained a status of enormous significance

---

[20] Shakespeare, *supra* note 15, p. 28.

[21] Campbell and Oliver, *supra* note 1; Finkelstein, V. (1980). *Attitudes and Disabled People: Issues for Discussion*. New York: World Rehabilitation Fund; Oliver, M. (1990). *The Politics of Disablement*. Basingstoke: Macmillan.

[22] Barnes, C. (1991). *Disabled People in Britain and Discrimination: A Case for Anti-discrimination Legislation*. London: Hurst & Co; Barnes, C. and Mercer, G. (2003). *Disability*. Cambridge: Polity; Thomas, *supra* note 3.

[23] Oliver, *supra* note 18, p. 21.

[24] Thomas, *supra* note 17.

in Britain, both within the disabled people's movement and in disability studies. Internationally, a large number of disability scholars and activists, among them *Disabled People's International*, have associated "the social model" with this formulation of disability.

The social model has been critically important for disabled people and the disability movement, both in Britain and elsewhere in the world. The most important impact of the social model is probably on disabled people themselves. Replacing the traditional deficit understanding with a social oppression approach is very liberating for disabled individuals. Instead of identifying the individual's deficit as the problem, it is society that is at fault. People do not need to be ashamed of being "abnormal" or feel sorry for themselves, instead they could be angry at society for discriminating against them. As a result, disabled people can think of themselves in different ways and become empowered to mobilise for social change, and could argue that it is society that needs to change, not disabled people.[25] Another important contribution made by the British social model of disability is its articulation of a simple, clear and easily understandable political strategy. Disabled people are disabled by society. Thus, the priority is to remove the disabling barriers. Rather than demanding better rehabilitation services, cure, therapy and training, the strategy should be social change.[26]

Despite the fact that the British social model has been extremely influential in Britain as well as internationally, it is not uncontested. In fact, it is highly controversial and many of the current debates in disability studies centre around it and there have been lively debates about the model's conceptual and practical merits, both within disability studies and the disability movement.[27] Below is a brief account of some of these criticisms and debates.

A common criticism of the British social model is that it places too much emphasis on social and structural barriers while ignoring the importance of cultural and experiential dimensions of disability.[28] The social model has also been criticized for not reflecting or articulating the experiences, needs and interests of people with particular kinds of impairments such as people with

---

[25] Shakespeare, *supra* note 15; Thomas, *supra* note 3.

[26] Barnes, C. and Mercer, G. (2001). The Politics of Disability and the Struggle for Change. In L. Barton (ed.). *Disability, Politics and the Struggle for Change* (pp. 11–23). London: David Fulton; Barnes and Mercer, *supra* note 22.

[27] An overview of these debates can be found in Shakespeare, *supra* note 15.

[28] Corker, M. and French, S. (eds.) (1999). *Disability Discourse*. Buckingham: Open University Press; Gustavsson et al., *supra* note 4; Shakespeare, T. and Watson, N. (2001). The Social Model of Disability: An Outdated Ideology? In S. Barnatt and B.M. Altman (eds.), *Exploring Theories and Expanding Methodologies: Where We Are and Where We Need to Go*. Research in Social Sciences and Disability, (pp. 9–28). London: Elsevier Science.

intellectual disabilities and deafness.[29] It has furthermore been argued that this model excludes or marginalizes large groups of disabled people on the basis of sexuality, ethnicity and gender.[30] Some have stated that although the British social model has provided an important rallying point for the disabled people's movement and associated political action, it has several inconsistencies and is flawed if not inadequate as a foundation for social theory.[31]

Feminists have been among those criticizing the British social model.[32] One aspect of the feminist criticism has to do with the distinction social modelists make between impairment (the biological) and disability (the social). Feminists have pointed out that in doing this, the model ignores the importance of the impairment itself, both in people's everyday lives as well as in disability theory.[33] Some feminists view this aspect of the model as dualistic thinking rooted in essentialism and modernism.[34] Another feminist criticism of the British social model of disability is related to the place of the personal, in particular personal experiences of impairment. Writers such as Liz Crow and Jenny Morris have argued that defining impairment as "private and personal" reflects a traditional patriarchal thinking which separates the personal from the public and the private from the social.[35] On a similar note Carol Thomas criticizes the social model for its preoccupation with "restrictions of activity" in the material world and argues for the importance of developing a "social relational approach" which can better account for the psycho-emotional dimensions of disability.[36]

---

[29] Corbett, J. (1996). *Bad Mouthing: The Language of Special Needs*. London: Falmer Press; Corker, M. (1998). *Deaf and Disabled or Deafness Disabled?* Buckingham: Open University Press; Goodley and Van Hove, *supra* note 8.

[30] Thomas, *supra* note 3.

[31] Shakespeare and Watson, *supra* note 28; Shakespeare, T. (2004). Social Models of Disability and Other Life Strategies. *Scandinavian Journal of Disability Research*, 6(1), 8–21.

[32] See feminist disability scholar Carol Thomas for an overview of this critique; Thomas, *supra* note 3.

[33] Thomas, *supra* note 3; Crow, L. (1996). Including All of Our Lives: Renewing the Social Model of Disability. In J. Morris (ed.) *Encounters with Strangers: Feminism and Disability* (pp. 206–226). London: The Women's Press.

[34] Corker, *supra* note 29; Corker and French, *supra* note 28.

[35] Crow, *supra*, note 33, Thomas, C. (2001). Feminism and Disability: The Theoretical and Political Significance of the Personal and the Experiential. In L. Barton (ed.), *Disability, Politics and the Struggle for Change* (pp. 48–58). London: David Fulton.

[36] Thomas, *supra* note 3; Thomas, C. (2002). Disability Theory: Key Ideas, Issues and Thinkers. In C. Barnes, M. Oliver, and L. Barton, (eds.), *Disability Studies Today* (pp. 38–57). Cambridge: Polity Press; Thomas, C. (2004). Rescuing the Social Relational Understanding of Disability. *Scandinavian Journal of Disability Research*, 6(1), 22–36.

4.2 *The Nordic Relational Approach to Disability*

How disability is understood in the Nordic countries is closely related to fundamental ideas about citizenship and equality which are long-standing basic principles and values of the Nordic welfare states.[37] A central part of this understanding in relation to disabled people can be traced back to the 1960s when Nordic authors were formulating the principle of normalization.[38] The context of the Nordic welfare state was crucial for the early development of the principle of normalization in the Nordic countries. Early critiques of long-stay institutions often focused on violations of human rights and unacceptable living conditions,[39] and one way to understand the development of normalization in the 1970s is to view it as an attempt to ensure that welfare provisions and citizenship rights should be extended to the entire population, including groups previously excluded such as disabled people.[40] This was accompanied by a fundamental challenge to the dominant biomedical/therapeutic perspective of the time and led to a rethinking of disability and disability policy in the 1970s where normalization became the steering principle. The new policies outlined the rights of disabled people, called for an end to segregated services, and argued that efforts should not address how to change disabled people, but rather that environments and societies should be adapted so that people with impairments could be included. Such thinking drew attention to the importance of the environment and that social change was important in order for disabled people to be included in everyday life.[41] This shift did not imply there was one single Nordic approach to understand disability, but is rather a family of ideas which locates the focus of problem-definition and target of solutions in the environment and the social context, in contrast to a view that locates the problem in the individual and its associated therapeutic discourses. Despite the Nordic emphasis on the social-contextual aspects of disability this new approach did not make a distinction between the biological *impairment* and the social-relational *disability* that is so critical to the British social model. In fact, many have found it difficult to make this distinction in the Nordic languages and the Nordic concepts that are

---

[37] Gustavsson et al., *supra* note 4.

[38] Bank-Mikkelsen, *supra* note 6; Grünewald, *supra* note 6.

[39] Grünewald, K. (ed.) (1971). *Manniskohantering på totala vårdinstitutioner: Från dehumanisering til normalisering. (Treatment of People in Total Institutions: From Dehumanization to Normalization).* Stockholm: Natur och Kultur.

[40] Grünewald, K. (ed.) (1989). *Medicinska omsorgsboken (The Book of Medical Care).* Stockholm: Natur och Kultur; Kristiansen, K. (1993). *Normalisering og verdsetjing av social rolle (Normalization and Social Role Valorization)* Oslo: Kommuneforlaget; Stangvik, G. (1987). *Livskvalitet for funksjonshemmede (Quality of Life for the Disabled).* Oslo: Universitetsforlaget.

[41] Tøssebro, J. and Kittelsaa, A. (eds.) (2004). *Exploring the Living Conditions of Disabled People.* Lund: Studentlitteratur.

equivalent to the English term "disability" are commonly used as umbrella terms to refer to groups of people with various impairments.

Norwegian sociologist Jan Tøssebro refers to the most common Nordic understanding of disability as "the relational approach." Although not a uniform Nordic understanding of disability, this approach appears to be fairly common in terms of the underlying ideology, principles and definitions, both in social science literature and in government policy documents in all of the Nordic countries. Tøssebro has summarised the main characteristics of this approach, as follows:[42]

First, disability is a person-environment mismatch or a "poor fit" between the individual's capabilities and the demands of the broader societal environment. This occurs because the person does not have capacities within the typical range, but also because the environment is not adapted to the whole range of human diversity. Accordingly, an individual is defined as disabled if a limitation, disease or impairment causes him or her to experience significant barriers in everyday life. Thus, disability is a relationship between individuals and the larger society.

Second, disability is situational or contextual. Whether a specific impairment is disabling or not depends on the situation or context. For example, deafness would not be a disability if everyone spoke sign language, and a blind person is not disabled when speaking on the telephone.

Third, disability is relative. Tøssebro uses intellectual disability as an example. During the 20th century the cut-off point for receiving this diagnosis varied throughout Europe from IQ=50 to IQ=85. Depending on the definition, somewhere between 0.5% and 15% of the population would be classified as intellectually impaired. Tøssebro argues that this also illustrates the constructionist element of disability definitions, including the arbitrariness of our dichotomies as an important aspect of our socially constructed understandings of disability.[43]

The Nordic understanding of disability stresses the complex and situated interaction between individual factors and the environment. This relational approach has been widely adopted in the Nordic countries and can now be found in most policy documents. However, it is underdeveloped as a theoretical understanding of disability and it has proven difficult to operationalize the relational concept when it comes to welfare provisions, special education and other services, which continue to rely on medical diagnoses and psychological

---

[42] Tøssebro, J. (2002). Leaving the Individual Out: Practical and Logical Problems. Paper presented at a Plenary Symposium "Understanding Disability: The UK Social Model and the Nordic Relational Approach" at the 6th NNDR Conference, *Disability Research, Theory and Practice*, 22–24 August, Reykjavík, Iceland; Tøssebro, J. (2004). Understanding Disability: Introduction to the Special Issue of SJDR. *Scandinavian Journal of Disability Research*, 6(1), 3–7.

[43] Tøssebro (2002), *ibid.*

tests to determine who qualifies for such services.[44] Although there are some obvious differences between the UK social model of disability and the Nordic relational approach, there are clearly strong similarities. Also, the debates and controversies around the British social model have inspired the Nordic discourse on the meaning of disability and have provided Nordic scholars and activists with a new perspective in the continuing work of developing a social-relational understanding of disability.[45]

4.3 *The North American Minority Group Approach*

The roots of the radical social-contextual understanding of disability in the USA are in disability activism in the 1960s, which among other things led to the development of the independent living approach and antidiscrimination legislation.[46] North American scholars and activists have developed a social understanding of disability but their re-defining of "disability" has not been as far reaching as in the British social model. UK social modelists have conceptualized disability as social oppression while North American approaches have mostly developed the notion of disabled people as a minority group, within the tradition of the North American thought. Many North American writers have argued that prejudice and discrimination against disabled people have to be combated through civil rights legislation, which will guarantee people's rights.[47] The work of North American theorists has also explored the important social, cultural and political dimensions of disability.[48] This scholarship, however, has not made the firm distinction between the biological (impairment) and the social (disability), a distinction that is a key element of the British social model of disability. Hence in North America the phrase "people with disabilities" is more common than the British politically correct "disabled people" indicating that people are disabled by society, locating disability in the social context and not as an attribute of the individual.

Despite the differences between the British, the Nordic and the North American approaches to disability, it is clear that the North American understanding places a major emphasis on the role of the social environment. As early as 1978,

---

[44] Tøssebro and Kittelsaa, *supra,* note 41.

[45] Gustavsson, Tøssebro and Traustadóttir, *supra*, note 4.

[46] Albrecht, *supra* note 5; DeJong, *supra* note 12; Hahn, *supra* note 1.

[47] Hahn, *supra* note 1; Rioux, M.H. (2002). Disability, Citizenship and Rights in a Changing World. In C. Barnes, M. Oliver, and L. Barton (eds.), *Disability Studies Today* (pp. 210–227). Cambridge: Polity Press.

[48] Hahn, *supra* note 1; Ingstad, B. and Whyte, S.R. (eds.) (1995). *Disability and Culture*. Berkeley: University of California Press; Rioux, *ibid.*; Snyder, Brueggemann and Thomson, *supra* note 9; Snyder and Mitchell, *supra* note 10.

Frank Bowe identified six forms of social barriers: architectural, attitudinal, educational, legal, occupational and personal.[49] Other scholars such as Amundsen also examine how the environment restricts people with disabilities rather than the inability of the individual.[50] Much of the current writings in North American disability studies echoes the same social and relational concerns found in Britain and the Nordic countries, and the North American overall orientation is social and cultural; not medical or individualistic.

Thus, although "the social model" has been conceptualized and articulated in different ways in different countries, there are also many common characteristics. The debates within the group of those promoting a social-contextual understandings of disability can be confusing. However, those concerned with human rights of disabled people and legal development to support these rights share an overall common understanding that can unite people across academic and geographical boarders.

5 *Disability Studies and Legal Development*

Disability studies has influenced legal developments in various ways, most importantly by re-defining the "problem" by directing the focus away from the individual bio-medical understanding towards a social-contextual view of disability. This has changed the way disability is defined and articulated in international documents and classification systems such as the International Classification of Impairments, Disabilities, and Handicaps (ICIDH)[51] and the International Classification of Functioning, Disability and Health (ICF).[52] The social understanding of disability was also an important aspect of the UN Standard Rules on the Equalization of Opportunities for Persons with Disabilities were this new social-contextual understanding of disability is articulated in the following manner:

> Towards the end of the 1960s organizations of persons with disabilities in some countries started to formulate a new concept of disability. That new concept indicated the close connection between the limitation experienced by individuals with

[49] Bowe, F. (1978). *Handicapping America.* New York: Harper and Row.

[50] Amundsen, R. (1992). Disability, Handicap, and the Environment. *Journal of Social Philosophy,* 23(1), 105–118.

[51] International Classification of Impairments, Disabilities, and Handicaps, World Health Organization (1980).

[52] International Classification of Functioning, Disability and Health, World Health Organization (2001).

> disabilities, the design and structure of their environments and the attitude of the general population.[53]

The social understanding of disability is also one of the cornerstones of the CRPD where the attention is on the importance of a social-relational approach with an emphasis on the interaction between the person and the social environment. The preamble to the Convention outlines its foundations and states that it is recognized:

> ...that disability is an evolving concept and that disability results from the interaction between persons with impairments and attitudinal and environmental barriers that hinders their full and effective participation in society on an equal basis with others...[54]

The Convention articulates a stronger emphasis on social barriers than the Standard Rules, indicating a firmer commitment to a social understanding which implies that many, and even most, of the difficulties experienced by disabled people are caused by social barriers.

6 *Conclusion*

This chapter has examined the relations between the disability rights movement, disability studies, the social model of disability and legal development. It has, in particular, explored the political and academic origin of "the social model" and outlined some of the diverse ways in which new approaches have conceptualized the social-contextual and relational nature of disability. The chapter has also discussed the origins and main characteristics of disability studies and how it has informed, as well as having been informed, by the disabled people's movements' social and political actions. The most important contribution disability research and scholarship has made to the disability rights movement is a re-definition of disability and the articulation of a new social understanding of disability. Disability studies scholars have theorized disability and the social oppression of disabled people as outcomes of the way fundamental activities are organized in society thus creating a new social-contextual understanding of disability. This conceptualization, usually referred to as "the social model" has provided the knowledge base which has informed the international legal development aimed at full participation and human rights of disabled people.

---

[53] Standard Rules on the Equalization of Opportunities for Persons with Disabilities, GA Res. 48/96 (1993), Introduction, para. 5.

[54] Convention on the Rights of Persons with Disabilities, GA Res. 61/106 (2007), Preamble, para. e.

Future Prospects for the United Nations Convention on the Rights of Persons with Disabilities

Michael Ashley Stein & Janet E. Lord

On December 13, 2006, the General Assembly adopted the United Nations Convention on the Rights of Persons with Disabilities (CRPD, or Convention)[1] along with its Optional Protocol[2] by general consensus.[3] The CRPD opened for signature on March 30, 2007, and entered into force on May 3, 2008.[4] As such, the Convention is the first human rights treaty of the twenty-first century, as well as the first legally enforceable United Nations instrument specifically directed at persons with disabilities.[5]

This chapter provides an overview of the background to the Convention's adoption, summarizes the contents of the CRPD, and then assesses its future

---

1 Convention on the Rights of Persons with Disabilities, G.A. Res. 61/106 (2007) [hereinafter CRPD].

2 Optional Protocol to the Convention on the Rights of Persons with Disabilities, G.A. Res. 61/106 (2007), entered into force 3 May 2008 [hereinafter Optional Protocol].

3 *See General Assembly Adopts Groundbreaking Convention, Optional Protocol on Rights of Persons with Disabilities: Delegations, Civil Society Hail First Human Rights Treaty of Twenty-First Century*, GA/105554 (United Nations Department of Public Information December 13, 2006), *available online at* <http://www.un.org/News/Press/docs/2006/ga10554.doc.htm>.

4 The CRPD text, along with its drafting history, resolutions, and updated list of States Parties is posted on the United Nations Enable website, *available online at* <http://www.un.org/esa/socdev/enable/rights/convtexte.htm>.

5 The CRPD required ratification by twenty States Parties to enter into force and trigger the establishment of a monitoring Committee on the Rights of Persons with Disabilities. *See* CRPD, *supra* note 1, at art. 45(1) ("The present Convention shall enter into force on the thirtieth day after the deposit of the twentieth instrument of ratification or accession."); *id.* at art. 45(2) ("For each State or regional integration organization ratifying, formally confirming or acceding to the Convention after the deposit of the twentieth such instrument, the Convention shall enter into force on the thirtieth day after the deposit of its own such instrument."); Optional Protocol, *supra* note 2, at art. 13(1) ("Subject to the entry into force of this Convention, the present Protocol shall enter into force on the thirtieth day after the deposit of the tenth instrument of ratification or accession.").

prospects for improving the lives of the six hundred and fifty million individuals with disabilities worldwide.[6] When looking forward we focus on three areas where we believe the Convention will have the most immediate impact, beginning with more abstract notions that include reconceptualizing disability as a human rights issue and moving thereafter towards more concrete results.[7]

1 *Toward a Disability Human Rights Convention*

From the time of its establishment in the wake of World War II through the end of the last century, the United Nations promulgated seven core human rights conventions.[8] Each of these treaties contains legal obligations that theoretically apply to persons with disabilities, but they are rarely applied in practice.[9] To

---

[6] Gerard Quinn & Theresia Degener, Human Rights and Disability: The Current Use and Future Potential of United Nations Human Rights Instruments in the Context of Disability 1 (2002), *available online at* <http://www.nhri.net/pdf/disability.pdf>.

[7] For earlier accounts that were drawn upon for this chapter, see Janet E. Lord & Michael Ashley Stein, *The Committee on the Rights of Persons with Disabilities*, in The United Nations and Human Rights: A Critical Appraisal ____ (Philip Alston & Frédéric Mégret eds., forthcoming Oxford University Press); Michael Ashley Stein, *Disability Human Rights,* 95 Cal. L. Rev. 75 (2007).

[8] Prior to the adoption of the CRPD, which represents the eighth UN hard law treaty, the core human rights treaties included: International Covenant on Civil and Political Rights, G.A. Res. 2200A (XXI), U.N. GAOR, Supp. No. 16 at 52, U.N. Doc. A/6316 (1966) [hereinafter ICCPR]; International Covenant on Economic, Social and Cultural Rights, G.A. Res. 2200A (XXI), U.N. GAOR, Supp. No. 16 at 49, U.N. Doc. A/6316 (1966) [hereinafter ICESCR]; Convention against Torture and Other Cruel, Inhuman or Degrading Treatment or Punishment, G.A. Res. 39/46, U.N. GAOR, 39th Sess., Annex, Supp. No. 51 at 197, U.N. Doc. A/39/51 (1984) [hereinafter CAT]; Convention on the Elimination of All Forms of Discrimination against Women, G.A. Res. 34/180, U.N. GAOR, 34th Sess., Supp. No. 46, at 193, U.N. Doc. A/34/46 (1981) [hereinafter CEDAW]; International Convention on the Elimination of All Forms of Racial Discrimination, G.A. Res. 2106 (XX), U.N. GAOR, Supp. No. 14, at 47, U.N. Doc. A/6014 (1966) [hereinafter CERD]; International Convention on the Protection of the Rights of All Migrant Workers and Members of their Families, G.A. Res. 45/158 of 18 December 1990 [hereinafter ICRMW]; Convention on the Rights of the Child, G.A. Res. 44/25, U.N. GAOR, 44th Sess., Supp. No. 49, at 16, U.N. Doc. A/44/49 (1989) [hereinafter CRC]. A ninth core convention has also recently been adopted but not yet entered into force: International Convention for the Protection of All Persons from Enforced Disappearance, G.A. Res. 61/177, 20 December 2006.

[9] For example, in the decade 1994–2003, seventeen disability-related complaints were asserted under the seven core United Nations instruments, but thirteen were declared inadmissible by their respective monitoring committees. The website maintained by the Office of the High Commissioner for Human Rights (OHCHR) contains detailed information on the operation of the United Nations human rights treaty bodies, and is *available online at* <http://www.ohchr.org/english/bodies/>. The general comments of the human rights treaty bodies and other work

invoke protection under any of these core instruments, a disabled person must either fall under a universal provision that by inference includes her as a person, or possess a separately protected characteristic in addition to her disability.[10] The principal difficulty with this approach is that existing human rights obligations are not tailored to address the specific barriers faced by persons with disabilities in the realization of their human rights. As such, human rights obligations have not been effectively utilized to address the situation of persons with disabilities, for example, regarding their access to justice or non-discrimination in the workplace.

Specifically, the International Covenant on Civil and Political Rights (ICCPR),[11] the International Covenant on Economic, Social, and Cultural Rights (ICESCR),[12] and the Convention against Torture and Other Cruel, Inhuman, or Degrading Treatment or Punishment (CAT)[13] are each universal in scope and so implicitly include persons with disabilities within their purview.[14] By comparison, the International Convention on the Elimination of All Forms of Racial Discrimination (CERD),[15] Convention on the Elimination of All Forms

product may be accessed through the OHCHR website, as well as the Netherlands Institute of Human Rights web page, *available online at* <http://sim.law.uu.nl/sim/Dochome.nsf>.

[10] *See generally* Gerard Quinn, *The International Covenant on Civil and Political Rights and Disability: A Conceptual Framework,* in Human Rights and Disabled Persons 69 (Theresia Degener & Yolan Koster-Dreese eds., Kluwer Academic Publishers 1995) [hereinafter Human Rights and Disabled Persons]; Philip Alston, *Disability and the International Covenant on Economic, Social, and Cultural Rights,* in Human Rights and Disabled Persons, *id.*, at 94; Manfred Nowak & Walter Suntinger, *The Right of Disabled People Not to be Subjected to Torture, Inhuman and Degrading Treatment or Punishment,* in Human Rights and Disabled Persons, *id.*, at 117.

[11] *See, e.g.*, ICCPR, *supra* note 8, at pmbl. (averring that "recognition of the inherent dignity and of the equal and inalienable rights of all members of the human family is the foundation of freedom, justice and peace in the world").

[12] *See, e.g.*, ICESCR, *supra* note 8, at art. 2, para. 2 (the rights enumerated in the ICESCR "will be exercised without discrimination of any kind as to race, colour...or other status").

[13] *See, e.g.*, CAT, *supra* note 8, at art. 1(1) (implicitly covering disability-based discrimination within its definition of torture which is "any act by which severe pain or suffering, whether physical or mental, is intentionally inflicted on a person for such purposes as obtaining from him or a third person information or a confession, punishing him for an act he or a third person has committed or is suspected of committing, or intimidating or coercing him or a third person, *or for any reason based on discrimination of any kind.*") [emphasis added].

[14] For a discussion of the application of existing human rights obligations to persons with disabilities, see National Council on Disability, *A White Paper – Understanding the Role of an International Convention on the Human Rights of People with Disabilities* (Janet E. Lord, principal author, Washington DC, June 12, 2002), *available online at* <http://www.ncd.gov/newsroom/publications/2002/unwhitepaper_05-23-02.htm>.

[15] *See, e.g.*, CERD, *supra* note 8, at art. 1 (implicitly prohibiting discrimination against persons with disabilities who face racial discrimination defined as "any distinction, exclusion, restriction or preference based on race, colour, descent, or national or ethnic origin which has the purpose

of Discrimination against Women (CEDAW),[16] the Convention on the Rights of the Child (CRC),[17] and the International Convention on the Protection of the Rights of All Migrant Workers and Members of their Families (ICPMW),[18] each target a specific identity characteristic that can overlap with an individual also having a disability,[19] but otherwise are not directed toward persons with disabilities.[20]

---

or effect of nullifying or impairing the recognition, enjoyment or exercise, on an equal footing, of human rights and fundamental freedoms in the political, economic, social, cultural or any other field of public life.")

16 *See, e.g.*, CEDAW, *supra* note 8, at arts. 1–2 (implicitly covering discrimination against women with disabilities insofar as Article 2 of CEDAW provides that "States Parties condemn discrimination against women in all its forms" and defines the term "discrimination against women" in Article 1 as "any distinction, exclusion or restriction made on the basis of sex which has the effect or purpose of impairing or nullifying the recognition, enjoyment or exercise by women, irrespective of their marital status, on a basis of equality of men and women, of human rights and fundamental freedoms in the political, economic, social, cultural, civil or any other field.")

17 *See, e.g.*, CRC, *supra* note 8, at art. 2 (providing that the rights of the child in the CRC are to be respected and ensured "without discrimination of any kind, irrespective of the child's or his or her parent's or legal guardian's race, colour, sex, language, religion, political or other opinion, national, ethnic or social origin, property, disability, birth or other status."). While its non-discrimination clause identities disability as a specific prohibited ground of discrimination, Article 23 of CRC addresses the rights of the disabled child, recognizing in art. 23(1) "that a mentally or physically disabled child should enjoy a full and decent life, in conditions which ensure dignity, promote self-reliance and facilitate the child's active participation in the community.").

18 *See, e.g.*, ICRMW, *supra* note 8, at art. 7 (providing that the rights of "all migrant workers and members of their families" should be respected and ensured "without distinction of any kind such as to sex, race, colour, language, religion or conviction, political or other opinion, national, ethnic or social origin, nationality, age, economic position, property, marital status, birth or other status.")

19 These provisions can be seen as a mixed blessing. They provide an added avenue of protection for disabled persons experiencing multiple forms of discrimination. For example, a person may suffer prejudice as a result of having a disability and due to aboriginal heritage. Yet, these instruments only protect those individuals encountering serial discrimination. And because disability is almost uniformly relegated to the universal "other" status, disability-specific rights are frequently overlooked. An example of such disregard is the Declaration that proceeded from the 2001 World Conference Against Racism, Racial Discrimination, Xenophobia and Related Intolerance that was convened in Durban, South Africa. *See* World Conference Against Racism, Racial Discrimination, Xenophobia & Related Intolerance, Aug. 31–Sept. 8, 2001, Durban Declaration and Programme of Action, U.N. Doc. No. A/CONF.189/12, *available online at* <http://www.unhchr.ch/pdf/Durban.pdf>. The Declaration encouraged the General Assembly to enact disability-specific human rights protection but did not itself include disability among the otherwise inclusive catalog of identity statuses it deemed to suffer discrimination. *See id.* at para. 180. Consequently, individuals whose rights are violated "solely" due to their disability identity receive no added protection.

20 The CRC alone among these identity-specific treaties contains a distinct disability-related article. *See* CRC, *supra* note 8, at art. 23, para. 1. (States Parties must recognize the rights of

While some progress was made in the formulation of international standards relating to disability and the placement of disability issues on the international agenda, these efforts did not culminate in legally binding measures. Early initiatives include the adoption of the Declaration on the Rights of Mentally Retarded Persons[21] and the Declaration on the Rights of Disabled Persons during the 1970s.[22] These were significant steps in terms of raising awareness about the human rights of people with disabilities, but they reflected medical and charity models of disability and were heavy-laden with paternalism.

Significant progress was made during the 1980s with designations of the International Year of the Disabled in 1981[23] and the International Decade of Disabled Persons from 1982–1991.[24] In 1982, the General Assembly adopted a World Programme of Action Concerning Disabled Persons[25] to encourage national level programs aimed at achieving equality for people with disabilities.[26] In 1993,

children with disabilities to enjoy "full and decent" lives and participate in their communities.). However, this obligation is tempered by the relative financial constraints of States Parties, and also does not mandate that children with disabilities be treated or considered equal to children without disabilities. *See id.* at art. 23, paras. 1–3 ("[T]he disabled child has effective access to and receives education, training. . . preparation for employment and recreational opportunities in a manner conducive to the child's achieving the fullest possible social integration and individual development. . ."). *See generally* Thomas Hammarberg, *The Rights of Disabled Children – The UN Convention on the Rights of the Child, in* Human Rights and Disabled Persons, *supra* note 10, at 147.

[21] Declaration on the Rights of Mentally Retarded Persons, G.A. Res. 2856 (XXVI), U.N. GAOR, Supp. No. 29 at 93, U.N. Doc. A/8429 (1971). This document soon came under heavy criticism by the disability community for qualifying the scope of rights for people with intellectual disabilities both in providing that "the mentally retarded person has, to the maximum degree of feasibility, the same rights as other human beings" and in terms of its goal for societies which is to promote "their integration as far as possible in normal life." *Id.* at art. 1; preamble para. 5.

[22] Declaration on the Rights of Disabled Persons, G.A. Res. 3447 (XXX), U.N. GAOR, Supp. No. 34 at 88, U.N. Doc. A/10034 (1975).

[23] International Year of Disabled Persons, G.A. Res. 36/77, U.N. GAOR, 36th Sess., Supp. No. 77 at 176, U.N. Doc. A/RES/36/77 (1981).

[24] Implementation of the World Programme of Action Concerning Disabled Persons, G.A. Res. 37/53, U.N. GAOR, 37th Sess., Supp. No. 53 at 186–87, para. 11, U.N. Doc. A/RES/37/53 (1982).

[25] World Programme of Action Concerning Disabled Persons, G.A. Res. 37/52, U.N. GAOR, 37th Sess., Supp. No. 51 at 185, U.N. Doc. A/RES/37/52 (1982).

[26] *Id.* The World Programme of Action identifies the general situations of persons with disabilities across the full spectrum of life and articulates proposals aimed at implementing a full range of programming to integrate disabled people into their communities. For proposals identifying national level action, see *id.* at paras. 87–90 (providing, *inter alia*, that "Member States should urgently initiate national long-term programmes to achieve the objectives of the World Programme of Action; such programmes should be an integral component of the nation's general policy for socio-economic development.").

the United Nations Standard Rules on the Equalization of Opportunities for Persons with Disabilities[27] were adopted as a blueprint for policy-making and to provide a basis for technical and economic cooperation among states. The Standard Rules establish a monitoring mechanism through the appointment of a Special Rapporteur who reports to the Commission on Social Development.[28]

The drawbacks to these initiatives are that they lack legally binding character, and also set forth an outmoded, medical and charity-based understanding of disability.[29] Consequently, prior to the adoption of the CRPD, the human rights of persons with disabilities were in theory covered by human rights treaty obligations and addressed in non-binding resolutions and declarations, but in practice were protected by neither. This situation led Special Rapporteur Leandro Despouy to caution that in the absence of specific treaty protection, human rights abuses against disabled persons likely would continue without redress.[30]

Acting on previous proposals to address the lack of specific human rights protection for disabled persons,[31] in December 2001 the General Assembly established an Ad Hoc Committee to consider enacting a disability-based human

---

[27] Standard Rules on the Equalization of Opportunities for Persons With Disabilities, G.A. Res. 48/96, at 202, U.N. GAOR, 48th Sess, Supp. No. 49 at 68, U.N. Doc. A/RES/48/96 (1993) [hereinafter Standard Rules].

[28] *See generally* United Nations Enable, The Special Rapporteur on Disability of the Commission for Social Development, *available online at* <http://www.un.org/esa/socdev/enable/rapporteur.htm>. For an insider's perspective on the role of the Special Rapporteur, see Bengt Lindqvist, *Standard Rules in the Disability Field – A New United Nations Instrument*, in Human Rights and Disabled Persons, *supra* note 10, at 63.

[29] Whether human rights treaties are actually enforceable is the subject of heated academic debate. *Compare, e.g.*, Oona A. Hathaway, *The Cost of Commitment*, 55 Stan. L. Rev. 1821 (2003) (maintaining that traditional understandings of treaty ratification do not adequately account for the likelihood of State compliance); Oona A. Hathaway, *Do Human Rights Treaties Make a Difference?*, 111 Yale L.J. 1935 (2002) (asserting that some number of States ratify human rights treaties as a means of avoiding observance), *with* Ryan Goodman & Derek Jinks, *How to Influence States: Socialization and International Human Rights Law*, 54 Duke L.J. 621 (2004) (arguing that international human rights treaties encourage domestic legal norm changes); Ryan Goodman & Derek Jinks, *Measuring the Effects of Human Rights Treaties*, 13 Euro. J. Int'l. L.171 (2003) (same, while also critiquing the empirical evidence upon which Hathaway based her conclusions). For a harmonizing approach, see Alex Geisinger & Michael Ashley Stein, *A Theory of Expressive International Law*, 60 Vand. L. Rev. 77 (2007).

[30] Leandro Despouy, Report on Human Rights and Disabled Persons paras. 280–81 (1993), *available online at* <http://www.un.org/esa/socdev/enable/dispaperdes0.htm > (noting that "persons with disabilities are going to find themselves in a legal disadvantage in relation to other vulnerable groups" because "unlike the other vulnerable groups, they do not have an international control body to provide them with particular and specific protection").

[31] Notably, in 1987, Italy proffered a convention draft during the forty-second session of the General Assembly. *See* U.N. GAOR, 42nd Sess., 16th mtg., U.N. Doc. A/C.3/42/SR.16 (Oct. 19,

rights instrument.[32] The Ad Hoc Committee in turn established a working group to draft a foundational text that would form the basis of future negotiations.[33] On January 16, 2004, the working group issued draft CRPD articles for consideration beginning with the next, third, Ad Hoc session; on August 25, 2006, the last day for negotiating and amending the proposed Convention at the eighth session, the Ad Hoc Committee adopted the CRPD.[34]

2 *An Overview of the Convention*

The CRPD is modeled after recent United Nations human rights conventions, and especially the CRC, in two significant substantive ways.[35] Adhering to the central objective of the human right to development,[36] the Convention holistically

---

1987). Sweden did the same two years later at the General Assembly's forty-fourth session. *See* U.N. GAOR, 44th Sess., 16th mtg., U.N. Doc. A/C.3/44/SR.16 (Oct. 24, 1989).

[32] Comprehensive and Integral International Convention to Promote and Protect the Rights and Dignity of Persons with Disabilities, G.A. Res. 56/168, U.N GAOR, 56th Sess., Supp. No. 168, U.N. Doc. A/RES/56/168 (Dec. 19, 2001). A detailed description of the political process behind the United Nations decision to go forward with a disability human rights convention is set forth in the National Council on Disability, Newsroom, *UN Disability Convention – Topics at a Glance: History of the Process, available online at* <http://www.ncd.gov/newsroom/publications/2003/history_process.htm>.

[33] Ad Hoc Comm. on a Comprehensive and Integral International Convention on the Prot. & Promotion of the Rights & Dignity of Pers. with Disabilities, Report of the Working Group to the Ad Hoc Committee, U.N. Doc. A/AC.265/2004/WG.1 para. 1 (Jan. 27, 2004). The working group included twelve nongovernmental organizations ("NGOs"). *See id.* at para. 2. The inclusion of NGOs at this stage was unprecedented in the normal course of treaty development at the United Nations, and can be interpreted as acquiescence to NGOs' assertion of "nothing about us without us."

[34] The Ad Hoc Committee held eight negotiating sessions in total, in addition to the January 2004 Working Group meeting. The sessions ran from 2002 until August 2006, after which the adopted draft Convention was submitted to a technical drafting committee to be reviewed and "cleaned" and made ready for submission to the entire General Assembly. The Convention was officially adopted by the General Assembly on Dec. 13, 2006. More on each session of the Ad Hoc Committee sessions is *available online at:* <http://www.un.org/esa/socdev/enable/rights/adhoccom.htm>.

[35] *See generally* Henry J. Steiner & Philip Alston, International Human Rights in Context: Law, Politics, Morals 136–322 (2d ed., Oxford University Press 2000).

[36] The General Assembly's Declaration on the Right to Development established development as a human right in 1986. *See* Declaration on the Right to Development, G.A. Res. 41/128, Annex, U.N. GAOR, 41st Sess., Supp. No. 53 at 183, U.N. Doc. A/RES/41/128 (1986). Subsequently, the 1993 Vienna Declaration proclaimed the right to development was "a universal and inalienable right" as well as "an integral part of fundamental human rights." World Conference on Human Rights, June 14–25, 1993, Vienna Declaration and Programme of

melds civil and political rights with economic, social, and cultural rights.[37] Put another way, the CRPD aspires to manifest the mandate that human rights are "indivisible, interrelated and interconnected."[38] It also emulates the CRC by articulating a comprehensive catalog of human rights obligations within the circumstances of a particular group, here, persons with disabilities.[39]

With a few notable variances, the structure of the CRPD likewise is similar to that of the CRC.[40] The Convention's articles are introductory,[41] of general application,[42] enumerate substantive rights,[43] set forth implementation and monitoring provisions,[44] and promulgate rules to govern the operation of the Convention.[45] An Optional Protocol governs communications and procedures of inquiry.[46]

Significant for a human rights treaty, the CRPD sets forth its explicit purpose.[47] Article 1 declares the Convention's objective is "to promote, protect and ensure the full and equal enjoyment of all human rights and fundamental freedoms by all persons with disabilities, and to promote respect for their inherent dignity."[48] It conceives of disability as being inclusive of, but not limited to "long-term physical,

---

Action, U.N. Doc A/CONF. 157/23, para. 10 (July 12, 1993), *available online at* <http://www.unhchr.ch/huridocda/huridoca.nsf/(Symbol)/A.CONF.157.23.En> [hereinafter Vienna Declaration]. *See generally* Philip Alston, *Making Space for New Human Rights: The Case of the Right to Development,* 1 Harv. Hum. Rts. Y.B. 3 (1988); Stephen P. Marks, *Emerging Human Rights: A New Generation for the 1980s?,* 33 Rutgers L. Rev. 435 (1981).

37 *See* Stein, *supra* note 7, at 94–98; Michael Ashley Stein & Penelope J. S. Stein, *Beyond Disability Civil Rights,* 58 Hastings L.J. 1203, 1212–14 (2007).

38 Vienna Declaration, supra note 36 at para. 63.

39 Beginning in the mid-1960s, the United Nations considered the disadvantage experienced by certain populations to human rights abuses that were not addressed with any degree of specificity in existing international human rights law and initiated human rights treaty drafting in respect of specific groups. *See* NCD White Paper, supra note 14, at Part II.

40 For instance, a separate article that announces its purpose, see CRPD, *supra* note 1, at art. 1, and the absence of a formal explanation of the protected class in the definition article, see *id.* at art. 2.

41 *See* CRPD, *supra* note 1, at preamble, arts. 1–2.

42 *See id.* at arts. 3–9.

43 *See id.* at arts. 10–30.

44 *See id.* at arts. 31–40.

45 *See id.* at arts. 41–50.

46 *See* Optional Protocol, *supra* note 2.

47 Articulation of general principles are a common feature of international environmental agreements, *see e.g.*, United Nations Framework Convention on Climate Change, 9 May 1992, entered into force 24 March 1994, reprinted in 31 I.L.M. 849 (1992), Article 4(1)(i), and other framework conventions, for instance the WHO Framework Convention on Tobacco Control, UN Doc. A56/8. Geneva: WHO, 2003 art 3, *available online at* <http://www.who.int/tobacco/framework/WHO_FCTC_english.pdf>.

48 CRPD, at art. 1.

mental, intellectual or sensory impairments."[49] Moreover, it firmly grounds the disability classification in the social model of disability by stating that as a condition it arises from "interaction with various barriers may hinder their full and effective participation in society on an equal basis with others" rather than as an inherent limitation.[50] Because these conceptual norms are set forth in the purpose article, it follows that States cannot enter permissible reservations to the normative contents of this article.[51]

"Disability" is not directly defined in Article 2.[52] Instead, Article 1 of the Preamble affirms the social construction of disability in which limitations arise from a person's interaction with environmental barriers rather than as the consequence of an individualized impairment.[53] Article 2 broadly defines the terms "communication,"[54] "language,"[55] and "universal design,"[56] and takes an expansive approach to two disability-specific terms central to the interpretation of non-discrimination principles as they apply to persons with disabilities. Accordingly, discrimination that ensues "on the basis of disability" includes "any distinction, exclusion or restriction on the basis of disability" that "has the purpose or effect

---

49 *Id.*

50 *See* CRPD, at art. 1

51 Article 19 of the Vienna Convention on the Law of Treaties prohibits a State from entering a reservation to a treaty, *inter alia*, where the "reservation is incompatible with the object and purpose of the treaty." Vienna Convention on the Law of Treaties, G.A. Res. 2166 (XXI) of 5 December 1966 and 2287 (XXII) of 6 December 1967, 1150 U.N.T.S. 331.

52 The same holds true for the European Union's employment discrimination directive. *See* Council of Europe Directive Establishing a Framework for Equal Treatment in Employment and Occupation, 200/78/EC (27 November, 2000) [hereinafter EU Framework Directive]; Lisa Waddington, *Implementing the Disability Provisions of the Framework Employment Directive: Room for Exercising National Discretion, in* Disability Rights in Europe: From Theory to Practice 107, 109 (Anna Lawson & Caroline Gooding eds., Hart Publishing 2005) ("EC directives set goals which Member States are obliged to achieve within a given period, but leave Member States free to select the most appropriate means of achieving those goals.").

53 *See* CRPD, *supra* note 1, at preambular para. (e) ("*Recognizing* that disability is an evolving concept and that disability results from the interaction between persons with impairments and attitudinal and environmental barriers that hinders their full and effective participation in society on an equal basis with others") (emphasis in original).

54 *See id.* at art. 2 (defining communication to include "languages, display of text, Braille, tactile communication, large print, accessible multimedia as well as written, audio, plain-language, human-reader and augmentative and alternative modes, means and formats of communication, including accessible information and communication technology").

55 *See id.* (defining language to include "spoken and signed languages and other forms of non spoken languages").

56 *See id.* (defining universal design as "the design of products, environments, programmes and services to be usable by all people, to the greatest extent possible, without the need for adaptation or specialized design" and not to "exclude assistive devices for particular groups of persons with disabilities where this is needed.").

of impairing or nullifying the recognition, enjoyment or exercise, on an equal basis with others, of all human rights and fundamental freedoms."[57] As such, the prohibition likely will extend both to individuals perceived as having a disability, as well as to non-disabled individuals associated with disabled persons.[58] Discrimination is also considered to include the "denial of reasonable accommodation,"[59] and is thus organically linked to the non-discrimination concept and so immediately applicable. Further, the CRPD defines the notion of reasonable accommodation as a "necessary and appropriate modification and adjustments not imposing a disproportionate or undue burden" that can ensure to disabled persons "the enjoyment or exercise on an equal basis with others of all human rights and fundamental freedoms."[60]

Article 3 enunciates the Convention's general principles as including respect for individual dignity, autonomy, and independence;[61] respect for difference and acceptance of disability as human diversity;[62] non-discrimination;[63] equal opportunity;[64] complete and meaningful social participation;[65] accessibility;[66] sexual equality;[67] respect for children's rights and support of their evolving capabilities.[68]

Article 4 sets forth the general obligations of States Parties to undertake measures aimed at ensuring the promotion and full realization of all human rights and fundamental freedoms under the CRPD for all persons with disabilities,[69] and to achieve these goals without discriminating in any way on the basis of disability.[70] States Parties must take measures to realize economic, social and cultural rights progressively to the maximum extent of their available resources.[71] Specifically, Article 4 enumerates the obligations of States Parties to: (i) adopt

---

57 *Id.*

58 *See, e.g., Equal Treatment Commission (Commissie Gelijke Behandeling)* 1.NL.117, Opinion 2004–67.

59 *See* CRPD, *supra* note 1, at art 2.

60 *Id.*

61 *See id.* at art. 3(a).

62 *See id.* at art. 3(d).

63 *See id.* at 3(b).

64 *See id.* at 3(e).

65 *See id.* at 3(c).

66 *See id.* at 3(f).

67 *See id.* at 3(g).

68 *See id.* at 3(h).

69 *See id.* at art. 4.

70 *See id.* at art. 4(1).

71 *See id.* at art. 4(2).

legislative, administrative and other measures to implement the Convention;[72] (ii) abolish or amend existing laws, regulations, customs and practices that constitute discrimination against persons with disabilities;[73] (iii) adopt an inclusive approach to protect and promote the rights of persons with disabilities in all policies and programmes;[74] (iv) refrain from conduct violative of the Convention and ensure that the public sector respects the rights of persons with disabilities;[75] (v) take measures to abolish disability discrimination by persons, organizations or private enterprises;[76] (vi) undertake research and development of accessible goods, services and technology for persons with disabilities and to promote others to undertake such research;[77] (vii) provide accessible information about assistive technology to persons with disabilities;[78] (viii) promote professional and staff training on Convention rights for those working with persons with disabilities on the Convention;[79] and (ix) consult with and involve persons with disabilities in developing and implementing legislation and policies and in decision-making processes concerning rights under the CRPD.[80]

States Parties are required by Article 5 to ensure the equality of persons with disabilities and to prohibit all forms of discrimination "on the basis of disability."[81] To achieve this goal, the CRPD provides broad mandates. Article 5 requires recognition by States Parties "that all persons are equal before and under the law" and thus entitled "to the equal protection and equal benefit of the law" free of any discrimination.[82] States Parties also must "prohibit all discrimination on the basis of disability" while guaranteeing that persons with disabilities have "equal and effective legal protection" versus all forms of discrimination.[83] At the same time, in order "to promote equality and eliminate discrimination,"

---

72 *See id.* at art. 4(1)(a).
73 *See id.* at art. 4(1)(b).
74 *See id.* at art. 4(1)(c).
75 *See id.* at art. 4(1)(d).
76 *See id.* at art. 4(1)(e).
77 *See id.* at art. 4(1)(f) & (g).
78 *See id.* at art. 4(1)(h).
79 *See id.* at art. 4(1)(i).
80 *See id.* at art. 4(3).
81 *Id.* at art. 5. For a discussion of the three main normative theories of equality (and by implication, non-discrimination) that are applied to the disability context, see Quinn & Degener, *supra* note 6, at 16–18. For different conceptions of disability-based equality within the context of the Americans with Disabilities Act, see Disability, Difference, Discrimination: Perspectives on Justice in Bioethics and Public Policy (Anita Silvers et al. eds., Rowman & Littlefield Publishers 1998).
82 CRPD, at art. 5(1).
83 *See id.* at art. 5(2).

States Parties are required to "take all appropriate steps to ensure that reasonable accommodation is provided."[84] Article 5, moreover, provides that any specific measures that "are necessary to accelerate or achieve de facto equality of persons with disabilities" may not themselves be construed as discriminatory.[85] Last, by prohibiting discrimination against "any person" on the basis of disability, rather than as only against individuals with disabilities, the CRPD empowers the CRPD to receive and consider complaints by individuals who have been discriminated against because they have mistakenly been regarded as having a disability,[86] or due to their association with a disabled person.[87]

Next among the articles of general application, and equally intended to be horizontally integrated across the CRPD, are provisions that especially underscore the rights of women with disabilities,[88] and children with disabilities.[89] By contrast, other individuals with disabilities subject to multiple forms of discrimination are acknowledged in the Preamble.[90]

Rounding out the articles of general application, Article 8 addresses some of the underlying determinants of disability discrimination by requiring States Parties to raise public awareness,[91] in support of which it provides a non-exhaustive list of

---

84 *Id.* at art. 5(3).

85 *See id.* at art. 5(4).

86 This is one form of protected coverage under the Americans with Disabilities Act. *See generally* Michelle A. Travis, *Perceived Disabilities, Social Cognition, and "Innocent Mistakes,"* 55 Vand. L. Rev. 481, 489–490 (2002).

87 *See, e.g., Equal Treatment Commission (Commissie Gelijke Behandeling)* Opinion 2004–67, 1.NL.117; *see also* Cases, Materials and Text on National, Supranational and International Non-Discrimination Law 166–67 (Dagmar Schiek et al. eds., Hart Publishing 2007).

88 *See* CRPD, *supra* note 1, at art. 6.

89 *See id.* at art. 7.

90 "*Concerned* about the difficult conditions faced by persons with disabilities who are subject to multiple or aggravated forms of discrimination on the basis of race, colour, sex, language, religion, political or other opinion, national, ethnic, indigenous or social origin, property, birth, age or other status." *Id.* at Preamble (p) (emphasis in original).

91 Such measures are identified in the Standard Rules as a condition precedent to the equalization of opportunities of persons with disabilities. *See* Standard Rules, *supra* note 27, at para. 1. They also are reflected in other human rights conventions addressing racial and other forms of discrimination. *See, e.g.*, CEDAW, art. 5, *supra* note 8 ("States Parties shall take all appropriate measures" in order to "modify the social and cultural patterns of conduct of men and women, with a view to achieving the elimination of prejudices and customary and all other practices which are based on the idea of the inferiority or the superiority of either of the sexes or on stereotyped roles for men and women."); ICERD, *supra* note 8 at art. 7 ("States Parties undertake to adopt immediate and effective measures, particularly in the fields of teaching, education, culture and information, with a view to combating prejudices which lead to racial discrimination.").

illustrative measures.[92] Article 9 seeks to dismantle barriers hindering the effective enjoyment of rights by persons with disabilities by addressing a broad spectrum of accessibility concerns[93] within both the public and private spheres.[94]

As a comprehensive human rights treaty, the CRPD's substantive articles cover the spectrum of life activities of persons with disabilities. In doing so, the Convention clarifies, within the context of disability, the human rights that all persons are entitled to under existing international human rights law instruments as well as under customary international law.[95] These elemental human rights include fundamental freedoms such as the right to life,[96] freedom from torture,[97] the right to education,[98] employment,[99] political participation,[100] legal capacity,[101] access to justice,[102] freedom of expression and opinion,[103] privacy,[104] participation in cultural life, sports and recreation,[105] respect for home and family,[106] personal integrity,[107] liberty of movement and nationality,[108] liberty and security of the person,[109] and adequate standard of living.[110]

---

[92] States Parties are directed to take "immediate, effective, and appropriate measures" to "raise awareness throughout society," to "combat stereotypes, prejudices and harmful practices relating to person with disabilities", and to "promote disability awareness." *Id.* at art. 8(1).

[93] *See id.* at art. 9. These include physical, technological, information, communication, economic and social accessibility. *See id.*

[94] *See id.* at art. 9(1) (obligating that public and private products or services be "open or provided to the public.").

[95] The right to non-discrimination, among other well-established human rights obligations, and its application to persons with disabilities may be considered part of customary international law. In that regard, the Convention codifies this fundamental disability rights obligation. Other, more progressive concepts set forth in the Convention may in time contribute to the crystallization of customary international law in this context.

[96] *See* CRPD, *supra* note 1, at art. 10.

[97] *See id.* at art. 15.

[98] *See id.* at art. 24.

[99] *See id.* at art. 27.

[100] *See id.* at art. 29.

[101] *See id.* at art. 12.

[102] *See id.* at art. 13.

[103] *See id.* at art. 21.

[104] *See id.* at art. 22.

[105] *See id.* at art. 30.

[106] *See id.* at art. 23.

[107] *See id.* at art. 17.

[108] *See id.* at art. 18.

[109] *See id.* at art. 14.

[110] *See id.* at art. 28.

Parenthetically, it bears noting that several articles appear at first blush to reflect newly created rights, but in fact were included for the purpose of clarifying the means through which other CRPD rights are realized.[111] For example, the articles on living independently,[112] personal mobility,[113] and habilitation and rehabilitation[114] are intrinsic to the attainment of historically recognized human rights.[115]

Implementation and monitoring measures are set forth in ten subsequent articles[116] and in the Optional Protocol.[117] Specially innovative for human rights treaties are provisions allowing the treaty monitoring body to receive collective complaints (and thus target systemic deficiencies as well as individual grievances),[118] elicit the expertise and input of NGOs[119] and UN specialized agencies and organs,[120]

---

111 A recurrent theme echoed throughout the Convention negotiations was the notion that the draft text did not reflect "new" rights but instead articulated existing human rights within the specific context of disability. This view is summarized by the United Nations Department of Economic and Social Affairs in its question and answer resource on the Convention which states: "The convention does not create any 'new rights' or 'entitlements.' What the convention does, however, is express existing rights in a manner that addresses the needs and situation of persons with disabilities." Convention on the Rights of Persons with Disabilities: Why a Convention?, *available online at* <http://www.un.org/disabilities/convention/questions.shtml#one>

112 *See* CRPD, *supra* note 1, at art. 19.

113 *See id.* at art. 20.

114 *See id.* at art. 26.

115 *See generally* Stein & Stein, *supra* note 37.

116 *See* CRPD, *supra* note 1, at arts. 31–40.

117 *See* Optional Protocol, *supra* note 2.

118 *See id.*at art. 1(1) (authorizing the Committee on the Rights of Persons with Disabilities to accept and deliberate upon individual and group complaints and communications regarding alleged violations of the CRPD).

119 *See* CRPD, *supra* note 1 at art. 4(3). Article 4(3) of the Convention makes consultations with disabled persons and their representative organizations a general obligation and is reinforced by the inclusion of participation as a general principle of the Convention in Article 3. NGO participation is implicitly provided for in the monitoring process, insofar as the Convention requires States Parties to include civil society in the monitoring process at the national level. *Id* at art. 33(3). Moreover, Article 34(3) calls on States Parties to consider consultations with NGOs in the formulation of Committee member nominations as well as in the preparation of reports (Article 35(4)).

120 *Id.* at art. 38(a) (mandating that UN specialized agencies and other UN organs "shall be entitled to be represented" during the course of considering implementation of Convention provisions "within the scope of their mandate."). *See also id.* (allowing the Committee on the Rights of Persons with Disabilities to "invite specialized agencies and other United Nations organs to submit reports on the implementation of the Convention in areas falling within the scope of their activities."). One body that might prove of especial utility is the newly formed Inter-Agency Support Group (IASG) on the Convention on the Rights of Persons with Disabilities.

conduct proactive inquiries,[121] and procedures to better manage reporting deadlines[122] and conduct Conferences of States Parties.[123]

The CRPD's final provisions address rules governing the operation of the Convention, including, inter alia, its entry into force, amendments, and the official languages in which the Convention is to be considered equally authentic.[124]

3 *Future Prospects for the Convention*

To assess the future prospects of the CRPD for improving the lives of the six hundred and fifty million individuals with disabilities worldwide, we focus on three areas where the Convention can have a more immediate impact, beginning with abstract rights notions and moving towards more concrete results.

The effects we identify include the expressive value of acknowledging disability-based human rights; the impact of requiring States Parties (and non States Parties) to reflect upon and engage with domestic-level disability laws and policies; and advances in social integration by persons with disabilities that will be facilitated through the CRPD's inclusive development mandate.

3.1 *The Convention as an Expressive Value Trigger*

The CRPD has expressive value insofar as it constitutes an acknowledgement by the global community of the equal dignity, autonomy, and worth of persons with disabilities.[125] The emerging field of expressive law explores the process

---

[121] *See* Optional Protocol, *supra* note 2, at art. 6 (providing for a procedure of inquiry to allow the Committee to initiate an inquiry on receipt by the Committee of "reliable information indicating grave or systematic violations by a State Party of rights set forth in the Convention.").

[122] *See* CRPD, *supra* note 1, at 35(4) (providing that "[a] State Party which has submitted a comprehensive initial report to the Committee need not, in its subsequent reports, repeat information previously provided.).

[123] *See id.* at art. 40 (providing that "States Parties shall meet regularly in a Conference of States Parties in order to consider any matter with regard to the implementation of the present Convention.").

[124] *See id.* at arts. 41–50.

[125] *See* Statement by H. E. Sheikha Haya Rashed Al Khalifa, President of the United Nations General Assembly, at the Adoption of the Convention on the Rights of Persons with Disabilities, United Nations Headquarters, New York, New York, 13 December 2006, *available online at*: <http://www.un.org/ga/president/61/statements/statement20061213.shtml> ("The adoption of this Convention is a great opportunity to celebrate the emergence of comprehensive guidelines the world so urgently needs. It is an opportunity to reaffirm our universal commitment to the rights and dignity of all people without discrimination. The Convention can also provide the much needed impetus for wider cultural changes in the way that the world perceives disabled people.").

whereby law can influence behavior by altering broader social perceptions and conventions.[126] Such lines of inquiry reveal how law carries with it a symbolic social meaning, and so influences the nexus between law, norms, and societal mores.[127] An expressive law analysis of the CRPD indicates that the treaty has the potential to legislate a belief change regarding persons with disabilities by better informing societies about persons with disabilities.[128] This approach relates well to the understanding in constructivist scholarship of actors who are "deeply social" and whose identities are shaped by the institutionalized norms, values and ideas of the social environment in which they act.[129]

These notions create the point of departure for understanding the Convention itself as a process[130] through which actor identities and interests may be shaped and reconstituted.[131] Viewed in this context, the CRPD should be understood as

---

[126] *See, e.g.*, Robert Cooter, *Expressive Law and Economics*, 27 J. Legal Stud. 585 (1998) (describing the role of law in the development of social norms, and socioeconomic law and economics, which seeks to inject psychological and social factors related to wealth and race into otherwise "neutral" economic analyses); Richard H. McAdams, *An Attitudinal Theory of Expressive Law*, 79 Or. L. Rev. 339 (2000) (highlighting the power of the approval or disapproval of law in shaping behavior); *see also* Lawrence Lessig, *The Regulation of Social Meaning*, 62 U. Chi. L. Rev. 943 (1998); Cass R. Sunstein, *On the Expressive Function of Law*, 144 U. Pa. L. Rev. 2021 (1996).

[127] *See generally* Alex Geisinger, *A Belief Change Theory of Expressive Law*, 88 Iowa L. Rev. 35 (2002). According to Geisinger, law impacts on an individual's certainty regarding the consequences of her actions either by providing additional information about that action, or through its influence on an individual's "inferential reasoning process." *Id.* at 63–65. This may occur because people were ambivalent about particular conduct, and the law's passage has now "tipped" those fence-sitters towards an equilibrium, or because individuals with little information regarding an activity have now updated their knowledge and beliefs subsequent to the law's passage. *Id.* at 68–69.

[128] For an account of the expressive law value of human rights treaties, see Geisinger & Stein, *supra* note 29. For an account of the expressive law value of the Americans with Disabilities Act, see Michael Ashley Stein, *Under the Empirical Radar: An Initial Expressive Law Analysis of the ADA*, 90 U. Va. L. Rev. 1151 (2004).

[129] International legal scholars, going back to Hugo Grotius, have long understood the international system as a social system. Hugo Grotius, *De Jure Belli ac Pacis: Libre Tres* (1625) in *Classics of International Law* (J. B. Scott, ed., Oxford University Press 1925). Moreover, the view of law as a social process is the particular foundation upon which the highly influential New Haven School of international law rests. *See, e.g.,* Myres McDougal & Florentino Feliciano, Law and Minimum World Public Order: The Legal Regulation of International Coercion (Yale University Press, 1961); Harold Lasswell & Myres McDougal, Jurisprudence for a Free Society (New Haven Press, 1992).

[130] On the understanding of international law as a process, see especially Rosalyn Higgins, Problems and Process: International Law and How We Use It (Clarendon Press, 1994).

[131] Alexander Wendt, *Constructing International Politics*, 20 Int'l. Security 71, 73 (1995) (positing that systems of shared ideas, beliefs and values work to influence social and political action within and across multilateral law-making processes). *See also* Christian Reus-Smit, *Constructiv-*

an instrument that seeks to recast disability as a social construction and articulates protections in specific application to the situation that disabled persons face in relationship to their human rights enjoyment. Previous human rights instruments that did not reflect a social model of disability, nor expressly link barriers in the realization of rights to the barriers experienced by persons with disabilities in their communities, were blunt instruments.

Moreover, while persons with disabilities were in theory possessed of full and equal human rights under existing United Nations core human rights treaties, recall that in practice these protections were only rarely asserted and even more rarely recognized.[132] The same may be said of other United Nations instruments, including the Charter of the United Nations[133] and the Universal Declaration of Human Rights.[134] It is equally true of the much vaunted, well lauded, United Nations Millennium Development Goals (MDGs).[135] Although the central aims of this program – poverty alleviation,[136] increased health status,[137] and improved

---

ism, in Theories of International Relations 209, 218 (Scott Burchill et al. eds., 2d ed. Palgrave MacMillan, 2001) (noting that "[i]nstitutionalized norms and ideas... condition what actors' consider necessary and possible, both in practical and ethical terms.").

132 *See* discussion *supra,* Part I.

133 *See, e.g.*, United Nations Charter, at art. 1(3). (expressing a core purpose of the UN to "achieve international co-operation in solving international problems of an economic, social, cultural, or humanitarian character, and in promoting and encouraging respect for human rights and for fundamental freedoms for all without distinction as to race, sex, language, or religion").

134 *See, e.g.*, Universal Declaration of Human Rights, G.A. Res. 217A (III), arts. 1–2, U.N. GAOR, 3d Sess., U.N. Doc. A/810 (1948) (proclaiming that "all human beings are born free and equal in dignity and rights" and are "entitled to all the rights and freedoms set forth in this Declaration, without distinction of any kind, such as race, colour, sex, language, religion, political or other opinion, national or social origin, property, birth or other status.").

135 The Millennium Development Goals, or "MDGs" were developed within the framework of the Millennium Development Summit in 2000 in which 89 member states of the United Nations agreed to help citizens in the world's poorest countries to achieve a better life by the year 2015. The MDGs were derived from the Millennium Declaration, adopted at the conference which have since become the centerpiece for achievement the goals of the Declaration. *See UN Millennium Declaration*, UN GA res. 55/2 (2000), *available online at* <http://www.unmillenniumproject.org/documents/ares552e.pdf> [hereinafter Millennium Declaration]. The official UN website for the MDGs sets forth all eight MDGs as derived from the Millennium Declaration and identifies key targets and benchmarks, along with successes and is *available online at*: <http://www.un.org/millenniumgoals/>. For the perspective of the Chair of the MDGs, from which disability also is absent, see Jeffrey D. Sachs, The End of Poverty: Economic Possibilities for Our Time (Penguin Press, 2005).

136 *See* MDGs, *supra* note 135, at Millennium Development Goal 1 (calling for the eradication of extreme poverty and hunger by 2017).

137 *See id.* at Millennium Development Goal 6 (calling for efforts to combat HIV/AIDS, malaria and other diseases).

education,[138] among others – are inextricably linked to disability,[139] the MDGs do not reference disability.[140]

The General Assembly's adoption of the CRPD and the Optional Protocol by consensus, along with the subsequent signature and ratification of the Convention by States Parties, sends a signal that the international community recognizes the place of disability within the human rights canon.[141] Moreover, the CRPD should be regarded as an educative tool insofar as it can serve to teach mainstream society about the life circumstances of persons with disabilities, by providing information regarding their relative position. Its potential may be fully realized provided the provisions in the Convention supporting its use as an educational tool are fully implemented by both State and non-State actors.[142] In this respect, the CRPD's narrative regarding the unnecessary and amenable nature of the historical exclusion of persons with disabilities across societies can serve a vital function beyond the particular implementation of its substantive obligations in law and policy.[143] And where the Convention's expressive value is

---

[138] *See id.* at Millennium Development Goal 2 (calling for the achievement of universal primary education).

[139] For a discussion of the MDGs and their implicit, but unstated, link to disability issues, see Janet E. Lord & Katherine N. Guernsey, *Inclusive Development and the Comprehensive and Integral International Convention on the Protection and Promotion of the Rights and Dignity of Persons with Disabilities* (IDDC Task Group in the UN Convention, January 2005), *available online at*: <http://www.un.org/esa/socdev/enable/rights/ahc5docs/ahc5iddc.doc>

[140] *See* MDGs, *supra* note 135. Notably, disability was not mentioned in a recent treatment by the Secretariat, cf. Report: Mainstreaming disability in the development agenda (E/CN.5/2008/6).

[141] *See Lauding Disability Convention as "Dawn of a New Era," UN urges Speedy Ratification"* (UN Press Release 13 Dec. 2006), *available online at*: <http://www.un.org/apps/news/story.asp?NewsID=20975&Cr=disab> (summarizing statements made on the adoption of the Convention and heralding its significance for persons with disabilities and for the development of international human rights law. *See also* UN Secretary General Kofi Annan Statement, *Secretary-General Hails Adoption of Landmark Convention on Rights of Persons with Disabilities*, 13 Dec. 2006, UN Doc. SG/SM/10797 HR/4911 L/T/4400, *available online at*: <http://www.un.org/News/Press/docs//2006/sgsm10797.doc.htm> ("This Convention is a remarkable and forward-looking document. While it focuses on the rights and development of people with disabilities, it also speaks about our societies as a whole – and about the need to enable every person to contribute to the best of their abilities and potential.").

[142] *See, e.g.*, CRPD, *supra* note 1, art. 8 (requiring States Parties "to adopt immediate, effective and appropriate measures… [t]o raise awareness throughout society, including at the family level, regarding persons with disabilities, and to foster respect for the rights and dignity of persons with disabilities…")

[143] *Id.* at prmbl. para. k (expressing concern that "persons with disabilities continue to face barriers in their participation as equal members of society and violations of their human rights in all parts of the world.").

made manifest in societal change, this stands to support, and be supported by, national level law and policy change.

3.2 *The Convention as a National Action Trigger*

The CRPD is designed to trigger among States Parties (and one might argue non-Parties due to the impact of customary international law),[144] national level engagement with disability law and policy.[145] Only some forty States have systemic disability rights laws,[146] of which many are outdated or of questionable value.[147] Consequently, the vast majority of States will be required to develop or substantially reform legal and social policies towards their respective domestic populations of persons with disabilities.[148] Given this underdevelopment of disability law and policy worldwide, the Convention is anticipated to serve as the impetus for law making and law reform that is unprecedented in modern human rights law. While this presents a remarkable opportunity, it likewise poses considerable challenges for effective national-level action.

State engagement with domestic-level disability laws and policies will necessarily manifest on at least three interrelated levels. First, each State must make

---

144 The essence of this argument is that States that do not enter into international treaties nonetheless can become bound by the precepts of those instruments when they reflect a codification of customary international law or where they, over time, acquire such status. *See* Louis B. Sohn, *The New International Law: Protection of the Rights of Individuals Rather than States*, 32 Am. U.L. Rev. 1, 16–17 (1982). *See also* Gerald J. Postema, *Custom in International Law: A Normative Practice Account,* in The Nature of Customary Law: Legal, Historical and Philosophical Perspectives 279 (Amanda Perreau-Saussine & James Bernard Murphy eds., Cambridge University Press 2007); John Tasioulas, *Customary International Law and the Quest for Global Justice, in id.* at 307.

145 The Convention's provisions on national-level implementation are quite novel among the core international human rights conventions. *See* CRPD, *supra* note 1 at art. 33.

146 Theresia Degener & Gerard Quinn, *A Survey of International, Comparative and Regional Disability Law Reform, in* Disability Rights Law and Policy: International and National Perspectives 3 (Mary Lou Breslin & Sylvia Yee eds. Transnational Publishers 2002), provides a catalogue.

147 For example, Morocco, like the majority of States, has no comprehensive disability law. Legislation dating to 1982 applies only to a limited number of rights in respect of persons with visual impairments, but not to persons with other types of disabilities. The Convention process, in which Morocco played a major role (both its government as well as NGOs) has promoted national-level planning and prompted national level legislative reform within the Government to remedy major gaps in national law and policy. *See* Secrétariat a'Etat Chargé de la Famille, de l'Enfance et des Personnes Handicapées, *Programme National de Réadaptation a Base Communitaire au Profit des Personnes Handicapées 2006–2008* (2006).

148 "Unfortunately, the continuing economic inequities and social exclusion of disabled persons worldwide severely calls into doubt the efficacy of these efforts. It also begs the question of whether any country adequately protects their disabled citizens." Stein & Stein, *supra* note 37, at 1203.

an independent judgment as to whether it will ratify the CRPD and Optional Protocol, and then adjust its own national level schemes (including the designation of focal points for monitoring and implementation)[149] accordingly,[150] adjust its national framework first, followed by ratification,[151] or adopt some intermediary measure.[152] Second, every State will need to reflect on its individual socio-legal circumstances to determine how best to balance antidiscrimination prohibitions with positive action.[153] Third, each State must resolve outstanding but unclear interpretations of disability-related principles (e.g., reasonable

149 *See* CRPD, *supra* note 1, at art. 33(1) (obligating States Parties to "designate one or more focal points within government" for "matters relating to the implementation of the present Convention"); art. 33(2) (requiring States Parties to "maintain, strengthen, designate or establish" one or more independent mechanisms to "promote, protect and monitor implementation" of the CRPD); and art. 33(1) (further requiring States to "give due consideration to the establishment or designation of a coordination mechanism within government to facilitate related action in different sectors and at different levels.").

150 Thus, Jamaica, the first State to ratify the Convention, has not acted to align its domestic legal framework with the Convention and remains a disability rights violator in a number of other areas. *See* US Department of State, Bureau of Democracy, Human Rights, and Labor Country Reports on Human Rights Practices (Washington, DC, March 6, 2007), *available online at*: <http://www.state.gov/g/drl/rls/hrrpt/2006/78897.htm> (emphasizing in the section entitled "Persons with Disabilities" that "[t]here were no laws prohibiting discrimination against persons with disabilities nor any laws mandating accessibility for persons with disabilities, and such persons encountered discrimination in employment and denial of access to schools."). *Id.*

151 New Zealand, one of the leading countries in the treaty negotiations, has some notably progressive domestic disability practices, but its legal framework remains underdeveloped in the comprehensive sense mandated by the Convention. *See* Anne-Marie Mooney Cotter, This Ability: An International Legal Analysis of Disability Discrimination 100–20 (Ashgate, 2007).

152 Mexico's Senate, for example, ratified the CRPD but made a declaration that it would not apply Article 12 because its domestic law on legal capacity exceeded the Convention's requirements. After well-publicized statements by two experts, the Senate acquiesced to reconsider its position. See Katia D'Artigues, *Mexico, Farol de la Calle, Oscuridad en Casa?*, El Universal (26 Oct. 2007), at A19 (describing the critiques offered by Professors Gerard Quinn and Michael Stein to the General Assembly of Human Rights Institutions of the Americas).

153 Take, for example, the EU Framework Directive, *supra* note 52, prohibiting discrimination in employment on the basis of disability. The Directive requires individual employers to take "appropriate measures" to provide reasonable accommodations. However, it is neutral as to whether Member States may support disabled employment through "specific measures" (i.e., equity modifiers). *Id.* at Article 7. An undetermined issue is how Member States with pre-existing programs – such as the employment quota system operated in Germany – will respond to the Directive's purely antidiscrimination mandate. *See generally* Waddington, *supra* note 52 (setting forth the Directive's requirements and assessing its implementation); Fiona Geist, et. al., *Disability Law in Germany*, 24 Comp. LAb. L. & Pol'y J. 563 (2003). The same dynamic is at play in Japan, where the government is under pressure by disability rights groups to supplement or supplant the existing quota system with anti-discrimination laws. *See* Stein & Stein *supra* note 37, at 1231–33.

accommodation[154] and access to justice)[155] and also grapple with rights that are implicit in the Convention and/or domestic law, but not previously endorsed (such as a right to mobility).[156]

An inherent danger in this process is that the pace of domestic law reform, in the haste to ratify the CRPD and the Optional Protocol or to bring national laws into alignment following ratification, may compromise both the quality of the process as well as the ultimate result. If the Convention is to realize its expressive value, domestic change must occur in a transparent and participatory process, one that necessarily is time intensive and not particularly efficient. In addition, the Convention does not foresee a made-to-measure legislative grafting according to which a particular template may be applied to all country contexts. And yet law reform processes, particularly those supported by the international donor community, all too frequently follow this perilous path.

The Convention's inclusive-development mandate offers opportunities for donor governments seeking to facilitate Convention implementation in less developed countries to do so responsibly, and in step with legal and cultural contexts whilst seeking alignment with the Convention framework and obligations. Successive adoptions of disability policies by donor governments suggests that technical assistance programming may well improve inclusion, not only in terms of fostering disability law reform projects, but also in terms of facilitating meaningful inclusion across the development spectrum in line with local participation and needs. Programming across development sectors must be made disability inclusive, whether in democracy and governance, environment, health, education, infrastructure, humanitarian emergencies or other programming.[157]

---

154 CRPD, *supra* note 1 at art. 2 (defining reasonable accommodation as "necessary and appropriate modification and adjustments not imposing a disproportionate or undue burden, where needed in a particular case, to ensure to persons with disabilities the enjoyment or exercise on an equal basis with others of all human rights and fundamental freedoms.").

155 *Id.* at art. 13 (providing that "States Parties shall ensure effective access to justice for persons with disabilities on an equal basis with others, including through the provision of procedural and age-appropriate accommodations, in order to facilitate their effective role as direct and indirect participants, including as witnesses, in all legal proceedings, including at investigative and other preliminary stages."). *See also* Tennessee v. Lane, 541 U.S. 509 (2004) (holding that one particular individual had a right to physically access one particular court, but leaving open the question of whether any other persons with disabilities could gain relief when denied access to other justice elements, for example, as witnesses or jurors).

156 CRPD, *supra* note 1, at art. 20 (providing that "States Parties shall take effective measures to ensure personal mobility with the greatest possible independence for persons with disabilities.").

157 For a study of the slow but increasing emergence of disability policies among donor governments, see Bill Albert, *Is Disability Really on the Development Agenda?: A Review of Official Disability Policies of the Major Governmental and International Development Agencies* (September 2004), *available online at*: <http://www.disabilitykar.net/pdfs/disability_on_the_agenda.pdf.>

3.3 *The Convention as a Social Integration Trigger*

The CRPD does offer an opportunity to trigger the social integration of persons with disabilities into society through its mandate of inclusive development.[158] Current development practices have by and large excluded people with disabilities from their schemes,[159] thereby increasing an already wide equity gap between disabled and mainstream populations.[160]

By requiring that technical assistance, development aid, and humanitarian efforts by States Parties conform to the rest of the CRPD's principles, inclusive development aid – and especially that of the European Union, the world's largest donor[161] – can compel great strides towards making the socially constructed environment more accessible to disabled individuals in developing countries.

158 *See* CRPD, *supra* note 1 at art. 33 (providing that "States Parties recognize the importance of international cooperation and its promotion, in support of national efforts for the realization of the purpose and objectives of the present Convention, and will undertake appropriate and effective measures in this regard, between and among States... [which] measures could include... [e]nsuring that international cooperation, including international development programmes, is inclusive of and accessible to persons with disabilities.").

159 *See* Albert, *supra* note 155, at 7 (detailing the historical disregard of inclusive development practice among donor governments in their development assistance programming). *See also* Amy T. Wilson, *The Effectiveness of International Development Assistance from American Organizations to Deaf Communities in Jamaica*, 150 Am. Annals of the Deaf 292, 298 (2005) (describing how USAID, in working "on behalf" of deaf-based development, did not work in conjunction with the local deaf community).

160 *See British Council of Disabled People's International Committee Improving DFID's Engagement with the UK Disability Movement*, report prepared for the Department for International Development 4 (March 2005), *available online at*: <http://www.dfid.gov.uk/pubs/files/bcodp-dfid-disability.pdf> (emphasizing that "[t]he disability movement in the UK has been concerned for some time about DFID's approach to disability" and detailing the following areas of concern: (i) "disability is not afforded the importance it merits nor is it mainstreamed within DFID"; (ii) "DFID does not have disabled people represented in its work force"; (iii) "DFID does not have policies and procedures to ensure that disability is included either in its HR or development practice"; (iv) "where it is included, disability is addressed without the engagement of the disability movement and the involvement of disabled people from both the North and the South"; (v) "without the meaningful inclusion of these disabled people and their organisations as well as a more deliberate approach to disability issues it is unlikely that the MDG's, particularly the headline goal of poverty reduction, will be met.").

161 Donor governments are beginning to adopt inclusive development policies. *See, e.g.,* U.S. Agency for International Development, *USAID Disability Policy Paper* (1997) *available online at* <http://pdf.dec.org/pdf_docs/PDABQ631.pdf>. *See also* U.S. Agency for International Development, *USAID Disability Policy – Assistance* (2004), *available online at* <http://www.usaid.gov/about_usaid/disability>; U.S. Agency for International Development, USAID Acquisition and Assistance Disability Policy Directive (2004), *available online at* <http://www.usaid.gov/about_usaid/disability/>; U.S. Agency for International Development, *USAID Acquisition and Assistance Policy Directive (Disability Policy on New Construction)* (2005), *available online at:*

Experience has shown that increasing social participation to the physically constructed environment, as well as to the policies and procedures that aid-sponsored programs enact, can help make persons with disabilities more visible,[162] and thereby facilitate the enjoyment of other fundamental rights.[163] The CRPD's provisions may therefore serve to lessen the identity of persons with disabilities as "other,"[164] increase non-disabled familiarity with the group,[165] and manifest closer in reality the Vienna Declaration's oft repeated refrain that human rights are "indivisible, interrelated and interconnected."[166]

4 *Conclusion*

This chapter provided an overview of the Convention's background, summarized its substantive content, and considered some of the more immediate ways that the CRPD may positively impact the lives of persons with disabilities worldwide. The three areas we identified as potential catalysts for progressive change include the Convention's ability to trigger expressive value, prompt national level action, and advance the social integration of persons with disabilities in society through its inclusive development mandate.

<http://www.usaid.gov/about_usaid/disability/>; U.K. Department for International Development, *Disability, Poverty and Development*, (London, UK, February 2000), *available online at:* <http://www.dfid.gov.uk/pubs/files/disability.pdf>.

162 "People with disabilities were often virtually invisible citizens of many societies," and "have been marginalized in nearly all cultures throughout history." Quinn & Degener, *supra* note 6, at 23. *See also* Mark C. Weber, Disability Harassment 6 (NYU Press 2007) ("Lack of daily contact at a level of true equality with persons with disabilities promotes and constantly reinforces stereotypes.").

163 National Council on Disability, The Impact of the Americans with Disabilities Act: Assessing the Progress Toward Achieving the Goals of the ADA (July 26, 2007), *available online at*: <http://www.ncd.gov/newsroom/publications/2007/pdf/ada_impact_07–26–07.pdf>.

164 This is a standard sociological argument. The classic treatment is Erving Goffman, Stigma: Notes on the Management of Spoiled Identity 5 (Prentice-Hall, 1963) (asserting that stigma manifests when "we believe the person with a stigma is not quite human"); *see also* Jonathan C. Drimmer, *Cripples, Overcomers, and Civil Rights: Tracing the Evolution of Federal Legislation and Social Policy For People With Disabilities,* 40 UCLA L. Rev. 1341 (1993) (identifying intolerance and discrimination as part and parcel of the reasons for excluding people with disabilities' equal social participation).

165 For an argument on this ground in favor of employing greater numbers of persons with psycho-social disabilities, see Michael E. Waterstone & Michael Ashley Stein, *Disabling Prejudice*, 102 NW. U. L. Rev. 1351 (2008).

166 Vienna Declaration, *supra* note 36 at para. 63.

Ultimately, the extensive rights catalogue contained in the Convention will only manifest with commitments from individual States Parties to alter the historical treatment of persons with disabilities in their respective societies, along with support from a proactive and long-viewed CRPD monitoring Committee.[167] Such efforts must be supported by an equally vigorous commitment from civil society – disabled peoples organizations and their allies – and individual advocates alike to educate and advocate within the rights-based framework offered by the Convention.

[167] *See* Lord & Stein, *supra* note 7.

A Future of Multidimensional Disadvantage Equality?

Oddný Mjöll Arnardóttir

1 *Introduction*

The UN Convention on the Rights of Persons with Disabilities (CRPD) is the first human rights convention adopted in the 21st century.[1] By tailoring the existing human rights catalogue to the unique situation of persons with disabilities it represents a giant leap forward in the protection of the rights of persons with disabilities. At a more abstract level the Convention is an extremely important contribution to a paradigm change that is taking place and moves the approach of international human rights law from a concept of formal equality to a concept of multidimensional disadvantage equality.

This contribution argues that the principle of equality is the leitmotif of the CRPD, but that the significance of this can only be properly understood against the background of the development of the principle of equality in international human rights law and practice. It will be argued that the development of the principle of equality has occurred in three phases or eras that, although overlapping on some ways, can be outlined from a chronological perspective. These three eras of international legal protection of equality will be analysed against the backdrop of the elaboration of the principle of equality in legal theory. The focus is on the international human rights regime, with an emphasis on the United Nations and the Council of Europe.[2] The analysis will look at the legal

---

1 Convention on the Rights of Persons with Disabilities, GA Res. 61/106 (2007). The Convention and its Optional Protocol entered into force on 3 May 2008, see http://www2.ohchr.org/english/issues/disability/index.htm.

2 The themes and eras discussed also have a clear resonance in the development of the law of the European Union, but the EU regime will not be the subject of discussion in the present contribution. The reader is referred to Oddný Mjöll Arnardóttir, 'Non-discrimination in International and European Law: Towards Substantive Models' (2007) 25 *Nordisk Tidsskrift for Menneskerettigheter*, 140 and the contributions of Anna Lawson and Lisa Waddington in the present volume. Although developed independently of it, the themes and eras outlined in this contribution also resonate with Jill Lovecy's account of the women's rights discourse at the Council of Europe, *cf.* Jill Lovecy, 'Gender Mainstreaming and the Framing of Women's Rights

practice from two perspectives; firstly from the perspective of the development of discrimination grounds and the related scope of protection offered by international human rights law and secondly from the perspective of the concepts of equality that emerge in the law and its application. In particular, the advent of the CRPD will be placed in this context with the aim to elaborate what kind of equality the Convention reflects and the related consequences. It will be argued that the CRPD and its approach to equality is the logical result of previous developments in international law and that it reflects a substantive and multidimensional disadvantage approach to equality, which is informed by an understanding of disability as a social construct. It will also be argued that the CRPD decisively places disability on the list of internationally suspect discrimination grounds.

2 *The Principle of Equality as the Leitmotif of the CRPD*

Article 1 of the Universal Declaration of Human Rights (UDHR) proclaims that: "All human beings are born free and equal in dignity and rights."[3] Further, Article 2 stipulates that everyone is entitled to all the rights and freedoms set forth in the Declaration without distinction of any kind. The opening of the UDHR exhibits the central place of the idea of equality in human rights discourse.[4] Indeed, human rights are essentially conceived of as rights owed equally to all human beings by virtue simply of their equal humanity. The principle of equality is reflected in some form or another in all the major international human rights instruments and its importance is further reflected in scholarly discourse as to whether the principle, or some more narrowly construed aspect of it, have the character of a *jus cogens* norm.[5] It can, therefore, be stated without hesitation that the principle of equality is a fundamental principle that lies at the heart of the international protection of human rights.

---

in Europe: The Contribution of the Council of Europe', (2002) 10 *Feminist Legal Studies*, 271. She argues that the first phase between the 1950s and 1970s focused on the political rights and legal position of women (276), that the second phase in the 1980's was characterised by focus on the socio-economic status of women (276) and controversies about positive action and quotas in relation to political representation (279), and finally that this was replaced by the gender mainstreaming approach originating in the 1990s (280).

[3] Universal Declaration of Human Rights, GA Res. 217 A III (1948).

[4] See for example Hersch Lauterpacht, *An International Bill of the Rights of Man* (Columbia University Press, New York 1945) 115: "The claim to equality before the law is in a substantial sense the most fundamental of the rights of man. It occupies the first place in most written constitutions. It is the starting point of all other liberties."

[5] See for example Warwick McKean, *Equality and Discrimination under International Law* (Clarendon Press, Oxford 1983) 277–284, with references. See also Hilary Charlesworth and Christine Chinkin, 'The Gender of Jus Cogens' (1993) 15 *Human Rights Quarterly* 63.

Conceptually, equality and non-discrimination connote the same idea and can be seen as simply the positive and negative statements of the same principle.[6] While legal instruments often are formulated with reference to that which is prohibited, i.e. discrimination, the ban is intended to secure the ideal of equality that lies behind. For example, in the context of the European Convention on Human Rights (ECHR), this is expressed in the explanatory report to its Protocol No. 12.[7] The explanatory report to Protocol 12 refers to the general principle of equality and non-discrimination and states:

> [...] it should be noted that the non-discrimination and equality principles are closely intertwined. For example, the principle of equality requires that equal situations are treated equally and unequal situations differently. Failure to do so will amount to discrimination unless an objective and reasonable justification exists. [...] The Court, in its case-law under Article 14, has already made reference to the "principle of equality of treatment" [...][8]

It is clear, therefore, that the principle of equality and non-discrimination requires the equal treatment of equal situations and the different treatment of unequal situations. Based on this core content of the fundamental principle of equality and non-discrimination in international law, it is clear that equality theory must not only examine equality and sameness but also inequality and difference/disadvantage. This examination includes questions of what constitutes unequal (different/disadvantaged) situations and, following the establishment of such situations, what kind of treatment the equality principle requires for non-discrimination to prevail. Chapter 3 *infra* elaborates how equality theory and international practice has dealt with these and related questions. At this point it suffices to establish this core content of the principle of equality, accepted by theory and practice alike.[9]

---

[6] Anne F. Bayefsky, 'The Principle of Equality or Non-Discrimination in International Law' (1990) 11 *Human Rights Law Journal* 1, at p. 1, footnote 1 with references.

[7] Convention for the Protection of Human Rights and Fundamental Freedoms, CETS No. 5 (1950). Protocol No. 12 to the Convention for the Protection of Human Rights and Fundamental Freedoms, CETS No. 177 (2000).

[8] Protocol No. 12 to the Convention for the Protection of Human Rights and Fundamental Freedoms, explanatory report, CETS No. 177 (2000), para. 15, available at http://Conventions.coe.int/Treaty/en/Reports/Html/177.htm (last visited 10 June 2008). See also para. 1.

[9] For example, in *Thlimmenos v. Greece* [GC], 06.04.2000, Reports 2000–IV, para. 44, the Europan Court of Human Rights stated: "The Court has so far considered that the right under Article 14 not to be discriminated against in the enjoyment of the rights guaranteed under the Convention is violated when States treat differently persons in analogous situations without providing an objective and reasonable justification [...] However, the Court considers that this is not the only facet of the prohibition of discrimination in Article 14. The right not to be discriminated against in the enjoyment of the rights guaranteed under the Convention is also violated when States without an objective and reasonable justification fail to treat differently persons whose situations are significantly different."

Turning to the CRPD more specifically, it is clear that the Convention is based on two main premises. First, it is clear that equality and non-discrimination is really the primary principle permeating the whole of the Convention. It is generally understood that the Convention does not explicitly aim to create new human rights and that instead it seeks to adapt the existing human rights protection to the unique situation of persons with disabilities. The aim is the enjoyment by persons with disabilities of all human rights on an equal footing with others. This approach was evidenced already in the General Assembly resolution which established the Ad Hoc Committee responsible for preparing the Convention. It placed great emphasis on the idea of the equalisation of opportunities for persons with disabilities and stated that the Convention should be: "based on the holistic approach in the work done in the fields of social development, human rights and non-discrimination [...]."[10] This idea that the Convention would not create new rights, but adapt existing rights to secure their equal enjoyment by persons with disabilities, became an omnipresent theme during its drafting.[11]

The Convention text itself is, of course, true to the mandate. The preamble repeatedly refers to the principles of equality and non-discrimination, *cf.* preambular letters a, b, c, e, f, h, p, r, and x. Article 1 of the Convention also declares the purpose of the Convention as being to promote, protect and ensure the full and equal enjoyment of all human rights by persons with disabilities and to promote respect for their dignity. And, finally, Article 3 lists the principles of the Convention in 8 items. Items b, e and g explicitly refer to non-discrimination, equality of opportunity and equality between men and women. The remaining items; a, c, d, f and h, all refer to issues that are in varying degrees also based on the principle of equality; most clearly the emphasis on inclusion

---

[10] General Assembly Resolution 56/168, 19 December 2001, A/RES/56/168, para. 1.

[11] The Ad Hoc Committee, for example, concluded its first session by adopting a recommendation for a General Assembly Resolution including the following statement: "*Reaffirming* the need to promote and protect the equal and effective enjoyment of all human rights and fundamental freedoms by persons with disabilities, aware of the contribution that a convention could make in this regard and thus convinced of the need to continue to consider proposals," *cf.* 'Report of the Ad Hoc Committee on a Comprehensive and Integral International Convention on Protection and Promotion of the Rights and Dignity of Persons with Disabilities', A/57/357. It has, however, been argued that this statement that the Convention does not create new rights is an oversimplification that: "...does not do justice to the multilayered normative reality of as rich an instrument as the Convention.", Frédéric Mégret, 'The Disabilities Convention: Human Rights of Persons with Disabilities or Disability Rights?' 30 *Human Rights Quarterly* 494, 498. The point here is not to contradict that analysis, but simply to describe the discourse surrounding the drafting process and to explicate how the principle of equality stands out as the most important guiding theme of the drafting process.

and accessibility, but also the respect for the dignity, diversity, autonomy and independence of persons with disabilities, and even the respect for the evolving capacities of children with disabilities.

The second premise of the Convention is the realisation that previous efforts to secure the human rights of persons with disabilities had been unsuccessful in fact. The classical non-discrimination clauses in the UN Covenants; Articles 2 and 26 of the International Covenant on Civil and Political Rights (ICCPR),[12] and Article 2, Paragraph 2 of the International Covenant on Economic, Social and Cultural Rights (IESCR),[13] are directed against discrimination of any kind, but list the following as the most important examples of discrimination grounds: race, colour, sex, language, religion, political or other opinion, national or social origin, property, birth or other status. Article 14 ECHR lists the same discrimination grounds, with the addition of association with a national minority. There is no mention of disability. The existing UN Conventions specifically directed against discrimination also only focused on race (ethnic origin) and sex (gender), *cf.* the UN Convention on the Elimination of All Forms of Racial Discrimination (CERD)[14] and the UN Convention on the Elimination of All Forms of Discrimination against Women (CEDAW).[15]

Clearly, there was a vacuum there to be filled in the context of disability. As explained in the contribution of Michael Stein and Janet Lord, the efforts to fill this gap were originally confined to soft law declarations in the form of non-binding guidance for social policy. This, not surprisingly, proved ineffective and the General Assembly resolution mandating the drafting of a new convention explicitly recognised that the soft law principles and policy guidelines adopted since the early 1980s had not resulted in the full and effective participation and opportunities for persons with disabilities.[16] Similarly, the Preamble to the Convention itself acknowledges these soft law instruments and the hard law of the general human rights provisions as important steps in the developments leading up to the adoption of the Convention. But the preamble explicitly raises awareness that: "despite these various instruments and undertakings, persons with disabilities continue to face barriers in their participation as equal members of

12 International Covenant on Civil and Political Rights, 999 UNTS 172 (1966).

13 International Covenant on Economic, Social and Cultural Rights, 993 UNTS 4 (1966).

14 International Convention on the Elimination of All Forms of Racial Discrimination, 660 UNTS 212 (1965).

15 Convention on the Elimination of All Forms of Discrimination against Women, 1249 UNTS 14 (1979). Before the adoption of the CRPD, the only UN convention to include disability among the enumerated discrimination grounds was the Convention on the Rights of the Child, 1577 UNTS 44 (1989), *cf.* Article 2(1).

16 General Assembly Resolution 56/168, *supra* note 10, preamble.

society and violations of their human rights in all parts of the world."[17] On the occasion of the adoption of the CRPD, Ambassador Don MacKay, who chaired the Ad Hoc Committee negotiating the Convention, put this premise behind the adoption of the Convention clearly:

> Theoretically there was no need for a new convention, because the existing human rights instruments apply to persons with disabilities, in just the same way that they do to everyone else. The reality, unfortunately, has not followed the theory. [...] This does not mean that States have deliberately avoided their obligations. But many of the obligations under other instruments are set out in quite a broad and generic way, which can leave grey areas for their practical implementation in respect of particular groups.[18]

In conclusion it can be stated that it is clear that equality and non-discrimination is a long established fundamental principle of human rights protection and that the CRPD as a whole is firmly rooted in this principle. The original idea behind the principle of equality in human rights law was that it would secure human rights to all persons on an equal basis. The Convention, however, very powerfully drives home the realisation that experience has shown that in fact, the general "universal" human rights regime has not proved to be all that effective in the context of disability, or for that matter in the context of other marginalised groups.[19] The Convention's whole leitmotif is to address this imbalance. In doing so it is firmly based on the principle of equality, but it represents a deeper and more profound understanding of equality as the principle of equality reflected in the Convention clearly requires the express adaptation of what is perceived as universal rights to the unique situation of persons with disabilities. The Convention, thus, clearly showcases firstly the danger that the simple and superficial understanding of universal equality renders non-discrimination clauses empty and toothless in legal practice, and secondly the depth and complexities involved in the principle of equality as such and the need to bring this deeper understanding of equality to bear on legal practice.

[17] Preamble, letter k.

[18] 'Statement on behalf of New Zealand, by Ambassador Don MacKay (Chair of the Ad Hoc Committee), at the adoption of the Convention on the Rights of Persons with Disabilities by the United Nations General Assembly on 13 December 2006', available at http://www.un.org/disabilities/default.asp?id=155#nz (last visited 11 June 2008).

[19] The CRPD has been argued to be part of a wider trend of a "pluralization of human rights", whereby it is increasingly recognised that the general human rights regime needs to be tailored to be able to deal with the realities of specific groups, see Mégret, *supra* note 11, 495–497.

3 *The Rights of Persons with Disabilities in light of the Development of the Principle of Equality in Human Rights Law*

The deeper understanding of equality reflected in the CRPD is rooted in the way the concept of equality has evolved in theory and in international human rights law and practice. To fully grasp the Convention's understanding of the principle of equality, it is necessary to look at how the CRPD is the "legitimate child" of these developments. The theoretical development of the principle of equality can be described as having occurred in three phases and it is argued here that each of these phases have subsequently had their impact on legal regulation and legal practice during a particular era. It can be said that feminist legal scholarship has led the theoretical elaboration of the principle of equality and informed other critical approaches as well as mainstream approaches to equality in law.[20]

3.1 *Universal Sameness: 1950s–1970s*

The first approach is the formal equality approach and its corresponding era. This era can be characterised by reference to the key terms of universality and sameness and it represents the foundational approach of the principle of equality in human rights law. This era is roughly defined by the adoption of the first international human rights instruments, the UDHR in 1948 and the ECHR in 1950, through the adoption of the two United Nations Covenants in 1966 and lasting until the mid 1970s.[21]

The theoretical equality model informing this era is the formal equality model, also referred to as the sameness approach or the symmetrical approach.[22] This approach focuses on the Aristotelian equality maxim that equals shall be treated equally and unequals unequally.[23] The formal approach does not challenge

---

[20] See e.g. Christine A. Littleton, 'Reconstructing Sexual Equality', (1987) 75 *California Law Review* 1279 (sameness/difference/acceptance); Catharine MacKinnon, *Toward a Feminist Theory of the State*, (Harvard University Press, Cambridge MA 1989) (sameness/difference/domination); Deborah L. Rhode, 'The Politics of Paradigms: Gender Difference and Gender Disadvantage', in Gisela Bock and Susan James (eds), *Beyond Equality and Difference: Citizenship, Feminist Politics and Female Subjectivity* (Routledge, London 1992) 149 (sameness/difference/disadvantage); Joan C. Williams: 'Deconstructing Gender', in Patricia Smith (ed), *Feminist Jurisprudence* (Oxford University Press, Oxford 1993), 531 (sameness/difference/deinstitutionalisation). A good overview is presented by Clíona J.M. Kimber, 'Equality or Self-determination', in Conor Gearty and Adam Tomkins (eds), *Understanding Human Rights*, (Mansell Publishing, London 1996) 266.

[21] The adoption of CERD in 1965 also belongs to this era chronologically, but it will be discussed with the "Specific Difference" era *infra.*

[22] This paragraph, with references, is in essence a re-print of Arnardóttir, *supra* note 2, 142–143.

[23] Aristotle, *Ethica Nicomachea*, V.3.: "...this is the origin of quarrels and complaints – when either equals have and are awarded unequal shares, or unequals equal shares.", cited from Louis

traditional constructions of equality/sameness and difference/otherness, and the focus on finding an appropriate comparator for equality analysis may exclude some acute equality issues such as pregnancy and disabilities completely from the realm of non-discrimination provisions.[24] The formal approach is void of normative content as it only guarantees consistency in treatment (procedural equality) but makes no demands on the content of that treatment (substantive equality).[25] It entails that the focus is on equal treatment regardless of the possible unequal results that may flow from it. The formal conception of equality, therefore, excludes indirect discrimination.[26] Within feminism, the formal model has been attributed to liberal feminism in line with a liberal conception of the state.[27] Its symmetry and focus on the same treatment is directly related to its focus on individualism in that individual merit and fault are instrumental in analysis and not the structural disadvantages pertaining to membership in a certain group. Therefore, positive measures designed to promote equality (hereinafter affirmative action) cannot be justified under the formal approach. Correlative is an emphasis on the passive role of the state and the idea of state neutrality.[28] Framing this emphasis in the terminology of international human rights law, the focus is on negative state obligations.

An important distinguishing characteristic of this era was the fact that non-discrimination was generally not perceived as an independent substantive right, but only as an accessory right with which to guarantee the equal enjoyment of the "real" substantive rights.[29] This clearly reflects the then prevailing understanding in mainstream legal scholarship that equality is normatively "empty" as a legal concept and can, at most, function to guarantee consistency in treatment.[30] Originally, therefore, the legal provisions of this era had only a vague normative

P. Pojman and Robert Westmoreland (eds), *Equality – Selected Readings* (Oxford University Press, Oxford 1997) 17, 20.

24 Kimber, *supra* note 20, 268–269.

25 *Ibid.*

26 Titia Loenen, 'Indirect Discrimination: Oscillating Between Containment and Revolution' in Titia Loenen and Peter R. Rodrigues (eds), *Non-Discrimination Law: Comparative Perspectives* (Kluwer Law International, The Hague 1999) 195, 198.

27 Stephanie Palmer, 'Critical Perspectives on Women's Rights: The European Convention on Human Rights and Fundamental Freedoms', in Anne Bottomley (ed), *Feminist Perspectives on the Foundational Subjects of Law* (Cavendish Publishing, London 1996) 223, 228.

28 Sandra Fredman, 'Reversing Discrimination' (1997) 113 *Law Quarterly Review* 575, 577.

29 *Cf.* Article 2 UDHR, Articles 2 and 3 ICCPR, Article 2, Paragraph 2 ICESCR and Article 14 ECHR. Article 26 ICCPR is the exception as it is expressly formulated in a manner that implies a substantive right. This was nevertheless originally disputed, *cf. infra.*

30 Alf Ross, *On Law and Justice* (Stevens & Sons, London 1958) 288. H.L.A. Hart, *The Concept of Law* (2nd edn Clarendon Press, Oxford 1994) 159.

content and it was unclear in what direction their interpretation might develop. The legal texts provided no precise guidance on that issue.

As to the scope of the legal protection in this era, all the key instruments belonging to this era (UDHR, ECHR, ICCPR, ICESCR) incorporated open-model non-discrimination clauses. Open models typically do not attempt to stipulate an exhaustive list of discrimination grounds but ban discrimination "on any ground" and possibly proceed to mention certain discrimination grounds by way of example. A non-exhaustive list of discrimination grounds has a very significant effect. It entails that distinctions of any kind may engage judicial scrutiny under the clause and the issue of whether or not it has been violated does not turn on questions such as whether the listed ground of sex includes pregnancy, sexual orientation or transsexualism. An open model also entails that the provision itself does not elaborate on the test for drawing the line between illegal discrimination and justified differentiations and it does not formally limit the possible justifications for differentiation. Open-model non-discrimination clauses are, therefore, generally blunt tools with which to combat discrimination. They do not automatically recognise the profound differences that exist in reality between the context and situation of socially privileged groups on one hand and marginalised groups on the other.

In conclusion on this era it seems clear that a genuine and benign belief in the utility of universal human rights norms and their potential to provide the same protection to everyone lay behind the international law adopted during this era. But the combination of the four key factors of 1) the perceived normative emptiness of the non-discrimination clauses, 2) the belief in the neutrality of the *laissez-faire* state, 3) the focus on individual merit and fault and 4) the focus on finding appropriate comparators without critically examining ideas of sameness and otherness, all these had a profound effect on how the principle of equality was understood in law. These factors rendered the principle of equality very assimilationist in character and legalised the approach that you had to be the same as the unquestioned standard representing the privileged groups in society before you could ever make a legal claim to non-discrimination. This approach had the effect to exclude all those who belonged to marginalised groups from the protection of the principle of equality. And, indeed, the ramifications for persons with disabilities stand out as the prime example of the shortcomings of the formal approach.

3.2 *Specific Difference: 1970s–1990s*

The next era runs approximately between the mid 1970s and the mid 1990s. The focus moved from the universal open-model non-discrimination clauses to more concrete and thorough treatment of specific discrimination grounds which were understood as natural or immutable and, thus, generally defined by biological indicators. Hence, this era can be characterised by reference to the key terms of specificity and difference.

The theoretical equality model informing this era can be described as the substantive difference model.[31] It builds upon the Aristotelian equality model, like the formal approach, but accommodates more clearly for differences/otherness. Under the formal approach differences lead to exclusion while the difference approach recognises that some differences must be acted upon to facilitate inclusion and achieve equality in fact. Classic examples include pregnancy and accommodation for persons with disabilities. The focus is on biological or immutable differences and accommodation for differences is generally seen as an exception to the rule of formal equal treatment.[32] This way the difference model imports a substantive normative element into the equality maxim and aims at producing equality of results in targeted areas.[33] A focus on equality of results can legitimate affirmative action programs and opens up the possibility to challenge indirect discrimination as different results as between groups, irrespective of intent, call for equality analysis and objective justification.[34] In the context of gender equality, the roots of the difference approach have been identified as lying in cultural feminism and its focus on the differences between men and women and on women's distinctive values and needs.[35] Correlative to the substantive difference approach is the view that a non-interventionist state only functions to perpetuate a *status quo* of unequal situations.[36] The difference approach, thus, reflects the development of international human rights law from a simple classical focus on protection from state interference and negative obligations, to its combination with a positive role for the state in implementing and ensuring human rights. The substantive difference approach, however, only targets specific differences and aims at equality of results in those areas. The main problem associated with this approach, relates to the question of which differences should be accommodated. Generally during this era the focus was on natural or immutable differences, which has a certain potential for the perpetuation of stereotypical views of group identity and otherness. Framing equality analysis in terms of difference from a comparator also maintains the approach that the prevailing groups in society are the unquestioned standard of measure. These

---

[31] This paragraph, with references, is in essence a re-print of Arnardóttir, *supra* note 2, 143–144.
[32] Kimber, *supra* note 20, 270–271.
[33] *Ibid.*, 271.
[34] Loenen, *supra* note 26, 199.
[35] Palmer, *supra* note 27, 229.
[36] Fredman, *supra* note 28, 578–579.

main characteristics of the difference approach, therefore, attracted criticism for its potential to entrench situations of privileges and disadvantages in society.[37]

Ideas about the inherent "emptiness" of the principle of equality and the right to non-discrimination started receding during this era. During the 1980s this issue was fiercely debated in the mainstream literature in some national jurisdictions and the literature on Article 26 ICCPR was highly concerned with the question as to whether Article 26 ICCPR contained an independent substantive right over and above the formal procedural guarantee of consistency.[38] The issue was settled in the affirmative in the 1989 ICCPR Human Rights Committee (HRC) General Comment on non-discrimination.[39] In fact, the shift in mainstream legal discourse, which now began to accept that there was normative substance in the right to non-discrimination, was spurred on by developments in the case law.[40]

With respect to racial discrimination, the specific difference approach was first evidenced as early as in the adoption of CERD in 1965. Chronologically it therefore belongs more to the previous era, but conceptually it is an exception to the typical characteristics governing that era and will therefore be counted with the present era.[41] Sex discrimination also received special attention during

[37] Kimber, *supra* note 20, 271–272.

[38] E.g. Peter Westen, 'The Empty Idea of Equality' (1982) 95 *Harvard Law Review*, 537 and Kent Greenawalt, 'How Empty is the Idea of Equality?' (1983) 83 *Columbia Law Review*, 1167. On the debates about Article 26 ICCPR see Asbjørn Eide and Torkel Opsahl, 'Equality and Non-Discrimination', cited from Asbjørn Eide, Jan Helgesen, Njål Høstmælingen and Erik Møse (eds), *Law and Equality, Selected Articles on Human Rights*, (Ad Notam Gyldendal, Oslo 1996) 165, 192 (with references).

[39] HRC General Comment No. 18, 'Non-Discrimination', 10.11.1989, available at http://www.unhchr.ch/tbs/doc.nsf/(Symbol)/3888b0541f8501c9c12563ed004b8d0e?Opendocument (last visited 19 June 2008). The General Comment interpreted all the provisions and concepts related to equality in the ICCPR together so as to constitute a basic and general principle and stated: "In the view of the Committee, article 26 does not merely duplicate the guarantee already provided for in article 2 but provides in itself an autonomous right. It prohibits discrimination in law or in fact in any field regulated and protected by public authorities. Article 26 is therefore concerned with the obligations imposed on States parties in regard to their legislation and the application thereof. Thus, when legislation is adopted by a State party, it must comply with the requirement of article 26 that its content should not be discriminatory. In other words, the application of the principle of non-discrimination contained in article 26 is not limited to those rights which are provided for in the Covenant.", *cf.* para. 12.

[40] Particularly the views of the HRC in *Broeks v. the Netherlands*, 09.04.1987, Comm. No. 172/1984, CCPR/C/29/D/172/1984 and *Zwaan-de Vries v. the Netherlands*, 09.04.1987, Comm. No. 182/1984, CCPR/C/29/D/182/1984.

[41] The emphasis on racial equality represented in the early adoption of CERD in 1965 has its historical explanations. Firstly, it is explained by the establishment of the UN and the adoptions of its human rights treaties being in effect a response to the atrocities of, particularly,

this era as reflected by the adoption of CEDAW in 1979. The case law of the ICCPR Human Rights Committee (HRC) and the European Court of Human Rights (ECtHR) mirrored these theme-specific developments. Although based on the general open-model non-discrimination clauses of Article 26 ICCPR and Article 14 ECHR, the case law singled specific discrimination grounds out for more thorough treatment and asserted the need for particularly convincing reasons before different treatment based on these discrimination grounds could be justified, thus asserting the strict scrutiny of discrimination based on specific "suspect" discrimination grounds. The categories of discrimination subject to strict scrutiny established under by the ECtHR during this era reached the biological categories of "illegitimacy" and sex.[42] Similarly, the HRC established sex as a suspect discrimination ground.[43] The traditional emphasis placed by international law on the eradication of racial discrimination also entailed that it was generally understood that racial discrimination would be subject to strict scrutiny.[44] International case law, however, proved ill equipped to identify various covert structural barriers relating to ethnicity which can be argued to be due to the underdeveloped state of indirect discrimination analysis during this era.[45]

Conceptually, the legal provisions belonging to this era reflected the substantive difference model of equality. Contrary to the general open-model discrimination clauses, Article 1 CERD and Article 1 CEDAW contained an

World War II, *cf.* e.g. the preamble to the UN Charter which opens on this statement: "We the peoples of the United Nations determined to save succeeding generations from the scourge of war, which twice in our lifetime has brought untold sorrow to mankind and to reaffirm faith in fundamental human rights [...]", Charter of the United Nations, 1 UNTS 16 (1945). Secondly, it can be explained by the emphasis on decolonisation also particularly relevant for historical reasons at the time of its adoption, *cf.* CERD, Preamble.

42 *Marckx v. Belgium*, 13.06.1979, Series A, No. 31 (illegitimacy) and *Abdulaziz, Cabales and Balkandali v. The United Kingdom*, 28.05.1985, Series A, No. 94 (sex).

43 *Mauritian Women v. Mauritius*, 09.04.1981, Comm. No. 35/1978, CCPR/C/12/D/35/1978, *Broeks v. the Netherlands*, 09.04.1987, *supra* note 40 and *Zwaan-de Vries v. the Netherlands*, 09.04.1987, *supra* note 40.

44 Bayefsky, *supra* note 5, 19–20, citing *inter alia* the opinion of the European Commission of Human Rights in *East African Asians v. the United Kingdom*, 14.12.1973, 3 EHRR 76, where the Commission stated that it was generally recognised that racial discrimination should receive special attention and might be capable of constituting degrading treatment, *cf.* para 207.

45 In *Gueye v. France*, 06.04.1989, Comm. No. 196/1985, CCPR/C/35/D/196/1985, the HRC found discrimination in the fact that pension rights were different for former soldiers of French nationality and those of Senegalese nationality who served in the French army prior to the independence of Senegal. The Committee, however, did not label this discrimination as being based on race, but on nationality ("other status"). In *Abdulaziz, Cabales and Balkandali v. The United Kingdom, supra* note 42, a minority of the European Commission of Human Rights found the contested immigration rules indirectly racist, but the Court found no such discrimination established.

express definition of discrimination which referred to the purpose "or effect" of discriminatory measures, but the reference to effects in this terminology of international law reflects the concept of indirect discrimination as it is known to the law of the European Union and many domestic jurisdictions. While the primary focus remained on negative state obligations and the equal treatment principle, the need for positive state obligation, appropriately accommodating for differences and affirmative action was also expressly recognised, *cf.* Articles 1(4) and 2(2) CERD and Article 4 CEDAW. In the context of the ICCPR, these inherent characteristics of the protection against discrimination were also expressly recognised in HRC General Comments, first in 1981 with regard to the equality between the sexes under Article 3 ICCPR, and then in 1989 with regard to non-discrimination more generally.[46] The HRC case law based on Article 26 ICCPR and the ECtHR case law on Article 14 ECHR also began recognising some exceptions to formal equal treatment during this era.[47]

In conclusion on this era it can be said that it is clear that the specific difference approach was based on the premise that discrimination law intervenes in an otherwise simple and neutral situation where the two individuals compared are alike in all relevant respects other than with regard to the one specific identity marker singled out as "the difference" to be corrected for. This correction for a specific difference could, depending on context, take the form of strict scrutiny of invidious differentiations or the form of reasonable accommodations and affirmative action to facilitate inclusion. The legitimacy of affirmative action, nevertheless, remained highly controversial during this era and all departures from formal and symmetrical equality were conceptualised as exceptions.[48] In mainstream legal practice, the differences meriting this treatment were generally understood with references to biological identity markers. In essence, the approach was that if it was biology and immutable natural differences that intervened in the otherwise presumed neutral social playing field, the law was prepared to correct for that as this implied no element of choice or fault on behalf of

---

[46] HRC General Comment No. 4, 'Equality between the sexes (Art. 3)', 30.07.1981, available at http://www.unhchr.ch/tbs/doc.nsf/(Symbol)/14424a74d091ad7cc12563ed0046a8f2?Opendocument (last visited 19 June 2008), para. 2 (affirmative action) and para. 3 (positive obligations). HRC General Comment No. 18, *supra* note 39, para. 7 (indirect discrimination) and para. 10 (affirmative action).

[47] *Stalla Costa v. Uruguay*, 09.07.1987, Comm. No. 198/1985, CCPR/C/30/D/198/1985, where it was held that the preferential re-hiring of civil servants who had been unfairly dismissed under a military regime was not in violation of Article 26 ICCPR. Also *Rasmussen v. Denmark*, 28.11.1984, Series A, No. 87 and *Schuler-Zgraggen v. Switzerland*, 24.06.1993, Series A, No. 263, where the same presumption on the primary role of women in childcare functioned to the detriment of a woman and a man respectively, and met different levels of scrutiny.

[48] E.g. Theodor Meron, *Human Rights Law-Making in the United Nations* (Clarendon Press, Oxford 1986) 36.

the individuals concerned. The assumption was that as between the individuals compared all things were equal except for the singled out identity marker. Therefore, the law during this era located the "problem" that non-discrimination provisions were supposed to address with the marginalised individual herself and her specific natural or biological difference, and not with structural societal factors. The non-discrimination law, thus, in effect could only address the needs of the sub-groups within socially marginalised groups who were most alike the prevailing standard. The difference of disability, however, was perceived as so profoundly incomparable to the prevailing standard, that under international law it remained largely unnoticed as an equality issue.

3.3 *Multidimensional Disadvantage: Current Trends*

The third and last era runs from the mid 1990s to date. This era has been characterised by the strengthening of protection against discrimination, an increased awareness of the complex structural social factors that intervene in the playing field that the law previously presumed was neutral and an increased awareness of how individual and group identities that create vulnerabilities to discrimination are multidimensional. Therefore, this present era can best be described by reference to the concepts of multidimensionality and structural disadvantage.

The theoretical equality model informing this era can be labelled the substantive disadvantage model.[49] It is a contextual approach that focuses on the asymmetrical structures of power, privilege and disadvantage that are at work in society. It aims clearly at the equality of results and the eradication of practices and policies that increase or maintain disadvantage. It does not see tools and techniques to achieve this change as exceptions from the main rule of identical treatment but as simply sometimes required to eliminate discriminatory social and political structures.[50] This is a similar take to that of the difference approach, but its ingredients are taken to their fullest capacity. This approach has been elaborated as a response to the weaknesses of the other approaches that frame questions of equality in terms of the comparative concepts of sameness or difference. It has been developed in the feminist scholarship proceeding to move forward from the focus on sameness or difference *per se* onto the structural or systemic consequences of gender.[51] As such it can be lumped together under the heading of social constructionist feminism.[52] In a wider context than that

[49] This paragraph, with references, is in essence a re-print of Arnardóttir, *supra* note 2, 144–145.

[50] Kimber, *supra* note 20, 273.

[51] Palmer, *supra* note 27, 230.

[52] The social construction of gender has been described as a theoretical perspective: "...which informs a feminist understanding of the systemic aspects of the position of women in society and also integrates empirical research to demonstrate this reality in women's and men's lives.",

of gender discrimination it can be argued that theories of social construction generally form the backbone to the disadvantage approach. In fact, social construction theory seems tailor-made to fit this kind of substantive equality analysis. As elaborated by Ian Hacking, social construction work raises awareness that: "the existence or character of X is not determined by the nature of things. X is not inevitable. X was brought into existence or shaped by social events, forces, history, all of which could have been different."[53] Social construction theory thus rejects essentialism, the claim that certain traits or identity markers are natural or immutable, and focuses attention on them being social constructs as well as critically focusing attention on the systemic patterns of power, dominance and disadvantage that exist in society. The disadvantage approach, thus, clearly rejects the focus on individualism and the laissez-faire state inherent in the formal approach as they may be conducive towards maintaining discrimination. Correlative in human rights discourse is an increased emphasis on the positive role and positive obligations of states.

During the present era, the remnants of the idea that equality and non-discrimination were in essence empty as a substantive right and only apt to ensuring procedural consistency in the application of the "real" substantive law were finally completely silenced. This occurred in 2000 by the advent of Protocol 12 to the ECHR, which added an independent and general ban against discrimination to the otherwise restricted scope of protection provided by Article 14.[54]

Of course, the legal response to the important discrimination grounds of sex and race continues to be developed during the present era.[55] It is, however, an

---

cf. Judith Lorber and Susan A. Farrell (eds): *The Social Construction of Gender* (Sage Publications, Newbury Park CA 1991) 1.

[53] Ian Hacking: *The Social Construction of What?* (Harvard University Press, Cambridge MA 1999) 6–7.

[54] Article 14 of the ECHR is only an accessory right that guarantees non-discrimination in the enjoyment of the other rights and freedoms protected by the Convention. Although there is in fact no watertight division between civil and political rights on one hand and economic, social and cultural rights on the other, the accessory nature of Article 14 has had the effect to exclude large areas of socioeconomic rights from the scope of the protection against discrimination under the ECHR. This was remedied by Protocol 12. The explanatory report to Protocol 12 explains that the expansion reaches discrimination in the following fields: "i. in the enjoyment of any right specifically granted to an individual under national law; ii. in the enjoyment of a right which may be inferred from a clear obligation of a public authority under national law, that is, where a public authority is under an obligation under national law to behave in a particular manner; iii. by a public authority in the exercise of discretionary power (for example granting certain subsidies); iv. by any other act or omission by a public authority (for example, the behaviour of law enforcement officers when controlling a riot).", *cf.* Protocol 12, explanatory report, *supra* note 8, para. 22.

[55] Important recent examples on race from the case law of the ECtHR include e.g. *Cyprus v. Turkey* [GC], 10.05.2001, Reports 2001–IV, where the Court found widespread and serious

important characteristic of this era that the suspect discrimination grounds under the open-model discrimination clauses of international law have been expanded from encompassing only sex (gender), race (ethnicity) and "illegitimacy" (being born to unmarried parents). Under the ECHR the list of suspect discrimination grounds now also includes nationality, religion, and sexual orientation.[56] Under the ICCPR, the Human Rights Committee has also expanded the repertoire of cases that indicate strict scrutiny from cases concerning sex to other discrimination grounds. Currently, violations of Article 26 are primarily found in cases concerning discrimination based on sex, religion/belief, nationality/citizenship and political opinion.[57] The discrimination ground of disability has also been under development in the present era. Already in 1989, the Convention on the Rights of the Child (CRC) included disability in its list of discrimination grounds, *cf.* Article 2(1).[58] In the European human rights regime, the revised European Social Charter of 1996 (ESC) added health to the usual list of discrimination grounds when framing the new general non-discrimination clause of the Charter, *cf.* Article E. The revised Article 15 ESC also replaced the former right to: "vocational training, rehabilitation and resettlement" with a right to "independence, social integration and participation in the life of the community."[59] The combination

discriminatory treatment based on race established and concluded that it amounted to degrading treatment in violation of Article 3 ECHR, and *D.H. and Others v. the Czech Republic* [GC], 13.11.2007, unpublished, available at http://cmiskp.echr.coe.int/tkp197/view.asp?action=html&documentId=825443&portal=hbkm&source=externalbydocnumber&table=F69A27FD8FB86142BF01C1166DEA398649 (last visited 20 June 2008), where the Court for the first time clearly analysed a case from the perspective of indirect discrimination under Article 14 ECHR and found racial discrimination established under that approach. The judgment also reiterated the previously established approach that racial discrimination should be subject to strict scrutiny, *cf.* paras. 175–176. In the context of sex (gender) equality, the judgment in *Stec and Others v. the United Kingdom* [GC], 12.04.2006, unpublished, available at http://cmiskp.echr.coe.int/tkp197/view.asp?action=html&documentId=794149&portal=hbkm&source=externalbydocnumber&table=F69A27FD8FB86142BF01C1166DEA398649 (last visited 20 June 2008) exhibited that the Court is becoming increasingly aware of how the social context of cases can justify departures from formal and symmetrical equality. Correspondingly, the Court placed positive action to: "correct the disadvantaged economic position of women" under rather lenient scrutiny, *cf.* para. 66.

56 See the analysis of the case law in Oddný Mjöll Arnardóttir, *Equality and Non-Discrimination under the European Convention on Human Rights* (Martinus Nijhoff Publishers, The Hague 2003), 150–155.

57 See the analysis of the case law in Manfred Nowak, *U.N. Covenant on Civil and Political Rights CCPR Commentary* (2nd ed. N.P. Engel Verlag, Kehl 2005), 608–629.

58 In 1990, Anne F. Bayefsky argued that international law would continue to expand the list of suspect discrimination grounds, and that the inclusion of disability on the CRC list of discrimination grounds provided evidence of that process, Bayefsky, *supra* note 6, 24.

59 European Social Charter, CETS No. 35 (1961) and European Social Charter (Revised), CETS No. 163 (1996).

of these innovations in the ESC had the effect that the systemic absence of persons with disabilities from the mainstream is no longer accepted under the ESC and disability is now dealt with under a non-discrimination approach.[60] Disability was, however, not added to the list of discrimination grounds in the new Protocol 12 to the ECHR in 2000. The question of whether to add the discrimination grounds of disability, sexual orientation and age to the express list of discrimination grounds was raised during the drafting of Protocol 12 to the ECHR, but unfortunately answered in the negative. The explanatory report, however, explained that this was: "not because of a lack of awareness that such grounds have become particularly important in today's societies as compared with the time of drafting of Article 14 of the Convention [...]",[61] but rather for reasons related to legislative techniques. In this context it is also necessary to keep in mind that Article 14 has been applied to discrimination grounds not included on the list,[62] and that the ECtHR has indeed subjected some of them to strict scrutiny. Therefore, the fact that no "new" discrimination grounds were added in Protocol 12 should not be construed as indicating that they could not be considered members of the list of internationally suspect discrimination grounds. The adoption of the CRPD clearly fits into this current trend of expressly or implicitly expanding the suspect discrimination grounds that the law can correct for, either by placing invidious differentiations under strict scrutiny, or by requiring or allowing reasonable accommodation and affirmative action. Against this background of current trends and earlier developments in the hard law of international human rights protection, it is concluded here that the advent of the CRPD decisively places disability onto the list of internationally suspect discrimination grounds.

Underlying these legal developments on discrimination based on, particularly, sex (gender), race (ethnicity), disability and sexual orientation, is an increased awareness of the social construction of these identity markers. This awareness has been informed by, respectively, feminist theory, critical race theory, disability studies and queer studies and it is beginning to strike through to the level of international law and legal practice. For example, it can be argued that the ECtHR has begun to conceptualise the previously biologically constructed discrimination ground of sex in terms of socially constructed gender. There are certainly some signs of development in that direction, although not (yet) directly related

60 For an in depth discussion see Gerard Quinn, 'The European Social Charter and EU Anti-discrimination Law in the Field of Disability: Two Gravitational Fields with One Common Purpose', in Grainne de Búrca and Bruno de Witte, (eds), *Social Rights in Europe* (Oxford University Press, Oxford 2005) 279 and the contribution of Colm O'Cinneide in the present volume.

61 Protocol 12, explanatory report, *supra* note 8, para. 20.

62 *Ibid.*

to Article 14 ECHR.[63] The Committee on the Elimination of Discrimination against Women also reflected the social construction of gender in a General Recommendation adopted in 2004.[64] Similarly, while racial discrimination has probably to some extent ever since the adoption of CERD in 1965, *cf.* Article 1(1), been understood as encompassing both biological indicators relating to appearances and ancestry on one hand, and social factors relating to history and culture on the other, it is possible to discern an increased emphasis on the social construction of ethnicity in legal practice. Already in 1990 the Committee on the Elimination of Racial Discrimination concluded in a General Comment that the question whether an individual belongs to a particular racial or ethnic group should be based on the person's own self-identification[65] and in 2000 it elaborated descent as a social construct, as part of its concept of racial discrimination under Article 1(1) CERD.[66] This awareness of the social construction of race was also evidenced clearly under the ECHR in 2005, when the ECtHR elaborated how the term racial discrimination should be understood in the jurisprudence of the Court.[67] The CRPD is a particularly clear example of this trend as it is expressly

---

[63] The most powerful sign of this development is to be found in *Christine Goodwin v. The United Kingdom* [GC], 11.07.2002, Reports 2002–VI, where in the context of a transsexual's right to marry under Article 12, which expressly stipulates this right in terms of "men and women": "The Court [was] not persuaded that at the date of this case it can still be assumed that these terms must refer to a determination of gender by purely biological criteria…", *cf.* para. 100. Reflective of a wider trend in this direction, Robert Wintemute, 'Filling the Article 14 "Gap": Government Ratification and Judicial Control of Protocol No. 12 ECHR' (2004) 5 *European Human Rights Law Review* 484, 492, has also suggested this as a possible development under Article 14 ECHR, without particular reference to the *Christine Goodwin* judgment.

[64] Committee on the Elimination of Discrimination against Women, General Recommendation No. 25, 'on article 4, paragraph 1, of the Convention on the Elimination of All Forms of Discrimination against Women, on temporary special measures', thirtieth session, 2004, available at http://www.un.org/womenwatch/daw/cedaw/recommendations/General%20recommendation%2025%20(English).pdf (last visited 22 June 2008), paras. 8 and 11.

[65] Committee on the Elimination of Racial Discrimination, General Comment No. 8, 'Identification with a particular racial or ethnic group (Art.1, par. 1 & 4)', 22.08.1990, available at http://www.unhchr.ch/tbs/doc.nsf/(Symbol)/3ae0a87b5bd69d28c12563ee0049800f?Opendocument (last visited 21 June 2008).

[66] Committee on the Elimination of Racial Discrimination, General Comment No. 29, 'Article 1, paragraph 1 of the Convention (Descent)', 01.11.2002, available at http://www.unhchr.ch/tbs/doc.nsf/(Symbol)/f0902ff29d93de59c1256c6a00378d1f?Opendocument (last visited 22 June 2008), para. 1.

[67] *Timishev v. Russia*, 13.12.2005, unpublished, available at http://cmiskp.echr.coe.int/tkp197/view.asp?action=html&documentId=790924&portal=hbkm&source=externalbydocnumber&table=F69A27FD8FB86142BF01C1166DEA398649 (last visited 21 June 2008). The Court reasoned: "Ethnicity and race are related and overlapping concepts. Whereas the notion of race is rooted in the idea of biological classification of human beings into subspecies according to morphological features such as skin colour or facial characteristics, ethnicity has its origin in

based on the social model of disability.[68] Article 1 stipulates that: "Persons with disabilities include those who have long-term physical, mental, intellectual or sensory impairments which *in interaction with various barriers* may hinder their full and effective participation in society on an equal basis with others."[69] It is, thus, not the impairment or the difference *per se* that governs the identity and functions as a trigger for discrimination analysis, but the social fact of the structural disadvantages persons with impairments face in their daily lives. Had CERD and CEDAW been drafted in the 21st century, like the CRPD, there seems little doubt that they too would have been phrased clearly in terms of the social construction of gender and ethnicity.

During the present era, it is also possible to discern an ever increasing acceptance of asymmetrical approaches to equality under the law. This was, for example, elaborated particularly clearly in the context of CEDAW by the Committee on the Elimination of Discrimination against Women in 2004.[70] Its General Recommendation No. 25 unequivocally states that an asymmetrical approach is not an exception to the principle of equality and non-discrimination, but part and parcel of the norm itself.[71] Since the beginning of the 21st century the ECtHR has, specifically in the context of the suspect discrimination grounds, also increasingly accepted and acted upon asymmetrical approaches to equality. It has decisively established that the concept of discrimination can be approached from the perspective of a lack of reasonable accommodation[72] and/or from the perspective of indirect discrimination analysis.[73] It has also proved to be rather open to affirmative action programs, applying a fairly relaxed objective justification test to such programs when challenged as discriminatory.[74]

the idea of societal groups marked by common nationality, tribal affiliation, religious faith, shared language, or cultural and traditional origins and backgrounds.", *cf.* para. 55. The Court continued to assert that: "Discrimination on account of one's actual or perceived ethnicity is a form of racial discrimination [...]", *cf.* para. 56.

68 On the social model, see the contribution of Rannveig Traustadóttir in the present volume.

69 Emphasis added. See also CRPD preamble, letter e.

70 Committee on the Elimination of Discrimination against Women, General Recommendation No. 25, *supra* note 64, e.g. paras. 7–10.

71 *Ibid.*, para. 14: "The Convention, targets discriminatory dimensions of past and current societal and cultural contexts which impede women's enjoyment of their human rights and fundamental freedoms. It aims at the elimination of all forms of discrimination against women, including the elimination of the causes and consequences of their de facto or substantive inequality. Therefore, the application of temporary special measures in accordance with the Convention is one of the means to realize de facto or substantive equality for women, rather than an exception to the norms of non-discrimination and equality."

72 *Thlimmenos v. Greece* [GC], *supra* note 9.

73 *D.H. and Others v. the Czech Republic* [GC], *supra* note 55.

74 *Stec and Others v. the United Kingdom* [GC], *supra* note 55.

The CRPD provides the logical next step in the development of these trends. Similarly to CERD and CEDAW, it is the underlying premise of the CRPD that the universal principle of equality needs adaptation to the realities of specific groups that are vulnerable to discrimination. This simply calls for departures from formal symmetrical equality, not as an exception, but as a logical requirement to effectuate the true substance of the principle of equality and non-discrimination itself. This is expressed clearly in the operative provisions of the CRPD itself. Article 2(4) defines discrimination with reference to the concepts of direct and indirect discrimination (purpose or effect), as well as with reference to denial of reasonable accommodation. Reasonable accommodation is defined in Article 2(5) as necessary and appropriate modification and adjustments, that do not impose a disproportionate or undue burden, where needed *in a particular case*. Reasonable accommodation is therefore directed towards real persons in real life situations. Framing the concept of discrimination in terms of a denial of reasonable accommodation with reference to individual cases clearly establishes an individual right to reasonable accommodation. Further, Article 5(3) stipulates that in order to promote equality and eliminate discrimination States Parties shall take all appropriate steps to ensure that reasonable accommodation is provided. The CRPD, therefore, clearly establishes a positive obligation upon the States Parties to act to accommodate for disabilities on an individual basis where relevant.[75] Article 5(4) also legitimates affirmative action programs as it stipulates that they shall not be considered discrimination under the terms of the Convention. It, however, does not go as far in the direction of elaborating a positive obligation to adopt them, as it does in the context of reasonable accommodations. Therefore, it remains to be seen whether the Committee on the Rights of Persons with Disabilities will construe the CRPD as entailing a positive obligation to enact affirmative action programs and how it will construe the dividing line between the clearly justiciable individual rights claim of denial of reasonable accommodation under the Convention and the more elusive constituency of affirmative action. The whole issue will have to be approached from the perspective of an informed awareness that the international human rights law of the present era generally places an ever increasing importance on the positive obligations of states as a necessary element of the effective protection of human rights.[76] Correlative is the realisation that positive obligations are a necessary

---

[75] A similar positive obligation to accommodate for different/disadvantaged situations was established under the ECHR in *Thlimmenos v. Greece* [GC], *supra* note 9.

[76] See e.g. HRC General Comment No. 31, 'Nature of the General Legal Obligation Imposed on States Parties to the Covenant', 26.05.2004, available at http://www.unhchr.ch/tbs/doc.nsf/(Symbol)/CCPR.C.21.Rev.1.Add.13.En?Opendocument (last visited 22 June 2008), paras. 5–8.

component of effective protection against discrimination.[77] It is nevertheless also clear that transformation to justiciable individual rights is no straightforward task. The current approach to affirmative action programmes generally settled upon in the case law of the international monitoring bodies is a middle ground between the more moderate and the more transformative approaches to equality, *allowing* the programmes that states may choose to adopt, and even possibly subjecting them to fairly lenient objective justification scrutiny when challenged, while not asserting, in the context of judicial or quasi-judicial review, a positive obligation to enact them.[78] This, of course, may possibly change in future with regard to particular discrimination grounds and in particular contexts, but it is foreseeable that to the extent that this may exceed reasonable individual accommodations, the monitoring bodies will be very careful in transforming the more programmatic and abstract notions of a positive obligation to promote equality and combat structural disadvantage through affirmative action into justiciable individual rights.[79]

A further characteristic of the present era is the development of the concept or practical tool of mainstreaming. Gender mainstreaming has been defined as: "...the (re)organisation, improvement, development and evaluation of policy processes, so that a gender equality perspective is incorporated in all policies at

---

[77] See e.g. HRC General Comment No. 28, 'Equality of rights between men and women (article 3)', 29.03.2000, available at http://www.unhchr.ch/tbs/doc.nsf/(Symbol)/13b02776122d4838802568b900360e80?Opendocument (last visited 22 June 2008), para. 3 and Committee on the Elimination of Discrimination against Women, General Recommendation No. 25, *supra* note 64, para. 24.

[78] E.g. *Stec and Others v. the United Kingdom* [GC], *supra* note 55.

[79] It is unequivocally stated in the context of Protocol 12 to the ECHR that no such positive obligation will arise, *cf.* Protocol 12, explanatory report, *supra* note 8, para. 16: "However, the present Protocol does not impose any obligation to adopt such measures. Such a programmatic obligation would sit ill with the whole nature of the Convention and its control system which are based on the collective guarantee of individual rights which are formulated in terms sufficiently specific to be justiciable." The Committee on the Elimination on Discrimination against Women, however, goes quite far in the direction of stating that there exists a positive obligation to adopt affirmative action, *cf.* Committee on the Elimination of Discrimination against Women, General Recommendation No. 25, *supra* note 64, para. 24: "[...] the Committee considers that States parties are obliged to adopt and implement temporary special measures in relation to any of these articles if such measures can be shown to be necessary and appropriate in order to accelerate the achievement of the overall, or a specific goal of, women's de facto or substantive equality." It is unclear, however, how this might operate in legal practice if an individual claimed she was the victim of discrimination because of denial of affirmative action under the CEDAW individual complaints procedure. The clear elaboration in terms of an individual right in the Convention text itself, such as exists with respect to reasonable accommodation under the CRPD, would be lacking.

all levels and at all stages, by the actors normally involved in policy-making".[80] The concept of mainstreaming can obviously refer to other equality perspectives *mutatis mutandis,* and has indeed informed claims to the mainstreaming of other perspectives as well. For example, the Council of Europe Action Plan on disability places great emphasis on mainstreaming disability within its human rights framework and in all policy areas[81] and the UN is increasingly looking towards mainstreaming a disability perspective in various areas of activity.[82] The focus on mainstreaming which has carried the day in equality discourse during this present era can be argued to have provided a practical and less radical solution to the impassé of the ideological controversies about affirmative action which characterised the previous era somewhat. In the context of gender equality, Jill Lovecy has argued that the mainstreaming approach does not claim to radically change the composition of actors normally involved in policy-making, but provides instead: "a pathway for integrating gender perspectives into the *established* institutional framework, personnel and organisational procedures of policy-making."[83] It is also noticeable that the mainstreaming approach generally does not come equipped with clear individual rights claims or active enforcement mechanisms in law, which of course confirms its non-threatening conciliatory input into the old controversies about affirmative action in mainstream legal discourse. Awareness of the concept of mainstreaming, nevertheless, puts in sharp focus how social structures and decision making processes can in countless covert ways function to maintain disadvantage and marginalisation. From a legal realist perspective, it seems obvious how this awareness can profoundly influence how a judge might approach and analyse a claim of discrimination.

Finally, the current era has also been characterised by an increased awareness of the limits of traditional non-discrimination law that usually analyses discrimination cases in terms of the sameness/difference/disadvantage experienced on basis of only one identity marker at a time. As individuals are multidimensional and belong to more than one group at the same time (e.g. a black woman with a disability), the intersection of her identity markers can create unique synergetic vulnerabilities to discrimination. It has been pointed out how traditional non-

[80] 'Gender Mainstreaming, Conceptual framework, methodology and presentation of good practices', Strasbourg May 1998, *EG-S-MS (98) 2*, 15.

[81] 'The Council of Europe Action Plan to Promote the Rights and Full Participation of People with Disabilities in Society: Improving the Quality of Life of People with Disabilities in Europe 2006–2015', published as an appendix to Recommendation of the Committee of Ministers, Rec (2006) 5, *cf.* e.g. chapters 1.2.2. and 2.4.

[82] E.g. 'Mainstreaming disability in the development agenda', Commission for Social Development, forty-sixth session, 6–15.02.2008, E/CN.5/2008/6.

[83] Lovecy, *supra* note 2, p. 281, emphasis added.

discrimination law misses this complexity of human identity and human experiences and can therefore leave the most serious forms of discrimination undetected in the margins.[84] Already in 1991, the Committee on the Elimination of Discrimination against Women, identified the danger of double discrimination against women with disabilities, and called for specific reporting on disabled women and their equal access and participation in society.[85] Subsequently the issue of multidimensionality was decisively placed on the international human rights agenda following the Fourth World Conference on Women in Beijing 1995,[86] and at the UN Expert Group Meeting on Gender and Race Discrimination in 2000.[87] At present, issues related to multidimensional equality figure prominently in the contemporary mainstream equality and human rights discourse[88] and it can be argued that the ECtHR managed to respond effectively to a multidimensional situation in one of its judgments in 2000.[89] The CRPD places great emphasis on the issue of multidimensional equality. The preamble, letter p, expresses concern about the multiple or aggravated forms of discrimination often faced by persons with disabilities on the basis of the combination of disability with their race, colour, sex, language, religion, political or other opinion, national, ethnic, indigenous or social origin, property, birth, age or other status. Article 6 in the operative part of the Convention also specifically addresses the multiple discrimination faced by women and girls with disabilities and requires states to

---

[84] See e.g. Kimberlé Crenshaw, 'Demarginalizing the Intersection of Race and Sex: A Black Feminist Critique of Antidiscrimination Doctrine, Feminist Theory and Antiracist Politics', (1989) *The University of Chicago Legal Forum*, 139 and Sarah Hannett, 'Equality at the Intersections: the Legislative and Judicial Failure to Tackle Multiple Discrimination', (2003) 23 *Oxford Journal of Legal Studies*, 65.

[85] Committee on the Elimination of Discrimination against Women, General Recommendation No. 18, tenth session 1991, available at http://www.un.org/womenwatch/daw/cedaw/recommendations/recomm.htm#recom18 (last visited 22 June 2008).

[86] 'Beijing Declaration and Platform for Action', Report of the Fourth World Conference on Women, Beijing 4–15 September 1995, A/CONF.177/20.

[87] 'Gender and racial discrimination', Report of the Expert Group Meeting, 21–24 November 2000, Zagreb Croatia, available at http://www.un.org/womenwatch/daw/csw/genrac/report.htm (last visited 23 June 2008) and Kimbelé Crenshaw (2000) 'Background Paper for the Expert Meeting on the Gender-Related Aspects of Race Discrimination, November 21–24 2000, Zagreb, Croatia', available at http://wicej.addr.com/wcar_docs/crenshaw.html (last visited 23 June 2008).

[88] See e.g. Dagmar Schiek and Victoria Chege (eds), *European Union Non-Discrimination Law: Comparative Perspectives on Multidimensional Equality Law* (Routledge-Cavendish, London 2008). On the ability of the ECtHR to adopt a multidimensional approach under Article 14 ECHR, see Oddný Mjöll Arnardóttir, 'Multidimensional equality from within: Themes from the European Convention on Human Rights', in Schiek and Chege (eds), *ibid.*, 53.

[89] *Thlimmenos v. Greece* [GC], *supra* note 9, see also Arnardóttir, *ibid.*, 61.

take all appropriate measures to ensure the full development, advancement and empowerment of women.

In conclusion, the present era, characterised by the key themes of disadvantage and multidimensionality, is concerned with the themes and concepts of equality associated with the previous era discussed in chapter 3.2 *supra.* These themes include the further development of positive state obligations in the context of equality, departures from formal symmetrical equality and the development of the concepts of indirect discrimination, reasonable accommodation and affirmative action to correct for factual inequalities. The current era is, however, additionally informed by a deeper understanding of structural disadvantage. This moves the focus of attention from the individual herself as the "problem" the law should address and correct for onto social factors that function to keep marginalised groups in the margins. This strikes through to the legal regulation and legal practice in the form of enhanced protection against discrimination for structurally disadvantaged groups. Thus, the principle of equality in the international human rights law of today, while not abandoning the ideal of universal equality for all, recognises that equality itself needs to be developed and tailored to the specific realities and experiences of those whom it is supposed to serve.

4 *Conclusions*

From the analysis *supra,* it is very clear that it is a basic and underlying premise of the Convention to reject formal and symmetrical equality. The underlying requirement of assimilation to an unquestioned standard is correspondingly rejected and the Convention as a whole provides a strong example of the balanced respect for diversity that the human rights law of the 21st century should strive to attain. This basic approach of the Convention is without doubt a very important contribution to the development of the principle of equality in human rights discourse.

The question whether it is substantive difference equality or substantive disadvantage equality that is represented in the Convention can be debated. The two models focus attention on the same issues in discrimination law and the difference between them is more one of degree than of principle. On the face of it, the difference approach may seem represented by the concept of reasonable accommodation which can be understood with reference to a concept of difference, but the defining factor does not lie in the concept of reasonable accommodation or difference *per se* but in how the situations that are seen as requiring action and accommodation are perceived. It is the awareness in legal practice of the social construction of disability and the situated context of the individuals or groups in question that would represent the disadvantage approach. The fact that the

Convention so aptly focuses attention on these factors renders it the single most powerful example of the cursor of international law moving ever further in the direction of the multidimensional disadvantage approach.

There remain quite a few difficulties in transforming the multidimensional disadvantage approach into hard non-discrimination law and individually justiciable rights. Categorising into disadvantaged groups can raise similar problems as categorising into different groups and an element of comparison with other groups remains an inherent characteristic of equality analysis. Another issue that international law cannot disregard in this context is the proper role of international courts and monitoring bodies in light of the principle of subsidiarity.[90] Also, it must be borne in mind that social construction analysis is of a different nature from that which these bodies traditionally encounter, although concepts like indirect discrimination and related approaches to the burden of proof in discrimination cases can do a lot to bring covert structural disadvantages to light.[91] In addition, the analysis of judicial or quasi-judicial bodies of a situation may be very different from that of the individuals concerned.[92] Some of the issues raised by multidimensional situations may also be too complex for the law as it is an inherent tendency of the law to simplify and compartmentalise complex issues.[93] Despite all these complications, it has been exhibited by the analysis *supra* that international law is already to some extent responding to the issues related to multidimensionality and disadvantage. The response may not be able to react to all the depth and subtlety of the theory, but a certain awareness can nevertheless be exhibited to strike through to international law. A non-discrimination approach will, however, always be limited by the factors identified *supra*. This is why it is another extremely important aspect of the CRPD that it takes the underlying leitmotif of the principle of equality and elaborates it into specific individual rights applicable in specific situations, such as the elaboration of the right to equal recognition before the law in Article 12 and the right to an inclusive education system in Article 24. In future practice the real strength of the CPRD will arise from the interaction of an informed understanding of the multidimensional disadvantage equality model underlying the Convention and the interpretation and application of these specifically elaborated rights.

The question posed in the title of this contribution is whether the future promises multidimensional disadvantage equality. On an optimistic finishing

---

[90] See e.g. Dinah Shelton, 'Subsidiarity and Human Rights Law' (2006) 27 *European Human Rights Reports* 4 and Paolo Carozza, 'Subsidiarity as a Structural Principle of International Human Rights Law' (2003) 97 *American Journal of International Law* 38.

[91] See e.g. *D.H. and Others v. the Czech Republic* [GC], *supra* note 55.

[92] See also Kimber, *supra* note 20, 275.

[93] See also Hannett, *supra* note 84, 85–86.

note it is concluded that it does, but that this will not happen easily or overnight. But if developed carefully, the law of the CRPD may do more to move the law forward to that future than any other currently existing instrument of international law. As a whole, it can be concluded that the CRPD represents the more complex and layered human rights law appropriate to the challenges of the 21st century.

From Invisibility to Indivisibility: The International Convention on the Rights of Persons with Disabilities

*Ida Elisabeth Koch**

1 *Introduction*

Human rights are sometimes mistakenly referred to as *invisible rights*, and with regard to human rights of persons with disabilities it is in fact a very precise designation. Or it has been, because a lot has changed with the adoption of the International Convention on the Rights of Persons with Disabilities (CRPD). This Convention has indeed made visible the rights of persons with disabilities. Moreover, in the CRPD socio-economic rights coexist with civil-political rights, and the Preamble reaffirms the indivisibility, interdependence and interrelatedness of all human rights and fundamental freedoms.[1] This and the fact that an individual complaints mechanism is likely to be established may have an impact on the justiciability[2] of half the rights, namely economic, social and cultural rights, and the development is indeed promising. Maybe human rights for persons with disabilities are about to become invincible. These issues on indivisibility and justiciability *will be subject to discussion in the following and my intention is*

---

* Ph.D., Senior Researcher, The Danish Institute for Human Rights.

[1] The International Convention on the Rights of Persons with Disabilities, Preamble, letter c.

[2] The notion of 'justiciability' is commonly used in the discussion of the normative character of socio-economic rights in particular with regard to the question whether or not these rights can be enforced by judicial or quasi-judicial bodies. It does not have an unambiguous meaning and it does not appear in ordinary dictionaries over English language. Those of us who deal with socio-economic rights have to put up with the spelling control on a daily basis suggesting 'justifiability' or the like in stead. The concept of 'justiciability' is discussed by Martin Sheinin, who identifies a variety of different possible meanings; cf. Martin Scheinin, 'Justiciability and the Indivisibility of Human Rights' in John Squires et al. (eds.), *The Road to a Remedy: Current Issues in the Litigation of Economic, Social and Cultural Rights*, Australian Human Rights Centre, The University of New South Wales, pp. 17–26.

to illustrate that although there might be a difference between the two sets of rights it is highly overestimated.

2 *An Integral Convention?*

As mentioned above, the Preamble of the Convention refers to the notions of the indivisibility, interdependence and interrelatedness of all human rights, it refers to all the UN conventions and it concludes with the following statement:

> Convinced that a comprehensive and *integral* international convention to promote and protect the rights and dignity of persons with disabilities will make a significant contribution to redressing the profound social disadvantage of persons with disabilities and promote their participation in the civil, political, economic, social and cultural spheres with equal opportunities, in both developing and developed countries.[3]

However, Article 4 (2) includes a provision very much similar to Article 2 (1) of the International Covenant on Economic, Social and Cultural rights (CESCR) in the sense that it underlines the progressive character of socio-economic rights. It runs as follows:

> With regard to economic, social and cultural rights, each State Party undertakes to take measures to the maximum of its available resources and, where needed, within the framework of international cooperation, with a view to achieving progressively the full realization of these rights, without prejudice to those obligations contained in the present Convention that are immediately applicable according to international law.

Thus, the Convention applies the traditional distinction between obligations which are immediately applicable and those which are to be realised progressively, and the various provisions on e.g. health and adequate standard of living and social protection[4] apply the traditional means and ends approach that we know from CESCR. Economic, social and cultural rights are often not formulated as individual legal rights. There is no link between the facts and the legal consequence but merely a relation between an end and the means supposed to lead to that end.[5] E.g. Article 28 of the CRPD recognises the rights of persons with

[3] Cf. letter y, italics made by author.

[4] Article 25 and 28.

[5] Amartya Sen speaks of *metarights*. He explains that '[a] *metaright* to something *x* can be defined as the right to have *policies* p. (*x*) that genuinely pursue the objective of making the right to *x* realisable.' The metaright *e.g.* to food serves the purpose of giving 'a person the right to demand that policy be directed towards securing the objective of making the right to adequate means

disabilities to an adequate standard of living and stipulates that States shall take 'appropriate steps to safeguard and promote the realisation of this right without discrimination on the basis of disability.' Civil and political rights on the other hand are often norm rational, as there is usually a link between the facts and the legal consequences. They follow what could be described as an 'if-then formula'. According to Article 17 of the CRPD, by way of example, '[e]very person with disabilities has a right to respect for his or her physical and mental integrity on an equal basis with others.'

Accordingly, it seems as if the CRPD has adopted the overall scepticism towards giving socio-economic rights the same protection as civil and political rights. This may be due to what Craig Scott has designated as 'implementation-based reasons'.[6] The implementation based reasons relate to the perception of the two sets of rights as fundamentally different in their normative character as civil and political rights are considered 'negative', precise and cost free rights subject to immediate implementation whereas economic, social and cultural rights are regarded as 'positive', vague and resource demanding rights subject to progressive realisation. Holger Kallehauge puts it like this:

> The civil and political rights provided by the convention enter into force immediately when the convention is ratified, while the economic, social and cultural rights will have to be implemented progressively, according to the economic strength of a country.[7]

The question is, however, whether it is possible to uphold this distinction between resource demanding rights and rights without significant budgetary consequences. Another question is whether it is possible to discern economic, social and cultural rights from civil and political rights of the CRPD. A closer look at the individual provisions of the Convention may provide an answer.

---

a realisable right, even if that objective cannot be immediately achieved. It is a right of a different kind: not to *x* but to p. (*x*). I propose to call a right to p. (*x*) a *metaright* to *x*', Amartya Sen, 'The right not to be hungry' in P. Alston et al. (eds.), *The Right to Food*, Martinus Nijhoff Publishers, 1984, p. 70.

6 Cf. Craig Scott, 'The Interdependence and Permeability of Human Rights Norms: Towards a Partial Fusion of the International Covenants on Human Rights' in *Osgoode Hall Law Journal*. Vol. 27, No. 4, 1989, p. 794 ff.

7 Holger Kallehauge, The Genesis of a New Human Rights Convention – A Convention on the Rights of Persons with Disabilities, in Implementing Human Rights, Essays in Honour of Morten Kjærum, Rikke Frank Jørgensen & Klaus Slavensky (eds.), The Danish Institute for Human Rights, 2007, p. 346.

3 All Rights have Costs

It has been asserted that all rights require *some* sort of 'positive' measure. As pointed out by Holmes and Sunstein *all* rights are 'positive' in the sense that they have budgetary implication.[8] Obligations not to interfere require that public officials are given the necessary guidance and education with regard to the legal content of the obligations in question, and at any rate the administration and monitoring of human rights compliance bear upon the economic interest of the State.

In fact, a 'positive' obligation to *create institutional machinery essential to the realisation of rights* is always a necessary precondition for human rights protection, and if one were to speak of a fundamental human rights obligation this would be the one. Human rights cannot be implemented if there is no one to do it, and the question is how this is reflected in the CRPD.

It is not disputed that provision of healthcare facilities, education, housing, social benefits etc. has budgetary consequences for the States Parties. However, many seem to assume that it is cost free to ensure persons with disabilities their civil and political rights. It is not. Where exactly the dividing line between the cost free and the resource demanding rights goes is uncertain, but is does certainly not follow the CCPR/CESCR distinction. *Let us in stead look at a few examples.*

Article 10 on the right to life is traditionally regarded as a civil right. It runs like this:

> States Parties reaffirm that every human being has the inherent right to life and shall *take all necessary measures* to ensure its effective enjoyment by persons with disabilities on an equal basis with others [italics by author].

Now, the States Parties 'shall *take all necessary measures* to ensure' the effective enjoyment of the right to life, and the question is whether it is possible to take such measures without effecting public expenditure. That is hardly the case. At least it obliges the States Parties to *create institutional machinery essential to the realisation of the right to life* i.e. that public officials are given the necessary guidance and education with regard to the legal content of the right to life; an obligation which bears upon the economic interest of the States Parties.

---

[8] Stephen Holmes and Cass R. Sunstein, *The Cost of Rights*: Why Liberty Depends on Taxes, W.W. Norton and Company, 1999, Chapter 1.

Similarly Article 15 (2) about freedom from torture or cruel, inhuman or degrading treatment obliges States Parties to 'take all effective legislative, administrative, judicial or other measures to prevent persons with disabilities, on an equal basis with others, from being subjected to torture or cruel, inhuman or degrading treatment or punishment.'

If this provision is to be interpreted in line with other prohibitions against torture and degrading treatment or punishment, there is absolutely no doubt that the budgetary consequences for the States Parties will be considerable. Thus, similar provisions like Article 7 of the UN Covenant on Civil and Political Rights (CCPR) leave no doubt that positive and resource demanding measures are required. The Human Rights Committee (HRC) has repeatedly held 'that States parties are under an obligation to observe certain minimum standards of detention, which include provision of medical care and treatment for sick prisoners, in accordance with rule 22 (2) of the Standard Minimum Rules for the Treatment of Prisoners.'[9] This is of course resource demanding but nevertheless mandatory. The HRC puts it like this:

> It should be noted that these are minimum requirements which the Committee considers should always be observed, even if economic or budgetary considerations may make compliance with these obligations difficult.[10]

Freedom of expression and access to information are traditionally considered 'negative', budgetary neutral rights. However, for persons with disabilities to be able to enjoy these rights on an equal footing with persons without disabilities, it is necessary that certain measures be taken to facilitate the enjoyment. This is reflected in Article 21 CRPD:

> States Parties shall take all appropriate measures [....] including by:
> (a) Providing information intended for the general public to persons with disabilities in accessible formats and technologies appropriate to different kinds of disabilities in a timely manner and without additional cost;
> (b) Accepting and facilitating the use of sign languages, Braille, augmentative and alternative communication, and all other accessible means, modes and formats of communication of their choice by persons with disabilities in official interactions; [....]
> (e) Recognizing and promoting the use of sign languages.

While freedom of expression and access to information in general may not require public expenditure to any great extent, the situation is different with regard to persons with disabilities. It is very costly to provide the assistance referred to

[9] *Leon R. Rouse v. The Philippines*, views adopted on 25 July 2005, Comm. No.1090/2002

[10] *Albert Womah Mukong v. Cameroon*, views adopted on 10 August 1994, Comm. No. 458/1991.

in Article 21, and one may ask what is the difference with regard to resources between this article and socio-economic rights in general. The article confirms that it is difficult if not impossible to uphold the traditional compartmentalised perception of the two sets of rights. Human rights are there for the sake of persons; they must reflect and respect the factual conditions of human life and the complexity of human activity. The various elements of our lives are inextricably intertwined, and human experience rarely confines itself into neat categories. Transporting a highly disabled person e.g. to another country in order for him to be able to enjoy his freedom of expression e.g. at a conference may be en extremely costly affaire. Most of us can enjoy this right with limited expenses, whereas a person who is unable to move may need not only a wheel chair but also several assistants who have to be available night and day.

Similar observations can be made with regard to other rights in the Convention which are traditionally considered civil and political rights. Respect for home and family requires effective and appropriate measures, cf. Article 23, and for persons with disabilities to be able to participate in political and public life extra measures are required, cf. Article 29. In domestic legislation such measures are often regulated in social, educational or health legislation and it is tempting to say that civil and political rights in the CRPD all have a strong socio-economic component. However, they are hardly encompassed by Article 4 (2) in which it is held that economic, social and cultural rights (but not civil and political rights) are subject to progressive realisation. Nevertheless, one might as well ask whether resource demanding civil and political rights such as Article 21 of the CRPD is justiciable or whether is should be left entirely to States Parties to implement the right according to the economic strength of the State Party in question. In that respect it is noteworthy that the above mentioned provisions do not follow the if-then formula, which is otherwise characteristic for civil and political rights. Rather, they follow a means and ends approach like many economic, social and cultural rights in that they prescribe 'appropriate measures' to promote, protect and ensure human rights.

Accordingly, rights in general have costs and rights of disabled persons have additional costs. It has to be that way if persons with disabilities are to enjoy human rights equally. Likewise, for elderly people to be able to enjoy their human rights special measures are sometimes required and something similar applies to other groups against which States must not discriminate. Non-discrimination has budgetary consequences, and that is anticipated in the objects clause in Article 1 which presents the purpose of the Convention as that to 'promote, protect and ensure the full and equal enjoyment of all human rights and fundamental freedoms by all persons with disabilities [....]'.

The CRDP is one of the finest examples of the fact that human rights necessarily have to be indivisible, interrelated and interdependent, if one aims to address the factual situation of persons with disabilities instead of insisting on a categorisation of rights which have no foundation in fact.

4 *The Justiciability of Indivisible Rights*[11]

An Optional Protocol to the Convention on the Rights of Persons with Disabilities has been adopted together with the CRPD according to which the Committee on the Rights of Persons with Disabilities (the Committee) can receive communications from or on behalf of individuals or groups of individuals who claim to be victims of a violation of the Convention. As of 19 December 2008 the Optional Protocol has been signed by 81 States Parties and ratified by 27. According to Article 13 of the Protocol it entered into force 3rd of May 2008, after the deposit of the tenth instrument of ratification or accession. It is therefore possible to file communications not only with regard to the civil and political rights of the CRPD *but also with regard to the economic, social and cultural rights listed in the Convention.*

It is of course difficult to make predictions particularly about the future, and we will have to wait and see how the Committee chooses to go about the issue of justiciability or quasi-justiciability of resource demanding rights whether placed in the socio-economic sphere or the civil-political sphere. However, it is likely that the Committee – to which individuals will be able to file complaints – will draw on the practice not only of other UN monitoring bodies such as the Human Rights Committee (HRC) and the International Committee on Economic, Social and Cultural Rights (ICESCR) but also allow itself to be inspired from regional bodies such as the European Court of Human Rights and the European Committee of Social Rights.

Judicial and quasi-judicial bodies influence one another, and what we witness these years is in fact a global dialogue on the issue of justiciability not only between legal scholars but also between judicial and quasi-judicial bodies worldwide.[12] One cannot exclude the possibility that the acceptance of justiciability in one context will have an indirect bearing in other contexts, as it contributes to the gradual softening of the strict categorisation of rights as belonging either in the socio-economic or the civil-political sphere.

There is little mentioning of persons with disabilities in the UN human rights conventions in force. Nevertheless, it is beyond doubt that disabilities are encompassed by the notion 'or other status' in the CCPR Article 2 (1) and CESCR Article 2 (2) both non-discrimination clauses which are *not* subject to

---

[11] Cf. Ida Elisabeth Koch, 'The Justiciability of Indivisible Rights', *Nordic Journal of International Law*, Vol. 72, No. 1, 2003, pp. 3–39.

[12] At its 59th session in 2003 the Human Rights Commission decided to establish an open-ended working group with a view to considering options regarding the elaboration of an optional protocol to the CESCR, UN Doc. E/CN.4/RES2003/18. After lengthy discussions this initiative has in December 2008 resulted in the adoption by the UN General Assembly of an optional protocol to the CESCR.

progressive realisation, cf. the Limburg Principles according to which '[a]rticle 2(2) calls for immediate application and involves an explicit guarantee on behalf of the States parties. It should, therefore, be made subject to judicial review and other recourse procedures.'[13] Moreover, the Committee on Economic, Social and Cultural Rights (ICESCR) has adopted a General Comment on persons with disabilities[14] from which it clearly appears that equality requires resources. The ICESCR states as follows:

> The obligation in the case of such a vulnerable and disadvantaged group is to take positive action to reduce structural disadvantages and to give appropriate preferential treatment to people with disabilities in order to achieve the objectives of full participation and equality within society for all persons with disabilities. *This almost invariably means that additional resources will need to be made available for this purpose* and that a wide range of specially tailored measures will be required [italics by author].[15]

This statement is very much in line with the Limburg principles according to which positive measures taken 'for the sole purpose of securing adequate advancement of certain groups or individuals requiring such protection as may be necessary in order to ensure to such groups or individuals equal enjoyment of economic, social and cultural rights shall not be deemed discrimination, provided, however, that such measures do not, as a consequence, lead to the maintenance of separate rights for different groups and that such measures shall not be continued after their intended objectives have been achieved.'[16] The General Comment continues as follows in para. 17.

> Anti-discrimination measures should be based on the principle of equal rights for persons with disabilities and the non-disabled, which, in the words of the World Programme of Action concerning Disabled Persons, 'implies that the needs of each and every individual are of equal importance, that these needs must be made the basis for the planning of societies, and that *all resources must be employed in such a way as to ensure, for every individual, equal opportunity for participation*. Disability policies should ensure the access of [persons with disabilities] to all community services' [italics by author].[17]

---

[13] The Limburg Principles on the Implementation of the International Covenant on Economic, Social and Cultural Rights,UN doc. E/CN.4/1987/17, Annex; and Human Rights Quarterly, Vol. 9, 1987, pp. 122–135.

[14] CESCR General Comment 5 on Persons with Disabilities, 1994.

[15] Ibid., para. 9.

[16] The Limburg Principles, supra note 13, para. 39.

[17] World Programme of Action concerning Disabled Persons, adopted by the General Assembly by its resolution 37/52 of 3 December 1982, para. 25.

Thus, the General Comment No 5 chooses to take its point of departure in what disabled persons actually need, and consider what it takes to achieve de facto equality, cf. CRPD Article 3 and 5 according to which those measures which are necessary to accelerate or achieve de facto equality of persons with disabilities shall not be considered discrimination. It follows that the CRPD's non-discrimination notion is rather wide and that resources are needed in order for the States Parties to comply. How does that impact the justiciability of the rights of the CRPD?

If the Committee on the Rights of Persons with Disabilities chooses to lean on already existing case law from other UN treaty bodies, such as the HRC, it is likely to exercise a similar self-restraint in its review. The HRC has adopted a long series of views on the basis of the general non-discrimination clause in CCPR Article 26, and the HRC shows little reticence despite the fact that the views have had serious budgetary consequences for the States in question. Article 26 of the CCPR is a general non-discrimination clause in the sense that it prescribes that '[a]ll persons are equal before the law and are entitled without any discrimination to the equal protection of the law'. It demands that 'the law shall prohibit any discrimination and guarantee to all persons equal and effective protection against discrimination on any ground [....]', one implication being that the provision reaches into the sphere of socio-economic rights. Case law is rich and a couple of examples will suffice.

In *Zwaan-de-Vries v. the Netherlands* and *Broeks v. the Netherlands* did the HRC find violations of Article 26 because married women unlike married men had to prove their obligations as breadwinners in order to obtain unemployment benefit. The HRC held that 'such differentiation is not reasonable' and found a violation of Article 26.[18]

In *Ibrahima v. France* retired soldiers of Senegalese nationality, who had served in the French army, were subject to a difference in pension treatment. The main question before the HRC was whether it was in conformity with Article 26 to differentiate in pension treatment, based on whether the retired soldiers were French nationals or not. The HRC concluded that the difference in treatment of the authors was not based on reasonable and objective criteria and constituted discrimination prohibited by the Covenant.[19]

In *Pauger v. Austria* the author complained that the Pension Act granted preferential treatment to widows, as they would receive a pension, regardless of their income, whereas widowers could receive pensions only if they did not have

[18] *Zwaan-de-Vries v. the Netherlands* and *Broeks v. the Netherlands*, views adopted on 9 April 1987, Comm. Nos. 172/1984 and 182/1984.

[19] *Ibrahima Gueye and 742 other retired Senegalese members of the French army v. France*, views adopted on 3 April 1989, Comm. No. 196/1985.

any other form of income. The author's claim for pension was rejected since he was gainfully employed. The HRC found that 'men and women, whose social circumstances are similar, are being treated differently, merely on the basis of sex. Such a differentiation is not reasonable [....]',[20] and the HRC found Article 26 to be violated.

In *Johannes Vos v. the Netherlands* the pension paid to the author as a married male former civil servant whose pension accrued before 1985 was lower than the pension paid to a married female former civil servant whose pension accrued at the same date. The HRC found this to be a violation of article 26 of the Covenant.[21] And in *Young v. Australia* the State party provided 'no arguments on how this distinction between same-sex partners, who are excluded from pension benefits under law, and unmarried heterosexual partners, who are granted such benefits, is reasonable and objective [....].'[22] Moreover, there was no evidence which would point to the existence of factors justifying such a distinction. In this context, the HRC found that Australia had violated article 26 of the Covenant by denying the author a pension on the basis of his sex or sexual orientation.

It is remarkable although logical, cf. CCPR art. 26 that the HRC finds itself competent to reach such conclusions, and at any rate it illustrates that the traditional dichotomous perception of the two sets of rights is misleading.

5 *Conclusion*

The CCPR does not specifically prohibit discrimination with regard to disability. However, the discrimination grounds in Article 26 are not exhaustive. It requires that the law shall prohibit 'any discrimination and guarantee to all persons equal and effective protection against discrimination on any ground such as race, colour, sex, language, religion, political or other opinion, national or social origin, property, birth or other status.' There is no doubt that persons with disabilities fall within the category 'other status'[23] in the same way as e.g. homosexuals, and if cases concerning discrimination against persons with disabilities were to be dealt with on the merits by the HRC, there is hardly any

[20] *Pauger v. Austria*, views adopted on 26 March 1992, Comm. No. 415/1990, at para at para. 7.4.
[21] *A.P. Johannes Vos v. the Netherlands*, views adopted on 26 July 1999, Comm. No. 786/1997.
[22] *Edward Young v. Australia*, views adopted on 6 August 2003, Comm. No. 941/2000, at para. 10.4.
[23] *F, on behalf of her son, C v. Australia*, Admissibility decision of 25 July 2001, Comm. No. 832/1998.

doubt that the review would be as intensive as in previous case law concerning discrimination because of sex, sexual orientation, national origin etc.

Therefore I see no reason why the Committee, which is to monitor the compliance of States Parties with the CRPD, should exercise more self-restraint than the HRC with regard to issues, which that have a bearing on the economy of the States Parties than the HRC. The Committee, which hopefully soon will begin its work, should allow itself to be inspired by the HRC and other judicial and quasi-judicial bodies, which have a long tradition for dealing with discrimination issues. Of course the Committee will have to allow States Parties a certain margin of appreciation, but there is all the reason to believe that persons with disabilities can look forward to a much stronger human rights protection. There is a long way from invisibility to invincibility, but the CRPD is until now one of the strongest manifestation of the notion of human rights as indivisible rights.

Part II

The European Context

The UN Convention on the Rights of Persons with Disabilities and European Disability Law: A Catalyst for Cohesion?

Anna Lawson

1 *Introduction*

As will be evident from other chapters in this volume, disability-related law and policy has emerged from both the European Community and from the Council of Europe. Its emergence, however, has not reflected a clear, unified and comprehensive European response to the Disability Movement's claims for equality and respect for human rights. Despite very positive developments, some needless inconsistencies of approach and coverage remain.

The traditionally fractured nature of European disability law reflects certain deeply grooved structural divisions. Most prominent amongst these is perhaps the division between the European Community, with its origins in economic co-operation, and the Council of Europe, with its emphasis on the protection of human rights.[1] The past decade has witnessed some blurring of the disability-related ramifications of this distinction as a result of the considerable strengthening of the profile of human rights concerns within the EC.[2] Thus, although 'separated at birth', the two institutions may fairly be described as 'twins'.[3]

Another significant distinction, in the context of European disability law, is the traditional dichotomy between human rights which are classified as civil or political on the one hand, and those which are classified as social, economic or cultural on the other. It is this distinction which underlies the division between

---

1 Statute of the Council of Europe 1949, art. 1(b).

2 See further, G. More, 'The Principle of Equal Treatment: from Market Unifier to Fundamental Right?' in P. Craig and G. de Burca (eds), *The Evolution of EU Law* (Oxford, Oxford University Press, 1999); P. Alston (Ed.) The EU and Human Rights (Oxford, Oxford University Press, 1999); and P. Craig and G. de Burca, *EU Law: Text, Cases, and Materials* (Oxford, Oxford University Press, 2007) pp. 379–427.

3 G. Quinn, 'The European Union and the Council of Europe on the Issue of Human Rights: Twins Separated at Birth?' (2001) 46 McGill Law Journal 845.

the Council of Europe's two principal instruments – the European Convention on Human Rights (ECHR) and the European Social Charter (ESC). The disability-related jurisprudence associated with these two instruments contains marked differences of approach.

It is not the purpose of this chapter to provide a detailed analysis of the disability-related law which has emerged in the specific contexts of the EC, the ECHR and the ESC. That purpose is fulfilled by other chapters in this book. This chapter aims instead to provide a broader overview of disability law at the European level and to assess the potential impact of the new United Nations Convention on the Rights of Persons with Disabilities (CRPD) upon it. It will focus, in particular, on the question of whether the CRPD might act as a catalyst to the development of a more comprehensive and cohesive European approach. It will be suggested that the CRPD is indeed likely to operate in this way and thereby to manifest the dynamic and cyclical nature of the relationship between European and UN disability law and policy – the EC, drawing upon the former, played a highly influential role in the elaboration of the CRPD and that instrument is now in its turn likely to play a highly influential role in the further development and strengthening of disability-related law and policy at the European level.

The chapter will contain four substantive sections. The first of these, Section 2, will highlight the broad disability policy frameworks operating within the EC and the Council of Europe. It will draw attention to the powerful similarity between them. Section 3 will examine the extent to which the principle of inclusion is reflected in EC, ECHR and ESC law. Section 4 will address the extent to which the concept of reasonable accommodation has been accepted in the law emerging from these three sources. Finally, Section 5 will address the material scope of current EC disability equality law and compare this with the coverage of the ECHR and the ESC. The impact of the CRPD will be considered throughout.[4]

2 *Policy Background*

As mentioned above, the origins of the European Community lie in the furtherance of principles, not of human rights, but of market economy. The profile of

---

[4] Some of the ideas considered here are further developed in A Lawson, 'Disability, Degradation and Dignity: The Role of Article 3 of the European Convention on Human Rights' (2006) 56 Northern Ireland Legal Quarterly 462; A. Lawson, 'The United Nations Convention on the Rights of Persons with Disabilities: New Era or False Dawn?' [2007] Syracuse Journal of International Law and Commerce 101; and A. Lawson, *Disability and Equality Law in Britain: The Role of Reasonable Adjustment* (Oxford, Hart Publishing, 2008).

human or fundamental rights, however, has grown significantly in recent years. This is demonstrated by the proclamation of the Charter of Fundamental Rights of the European Union (initially in 2000)[5] and also by the establishment of the Fundamental Rights Agency in 2007.[6]

The Charter draws on instruments such as the ECHR and the ESC and aims to set out all the civil, political, economic and social rights to which European citizens and residents are entitled.[7] Article 21 of the Charter lists disability as one of the grounds on which discrimination must be prohibited. The sphere of operation of this Article is wide. It is not restricted either to a particular context (such as employment) or to the enjoyment of the rights conferred by the Charter. It is supplemented by article 26, according to which:

> The Union recognises and respects the right of persons with disabilities to benefit from measures designed to ensure their independence, social and occupational integration and participation in the life of the community.

The Charter was initially proclaimed on 7 December 2000 and then again, after amendments, on 12 December 2007.[8] It would have been incorporated by reference into the draft EU constitution which was rejected by 'No' votes in referenda in France and the Netherlands in 2005. It remains an integral part of the proposals for EU reform now contained in the Treaty of Lisbon. That Treaty was signed by national government representatives on 13 December 2007.[9] It will enter into force if it is ratified by all the Member States.[10] If adopted, the Lisbon Treaty will have the effect of making the Charter's provisions binding on

---

5 See below n. 8.

6 Regulation No. 168/2007/EC establishing a European Union Agency for Fundamental Rights. See generally http://fra.europa.eu/fra/index.php?fuseaction=content.dsp_cat_content&catid=2 (last accessed 6 May 2008); and P. Alston and O. De Schutter (eds), *Monitoring Fundamental Rights in the EU: The Contribution of the Fundamental Rights Agency* (Oxford, Hart Publishing, 2005).

7 See generally S. Fredman, C. McCrudden and M. Freedland, 'An EU Charter of Fundamental Rights' [2007] *Public Law* 178; B. Hepple, 'The EU Charter of Fundamental Rights'(2001) 30 *Industrial Law Journal* 225; T. Hervey and J. Kenner (eds), *Economic and Social Rights under the EU Charter of Fundamental Rights* (Oxford, Hart Publishing, 2003); B. Bercusson, 'Episodes on the Path Towards the European Social Model: The EU Charter of Fundamental Rights and the Convention on the Future of Europe' in C. Barnard, S. Deakin and G.S. Morris (eds), *The Future of Labour Law* (Oxford, Hart Publishing, 2004); P. Alston and O. De Schutter (eds), *Monitoring Fundamental Rights in the EU: The Contribution of the Fundamental Rights Agency* (Oxford, Hart Publishing, 2005); and S. Fredman, 'Transformation or Dilution: Fundamental Rights in the EU Social Space' (2006) 12 *European Law Journal* 41.

8 OJ C364, 18.12.2000; and OJ C303, 14.12.2007 respectively.

9 OJ C306.50, 17.12.2007.

10 The Treaty was rejected in the 2008 Irish Referendum. In the EU Summit of 12 December 2008, however, the Irish Government agreed to hold another referendum on the issue after

all the institutions of the EU and also on all but two of the Member States in their implementation of EU law.[11] It would amend Article 6.1 of the Treaty on European Union so as to require the provisions of the Charter to be recognised and to be given the same 'legal value' as the Treaties themselves.

Even in the absence of the additional force which would be conferred upon it by implementation of the Lisbon Treaty, the Charter remains 'an influential form of soft law'.[12] Indeed, it may well have played an important role in shaping the EU's negotiating positions in the discussions leading to the CRPD.[13]

The Lisbon Treaty also makes provision for the accession of the EU to the European Convention on Human Rights.[14] Disappointingly, however, it does not provide for accession to the Revised European Social Charter.[15] Nevertheless, the practical implications of this omission in the disability context are likely to be minimal given the plans of the European Commission to ratify the CRPD.[16]

Equality features large both in the Charter of Fundamental Rights and also in more firmly established documents such as the Treaty of Amsterdam and its ensuing directives.[17] The EC's interest in promoting equality may be attributed to the two underlying rationales of facilitating the market economy by reducing

---

certain assurances (not of direct concern for present purposes) had been made to allay the major concerns of the Irish public.

11 Provision is made for the UK and Poland to opt out of the Charter by a protocol to the Lisbon Treaty – Protocol on the Application of the Charter of Fundamental Rights of the European Union to Poland and to the United Kingdom.

12 P. Craig and G. de Burca (eds), *The Evolution of EU Law* above n. 2, p. 380. See also ECJ 27 June 2006, Case C-540/03 *European Parliament v. Council of the European Union* [2006] ECR I-5769.

13 Opinion of the European Economic and Social Committee on the Communication from the Commission Towards a United Nations legally binding instrument to promote and protect the rights and dignity of persons with disabilities of 24 January 2003, COM 16 final, 26 March 2003.

14 By virtue of its amendments to Art. 6(2) of the Treaty on European Union.

15 O. de Schutter, 'Anchoring the European Union to the European Social Charter: The Case for Accession' in G. de Burca and B. de Witte (eds), *Social Rights in Europe* (Oxford, Oxford University Press, 2005).

16 European Commission, 'Situation of Disabled People in the European Union: the European Action Plan 2008–2009' Communication from the Commission to the Council, the European Parliament, the European Economic and Social Committee and the Committee of the Regions, COM 738 final, 26 November 2007. See generally L. Waddington, 'Breaking New Ground: The Implications of the UN Convention on the Rights of Persons with Disabilities for the European Community' in O. Arnardóttir and G. Quinn (eds), *The UN Convention on the Rights of Persons with Disabilities: European and Scandinavian Perspectives* (Leiden, Martinus Nijhoff, 2009).

17 See generally, M. Bell, *Anti-Discrimination Law and the European Union* (Oxford University Press, Oxford, 2002); and E. Ellis, *EU Anti-Discrimination Law* (Oxford, Oxford University Press, 2005).

irrational prejudice and of protecting the human rights of individual citizens to fulfil their potential free from arbitrary discrimination.[18] Unsurprisingly perhaps, this growing emphasis on human rights and equality has occurred in tandem with an increasing emphasis on a social model conception of disability.[19]

The traditional medical or individual model conception of disability shaped documents such as the Council of the European Communities' action plan for the rehabilitation of disabled workers in 1974.[20] Gradually, however, the emphasis has shifted away from policies grounded in the belief that the problem to be addressed lies primarily within the individual concerned and towards policies which also recognise the need to tackle the societal forces which operate to marginalise disabled people.[21] The importance of tackling such social barriers is stressed in the Commission's 2003 Action Plan.[22] According to this:

> The EU...sees disability as a social construct. The EU social model of disability stresses the environmental barriers in society which prevent the full participation of people with disabilities in society. These barriers must be removed...[23]

This Action Plan, which is due to run until 2010, details a variety of ways in which the Commission is working to bring about the removal of disabling social barriers. These include the three key 'operational objectives' of anti-discrimination, mainstreaming and accessibility. Principles of mainstreaming and accessibility underlie many important disability-related developments, including a number of

---

[18] See e.g. G. Quinn, 'Disability Discrimination Law in the European Union' in H. Meenan (ed), *Equality Law for an Enlarged Europe: Understanding the Article 13 Directives* (Cambridge, Cambridge University Press, 2007).

[19] M. Oliver, *The Politics of Disablement* (Basingstoke, Macmillan, 1990); M. Oliver, *Understanding Disability: From Theory to Practice* (Basingstoke, Macmillan, 1996); M. Priestley, 'Constructions and Creations: Idealism, Materialism and Disability Theory' (1998) 13 *Disability & Society* 75; V. Finkelstein, 'The Social Model of Disability Repossessed' (paper presented 1 December 2001, to the Manchester Coalition of Disabled People) Available at <http://www.leeds.ac.uk/disability-studies/archiveuk/finkelstein/soc%20mod%20repossessed.pdf>.

[20] Council Resolution of 27 June 1974, establishing the initial community action programme for the vocational rehabilitation of handicapped persons. See, in particular, the pre-amble where 'handicap' is defined as "any limitation, congenital or acquired, of a person's physical or mental ability which affects his daily activity and his work by reducing his social contribution, his employment prospects, his ability to use public services".

[21] See generally, G. Quinn, 'The Human Rights of People with Disabilities under EU Law' in P. Alston (ed), above n. 2, 281; D. Mabbett, 'The Development of Rights-Based Social Policy in the European Union' (2005) 43 Journal of Common Market Studies 97; and M.A. Priestley, 'In Search of European Disability Policy: Between National and Global' [2007] 1 European Journal of Disability Research 61.

[22] *Equal Opportunities for People with Disabilities: a European Action Plan*, COM 650 final, 30 October 2003.

[23] *Ibid.*, p. 4.

directives which enshrine principles of universal design in a variety of contexts.[24] The law emerging under the Community's anti-discrimination strategy is of particular significance for present purposes, however.

The Treaty of Amsterdam inserted a new Article 13 into the consolidated EC Treaty.[25] This authorised 'the Council, acting unanimously on a proposal from the Commission and after consulting the European Parliament', to take appropriate action 'to combat discrimination based on sex, racial or ethnic origin, religion or belief, disability, age or sexual orientation'. Such action was taken promptly and manifested itself in the Framework Employment Directive 2000.[26]

The Framework Employment Directive requires Member States to take steps to prohibit discrimination on a number of grounds including disability in the context of employment. The conduct to be prohibited includes direct and indirect discrimination as well as harassment and instructions to discriminate.[27] In addition, steps must be taken to ensure that reasonable accommodation is provided for disabled employees and that those associated with the bringing of a discrimination complaint are not victimised as a result.[28]

Like the EU, the Council of Europe has adopted an Action Plan on disability.[29] Although by no means its first initiative on disability equality,[30] this 10-year

---

[24] See e.g. Directive 2001/85/EC on vehicles carrying more than eight passengers; Directive 95/16/EC on lifts; Directives 2004/17/EC and 2004/18/EC on public procurement; Directive 1999/5/EC on radio and telecommunication terminal equipment; Directive 2002/21/EC on electronic communications networks and services; Directive 2002/22/EC on universal services and users' rights; Directive 2003/24/EC amending Council Directive 98/18/EC on safety rules and standards for passenger ships; Directive 96/48/EC on the interoperability of the trans-European high-speed rail system; Directive 2001/16/EC on the interoperability of the trans-European conventional rail system as modified by Directive 2004/49/EC (Railway Specific Directive); and Regulation 1107/2006/EC concerning the rights of disabled persons and persons with reduced mobility. For fuller accounts, see the chapter by L. Waddington in this volume, above n. 15; and A. Lawson and B. Matthews, 'Dismantling Barriers to Transport by Law: The European Journey' in C. Barnes and G. Mercer (eds), *Disability Policy and Practice: Applying the Social Model* (Leeds, Disability Press, 2005).

[25] OJ C340 10.11.1997, Art. 6A. See further, M. Bell, 'The New Article 13 EC Treaty: A Sound Basis for European Anti-Discrimination Law?', (1999) 6 Maastricht Journal of *European Law* 5; R. Whittle, 'Disability Discrimination and the Amsterdam Treaty' (1998) 23 European Law Review 50; and L. Waddington, 'Article 13 EC: Setting Priorities in the Proposal for a Horizontal Employment Directive' [2000] 29 *Industrial Law Journal* 176.

[26] Directive 2000/78/EC establishing a general framework for equal treatment in employment and occupation.

[27] Art. 2.

[28] Arts 5 and 11 respectively.

[29] 'The Council of Europe Action Plan to Promote the Rights and Full Participation of People with Disabilities in Society: Improving the Quality of Life of People with Disabilities in Europe 2006–2015', Recommendation of the Committee of Ministers, Rec (2006)5.

[30] See, e.g., 'A Coherent Policy for the Rehabilitation of Persons with Disabilities', Recommendation of the Committee of Ministers, Rec (92)6, 1992; and 'Malaga Political Declaration:

Action Plan to promote the rights and full participation of disabled people undoubtedly now represents the primary reference point in this area. The Plan was adopted by the Committee of Ministers on 5 April 2006 and formed the subject matter of a subsequent Recommendation to Member States.[31] Member States are thus urged to 'integrate as appropriate in their policy, legislation and practice the principles' and to 'implement the actions' set out in the Plan.[32] The Council of Europe undertakes to assist Member States in this regard by providing them with recommendations, advice and information.[33]

The Plan identifies, as its fundamental principles:

> Non-discrimination; equality of opportunities; full participation in society of all persons with disabilities; respect for difference and acceptance of disability as part of human diversity; dignity and individual autonomy including the freedom to make one's own choices; ... [and] participation of disabled people in all decisions affecting their lives, both at individual level and at society level through their representative organisations.[34]

'Universal Design principles, equality, training and mainstreaming' are described as 'vital elements' of its implementation strategy.[35] The need to ensure that laws and policies include the notion of 'reasonable adjustment' (or 'reasonable accommodation') is expressly mentioned in the contexts of access to culture, the arts, sport, leisure and tourism;[36] of education;[37] and of employment.[38]

Underlying the Action Plans of both the EU and the Council of Europe, then, are principles of equality, non-discrimination, mainstreaming and universal design. Such principles also underlie the CRPD. That Convention contains a number of Articles, in addition to the 26 paragraphs of its preamble, the function of which is to make clear its purpose and its underlying principles. According to Article 1, its purpose is:

> to promote, protect and ensure the full and equal enjoyment of all human rights and fundamental freedoms by all persons with disabilities, and to promote respect for their inherent dignity.

Improving the Quality of Life for People with Disabilities, Enhancing a Coherent Policy for and Through Participation', Second Council of Europe Ministerial Conference in Disability (Malaga, 2003).

31 'The Council of Europe Action Plan to Promote the Rights and Full Participation of People with Disabilities in Society', above n. 28.

32 *Ibid.*, para. (a).

33 *Ibid.*, para. 2.1.

34 *Ibid.*, para. 2.7.

35 *Ibid.*, para. 1.5. See also *ibid.*, Section 5.

36 *Ibid.*, para. 3.2.1.

37 *Ibid.*, para. 3.4.2.

38 *Ibid.*, para. 3.4.3.

The principle of equality is thus given a central place. The preamble refers to 'the profound social disadvantage' currently experienced by disabled people, to the fact that most of them live in conditions of poverty and to the fact that they continue to encounter 'barriers in their participation as equal members of society'.[39] It is acknowledged that, although the UN Charter recognises that 'all members of the human family' have 'equal and inalienable rights', there is a need for disabled people to be guaranteed the full enjoyment of these rights 'without discrimination'.[40] Further, paragraph (h) declares that discrimination against any person on the basis of disability is a violation of the inherent dignity and worth of the human person.

Article 3 contains eight paragraphs which set out the underlying principles of the CRPD and are intended to inform its interpretation. Paragraph (a) refers to respect for the 'inherent dignity', 'autonomy' and 'independence' of the individual, and paragraph (d) to respect for 'difference' and 'human diversity'. Other paragraphs refer to 'non-discrimination', 'equality of opportunity', 'accessibility' and 'full and effective participation and inclusion in society'.[41] Reference is also made to the principle of gender equality[42] and to that of respect for the identity and the evolving capacities of disabled children.[43]

Article 4 sets out the 'general obligations' of States under the Convention. Paragraph (1) lists a range of strategies which must be adopted in pursuance of the general obligation to ensure the full realisation of all human rights by disabled people. These include refraining from practices inconsistent with the Convention;[44] mainstreaming disability perspectives into all policies and programmes;[45] introducing legislative, administrative and other measures to secure relevant rights for disabled people;[46] and taking positive steps to promote the development and availability of universal design, of assistive technology and of professionals appropriately trained in the provision of relevant skills, essential to the realisation of human rights (for example, the use of assistive technology or mobility aids such as long canes, assistance dogs and wheelchairs).[47] These obligations are supplemented by the duty, imposed on States by Article 8, both to raise awareness of the contribution and potential of disabled people and also to counter stereotypes and to promote positive images of disability. Article 4(3)

---

39 Paras. (y), (t) and (k) respectively. See also para. (e).

40 Paras. (a) and (c).

41 Paras. (b), (e), (f) and (c) respectively.

42 Para. (g). See further art. 6.

43 Para. (h). See further art. 7.

44 Para. (d).

45 Para. (c).

46 Paras. (a) and (b).

47 Paras. (f) and (g) respectively.

requires States to 'closely consult with and actively involve' disabled people's organisations in their implementation of the CRPD and other policies affecting disabled people.

In relation to their over-arching disability policy, then, both the EU and the Council of Europe unsurprisingly appear to be very much in line with the vital force of the CRPD. It is therefore unlikely that the emergence of the CRPD will result in significant changes in direction in either of these European institutions. It is likely instead simply to confirm and to strengthen current policy approaches.

3 *Inclusion*

As the previous Section demonstrates, the idea that disabled people have a place in society's mainstream underlies the disability policy of the EU and the Council of Europe. The extent to which this principle of social inclusion is reflected in the law relating to the Framework Employment Directive, the ESC and the ECHR will now be addressed.

The Framework Employment Directive is firmly grounded on principles of equality and non-discrimination. Its focus is on mainstream employment and training. Indeed, so strong is this emphasis on the mainstream that the relevance of the Framework Employment Directive to segregated sheltered employment remains a matter of some uncertainty and, given the numbers of disabled people working in such settings, one of considerable concern.[48] The Directive aims to facilitate the integration of disabled people, not simply by the prohibition of direct and indirect discrimination against them, but also by the imposition of a reasonable accommodation duty. In elaborating on the nature of such a duty, the Directive explicitly states that workplaces must be adapted in order to facilitate the employment of disabled people.[49] In addition, the Directive adopts a permissive approach to disability-related positive action measures.[50]

According to Part 1 of the ESC, its aim is to attain conditions in which the rights set out in a number of specified principles may be effectively realised.

---

48 See e.g. the decision of the Danish High Court in Eastern High Court of Denmark, UfR, 2005, p. 1492 (discussed by G. Quinn, 'Disability Discrimination Law in the European Union', above n. 17, 262). It is worth contrasting this position with that of the European Committee on Social Rights which, in applying art 15 of the ESC, has insisted that 'the right to fair remuneration and just conditions of employment apply to all workers including workers with disabilities whether they are employed in sheltered facilities or in the open labour market' (Conclusions XVI-2, vol. 1 (2003), at 229).

49 Recital 20.

50 Art. 7.

These principles refer to rights such as the opportunity to earn a living in a freely chosen occupation;[51] the right to just working conditions;[52] and the right to benefit from measures designed to secure the highest possible standard of health. Article 15 deals specifically with disability. Its language, however, is not redolent of principles of inclusion. According to it, States undertake to provide training facilities for disabled people, including by means of 'specialized institutions', and to facilitate the placing of disabled people in employment by, for example, 'specialized placing services, facilities for sheltered employment and measures to encourage employers to admit disabled persons to employment'.

Under the Revised European Social Charter 1996, the language of Article 15 is very different. Although reference continues to be made to 'specialised institutions' and 'sheltered employment', a higher profile is clearly given to principles of mainstreaming and integration. Further, its scope is extended beyond training and employment to 'independence, social integration and participation' in the life of mainstream society more generally. Unsurprisingly, concepts of reasonable accommodation are clearly (if implicitly) drawn upon. Reference is made, for instance, to the need to 'adjust the working conditions to the needs of the disabled' and, more generally, to 'promote their full social integration and participation in the life of the community in particular through measures, including technical aids, aiming to overcome barriers to communication and mobility and enabling access to transport, housing, cultural activities and leisure'.

Gerard Quinn has succinctly encapsulated the shift in emphasis between the 1961 and the 1996 versions of Article 15 as one from 'rehabilitation with a nod toward equality' to 'equality with a nod toward rehabilitation'.[53] The heightened profile of equality is not confined to Article 15. In the 1961 version of the Charter, the principle of non-discrimination is mentioned only in the preamble. In the 1996 version, however, a non-discrimination requirement (very similar to that contained in Article 14 of the ECHR) is set out in Article E.

The European Committee on Social Rights, charged with the responsibility of overseeing the implementation of the ESC, has made some extremely valuable disability-related contributions. From 2003 onwards, its interpretation of the requirements of even the 1961 version of Article 15 prioritises the principle of inclusion and the creation of opportunity to participate in mainstream society.[54] Indeed, in that year, it concluded negatively against Denmark in relation to

---

51 Principle 1.

52 Principle 2.

53 G. Quinn, 'The European Social Charter and EU Anti-Discrimination Law in the Field of Disability: Two Gravitational Fields with one Common Purpose' in G. de Burca and B. de Witte (Eds), *Social Rights in Europe*, above n. 14, 279.

54 See further, *ibid.* 290–293.

the original Article 15 because it did not have legislation prohibiting disability discrimination in the employment sphere.[55]

Similarly, in the context of Article 15 of the revised Charter, the Committee concluded negatively against France for its failure to adopt legislation prohibiting disability discrimination in education[56] and asked it to provide further information as to the nature of any reasonable accommodation duties in its existing equality law.[57] Also worthy of note is the decision of the Committee in *Autisme-Europe v. France.*[58] This case was brought under the collective complaints protocol to the Charter[59] and challenged the level of educational provision made for autistic people both within the French mainstream and special education sectors. The Committee upheld this challenge and again drew attention to the importance of non-discrimination principles in facilitating the 'modern approach of mainstreaming'.[60]

The European Committee on Social Rights relied on the jurisprudence of the European Court of Human Rights (ECtHR) to support its decision in the *Autisme-Europe* case. This appears somewhat ironic given the fact that the reasoning of that Committee is clearly, in many respects, far more advanced on disability-related matters than is that of the ECtHR. This is illustrated by the contrast between the Committee's acceptance of the educational mainstreaming approach and the views of a Chamber of the Second Section of the ECtHR in *DH v. Czech Republic.*[61] That Chamber there suggested that decisions as to the establishment of segregated education for disabled children, and as to the curricula to be followed within that system, raised no equality or human rights issues. Such decisions, according to it, 'mainly [involve] questions of expediency on which it is not for the Court to rule'.[62]

---

55 Conclusions XVI-2, vol. 1 (2003), para. 229.

56 *Ibid.*, para. 158.

57 *Ibid.*, para. 168.

58 Decision of the European Committee of Social Rights, Collective Complaint 13 (2003). See also its decision in MDAC v Bulgaria, Complaint 41/2007, 3 June 2008.

59 Additional Protocol to the European Social Charter providing for a system of collective complaints, Council of Europe Treaty Series No. 158. See further R. Brillat, 'A New Protocol to the European Social Charter Providing for Collective Complaints' [1996] 1 European Human Rights Law Review 52; D. Harris, 'The Collective Complaints Procedure' in *Council of Europe: The Social Charter of the 21st Century* (Strasbourg, Council of Europe Publishing, 1997) 100; and H. Cullen, 'The Collective Complaints Mechanism of the European Social Charter' (2000) 25 *European Law Review Supplement (Human Rights Survey)* 18.

60 See further, Decision of the European Committee of Social Rights, Collective Complaint 13 (2003), para. [49].

61 App. No. 57325/00 (7 February 2006).

62 *Ibid.*, para. [47]. See also M. Bell, 'Direct Discrimination' in D. Schiek, L. Waddington and M. Bell (Eds), *Cases, Materials and Text on National, Supranational and International*

When referred to the Grand Chamber of the ECtHR, the views of the Second Section on this point were not reaffirmed.[63] Instead, the Grand Chamber indicated that it 'share[d] the disquiet of the other Council of Europe institutions who have expressed concerns about the more basic curriculum followed in these schools and, in particular, the segregation the system causes'.[64] On the facts of the case, however, it was not necessary for the Court to investigate the issue of the segregation of disabled children and the question therefore awaits further exploration in a future case.

Thus, while the principle of social inclusion is clearly enshrined in the Framework Employment Directive and in the reasoning of the European Committee on Social Rights, its recognition by the ECtHR is more equivocal. The approach of the ECtHR on this issue is particularly important because there is no explicit reference to disability in the ECHR itself. Unlike cases relating to the Framework Employment Directive and the ESC, there will therefore be no direct and specific statutory language on which disabled claimants will be able to rely.

The appearance of the CRPD is likely to add considerable weight to arguments that including disabled people in society's mainstream is a matter of equality and human rights with which the ECtHR should be concerned. In addition to the general aims and principles of the CRPD, outlined in the previous Section, reference to its treatment of education might also be helpful given the educational context in which these issues have arisen most prominently to date. Article 24 recognises the right of disabled people to an education. Paragraph (1) of this obliges States to provide an 'inclusive system of education and of life-long learning'. This requires them to ensure that disabled people are able to access an inclusive and good quality primary and secondary education, in their own communities, on an equal basis with others.[65] Disabled people receiving such education must be provided with appropriate support[66] and, at all levels of education, their needs must be accommodated wherever that would be reasonable. The emphasis of Article 24 is thus very firmly on the goal of fully supported educational inclusion.[67]

Non-Discrimination Law (Oxford, Hart Publishing, 2007) pp. 257–269 for discussion of whether segregation represents a form of direct discrimination.

63 App. No. 57325/00 (13 November 2007).

64 *Ibid.*, para. [198].

65 Art. 24(2)(a) and (b).

66 Art. 24(2)(d).

67 Although the provision which is made in art. 24(3) for the education of children with sensory impairments in the most appropriate modes and settings may authorise their education alongside others with similar impairments.

The ECtHR is by no means impervious to the influences of international law.[68] In the face of the CRPD, coupled with the Council of Europe's own disability policy as expressed in its Action Plan, it would therefore appear perverse for it to continue to insist (as its Second Chamber appears to have done in the *DH* case) that the segregation of disabled people raises no issue of human rights. An ECtHR acceptance of the fact that the claims of disabled people to a place in life's mainstream do indeed engage human rights questions would result in a more consistent, and therefore more cohesive, European approach.

4 *Reasonable Accommodation*

The success of any policy to promote the full inclusion of disabled people in mainstream society is likely to depend, in part, on the extent to which it is underpinned by effective reasonable accommodation obligations. Such obligations require duty-bearers (such as employers, providers of goods and services and public authorities) to take reasonable steps to adjust their policies, practices and premises in order to remove the disabling barriers which lie in the path of relevant individuals. They might also require duty-bearers to provide specific equipment, aids or services to enable disabled individuals to access workplaces, schools, transport systems or other facilities.

Turning first to the Framework Employment Directive, Article 5 imposes an explicit obligation on Member States to impose reasonable accommodation duties on employers. It demands that employers must be required to take reasonable steps to provide 'appropriate measures, where needed in a particular case, to enable a person with a disability to have access to, participate in, or advance in employment, or to undergo training, unless such measures would impose a disproportionate burden on the employer'. The significance of this obligation must not be under-estimated. Not only has it required an expansion of the domestic laws of the vast majority of Member States but it also represents an important expansion of EU equality law.[69] The Framework Employment Directive gives, for the first time at EC level, binding legal force to the concept of reasonable accommodation. This represents a significant deepening and enriching of the principle of equal treatment which underlies EC equality law. The power of Article 5 is limited, however, in that it operates to benefit disabled people only

---

[68] L. Wildhaber, 'The European Convention on Human Rights and International Law' (2007) 56 International and Comparative Law Quarterly 217.

[69] See further, L. Waddington, 'Reasonable Accommodation' in D. Schiek, L. Waddington and M. Bell (Eds), *Cases, Materials and Text on National, Supranational and International Non-Discrimination Law* above n. 61.

in the contexts of employment and occupation. This issue will be examined further in Section 5 below.

Finally, it should be noted that, although Article 5 couches the reasonable accommodation obligation clearly within the equal treatment principle, that duty is nowhere explicitly categorised as a non-discrimination measure. It appears that this omission may simply have been an accident of drafting.[70] Nevertheless, on the basis of the statutory language, there is no requirement to consider a failure to provide reasonable accommodation to be a form of unlawful discrimination.[71]

The concept of reasonable accommodation is not explicitly mentioned in either the ESC or the Revised ESC. Despite this, there are indications that the European Committee on Social Rights regards the concept as constituting a vital element of effective non-discrimination law. Thus, in *Autisme-Europe v. France*, the Committee declared that:

> Human difference in a democratic society should not only be viewed positively but should be responded to with discernment in order to ensure real and effective equality.[72]

In relation to the ECHR, the starting point for any consideration of reasonable accommodation is its non-discrimination provision – Article 14. According to this:

> The enjoyment of the rights and freedoms set forth in this Convention shall be secured without discrimination on any ground such as sex, race, colour, language, religion, political or other opinion, national or social origin, association with a national minority, property, birth or other status.

As will be immediately apparent, disability is not included in the list of protected grounds. There is no doubt, however, that it falls within the catch-all phrase of 'other status'.

Article 14 thus appears to affirm the view that human rights must be enjoyed by all on an equal basis. In order to ensure that this occurs, some notion of reasonable accommodation is required. To date, however, there has been no explicit acknowledgement that Article 14 embraces principles of reasonable accommoda-

---

70 G. Quinn, 'Disability Discrimination Law in the European Union', above n. 17, 258–259. See also, L. Waddington, *ibid.*, Section 6.1.2.

71 For an account of the variety of approaches which have been adopted to this issue in European countries, see L. Waddington, *ibid.*, Section 6.5.

72 Decision of the European Committee of Social Rights, Collective Complaint 13 (2003), para. [52]. See also e.g. European Social Charter (Revised), XVI-2, vol. 1 (2003 paras. 158, 168 and 229.

tion. The case in which the Court came closest to such an acknowledgement was *Thlimmenos v. Greece*.[73]

In *Thlimmenos*, the ECtHR accepted that non-discrimination required that, on occasion, it would be necessary to treat differently people whose material circumstances differed. Article 14 was held to have been violated where a State failed, without justification, to treat people differently from others despite the fact that their religion made a material difference to their circumstances. The potential of such reasoning for the development of a notion of reasonable accommodation is self-evident. To date, however, this potential has not been exploited.

Some hope for movement in the thinking of the ECtHR on equality issues is provided by the recent decision of the Grand Chamber in *DH v. Czech Republic*.[74] This case concerned the placement of Roma children in segregated schools for pupils with 'mental handicaps'[75] where, it was accepted, they received a 'substantially inferior education'[76] than that received by children in mainstream schools. It was argued that the rate of such placement was disproportionately high and that it amounted to a violation of the Article 14 right of Roma children to be free from discrimination in connection with their enjoyment of the right to education protected by Article 2 of Protocol 1. The Grand Chamber accepted this argument and, for the first time clearly acknowledged that Article 14 embraced the concept of indirect discrimination.[77]

Article 14 undoubtedly provides the most obvious site for the development of a concept of reasonable accommodation under the ECHR. It would, however, be dangerous to confine any consideration of reasonable accommodation related ECHR developments to this provision. It is entirely possible to interpret substantive ECHR rights in such a way as to incorporate some notion of reasonable accommodation.

The issue of reasonable accommodation, although not generally articulated as such, has arisen in a number of cases brought by disabled people claiming violations of Convention rights. The issue has arisen most obviously in cases concerning Articles 3, 8 and 6. The judicial response has varied.

---

[73] App. No. 34369/97 (6 April 2000) 31 EHRR 15. See also the discussion of the 'substantive' nature of equality under Art. 14 in A. Hendriks, 'The Significance of Equality and Non-Discrimination for the Protection of the Rights and Dignity of Disabled Persons' in T. Degener and Y. Koster-Dreese, (eds), *Human Rights and Disabled Persons: Essays and Relevant Human Rights Instruments* (Dordrecht, Martinus Nijoff Publishers, 1995) 52.

[74] App. No. 57325/00, (13 November 2007).

[75] This is the language used in the judgement. See e.g. *ibid.*, para. [41].

[76] *Ibid.*, para. [135].

[77] *Ibid.*, para. [184]. The Court cited, in support of this acknowledgement, its decisions in *Hugh Jordan v. UK* App No 24746/94, (4 May 2001) para. [154] and *Hoogendijk v. the Netherlands* App. No. 58461/00 (Admissibility Decision 6 January 2005) as well as the European Union's Council Directives 97/80/EC and 2000/43/EC.

The right to be free from inhuman and degrading treatment or punishment, protected by Article 3 of the ECHR, is an absolute right to which there are no exceptions or limitations. The Court has consequently set a high threshold for entry into its realms. Suffering must reach a certain minimum level before it can amount to an Article 3 violation. In assessing whether this level has been attained, the court must take into account all the circumstances of the case, including the health, age and sex of the victim.[78] This stress on the circumstances of the particular victim has been used by judges, at least in cases concerning the treatment of prisoners, to require States to pay due regard to the impairments of a disabled person in deciding whether Article 3 has been violated.

In *Price v. UK*,[79] which is perhaps the most important Article 3 case concerning disabled people, the ECtHR ruled that the UK had inflicted degrading treatment on Ms Price by its failure to accommodate the particular needs arising from her impairment. As a result of thalidomide, all four of her limbs were foreshortened and she had a number of associated health difficulties, including kidney problems. Her refusal to answer questions in County Court debt recovery proceedings resulted in her spending three nights in prison. She was refused permission to take the battery charger for her wheelchair to prison; she had to spend the first night in a cell which was dangerously cold for her and contained a bed she was unable to use; she had to be assisted in using the toilet by male staff (having been left sitting on the toilet for three hours on one occasion until she gave up hope of being assisted by a woman); and, at the end of her sentence, she required catheterisation due to lack of fluid and to urine retention caused by difficulties in using the toilet facilities.

The ECtHR found that Ms Price's Article 3 rights had indeed been violated, observing that:

> There is no evidence in this case of any positive intention to humiliate or debase the applicant. However, the Court considers that to detain a severely disabled person in conditions where she is dangerously cold, risks developing sores because her bed is too hard or unreachable, and is unable to go to the toilet or keep clean without the greatest of difficulty, constitutes degrading treatment.[80]

---

[78] *Ireland v. UK* App. No. 5310/71 (18 January 1978), para. [162].

[79] App. No. 33394/96 (10 July 2001) 34 EHRR 1285. For a similar decision in the UN context, see, *Hamilton v. Jamaica,* communication No. 616/ 1995, Views adopted by the Human Rights Committee on 28 July 1999 (CCPR/C/66/D/616/1995); discussed in T. Degener, 'Disability and Freedom: The International Covenant on Civil and Political Rights' in G. Quinn and T. Degener (eds), *Human Rights and Disability: the current use and future potential of United Nations human rights instruments in the context of disability,* (UN, Geneva, 2002) para. 4.1.4.

[80] *Ibid.*, para. [30].

Judge Greve, who delivered a separate concurring opinion, added that:

> In a civilised country like the United Kingdom, society considers it not only appropriate but a basic humane concern to try to ameliorate and compensate for the disabilities faced by a person in the applicant's situation.... The applicant's disabilities are not hidden or easily overlooked. It requires no special qualification, only a minimum of ordinary human empathy, to appreciate her situation and to understand that to avoid unnecessary hardship – that is, hardship not implicit in the imprisonment of an able-bodied person – she has to be treated differently from other people because her situation is significantly different.[81]

Price thus demonstrates clearly that, in order to comply with Article 3, States may have to adapt or alter mainstream conditions or regimes in order to accommodate the needs of disabled prisoners.[82] They must take into account the difference in circumstance created by an individual's impairment and provide them with correspondingly different treatment. It thus illustrates the operation of some form of reasonable accommodation duty in the implementation of the fundamental and absolute right to be free from inhuman and degrading treatment. It should be remembered, however, that the ambit of this right is extremely narrow and that it seems unlikely to avail disabled people outside the institutional context.[83]

Article 8, although subject to a form of justification defence, is much broader in scope than Article 3. It is therefore sometimes possible to establish a violation of the former but not the latter. Article 8 protects the right to respect for one's private and family life, one's home and correspondence. The ECtHR has given the concept of private life a wide interpretation. According to *Botta v. Italy*,[84] it embraces the 'physical and psychological integrity' of an individual and the 'development, without outside interference, of the personality of each individual in his relations with other human beings'. Unsurprisingly, this rich notion of 'private life' has generated a number of cases in which disabled people have claimed that their Article 8 rights have been violated by the failure of a State to remove access barriers or to provide them with facilitative aids and devices.

---

81 *Ibid.*

82 In cases such as *Mouisel v. France* App. No. 67263/01 (14 November 2002) it has been held that the illness or impairment of a prisoner may, on occasion, require that they be removed from the mainstream prison environment, either by being released or by being transferred into other conditions (such as those of a hospital). See also the UK case of *Napier v. Scottish Ministers* [2004] SLT 555.

83 See e.g. *Wainwright v. UK* App. No. 12350/04 (26 September 2006)in which the irregularities entailed in the strip-search of a disabled person visiting a relative in prison were not held to violate Art. 3. See also the domestic British case of *R (Bernard) v. Enfield LBC* [2002] EWHC (Admin) 2282.

84 App. No. 21439/93 (24 February 1998) 26 EHRR 241, para. [32]. See also *Niemietz v. Germany* App. No. 13710/88 (16 December 1992) 16 EHRR 97.

The leading case on this issue is *Botta* itself. Mr Botta (a wheelchair user) claimed that, in failing adequately to enforce laws requiring private beaches to provide physical access for disabled people, the state had not complied with its obligation to respect his private life and to allow him to develop his personality. The physical barriers to accessing the beaches in question rendered him unable to enjoy a 'normal social life' and 'to participate in the life of the community'.[85] The ECtHR accepted that compliance with Article 8 would sometimes require a state to adopt 'measures designed to secure respect for private life even in the sphere of the relations of individuals between themselves'.[86] Such an obligation, however, would arise only where there was a 'direct and immediate link between the measures sought by an applicant and the latter's private and/or family life'.[87] There was no such direct and immediate link in *Botta* – the right claimed there concerning 'interpersonal relations of such broad and indeterminate scope that there [could] be no conceivable direct link'.[88]

Similar reasoning was applied in *Zehnalova and Zehnal v. the Czech Republic*,[89] where a disabled person challenged the failure of the state to enforce laws requiring public buildings (including the post office, swimming pool and police station) to be made accessible. Though the buildings were in the town in which the applicant lived, the Court considered that there was insufficient evidence as to their everyday use by the applicant to establish the necessary direct and immediate link. Failure to take positive steps to make the buildings accessible could not therefore constitute an Article 8 violation.

In two other disability-related cases, however, the ECtHR has accepted the presence of a direct and immediate link sufficient to raise the possibility that the State would be required to take positive steps to protect the Applicants' private life. In neither of them, however, was a violation of Article 8 established because the State's failure to take the contested positive step was on each occasion found to have been justified under Article 8(2).

In the first of these cases, *Marzari v. Italy*,[90] Mr Marzari challenged the Italian authorities' failure to provide him with housing which he claimed to be suitable for somebody with his particular form of physical impairment. While the provision of appropriate accommodation was found to entail the necessary direct and immediate link, it was held that the State had not acted inconsistently with Article 8. To have ruled otherwise would have had considerable repercussions on Italian social housing policies. In addition, the authorities had offered Marzari

[85] *Ibid.*, para. [27].
[86] *Ibid.*, para. [33].
[87] *Ibid.*, para. [34].
[88] *Ibid.*, para. [55].
[89] App. No. 38621/97 (Admissibility Decision 14 May 2002).
[90] App. No. 36448/97 (Admissibility Decision 4 May 1999) 28 EHRR CD 175.

what an expert committee had judged to be suitable accommodation and had expressed willingness to make adaptations to his allocated apartment.

In the second of these cases, *Sentges v. the Netherlands*,[91] Mr Sentges challenged the Dutch authorities' refusal to supply him with a robotic arm which would have significantly reduced his otherwise total dependence on assistance from carers, thereby giving him some degree of privacy and independence. Again, the necessary direct and immediate link between the provision of such an aid and the claimant's private life was established. The expense which providing it would have entailed, however, was held to justify the State's refusal to provide it to him.

Thus in *Botta* and *Zehnalova*, where no direct and immediate link was found, the measures sought related to general access to public places. In *Marzari* and *Sentges* on the other hand, where such a link was found to exist, the contested measures were highly specific and personal in nature. Further, the effect of the measures in the latter two cases would extend to all aspects of the lives of the applicants and be felt on a relatively permanent basis rather than only on visits to public facilities.

The role of reasonable accommodation within the Article 8 jurisprudence has been fully explored by Olivier De Schutter.[92] He suggests that the introduction of the direct and immediate link requirement in *Botta* represents an attempt, by the ECtHR, to set the process of identifying Article 8 positive obligations on an objective basis and to set that process clearly apart from the process of determining whether an alleged violation is or is not justified. He describes this as an attempt to tame the notion of positive obligations. If allowed to run wild, that notion 'could have led to the imposition of a requirement to undertake wide-scale restructuring of the environment wherever such restructuring could contribute, at a reasonable cost, to facilitating the self-fulfilment of disabled individuals'.[93] The result, however, is morally questionable as well as unduly restrictive. In his words:

> [T]he *Botta* line of cases confronts us with an implicit view that certain activities in life (eg travelling, going on vacation, having the choice of which chemist to visit) are less worthy of protection, because they are less essential to the fulfilment of one's personality. Perhaps we should question this hierarchy. Perhaps we should challenge both the practicability of such a distinction – as if housing or employment, for instance, can be distinguished from public transportation or access to services of general interest – and, especially, the underlying idea that it would be

[91] *Sentges v. The Netherlands* App. No. 27677/02 (Admissibility Decision 8 July 2003).

[92] O. De Schutter, 'Reasonable Accommodations and Positive Obligations in the European Convention on Human Rights' in A. Lawson and C. Gooding (eds), *Disability Rights in Europe: From Theory to Practice* (Oxford, Hart Publishing, 2005) 35.

[93] *Ibid.*, p. 45.

> compatible with the requirement of autonomy to oblige a person to restrict him/herself to his or her immediate surroundings and deny him/her the opportunity of moving beyond them.[94]

Thus, although Article 8 appears to hold promise as a source of positive obligations to take steps which would facilitate the inclusion and participation of disabled people in mainstream society, that promise has not yet been realised. Its extent is tightly circumscribed by the direct and immediate link requirement and no relevant ECtHR cases have, to date, proved successful.[95]

Finally, in this connection, it is worth devoting a few words to Article 6. This protects the right to a fair trial and, although its potential scope is much narrower than that of Article 8, it has generated a number of interesting cases in which the central issue has in effect been the entitlement of a disabled litigant to reasonable accommodation. The approach which emerges from the Strasbourg cases is, however, disappointingly restrictive.

Malone v. UK[96] concerned the accessibility of court facilities to an Applicant who had rheumatoid arthritis and used a wheelchair. Ms Malone complained that, in connection with a housing dispute, she had been required to attend an inaccessible court in London which was some 500k away from where she lived. The long journey, which began at 4.30 am, caused her so much pain that she had to spend the next four days in bed. Because the building was inaccessible, she had to be carried by court officials up the steps into, and also inside, the court building. She suffered extreme discomfort as a result of the inaccessible toilet facilities – a problem intensified by the fact that, on one occasion, she had had to wait for nearly six hours before her case was heard. The case, she argued, should have been transferred to an accessible court in her hometown and the State's failure to do this amounted to a violation of her Article 6 rights.

Ms Malone's case was held to be inadmissible because she had failed to take adequate steps to bring her requirements to the attention of the court. She had not applied for a transfer until the case had been listed for London.

Malone is, as Clements and Read observe, 'an unsatisfactory decision'.[97] While disabled people should be expected to inform relevant authorities of their requirements, this should not absolve those authorities of all responsibility when, as in *Malone*, the disability is known to them and the consequences of failure to act

---

[94] *Ibid.*, p. 61.

[95] For discussion of disability-related British domestic cases which have succeeded in imposing positive Art. 8 obligations on the State, see A. Lawson, *Disability and Equality Law in Britain,* above n. 4, ch. 2.

[96] App. No. 25290/94 (Admissibility Decision 28 February 1996).

[97] L. Clements and J. Read, *Disabled People and European Human Rights: A Review of the Implications of the 1998 Human Rights Act for Disabled Children and Adults in the UK* (Bristol, Policy Press, 2003), 45.

will be serious for the disabled person. 'Equal treatment', they comment 'is not a special dispensation available only if booked in advance'.[98]

Another disappointing Strasbourg decision is *Stanford v. UK*.[99] There, the Applicant, who had a severe hearing impairment, had been tried for rape. He had been unable to hear the testimony of the victim. He had complained about this to his prison guard and also to his solicitor but his lawyers did not mention this to the judge. When he challenged the proceedings under Article 6, it was accepted that the right of an Accused to participate effectively in a trial conferred by that Article included, 'not only his right to be present, but also to hear and follow the proceedings'.[100] According to the ECtHR, however, Article 6 had not been infringed because the Applicant had not brought his hearing difficulty to the attention of the trial judge. Though he had mentioned it to his guard and his solicitor, they were not court officials and therefore the court itself was not at fault. Like *Malone*, this case appears to require a disabled Applicant to discharge a heavy burden (one which may indeed have been impossible for Stanford to discharge) before any form of reasonable accommodation duties will be triggered.

The more recent case of *Young v. UK*[101] also concerned a disabled prisoner. Ms Young, who had cerebral palsy, had been unable to provide a urine sample when required to do so for purposes of a drugs test. The authorities treated this as a deliberate refusal to co-operate and added three days to her sentence as a penalty. Ms Young challenged the fairness of these proceedings on a number of grounds, some of which were disability-related. She claimed that she had been unable to provide the sample because of the physical symptoms of her cerebral palsy and that the authorities had, both at that point and in the subsequent disciplinary proceedings, taken insufficient account of the linguistic and communication-related aspects of her impairment. A Chamber of the Court's Fourth Section found that the relevant disciplinary proceedings had violated Article 6 for reasons unrelated to Ms Young's impairment. It did not therefore need to address the disability-related arguments and chose not to do so. Disappointingly, therefore, *Young* does not expand the somewhat restrictive approach of the ECtHR to the notion of reasonable accommodation in the Article 6 context.

To conclude, the Article 3 jurisprudence contains clear and powerful recognition of the need to take steps to accommodate the needs of disabled people, at least if they are confined in institutions, in order to ensure that the way in which they are treated does not cause them disproportionate hardship. The ECtHR

---

98 *Ibid.*

99 App. No. 16757/90 (23 February 1994).

100 *Ibid.*, para. [26].

101 App. No. 60682/00 (16 January 2007).

approach to the issue of disability-related accommodations under Articles 6 and 8 has, however, been somewhat disappointing to date. A more expansive approach appears to be evident in UK domestic jurisprudence.[102] Although it is tempting to attribute this difference in approach to an overly cautious approach on the part of the ECtHR, it should be remembered that the more expansive British decisions tend to be of much more recent origin than their ECtHR counterparts. In a field which has been developing as rapidly as that of disability law, time is undoubtedly a significant factor. The well-recognised but uncomfortable fact that surprisingly few disability-related cases reach the ECtHR[103] means that there are relatively few opportunities to demonstrate a more confident and positive approach to the issue of disability-related accommodation duties. It is, perhaps, no accident that *Price v. UK*[104] is one of the most recent of the ECtHR cases considered here and that it is also the one in which such duties were most warmly embraced. Nevertheless, the most recent case is *Young* and it demonstrates that the Court is not keen to take advantage of any available opportunity to develop human rights law in a disability-sensitive manner.

It would certainly be unrealistically optimistic to attribute the apparent reluctance of the ECtHR to develop reasonable-accommodation-type positive obligations simply to the scarcity of recent cases raising such issues. The potentially obstructive fact remains that, unlike the ESC, the primary aim of the ECHR is not to confer rights carrying positive obligations. Such positive obligations as there are, 'emerge in the afterglow of essentially negative rights'.[105] In the context of disability, however, the classical distinction between positive and negative rights is an unhelpful one – a point which emerges with striking clarity from the approach of the CRPD.[106]

---

102 See e.g. the cases of *R (Bernard) v. Enfield LBC* [2002] EWHC (Admin) 2282; *R (A and B) v. East Sussex CC* [2003] EWHC (Admin) 167; and *R (King) v. Isleworth Crown Court* [2001] Administrative Court Digest 289. See, however, the case of *Wainwright v. UK* App. No. 12350/04 (26 September 2006) in which the ECtHR took a more expansive approach to Art. 8 than had the British House of Lords.

103 See e.g. L. Clements and J. Reid, 'The Dog that Didn't Bark: The Issue of Access to Rights under the ECHR by Disabled People' in A Lawson and C. Gooding (eds), above n. 91, 21.

104 App. No. 33394/96 (10 July 2001) 34 EHRR 1285.

105 G. Quinn, 'The European Social Charter and EU Anti-Discrimination Law in the Field of Disability' above n. 52, 298.

106 See, for powerful arguments to the effect that all human rights impose positive as well as negative obligations, S. Fredman, *Human Rights Transformed* (Oxford, Oxford University Press, 2008).

The concept of reasonable accommodation is firmly embedded in the CRPD. It is explicitly mentioned in the substantive Articles dealing with education,[107] employment,[108] liberty and security of person[109] and, though in slightly different terms, in the Article dealing with access to justice.[110] Further, largely as a result of Articles 2 and 5, it is an implicit element of almost every one of the substantive Articles.

Article 5(2) requires signatory States to 'prohibit all discrimination on the basis of disability'. Such discrimination is defined in Article 2 as follows:

> ...any distinction, exclusion or restriction on the basis of disability which has the purpose or effect of impairing or nullifying the recognition, enjoyment or exercise, on an equal basis with others, of all human rights and fundamental freedoms in the political, economic, social, cultural, civil or any other field. It includes all forms of discrimination, including denial of reasonable accommodation.

As will be apparent, this is an extremely broad definition.

Reasonable accommodation is itself defined in Article 2 as:

> ...necessary and appropriate modification and adjustments not imposing a disproportionate or undue burden, where needed in a particular case, to ensure to persons with disabilities the enjoyment or exercise on an equal basis with others of all human rights and fundamental freedoms.

This makes it clear that a duty to provide reasonable accommodation imposes positive obligations to identify barriers in the way of a disabled person's enjoyment of their human rights and to take appropriate steps to remove them. The emphasis is on the barriers which operate in a particular case and thus on the need to respond to the specific circumstances of the individual disabled person in question. The solutions required must be appropriate to that person. They may simply require cost-free changes to be made to standard practices but they may also require money to be spent on additional equipment or support or on the installation of improved physical access.

As already mentioned, unlike the Framework Employment Directive, Article 2 of the CRPD includes a failure to provide reasonable accommodation in the definition of discrimination. States are therefore required to prohibit such failures by Article 5(2) and to do so immediately as the right to be free from discrimination is a civil and political right to which the principle of progressive

---

[107] Arts. 24(2)(c) and 24(5).

[108] Art. 27(1)(i).

[109] Art. 14(2).

[110] Art. 13(1) This refers to the 'provision of procedural and age appropriate accommodations'.

realisation does not apply.[111] Unlike most other civil and political rights, however, reasonable accommodation obligations are likely to require States to spend money, thus blurring the distinction between traditionally positive and negative rights.

Because of the expenditure often associated with reasonable accommodation, its positioning within the domain of civil and political rights was not free from controversy in the CRPD negotiations. It should be stressed, however, that the concepts of 'reasonableness' and 'undue burden' will themselves inject some degree of progressive realisation into the implementation of reasonable accommodation duties. These concepts are inherently sensitive to the particular circumstances, not only of the disabled individual in need of an accommodation, but also to the circumstances of those on whom the duties fall. These circumstances are likely to change over time with the result that an accommodation that may at one time be considered to impose an undue burden will, at a later point, not be so regarded.

Finally, it is worth noting again the peculiar bridging role played by the concept of reasonable accommodation in the context of human rights law. As has been seen, it may legitimately be regarded as an integral element of non-discrimination. This situates it within the realms of civil and political rights. Its function, however, is to ensure that rights of all kinds – whether they are classified as economic, social or cultural rights or as civil or political ones – become available, in a meaningful sense, to disabled people. It thus directly challenges the traditional clear-cut division between civil and political rights, on the one hand, and economic, social and cultural ones, on the other – making it clear that all human rights will impose positive as well as negative obligations on States.

The CRPD thus provides an extremely helpful clarification of the role of reasonable accommodation in ensuring the full enjoyment of human rights by disabled people. It confirms its status as an integral element of non-discrimination and will, it is to be hoped, prove highly influential in the development of European disability law.

---

[111] Art. 4(2). This is consistent with the approach of other international human rights instruments – see, e.g., art. 4 of the Convention on the Rights of the Child; art. 2(1) of the International Covenant on Economic, Social and Cultural Rights; and General Comment No. 3 "The nature of States parties' obligations" adopted by the Committee on Economic, Social and Cultural Rights at its fifth session in 1990 (UN Doc E/1991/23).

5 *Material Scope*

Attention will now be turned to the areas covered by the Framework Employment Directive, the ESC and the ECHR. There is, as will be seen, some degree of overlap between them but, importantly, their associated enforcement mechanisms are quite distinct. In terms of enforcement and practical realisation, the rights conferred by the Framework Employment Directive are much stronger than those conferred by the ECHR or the ESC. The ECHR does entitle aggrieved individuals, as a last resort, to have recourse to the ECtHR. The ESC, however, cannot be enforced by individuals and collective complaints may be brought only against countries which have ratified the relevant protocol.[112]

The Framework Employment Directive is confined to the areas of employment and occupation. These phrases, however, are broadly conceived. It therefore operates in both the public and private sectors and applies to employment, self-employment, occupation, vocational guidance and training (which covers a substantial proportion of post-sixteen education), trade unions and professional bodies.[113]

Thus, despite its undoubted significance, the practical impact of the Framework Employment Directive is severely constrained by the narrow confines of its material scope. The provision of meaningful equality in the workplace is of little value if one is prevented from attaining the necessary qualifications by discriminatory education systems, or from travelling to it by inaccessible transport or housing systems. For this reason the European Disability Forum has long campaigned for an additional directive which would extend the prohibition of discrimination and the obligation to make reasonable accommodation beyond employment to areas such as education, transport, housing and goods and services generally and has produced a shadow directive to this effect.[114] Article 13 of the Amsterdam Treaty would clearly found such an expansion as is illustrated by the wider material scope of directives relating to race and gender.[115]

---

[112] See further, T. Novitz, 'Are Social Rights Necessarily Collective Rights? A Critical Analysis of the Collective Complaints Protocol to the European Social Charter' [2002] European Human Rights Law Review 52.

[113] Art. 3. See further, R. Whittle, 'The Framework Directive for Equal Treatment in Employment and Occupation: An Analysis from a Disability Rights Perspective' [2002] European Law Review 303, 320–321.

[114] *Proposal by the European Disability Forum for a Comprehensive Directive to Combat Discrimination against Persons with Disabilities* Doc EDF/0108 (Brussels, EDF, 2008) available at http://www.edf-feph.org/Page_Generale.asp?DocID=13854&thebloc=13856 (last accessed 12 May 2008).

[115] Directive 2000/43/EC implementing the principle of equal treatment between persons irrespective of racial or ethnic origin; and Directive 2004/113/EC implementing the principle of equal treatment between men and women in the access to and supply of goods and services.

The European Commission has now proposed a directive which would implement the principle of equal treatment (on grounds of disability, age, sexual orientation and religion and belief) outside employment.[116] Such an instrument would undoubtedly very significantly broaden and strengthen the protection available to disabled Europeans from discrimination and marginalisation.

The ESC is concerned with economic, social and cultural rights. It therefore covers areas such as employment, education, health and transport. Thus, although it is wider in scope than the Framework Employment Directive, there is a significant overlap.[117] Until such time as the Framework Employment Directive is expanded, the ESC, despite its traditionally 'twilight existence',[118] thus provides a useful fallback means of challenging inadequate State responses to the needs of disabled people in connection with social, economic and cultural rights which fall outside the realms of employment and occupation.

The ECHR deals with civil and political rights. However, as is evident from the discussion of *DH* above, it also extends to education and therefore overlaps, to some extent, with the ESC.

The non-discrimination protection afforded by Article 14 of the ECHR applies only to the enjoyment of the rights set out in the ECHR. Thus, although it does not require the discrimination concerned to amount to an actual violation of a substantive ECHR right, it does require it to amount to an interference with the enjoyment of such a right. The case must fall within the ambit of one of the substantive provisions of the ECHR before any issue of discrimination under Article 14 may be considered.[119]

Unsurprisingly, this aspect of Article 14 has attracted criticism.[120] It is addressed by Protocol 12, which confers the much broader right to be free from discrimination in 'the enjoyment of any right set forth by law'. It would thus require States

[116] 'Proposal for a Council Directive on Implementing the Principle of Equal Treatment Between Persons Irrespective of Religion or Belief, Disability, Age or Sexual Orientation' COM (2008) 426.

[117] G. Quinn, 'The European Social Charter and EU Anti-Discrimination Law in the Field of Disability', above n 52; and M. Bell, 'Walking in the Same Direction? The Contribution of the European Social Charter and the European Union to Combating Discrimination' in G. de Burca and B. de Witte (eds), *Social Rights in Europe*, above n. 14, 261.

[118] D. Harris and J. Darcy, *The European Social Charter* (Ardsley NY, Transnational Publishers, 2001), 12. For discussion of how its effectiveness might be further enhanced, see P. Alston, 'Assessing the Strengths and Weaknesses of the European Social Charter's Supervisory System' in G. de Burca and B. de Witte (eds), above n. 14, 45.

[119] See e.g. *Abdulaziz, Cabales and Balkandali v. UK* App. No. 9214/80; 9473/81; 9474/81 (28 May 1985) 7 EHRR 471; and *Botta v. Italy*, App. No. 21439/93 (24 February 1998) 26 EHRR 241.

[120] See e.g. K. Monaghan, 'Limitations and Opportunities: A Review of the Likely Domestic Impact of Article 14 ECHR' [2001] *European Human Rights Law Review* 167; R. Wintermute,

to ensure that citizens were not discriminated against in their enjoyment of a much wider range of rights than those covered by the ECHR.[121] It therefore has the potential to be a great resource to disabled people, particularly if the ECtHR were to accept that (in line with the CRPD) the concept of non-discrimination includes a principle of reasonable accommodation.

Protocol 12 came into force on 1 April 2005. It is thus still relatively recent. Regrettably, however, countries such as the UK have chosen not to ratify it.

The emergence of the CRPD may well have hastened the steps of the European Commission toward the implementation of a broad disability-specific directive. The fact that the EC has signed the Convention provides firm grounds for this hope. Indeed, as Lisa Waddington's chapter suggests, compliance with the CRPD may well oblige the EC to develop such an instrument.

A disability-specific directive extending to all the areas covered by the Race Directive[122] would greatly enhance the protection currently afforded to disabled people in Europe. It would reach not only employment and occupation, but also goods and services, education, health-care and social protection. A vast range of social, economic and cultural rights would thus fall within its scope, significantly increasing the overlap between EC law and the ESC. Various ECHR rights (such as the right to education and rights connected with the provision of a service) would also be covered, offering disabled individuals an alternative (and probably preferable) means of enforcement.

6 *Conclusion*

The CRPD is undoubtedly an 'extraordinarily far-reaching convention'.[123] Its aim was not the creation of new rights but the disability-sensitive articulation and clarification of existing ones. Nevertheless, the effect of the clarification it provides has the potential to be at least as powerful as many instruments which purport to be creating new rights. Indeed, the very fact that it simply represents

---

'Within the Ambit: How Big is the "Gap" in Article 14 ECHR?' [2004] *European Human Rights Law Review* 366.

121 See generally *Non-Discrimination: A Human Right – Proceedings, Seminar Marking the Entry into Force of Protocol No. 12 to the European Convention on Human Rights* (Strasbourg, Council of Europe Publishing, 2006); and J. Schokkenbroek, 'A New European Standard Against Discrimination: Negotiating Protocol No. 12 to the European Convention on Human Rights' in J. Niessen and I. Chopin (eds), *The Development of Legal Instruments to Combat Racism in a Diverse Europe* (Leiden, Martinus Nijhoff, 2004).

122 Directive 2000/43/EC implementing the principle of equal treatment between persons irrespective of racial or ethnic origin, [2000] OJ L 180/22.

123 Press conference on the adoption of the Convention on the Rights of Persons with Disabilities, UN Headquarters, New York, 6 December 2006.

a clarification of rights already conferred by pre-existing UN human rights conventions may add to its power. Countries reluctant to ratify the CRPD, but which have ratified earlier and more general human rights treaties, are likely to find that the rights to which they are already committed must now be understood and implemented in a manner consistent with the CRPD.

In the European context, the CRPD provides a number of insights which are likely to influence the development of disability law. It draws attention to the fact that participation in society's mainstream is a fundamental issue of human rights. Although similar messages are conveyed by the Action Plans of the EU and the Council of Europe, the CRPD's affirmation of this point is likely to help guide the ECtHR away from further pronouncements of the type made by its Second Section in *DH v. Czech Republic.*[124]

In addition, the CRPD will strengthen and reinforce awareness of the importance of the notion of reasonable accommodation and its centrality to disability equality. Unlike any of the European legal instruments, it states clearly that reasonable accommodation is an essential element of the non-discrimination principle as it applies to disabled people. This is likely to have significant implications for the interpretation of the non-discrimination provisions of the Framework Employment Directive, the ESC and, perhaps most significantly, the ECHR.

The CRPD is also likely to hasten efforts to extend the current scope of EC disability non-discrimination law. It thus brings closer the prospects of a broad disability directive, along the lines of the Race Directive, extending beyond employment to cover all the fields falling within the ambit of the Amsterdam Treaty. Such an instrument would undoubtedly broaden and strengthen the protection available to disabled Europeans from discrimination and marginalisation. It would indeed constitute a Europeans with Disabilities Act fit to 'rival the [Americans with Disabilities Act 1990] in scope and depth'.[125]

Many of the ideas and insights set out in the CRPD are not new to European institutions. Indeed, many of them are firmly rooted in such institutions and owe their inclusion in the CRPD partly to the influential role played by the EC in the process of elaborating that instrument. The CRPD is nevertheless likely to have a significant impact on the law of the region. It contains authoritative and high profile clarification of important disability equality concepts and their underlying rationales. It has raised awareness of the disability dimension of

---

[124] App. No. 57325/00 (7 February 2006).

[125] T. Degener and G. Quinn, 'A Survey of International, Comparative and Regional Disability Law Reform' in M.L. Breslin and S. Yee (eds), *Disability Rights Law and Policy: International and National Perspectives* (Ardsley New York, Transnational Publishers, 2002), 51.

human rights amongst disabled people themselves and amongst policy-makers, politicians and lawyers.

In addition, the Convention has generated a considerable momentum in the direction of reform. It is, in many ways, an instrument which has arisen from the grass-roots level. Its detail has been shaped by disabled people and their organisations. The process of its elaboration and adoption has itself also contributed to the development and strengthening of the international and the European disability movements.[126] It is, therefore, likely to be far more powerful and significant than an instrument born out of a purely top-down process.

The CRPD is thus well placed to perform the role of a catalyst for the development of a more comprehensive and more cohesive European disability equality law. Such a development, in turn, has the potential to make a significant difference to the lives of many thousands of disabled Europeans. The CRPD is, in many ways, an inspirational instrument. The important work of giving it concrete practical form, both at the European and national levels, must now begin.

---

[126] See further M.A. Priestley, 'In Search of European Disability Policy', above n. 20; T. Shakespeare, 'Disabled People's Self-Organisation: A New Social Movement?' (1993) 8 *Disability, Handicap and Society* 249; D. Driedger, *The Last Civil Rights Movement* (London, Hurst & Co., 1989); and, more generally, M.E. Keck and K. Sikkink, *Activists beyond borders: advocacy networks in international politics* (Ithica NY, Cornell University Press, 1998); and P. Evans, 'Fighting Marginalization with Trans-National Networks: Counter-Hegemonic Globalization' (2000) 29 *Contemporary Sociology – a Journal of Reviews* 230.

Breaking New Ground: The Implications of Ratification of the UN Convention on the Rights of Persons with Disabilities for the European Community

*Lisa Waddington**

The United Nations Convention on the Rights of Persons with Disabilities (CRPD)[1] is ground breaking in many respects: it is the first human rights Convention of the new century; it is not merely a non-discrimination convention, but also provides for a wide range of classical and substantive rights;[2] and, from a European perspective, it is the first human rights convention which the European Community (EC) negotiated and signed, and it will be the first such convention which the Community is expected to ratify. In the past only the

---

* European Disability Forum Chair in European Disability Law, Maastricht University (NLs). I am grateful to Reykjavik University and the Icelandic Human Rights Centre, and particularly Prof. Oddný Mjöll Arnardóttir, for organising the conference on The Human Rights of Persons with Disabilities – from Social Policy to Equal Rights, held in Reykjavik on 27–28 September 2007, as well as my fellow speakers and the participants. I am grateful to Profs. Gerard Quinn and Oddný Mjöll Arnardóttir for their helpful comments on an earlier version of this article. I am also grateful to a number of European Commission and Council officials who helpfully provided me with documents or background information when researching this paper, and to Joëlle Dek, Jantien Dekkers (both of Maastricht University) and Conor Burns (of the National University of Ireland, Galway), who assisted me in background research and/or in rendering the paper compliant with the relevant style sheet. This paper was completed on 17 May 2008 and does not include information which became available thereafter.

1 Convention on the Rights of Persons with Disabilities (adopted 13 December 2006, opened for signature 30 March 2007, entered into force on 3 May 2008).

2 Gerard Quinn, 'The UN Convention on the Human Rights of Persons with Disabilities', 10 June 2007, <http://www.nhri.net/2007/Berlin-Quinn2.pdf> accessed 16 November 2007, at 9, and Tara J. Melish, 'Perspectives on the UN Convention on the Rights of Persons with Disabilities: The UN Disability Convention: Historic Process, Strong Prospects, and Why the U.S. Should Ratify', (2007) 14 Human Rights Brief, 37 at footnote 11, who describes the Convention as adopting a 'hybrid approach'.

Member States have been party to human rights conventions.[3] Consequently, the CRPD will take on a completely new legal status within EC law, and will have to be respected in its totality, and not as a mere add on to be referred to in passing in Community instruments. The Community competence to negotiate, sign and ultimately ratify the Convention, alongside the Member States, resulted primarily from changes introduced by the Amsterdam Treaty. Under Article 13 EC the Community acquired powers to take action to combat disability discrimination. In addition EC competences exist in a number of other areas where a disability dimension exists, although no other specific mention of disability can be found in the main body of the current EU or EC Treaties.

As a consequence of this direct involvement with the Convention, the EC will, like other States Parties, be bound by its obligations. The goal of this paper is to give some first impressions as to what this implies for the EC and, specifically, what legal obligations ratification of the Convention will impose on the Community.

In essence, this analysis involves asking, and answering, three sets of questions:

1. What fields does the Convention cover and what kinds of obligations does it impose on States Parties in those fields?
2. In which of those fields does the EC have competence?

[3] However, this is not to say that human rights conventions have been completely ignored by the Community institutions, and references to such conventions can be found, for example, in preambles to the equality directives (Council Directive (EC) 2000/43 implementing the principle of equal treatment between persons irrespective of racial or ethnic origin [2000] OJ L180/22 and Council Directive (EC) 2000/78 establishing a general framework for equal treatment in employment and occupation [2000] OJ L303/16). See the Employment Equality Directive (Council Directive (EC) 2000/78) which refers to the Universal Declaration of Human Rights, the Convention on the Elimination of All Forms of Discrimination Against Women, the Covenant on Civil and Political Rights, the Covenant on Economic, Social and Cultural Rights, and ILO Convention 111 in recital 4 of its preamble. Infrequent references can also be found in European Court of Justice case law. In this context Rikki Holtmaat and Christa Tobler refer to Case 158/91 *Levy* [1993] ECR I-3287 as being the only case in which the ECJ has referred to the UN Convention on the Elimination of All Forms of Discrimination Against Women (CEDAW), CEDAW and the European Union's Policy in the Field of Combating Gender Discrimination, (2005) 12 Maastricht Journal of European and Comparative Law 4, 399. The authors also discuss the limited impact which CEDAW has had on EC gender equality law at 418–421. The Court has also occasionally made reference to other human rights instruments. In Case C-249/96 *Grant v. South West Trains Ltd.* [1998] ECR I-621 the Court referred to the International Covenant on Civil and Political Rights. However, the Covenant did not impact on its decision as the Court declined to follow the opinion of the Human Rights Committee established under the Covenant. One can conclude that the impact of such international conventions has certainly been very restricted thus far.

3. In those fields in which there is an overlap between the Convention and EC competence,
   – in how far do existing EC instruments meet the required standard?
   – what further initiatives is the EC required to take?

This paper is structured accordingly. However, given the brevity of this paper, these three topics can only be touched upon. Further research will be needed to fully explore the implications of the Convention for EC law.

Before commencing this analysis, a few words will be said on the interrelationship between EC and international law. This should help to put the discussion which follows in context.

1 *The Interrelationship between EC and International Law*

Under Article 310 EC the Community may conclude agreements with one or more States or international organisations 'establishing an association involving reciprocal rights and obligations, common action and special procedure'. The procedure to be followed when negotiating such agreements is set out in Article 300 EC and, in essence involves the Council giving the Commission a mandate to negotiate on behalf of the Community, with the Council taking the final decision to sign and/or ratify the agreement in question. The negotiation and signing of the CRPD by the Community reflects this procedure. The Community has the capacity to assume rights and obligations under international law, and it is expressly stated in Article 281 EC that the EC has legal personality.[4] However, the capacity of the EC to act on the international stage must be distinguished from its authority to do so. The former should be seen as 'a general potentiality to act on the international plane'[5], whilst the authority to act is derived from particular treaty provisions. In the case of the CRPD the authority to act, as will be noted later, derives from Articles 13 and 95 EC which address (disability) discrimination and the internal market respectively. While authority to act is a matter of internal EC law, the notion of capacity relates to the legal power to enter into an agreement, and is a matter international law.[6] The European Court

[4] In Case C-327/91 *France v. Commission* [1994] ECR I-3641, para. 24 the ECJ held 'it is the Community alone, having legal personality pursuant to article 21 [now Article 281 LW] of the Treaty, which has the capacity to bind itself by concluding agreements with a non-member country or an international organisation.'

[5] Maria Gavouneli, 'International Law Aspects of the European Union', (2000) 8 Tulane Journal of International and Comparative Law, 147 at 158.

[6] *Ibid.*, 158.

of Justice has elaborated on this division in its well known *ERTA* case.[7] Finally, it is worth noting that Article 302 EC requires 'the Commission to ensure the maintenance of all appropriate relations with the organs of the United Nations and of its specialised agencies.'

Many of the international agreements which the EC enters into, including the CRPD, involve concurrent jurisdictions of both the Member States and the EC. Such 'mixed agreements' have been described as unique in international relations since they 'involve[ ] a shared contractual relationship between an international organisation and its members and one or more third countries and/or international organisations', and such agreements are only used by the EC and its Member States.[8] Where the EC's competence to act is not exclusive, the Member States remain free to act collectively, individually or jointly with the Community to fulfill the obligations under an international agreement.[9] However, under Article 300(7) EC[10] international agreements which are concluded by the EC are binding on both the institutions of the EC and the Member States.[11] One can also argue that the Member States are bound to assist the EC in complying with its duties under a mixed agreement through their general duty of loyal cooperation.[12]

Attention will now be turned more specifically to the Convention, and its (potential) implications for the European Community.

---

7 Case 22/70 *Commission v. Council* [1971] ECR 263.

8 Delano Verwey, 'The European Community, the European Union and the International Law of Treaties', (2004) T.M.C. Asser Press, at 35.

9 See *Re: European Development Fund*, Case C-316/91 *European Parliament v. Council* [1994] ECR I-625.

10 See Case 194/81 *Kupferberg* [1982] ECR 3641.

11 In the case of mixed agreements, the Member States' obligations under Community law are naturally restricted to the areas which fall within the scope of Community law. Where Member States also ratify the agreement in their own right, as has already happened with regard to the CRPD in some cases, States naturally also assume responsibilities which do not fall under the scope of Community law.

12 Gavouneli, (n. 5) at 160. See also Article 10 EC and Opinion 1/94 *WTO* [1994] ECR I-5267, para. 108 in which the ECJ stated 'The obligation [on the Member States and the Community LW] to cooperate flows from the requirement of unity in international representation of the Community.' A failure to comply with this obligation by the Member States would arguably be a breach of their obligations under Community law, but not under international law. Instead, it would be the EC itself which would be in breach of its obligations under international law. See Verwey, (n. 8), 150.

2 *The UN Convention and the Obligations it Imposes*[13]

The Convention, as is appropriate for a human rights instrument, strongly reflects the social model of disability. Explicit recognition is made of the fact that 'disability results from the interaction between persons with impairments and attitudinal and environmental barriers that hinders their full and effective participation in society on an equal basis with others.'[14] The Convention therefore reflects the reality that disability stems primarily from the failure of the social environment to meet the needs and aspirations of people with impairments, and is the highest legal manifestation and confirmation of the social model of disability on the international stage.

Moreover, the scope of the Convention is extremely broad. The Convention does not simply prohibit disability discrimination, nor does it only cover civil or political rights or economic, cultural or social rights. Instead the Convention is underpinned by the principles of non-discrimination and equality, which embrace the right to a reasonable accommodation, and these are linked to a broad group of rights. These rights are both civil and political, such as the right to liberty,[15] as well as more substantive, such as the right to education.[16] It is, in fact, truly a human rights convention for the 21st century.

The principles of equality and non-discrimination run through the Convention like a red thread. They find their anchor in Article 3, which Gerard Quinn has described as providing the 'moral compass for change'[17] which the Convention embraces. This Article refers not only to non-discrimination and equality of opportunity, but a series of other principles which 'animate' the Convention, including dignity; individual autonomy; full and active participation and inclusion; respect for difference; and accessibility. The principles of non-discrimination and equality find repeated reference elsewhere in the Convention. In light of this, Article 2, which elaborates on key terms used in the Convention, contains a broad definition of 'discrimination on the basis of disability', and specifies that such discrimination includes the denial of a reasonable accommodation.

---

[13] For a more detailed discussion of the content of the Convention, including the provisions relating to equality and non-discrimination, see Anna Lawson, 'The United Nations Convention on the Rights of Persons with Disabilities: New Era or False Dawn?', (2007) 34 Syracuse Journal of International Law and Commerce, 563, at section IV (590–616).

[14] Preamble, recital (e) and Article 1.

[15] Article 14, which covers liberty and security of the person.

[16] Article 24.

[17] Quinn (n. 2), 3.

The principles of equality and non-discrimination also receive specific attention in Article 5. This Article embraces both a formal approach to equality ('equal before and under the law');[18] and a more substantive approach ('prohibit discrimination on the basis of disability';[19] provision of 'reasonable accommodation';[20] and positive action measures[21] 'shall not be considered discrimination'). States Parties are under an obligation to recognise and ensure protection of these rights. Elsewhere the Convention is 'sprinkled' liberally with references to non-discrimination, equality and reasonable accommodation. Article 6, another transversal article addressing the particular needs of women with disabilities, specifies that States Parties recognise that women and girls with disabilities are subject to multiple discrimination. Eliminating discrimination, in the sense of removing obstacles and barriers to accessibility, lies at the heart of Article 9. Article 12, on equal recognition before the law, and Article 13, on access to justice, refer to the need to recognise that people with disabilities 'enjoy legal capacity on an equal basis with others in all aspects of life', and that they have 'effective access to justice...on an equal basis with others' respectively. Explicit or implied references to reasonable accommodation can be found, amongst others, in Articles 20, on personal mobility and 21 on freedom of expression and opinion and access to information (both implicit references); and Articles 24 on education and 27 on employment (both explicit references).

Turning to the specific fields covered by the Convention, one finds a broad range of rights protected. The Convention covers classical rights, which include, in addition to those already mentioned, the right to life (Article 10); freedom from torture or cruel, inhuman or degrading treatment or punishment (Article 15); freedom from exploitation, violence and abuse (Article 16); protecting the integrity of the person (Article 17); and respect for privacy (Article 22). The Convention recognises that, in order to protect and respect some 'classical' rights, quite substantial action by States Parties is required. Whilst these 'classical' rights are certainly not irrelevant from the perspective of the European Community, they have traditionally fallen more within the scope of the Council of Europe, and under the European Convention of Human Rights, than been matters for regulation by EC law. For this reason, it is likely that the more substantive rights found in the text will be of particular importance for determining the implications of the Convention for the EC.

---

18 Article 5(1).

19 Article 5(2).

20 Article 5(3).

21 The Convention does not refer to positive action, but instead speaks of 'Specific measures which are necessary to accelerate or achieve de facto equality', Article 5(4).

Amongst the Articles addressing substantive rights that are likely to engage Community responsibility are Article 9 on accessibility and Article 27 on employment. These are both underpinned by the principles of non-discrimination and equality, and are discussed in more detail below.

Other articles address living independently and being included in the community (Article 19); personal mobility (Article 20); education (Article 24); health (Article 25); adequate standard of living and social protection (Article 28); and participation in cultural life, recreation, leisure and sport (Article 30).

Article 32 covers international cooperation, and recognises that such cooperation can be used to support national efforts to realize the purpose and objectives of the Convention. This includes ensuring that international development programmes are inclusive of and accessible to persons with disabilities.

Article 33 relates to implementation and monitoring, and requires States Parties to designate a focal point for matters relating to the implementation of the Convention, and establish a framework, including one or more independent mechanisms, to promote, protect and monitor implementation.

Finally,[22] Article 4 of the Convention sets out the general obligations of the States Parties, which include the requirement 'to adopt all appropriate legislative, administrative and other measures for the implementation of the rights recognized in the present Convention'. Gerard Quinn has concisely stated that this article 'converts the convention into a trigger for worldwide disability law reform'.[23] The same article notes that the Convention shall 'not affect any provisions which are more conducive to the realization of the rights of persons with disabilities',[24] meaning that implementation of the Convention cannot provide an excuse for reducing the existing level of protection provided.

3 *The Competences of the EC – Overlaps with the Convention*

Having provided a brief outline of the fields covered by the Convention, attention will now be turned to the question of which of those fields fall within the scope of EC law. It is appropriate to approach this analysis of the overlap of the EC competencies with the obligations contained in the Convention from three directions.

---

[22] Given that the purpose of this paper is to not to explore the implications of the Convention in full, the description of its contents has necessarily been brief and selective. Many important provisions, including those relating to the Committee on the Rights of Persons with Disabilities (Article 34), have not been touched on in this overview.

[23] Quinn (n. 2), 5.

[24] Article 4(4).

Firstly, a review of the 'opinion' of the Community institutions on this matter is helpful. As stated previously, the CRPD was the first human rights treaty to which the Community was party to negotiations and which it is expected to ratify. This results from the fact that the EC Treaty transfers competences to the Community which fall within the scope of the new Convention. Both the Commission and, more authoritatively, the Council, have adopted (legally binding) instruments in which (some of) the relevant Community competences are referred to and discussed, and where power is explicitly conferred on the Commission to negotiate and sign the Convention on the basis of specific EC Treaty Articles. As a consequence, insight into the 'Community' perspective can be gained through an examination of a variety of documents, ranging from the original communication of the Commission of 2003[25] which sets out why 'an active participation of the European Community in the development' of the Convention was 'indispensable'[26] to the Council Decision of 2007 on the signing, on behalf of the EC, of the Convention.

Secondly, in the past decade, the Community has adopted a number of legislative acts that specifically address the situation of disabled people. The most well known of these instruments is the Employment Equality Directive of 2000[27] which prohibits disability discrimination in the area of employment. However, a number of, primarily mainstream,[28] instruments, also contain specific requirements with regard to people with disabilities. An examination of these instruments, and specifically a consideration of the fields they cover and the legal bases utilized, can also help to reveal where the Community has competence to act with regard to disability.

Lastly, it is appropriate to return to the Convention to establish whether any areas not already revealed as falling within the scope of Community law through the preceding two analyses, present themselves. This may be because the Community has some competence in a specific area covered by the Convention, but has not yet exercised that competence in the context of disability.

---

[25] Commission (EC), 'Towards a United Nations legally binding instrument to promote and protect the rights and dignity of persons with disabilities' (Communication) COM (2003) 16 final, 24 January 2003.

[26] *Ibid.*, 2.

[27] Council Directive (EC) 2000/78 (n. 3). This directive is examined in more detail below.

[28] The instruments are mainstream in that they do not address exclusively the situation of persons with disabilities, but do include one or more provisions paying specific attention to the needs of this group.

3.1 *The EC Competence to Negotiate and Sign the Convention*

It is clear from the 2003 Commission Communication 'Towards a United Nations legally binding instrument to promote and protect the rights and dignity of persons with disabilities' that the Commission saw non-discrimination and equality as being the core principles to be embraced by any new Convention. The Communication recognised that, in principle, the then existing human rights treaties protected people with disabilities, but that, in practice, their rights were, far too often overlooked and ignored. The Commission, in common with the international community, saw a specific disability convention as being necessary to 'tailor the existing human rights implementation standards to the specific circumstances of people with disabilities, thereby improving access for people with disabilities to their rights.'[29] This was to be achieved through the non-discrimination and equality principles.

'A key tool in achieving equality is the *non-discrimination principle.* Equal access to the human rights can be guaranteed by ensuring that people with disabilities are not discriminated against on the grounds of their disability.'[30] (emphasis in original)

Turning to the question of Community competences to negotiate and, ultimately sign and ratify any disability convention, the only specific Treaty article referred to in the 2003 Communication is Article 13 EC, which addresses combating discrimination on a number of grounds, including disability. This may well explain the strong emphasis on non-discrimination and equality in the Communication. The Commission clearly saw Article 13 EC as giving it 'access' to the negotiating table, and that its primary area of concern should be to ensure appropriate references to non-discrimination and equality in the Convention. Moreover, its goal was to 'seek to ensure consistency between European internal and international action regarding disabled people'.[31] However, this does not mean that the Commission thought any convention should be confined to the areas of non-discrimination and equality – instead it stated that the instrument 'should refer to and identify the full spread of human rights including political and civil/fundamental rights as well as economic, social and cultural rights.'[32] As has been seen above, this is indeed what happened in practice.

---

29 Commission (EC) 'Towards a United Nations legally binding instrument to promote and protect the rights and dignity of persons with disabilities' (Communication) (n. 25), 3.

30 *Ibid.*, 10.

31 *Ibid.*, 12.

32 *Ibid.*, 11.

The Economic and Social Committee, in its Opinion on the Communication,[33] took a similar stance to the Commission, although it referred, in addition to Article 13 EC, to Articles 21 and 26 of the EU Charter of Fundamental Rights,[34] addressing respectively non-discrimination and integration of persons with disabilities. The Committee likewise requested that the Commission ensured adequate consistency between the new Convention and these provisions.

Whilst the Commission Communication set out the background to why Community involvement in the Convention was appropriate, it did not amount to a legally binding decision conferring competence on the Commission to enter negotiations on the behalf of the Community. This was done by a Council Decision,[35] which was itself based on an earlier Commission recommendation.[36] The Commission recommendation stated that 'The Community competence (to conduct negotiations on behalf of the European Community LW) is based on Article 13 of the EC Treaty…',[37] however, no specific reference to any Treaty Article seems to exist in the subsequent Council Decision.[38]

In line with its negotiating mandate, the European Commission was present throughout the negotiation and drafting of the Convention, and attended the crucial pre-sessional meetings during which the EU Presidency coordinated the common position of the EU Member States. The EU Member States therefore

33 Economic and Social Committee (EC) 'Opinion on the Communication from the Commission Towards a United Nations legally binding instrument to promote and protect the rights and dignity of persons with disabilities of 24 January 2003', COM (2003) 16 final, 26 March 2003.

34 *Ibid.*, para. 2.14.

35 Based on document 9066/1/04/ REV 1.

36 Commission (EC) 'Recommendation to the Council in order to authorise the Commission to participate in the negotiations of an international legally binding instrument to promote and protect the rights and dignity of persons with disabilities', (Recommendation) SEC (2003) 16 final.

37 Explanatory Memorandum.

38 The relevant Council Decision is not a publicly available document. However, in response to a request to the Council from the author, the Decision was partially declassified. The whole document was not declassified on the grounds that 'Disclosure of this information could weaken the future position of the European Union in the framework of similar international negotiations.' (Correspondence from Karel Jezek to author of 7 September 2007.) The information which was made available to the author was a note from the Council Working Party on Human Rights to Coreper / the Council of Ministers containing a Draft Council Decision to authorise the Commission to open and conduct negotiations on behalf of the EC on the UN Convention (but which did not include the negotiating directives). This did not make reference to any specific EC Treaty article. A further request for information on this point to the Council elicited the response: 'The requested information [relating to references to EC Treaty articles in the Council Decision] is not mentioned in the parts of document 9066/1/04 Rev 1 to which you were not granted access.' (Email from DG F – Transparency – Information to the Public Service to author of 27 September 2007).

negotiated in a multi-lateral fora as a bloc, and their work was coordinated by representatives of the State which held the Presidency of the Council of the EU[39] at the relevant time. This gave a significant amount of power to the EU Presidency. However, it can be assumed that the Commission also played a vital role at these pre-sessional meetings. As guardian of the Treaties, and in line with its mandate to ensure appropriate and EC compatible references to non-discrimination in the Convention, it may well have had the task of grounding the (confidential) discussions which led to the common negotiating stance, on current EC law, and, in particular, the Employment Equality Directive.

The latest set of documents in this series is the Commission proposal,[40] and the related Council Decision,[41] on the signing of the Convention by the Community. Interestingly the legal basis for this Decision is not only Article 13 EC, but also Article 95 EC that relates to the establishment and functioning of the internal market.[42] As will be seen in the next section of this paper, this is completely appropriate given the prior use of this Article by the Community with regard to disability, not to mention the wide scope of the Convention itself. Nevertheless, this is the first explicit reference to this Article in Community documents on the Convention, and it seems that it was only recognised, at this relatively late stage, that the Convention could engage Community obligations in areas beyond non-discrimination.

This story is not yet complete. Attached to the 2007 Council Decision was a declaration that the Council would reconsider the signing of the Optional Protocol to the Convention by the Community as soon as possible.[43] In addition, a further Council Decision will need to be taken in order to enable the Community to ratify the Convention.

---

39 Presidency of the Council of the European Union is rotated between European Union Member State every six months. There is no single president but rather the task is undertaken by an entire national government, which hence allows that state to influence the direction of *European Union* policy during the term of office.

40 Commission (EC), 'Proposal for a Council Decision on the signing, on behalf of the European Community, of the United Nations Convention on the Rights of Persons with Disabilities and its Optional Protocol', COM (2007) 77 final, 27 February 2007.

41 Council Decision (EC) on the signing, on behalf of the European Community, of the United Nations' Convention on the Rights of Persons with Disabilities, 20 March 2007, 7407/07.

42 A third legal basis was Article 300(2) EC. As was noted above, this Article addresses the procedure to be followed when the Community makes agreements with international organisations.

43 The original Commission proposal for a Council Decision specified that the Community should sign not only the Convention, but also the Optional Protocol. However, the latter proposal was not accepted by the Council, and the ultimate Decision reflected this.

3.2 *EC Competences to Adopt Legislation Specifically referring to Persons with Disabilities – Existing Instruments*

The key instruments and fields in which the EC has already exercised powers with regard to disability will now be briefly reviewed.

3.2.1 *Discrimination*

As a result of the 1997 Amsterdam Treaty, the Community acquired the power to take action to combat discrimination on a number of grounds, including disability. The new Article 13 EC[44] contained the first ever mention of disability to be found in the Treaty, and quickly revealed its potential by providing the legal basis for a 2000 directive addressing discrimination in the areas of employment and vocational training on the grounds, amongst others, of disability (henceforth Employment Equality Directive).[45] This Directive built on earlier Community initiatives in the area of disability which preceded the Amsterdam Treaty. In 1996 both the Commission and the Council had taken the first steps towards developing a broader disability policy and formally recognised and embraced the social model of disability. In July 1996 the Commission adopted a Communication on Equality of Opportunity for People with Disabilities, the subtitle of which was 'A New European Community Disability Strategy'.[46] This was the first comprehensive European Community strategy produced by the Commission and was inspired by the (non-binding) United Nations Standard Rules on the Equalization of Opportunities for Persons with Disabilities.[47] The Communication noted that the way in which society is organised serves to exclude disabled citizens,[48] and spoke of the evolution towards 'an equal opportunities model in the field of disability policy' within the Member States of the EU.[49] The Communication stated:

> The core value of equality – rendered here as equal opportunities – is now seen as the central benchmark against which economic and social structures must be assessed. It forms the essence of the rights-based approach to disability. The equal opportunities ideal is of course broader than that, but nevertheless subsumes the principle of non-discrimination.[50]

---

[44] The amendments brought about by the Amsterdam Treaty came into force in 1999, following ratification by all Member States.

[45] Council Directive (EC) 2000/78 (n. 3).

[46] Commission (EC), 'Communication on Equality of Opportunity for People with Disabilities' (Communication) COM (96) 406 final, 30 July 1996.

[47] United Nations General Assembly Resolution 48/46 (20 December 1993).

[48] Commission (EC), 'Communication on Equality of Opportunity for People with Disabilities' (n. 46), par. 2.

[49] *Ibid.*, par. 20.

[50] *Ibid.*, par. 18.

In December of the same year, the Council also approved a Resolution on Equality of Opportunity for People with Disabilities.[51] In this document, the Council too reaffirmed its commitment to the principles and values of the United Nations Standard Rules and the principles of equality of opportunity and eliminating negative discrimination on the sole grounds of disability.

The Community institutions have continued to regularly refer to the philosophical underpinning of disability policy and stress the commitment to the social model of disability. In 2003, for example, the European Commission reiterated its commitment to the model by stating:

> The EU's long-standing commitment towards its disabled citizens goes hand in hand with a new approach to disability: from seeing people with disabilities as the passive recipients of compensation, society has come to recognise their legitimate demands for equal rights and to realise that participation relates directly to insertion.[52]

This philosophy is reflected in the 2003 Communication on the UN Convention that stressed that the development of such a Convention was fully in line with EC disability policy.

3.2.2 *The Internal Market*

Article 95 EC provides the Community with the competence to adopt harmonizing measures which have as their object the establishment and functioning of the internal market. Given that the internal market is an extremely broad notion that encompasses the removal of all kinds of barriers to trade, it is not surprising to find that Article 95 EC has provided the legal basis for instruments addressing many different areas. In some cases these instruments have recognised a specific disability dimension. For example, Directive 2001/85[53] on vehicles carrying more than eight passengers requires the mandatory fitting of certain accessibility features for persons with reduced mobility and visually impaired persons; Directive 95/16/EC[54] on lifts refers to the need to ensure accessibility for disabled persons;

---

[51] Resolution of the Council and of the Representatives of the Governments of the Member States meeting within the Council of 20 December 1996 on equality of opportunity for people with disabilities, [1997] OJ C12/1.

[52] EU Disability Action Plan: Commission (EC), 'Equal opportunities for people with disabilities: a European Action Plan' (Communication) COM (2003) 650 final, 4, 30 October 2003.

[53] Council Directive (EC) 2001/85 relating to special provisions for vehicles used for the carriage of passengers comprising more than eight seats in addition to the driver's seat, and amending Directives 1970/156/EEC and 1997/27/EC [2002] OJ L43/1.

[54] Council Directive (EC) 1995/16 on the approximation of the laws of the Member States relating to lifts [1995] OJ L213/1 as amended.

Directives 2004/17[55] and 2004/18[56] on public procurement allow accessibility for disabled people and design for all requirements to be taken into account during the different stages of public procurement; Directive 1999/5[57] on radio and telecommunication terminal equipment provides that the Commission may decide that apparatus shall support features to facilitate their use by disabled persons; Directive 2002/21[58] on electronic communications networks and services requires national regulatory authorities to address the needs of disabled users in a variety of ways; and Directive 2002/22[59] on universal services and users' rights relating to electronic communication networks and services requires Member States to ensure that covered services are affordable for disabled users and that they have the same conditions of access as others. All of these instruments have, as their legal basis, Article 95 EC,[60] and therefore recognise the disability dimension to securing the internal market. They also amount to EC legislation containing a disability dimension in the fields of transport; building infrastructure; public procurement; digital television; and telecommunications – with the exception of public procurement, all of these fields are clearly covered by the Convention.

In order to understand how such references to disability can be included within legal instruments based on Article 95 EC, it is worth studying the (non-binding) preambles to some of the measures. For example, the preamble to Directive 2001/85, on vehicles used for the carriage of more than eight passengers, specifies that technical requirements relating to vehicles can differ from one Member State to another, and that such differences prevent vehicles being sold in the Community market. For that reason the Directive sets out harmonized requirements to facilitate the proper functioning of the internal market. Whilst the principal aim of the Directive is to guarantee the safety of passengers, the Directive recognises that it is also necessary to provide technical prescriptions to allow accessibility for persons of reduced mobility in accordance with Community transport and social policies. The aim of this Directive was therefore to create harmonized design standards to ensure a single market for such vehicles, and, at the same time, to ensure that these standards contributed to the safe

---

55 Council Directive (EC) 2004/17 coordinating the procurement procedures of entities operating in the water, energy, transport and postal services sectors [2004] OJ L134/1.

56 Council Directive (EC) 2004/18 on the coordination of procedures for the award of public works contracts, public supply contracts and public service contracts [2004] OJ L134/114.

57 Council Directive (EC) 1999/5 on radio and telecommunications terminal equipment and the mutual recognition of their conformity [1999] OJ L91/10.

58 Council Directive (EC) 2002/21 on a common regulatory framework for electronic communications networks and services (Framework Directive) [2002] OJ L108/35.

59 Council Directive (EC) 2002/22 on universal service and users' rights relating to electronic communications networks and services (Universal Service Directive) [2002] OJ L108/5.

60 In the case of Directive 2004/17 and 2004/18 on public procurement, Articles 47(2) and 55 EC are also legal bases in addition to Article 95 EC.

transport of passengers. With regard to the latter, the legislators recognised that certain travellers with a disability required specific safety measures, and included appropriate and additional standards within the Directive.

Similar arguments have been used, and can be used, to justify harmonization standards in other areas. These standards can specifically take account of the needs of disabled consumers when this is appropriate.[61]

3.2.3 *Transport*

The Community has been relatively successful in mainstreaming disability into its general legislation in the area of transport. Reference has already been made to Directive 2001/85 concerning vehicles used for the carriage of more than eight passengers which was based on Article 95 EC. However, Title V of the Treaty, which is devoted to Transport, is also relevant. Article 70 EC in Title V refers to a common transport policy and Article 71 EC confers legislative powers on the Community with the purpose of implementing Article 70 EC. This power is broad, and as well as allowing the Community to adopt common rules applicable to international and intra-Community transport and measures to improve transport safety, includes the adoption of 'other appropriate provisions'.[62] Article 80 EC specifies that the Title applies to rail, road and inland waterway transport,[63] and allows the Council to extend the measures to sea and air transport.[64]

A number of instruments addressing the needs of disabled travellers have found their legal basis in this Title. Significantly, Article 80(2) EC covering sea and air transport has been relied on, on three occasions. Undoubtedly the most important instrument in this context is Regulation 1107/2006.[65] This is a disability specific measure designed to protect the rights of disabled persons and

---

[61] Gerard Quinn has argued that a link between Article 13 EC and Article 95 EC can be established and that this might be compared to the link between section 5 of the 14th amendment and the Inter-State commerce clause in the US. A combination of these two provisions drove the US disability non-discrimination law, the Americans with Disabilities Act. Quinn has argued that the (disability) non-discrimination agenda in the EU is now also being linked more closely to the goals of the internal market. Ultimately, this approach may have implications for the European social model. See report on the European Day of Persons with Disabilities, 2007, People with disabilities: Active players in the internal market, Brussels 5 and 6 December 2007, 3.2, 13–14 (summary of presentation made by Gerard Quinn), available at <http://ec.europa.eu/employment_social/events/2007/eddp/eddp_2007_conference_eport_en.pdf.> accessed 17 May 2008.

[62] Article 71(1) (a), (c), and (d) EC respectively.

[63] Article 80(1) EC.

[64] Article 80(2) EC.

[65] Regulation (EC) 1107/2006 concerning the rights of disabled persons and persons with reduced mobility when travelling by air [2006] OJ L 204/1.

persons with reduced mobility when traveling by air. The Regulation specifies that disabled individuals cannot be denied boarding, or booking; they are entitled to receive assistance at the airport and when boarding and cannot be charged an additional fee for this; and establishes standards for providing assistance.

Two other mainstream instruments based on Article 80(2) EC pay specific attention to the needs of disabled travelers. Regulation 261/2004[66] which establishes rights to compensation and assistance for air passengers when they are denied board, face long delays, or their flights are cancelled, requires that air carriers pay particular attention to the needs of people with reduced mobility and those people accompanying them. Carriers are to give priority to carrying such persons and must provide 'care' to these passengers in the event of delay or cancellation as soon as possible. Meanwhile Directive 2003/24[67] requires Member States to take appropriate measures to enable persons with reduced mobility to have safe access to passenger ships and high speed passenger crafts.

Finally Article 156 EC, which relates to trans-European networks in the areas of transport, telecommunications and energy infrastructure, has provided the legal basis for two Directives on the inter-operability of rail systems and these both require that the infrastructure of covered railway stations and train carriages must be accessible for disabled passengers.[68]

As a result of this combination of disability specific and mainstream instruments which recognise the specific needs of disabled consumers, there can be little doubt that the Community has the competence to address transport related matters with regard to disability. It is also interesting to note the variety of legal bases which the Community has utilized in this respect.

3.2.4 *Employment*

As of the Amsterdam Treaty the Community and its Member States have sought to develop a 'coordinated' strategy for employment through the European Employment Strategy (EES). The Open Method of Coordination is now used in this context. This involves the adoption of employment guidelines by the Council, which then form the basis for National Reform Programmes[69] (NRPs)

---

[66] Regulation (EC) 261/2004 establishing common rules on compensation and assistance to passengers in the event of denied boarding and of cancellation or long delay of flights [2004] OJ L46/1.

[67] Council Directive (EC) 2003/24 amending Council Directive (EC) 98/18 on safety rules and standards for passenger ships [2003] OJ L123/18.

[68] Council Directive (EC) 96/48 on the interoperability of the trans-European high-speed rail system [1996] OJ L235/6 and Council Directive (EC) 2001/16 on the interoperability of the trans-European conventional rail system [2001] OJ L110/1 as modified by Council Directive (EC) 2004/49 (Railway Specific Directive) [2004] OJ L164/44.

[69] Previously known as National Action Plans.

produced by each Member State. The NRPs set out how each Member State intends to implement the guidelines and are commented on and the subject of a joint annual report by the Council and Commission. New guidelines and NRPs are adopted each year, although, since 2005, the practice has been to only fully review the guidelines once every three years and, in the meantime, to renew the previous year's guidelines.[70] This process now contributes to achieving the goals of the Lisbon Strategy, which in essence aims at promoting the competitiveness of the EU on the global stage, and stimulating employment, modernizing social protection and promoting social inclusion. The guidelines do make reference to the situation of disabled people. For example the 2005 Council Decision on the guidelines states: 'Particular attention must also be paid to significantly reducing employment gaps for people at a disadvantage, including disabled people…'.[71] In addition, the Commission has issued a report on Disability Mainstreaming in the European Employment Strategy,[72] although this concluded 'mainstreaming is still rarely applied' by Member States.[73]

3.2.5 *EC Funding*

The EC provides a vast amount of funding for a variety of projects within the Member States. This ranges from funding for infrastructure projects, employment and training, and cultural activities to farming and agricultural subsidies. Much of this funding is provided through the Structural Funds, which consume 35% of the EU budget, amounting to some 43 billion euros annually. The latest Regulation[74] on the use of the Funds[75] requires the Member States and Commission to take appropriate steps to prevent discrimination on the grounds of disability with regard to access to the Funds and specifies that accessibility for disabled persons shall be one of the criteria to be considered as relevant in deciding on the allocation of funds.

In addition, the EU and its Member States are the largest providers of international development aid in the world. As of the Amsterdam Treaty, a specific title is devoted to development cooperation in the EC Treaty.[76] A variety of

[70] See Council Decision (EC) 10237/07 on guidelines for the employment policies of the Member States SOC 239, ECOFIN 243, 19 June 2007, which maintained the existing guidelines.

[71] Council Decision (EC) 2005/600 of 12 July 2005 on Guidelines for the employment policies of the Member States [2005] OJ L205/21.

[72] Commission (EC), 'Disability mainstreaming in the European Employment Strategy', EMCO/11/290605, 1 July 2005.

[73] *Ibid.*, 15.

[74] Council Regulation (EC) 1083/2006 laying down general provisions on the European Regional Development Fund, the European Social Fund and the Cohesion Funds and repealing Regulation (EC) 1260/1999 [2006] OJ L210/25 as amended.

[75] Based on Article 161 EC.

[76] Title XX including Articles 170–181 EC.

legal instruments provide the basis for development aid programmes, including multilateral or bilateral international agreements or conventions and unilateral arrangements based on specific Treaty articles.[77] This research could find no evidence of any of these myriad legal instruments specifically targeting development aid at persons with disabilities or their organisations.[78] However, the Commission has issued a Guidance Note on Disability and Development which provides advice to EU delegations and services on how to address disability issues effectively within development cooperation,[79] although no data exists detailing how this Note has been used in practice.

3.3 *Further Possible EC Competences Falling within the scope of the Convention*

This analysis has already revealed that the EC has a variety of relevant competences in the disability field, going beyond combating discrimination, that might be potentially engaged as the result of the ratification of the Convention.

In addition the Community arguably has competences in a number of other areas which fall within the scope of the Convention, although it has thus far not exercised these in the field of disability. It is beyond the scope of this article to consider all the areas of potential Community competence which are also covered by the Convention, although a number of fields deserve specific mention.

The Community has not only taken legislative action to combat disability discrimination in the past, but has also addressed discrimination on the grounds of gender, and race and ethnic origin, amongst others. It is notable that the material scope of directives addressing these three forms of discrimination, is much wider than that covered by the Employment Equality Directive. Directive 2004/113[80] prohibits gender discrimination with regard to access to goods and

---

77 Article 133 EC, which governs the common commercial policy, provides the basis for the Generalised System of Preferences which allows access to the Community market of products from developing countries, and Article 308 EC has been used to allow the Community to develop financial and technical aid for Asian and Latin American countries.

78 Members of staff at the relevant Directorate General within the Commission were also unable to refer to any specific reference to disability in the various legal documents governing the distribution of EU development aid. However, some EU aid is directed towards education in developing countries and this may sometimes include provisions relating to the education of disabled children, and EU aid may support NGOs working in the field of disability. Further information was not available since the Commission does not currently monitoring how much, and whether, aid is distributed to disability related projects in developing countries.

79 Commission (EC), 'Guidance Note on Disability and Development, European Commission', July 2004,<http://ec.europa.eu/development/icenter/repository/Disability_en.pdf> accessed 17 May 2008.

80 Council Directive (EC) 2004/113 implementing the principle of equal treatment between men and women in the access to and supply of goods and services [2004] OJ L373/37.

services,[81] whilst Directive 2000/43,[82] which addresses equal treatment between persons irrespective of racial or ethnic origin, goes further and covers not only employment and access to goods and services, but also social protection, including social security and healthcare; social advantages; and education. Whilst the limits of the Community's competences in areas such as healthcare and education have certainly not been established yet, Directive 2000/43 does demonstrate that some Community competences exist in these areas, and that these clearly extend to taking action to prohibiting discrimination. One can conclude that the Community competence to combat disability discrimination also certainly extends beyond the limited employment related field covered by the current Employment Equality Directive, and the Community may have competencies related to access for persons with disabilities to goods and services, healthcare and education which go beyond combating discrimination.

In addition the UN Convention may well engage the responsibilities of the Community in a number of activities that it undertakes. Access to information, which falls under Article 21 of the Convention, is potentially relevant given the huge amount of documentation that is generated by the Community institutions and the already existing commitment to openness and transparency. The Community complies statistics on a regular basis, meaning that Article 31, addressing statistics and data collection, must also be considered. The Community will also be obliged to monitor its own activities in implementing the Convention under Article 33.

4 *Implications of the Convention for EC Law*

In considering the implication of the Convention for the EC it is important to distinguish between obligations relating primarily to non-discrimination and equality, and other obligations. As has been seen, the Commission entered into and pursued negotiations at the UN on the basis of a Council Decision which found its legal basis in Article 13 EC. The assumption throughout the negotiations seems to have been that the relevant competence resulted from the Community's powers in the area of discrimination. Furthermore, combating discrimination is the only area where the current Treaty confers explicit powers on the Community in the context of disability, and it is therefore in this area where it has the most solid claim to act. Nevertheless, many areas of the Convention extend beyond non-discrimination and this has, to some degree, been

[81] Other Community Directives prohibit gender discrimination in the areas of employment and social security.

[82] Council Directive (EC) 2000/43 (n. 3).

reflected in the dual legal basis of Articles 13 and 95 EC of the Council Decision on the signing of the Convention by the Community. It is therefore also important to consider what implications the CRPD has for the Community in areas extending beyond combating disability discrimination. Lastly, brief attention will be paid to the procedural obligations that the EC will be under with regard to monitoring its own implementation of the Convention, and involving civil society in this process.

In addition, in non-discrimination and other fields, it is important to consider both whether existing EC instruments meet the standards set by the Convention, and whether the Convention requires the adoption of additional legal instruments.

Lastly, should EC law set higher standards than those established in the Convention then, by virtue of Article 4(4) of the Convention, those standards should not reduced.

4.1 *Non-Discrimination and Equality*

4.1.1 *The Convention*

It has already been noted that discrimination and equality are prominent themes in the Convention. Since this is also an area where the Community clearly has competence to act, and indeed, has already done so with regard to employment, it is worth reflecting in more detail on the obligations imposed on States Parties by the Convention in this respect.

Article 2 of the Convention, which elaborates on key terms used in the text, defines 'discrimination on the basis of disability' very broadly to mean:

> ...any distinction, exclusion or restriction on the basis of disability which has the purpose or effect of impairing or nullifying the recognition, enjoyment or exercise, on an equal basis with others, of all human rights and fundamental freedoms in political, economic, social, cultural, civil or any other field.[83]

[83] It is worth noting that the EC approach to defining discrimination as including both direct and indirect discrimination was explicitly rejected during the negotiation of the Convention. Ireland, which held the EU Presidency at the relevant time, argued in favour of the Convention defining discrimination as including both direct and indirect discrimination, but this was rejected. See: <http://www.un.org/esa/socdev/enable/rights/ahcwgreporta7.htm> which contains the original draft of the Convention article dealing with discrimination, which did contain a reference to direct and indirect discrimination, and summarizes the discussions which took place within the relevant Working Group, and <http://www.un.org/esa/socdev/enable/rights/wgsuma7.htm> which contains a more elaborate overview of the arguments made by specific parties during the discussions within the relevant Working Group (both accessed on 17 May 2008).

Importantly, such discrimination includes the denial of a reasonable accommodation,[84] which is itself defined as meaning:

> ...necessary and appropriate modification and adjustments not imposing a disproportionate or undue burden, where needed in a particular case, to ensure to persons with disabilities the enjoyment or exercise on an equal basis with others of all human rights and fundamental freedoms.

Under Article 4, which establishes general obligations, States Parties are to, inter alia, 'take all appropriate measures to eliminate discrimination on the basis of disability by any person, organization or private enterprise'[85] and under Article 5 they are to promote equality and eliminate discrimination and 'take all appropriate steps to ensure that reasonable accommodation is provided.'[86]

Article 9, which addresses accessibility, does not specifically refer to discrimination, but does require States Parties

> ...take appropriate measures to ensure to persons with disabilities access, on an equal basis with others, to the physical environment, to transportation, to information and communications, including information and communications technologies and systems, and to other facilities and services open or provided to the public....

These measures include the 'identification and elimination of obstacles and barriers to accessibility' in a wide range of areas, and could certainly be interpreted as requiring, inter alia, measures to combat discrimination.[87]

---

[84] The question of whether to define explicitly a failure to make a reasonable accommodation as a form of discrimination or not received a lot of attention in the Working Group established to consider the provision addressing non-discrimination and equality (originally Article 7). The Working Group established a sub-group to examine the concept of reasonable accommodation and, specifically, its link to discrimination. During the deliberations of the sub-group, the EU Presidency, no doubt taking its lead from Article 5 of the Employment Equality Directive, argued that the concepts should be regarded as separate. Specifically, it was argued that a failure to provide a reasonable accommodation should not automatically trigger a finding of discrimination. In this context, the Report of the Chair of the Working Group dealing with discrimination notes that:

> [some] members of the Working Group considered that the Convention should not dictate the manner by which the concept of 'reasonable accommodation' should be achieved or framed under relevant domestic legislation. Specifically, they took the view that it was inappropriate for an international legal instrument designed primarily to engage State responsibility to frame a failure to 'reasonably accommodate' on the part of private entities as a violation of the non-discrimination principle. See: <http://www.un.org/esa/socdev/enable/rights/ahcwgreporta7.htm> accessed 17 May 2008.

[85] Article 4(1)(e).

[86] Article 5(3).

[87] For criticism of the Convention and, in particular Article 9 thereof, see Tracy R. Justesen and Troy R. Justesen, 'Perspectives on the UN Convention on the Rights of Persons with Disabilities:

Employment is addressed in Article 27 which requires States Parties meet the set obligations by 'taking appropriate steps, including through legislation', to, amongst others, prohibit disability discrimination in all employment related areas; protect the employment rights of persons with disabilities, such as the right to equal pay and protection from harassment, on an equal basis with others; ensure effective access to vocational training and related activities; and ensure reasonable accommodation is provided. States Parties are also to 'safeguard and promote the realization of the right to work' and this is to occur 'on an equal basis with others'.

Finally, whilst the Convention does not contain a definition of disability,[88] it is clearly founded upon the social model of disability as already noted, and underpins this by giving an indication of group of individuals who are protected:

> Persons with disabilities include those who have long-term physical, mental, intellectual or sensory impairments which in interaction with various barriers may hinder their full and effective participation in society on an equal basis with others.[89]

An Analysis of the Development and Adoption of the United Nations Convention Recognizing the Rights of Individuals with Disabilities: Why the United States Refuses to Sign this UN Convention', (2007) 14 Human Rights Brief, 36. Justesen and Justesen state: '…Article 9 suggests that member-states must independently create architectural design and construction standards for facilities to meet the accessibility requirements of the Convention. The article provides no additional support or technical assistance specifying which building elements and features must be accessible, or how and by when member-states should meet such standards. Likewise, there is no reasonable means for measuring a member-state's progress or lack thereof in this regard.' (footnotes omitted).

Justesen and Justesen also argue that US law provides stronger protection for disabled individuals, including technical accessibility standards.

[88] The question of whether to include a definition of disability in the Convention or not was controversial, and the penultimate (Seventh) Ad Hoc Committee meeting on the Convention was devoted almost exclusively to this issue. Ultimately it was decided not to include a definition, since any definition would necessarily exclude some people. The inclusion of a definition of disability was seen also as potentially undermining the Convention's commitment to the social model of disability. As a compromise, however guidance was included on who was to be regarded as a person with a disability under the Convention. For further discussion and elaboration of the background to this decision see Arlene S. Kanter, 'The Promise and Challenge of the United Nations Convention on the Rights of Persons with Disabilities', (2007) 34 Syracuse Journal of International Law and Commerce 287, at 292 and Anna Lawson, 'The United Nations Convention on the Rights of Persons with Disabilities: New Era or False Dawn?', (n. 13) at 593–595.

[89] Article 1 on Purpose.

4.1.2 *Existing Instruments*

It is important to bear in mind that the Commission, in negotiating the Convention, had the specific task of ensuring that any UN text was compatible with existing EC disability law and policy. Since the Employment Equality Directive of 2000, which prohibits disability discrimination in the area of employment and vocational training, is the 'flag ship' of European disability policy, it is natural that the Community's primary concern was to ensure that the CRPD was in line with this instrument. The Directive prohibits both direct and indirect discrimination, and harassment, and requires that reasonable accommodations be made for disabled individuals. Measuring the Directive against the standards set out in Article 27 of the Convention, one can conclude that EC law certainly appears to meet the set requirements. The Directive prohibits discrimination 'with regard to all matters concerning all forms of employment', it covers areas such as vocational training, career advancement, self-employment, the public and private sectors, and it includes an obligation to make reasonable accommodations.[90]

However, whilst the Directive is clearly based on the social model of disability, no definition of disability or disabled person, or even guidance on what is meant by these terms, is included within it. This has, however, been the subject of a 2006 decision of the European Court of Justice (*Chacón Navas*),[91] in which the Court was called upon to decide if an employee, who had been absent from work for some time as a result of illness, was to be regarded as a person with a disability for the purposes of the Directive. The Court responded by developing a 'uniform and autonomous' approach to disability in the context of the Directive and defined disability in that light as 'a limitation which results in particular from physical, mental or psychological impairments and which hinders the participation of the person concerned in professional life'.[92] According to this approach the cause of the disadvantage (or the 'limitation') is the 'impairment' which an individual has, and it is the 'impairment' which hinders participation in professional life. Therefore, the problem lies in the individual, and not in the reaction of society to the impairment or the organisation of society.[93]

---

[90] These requirements are set out in Article 27(1)(a), (d), (e), (f), (g), (h) and (i) of the Convention.

[91] Case C-13/05, *Chacón Navas v. Eurest Colectividades SA* [2006] ECR I-6467.

[92] *Ibid.*, para. 43.

[93] For criticism of the *Chacón Navas* judgment, including the argument that it is not in line with the new UN Convention see Lisa Waddington, 'Case C-13/05, *Chacón Navas v. Eurest Colectividades SA*, judgment of the Grand Chamber of 11 July 2006', (2007) 44 Common Market Law Review 487–499.

Unlike the Commission, Council and European Parliament, which have been showing increasing sensitivity to the social model of disability, the Court embraced a medical or individual model of disability[94] in its judgment by locating the cause of the 'limitation' clearly within the individual and the impairment. Furthermore, it is interesting to note that this judgment seems to have affected the Commission's negotiating stance on the Convention. Prior to the Court's judgment, the European Commission had argued that no definition of the term disability was required within the Convention, and referred to the Employment Equality Directive, to demonstrate that a human rights based instrument could cover disability and disabled people, without including any such guidance or elaboration. However, following the *Chacón Navas* judgment, the Commission, at the last negotiating session in New York in August 2006, withdrew its opposition to the inclusion of guidance on the meaning of the concept of disability and disabled persons in the Convention.[95]

Therefore, whilst the Employment Equality Directive seems to comply with the requirements of the new Convention, the 'definition' of disability developed by the European Court of Justice in the context of the Directive seems outdated and to require a revisit in light of the Convention. Further preliminary references to the Court from national courts seeking guidance on the concept of 'disability' will give it this opportunity. However, the Commission seems not to share the opinion that the Court was out of line with the Convention. In its Explanatory Memorandum accompanying its 2007 proposal for a Council Decision on the signing of the Convention, it stated:

> The Commission ensured that the provisions of the Convention are in line with relevant EU legislation and jurisprudence, for example the definitions of discrimination as well as the non discrimination in employment.... Disability is defined against a set of criteria which both reflect the social model of disability and the recent ECJ jurisprudence on the definition of disability (case C-13/05).

Given that the *Chacón Navas* judgment seems to be incompatible with the social model of disability, it is difficult to agree with the last statement.

4.1.3 *New Instruments*

Having argued that the Employment Equality Directive, with the exception of the definition of disability developed by the European Court of Justice, is in

94 There is a wealth of literature addressing theoretical models of disability. See, e.g. M. Oliver, *Understanding Disability: from theory to practice* (Macmillan Press Ltd., 1996), and M. Priestley, 'Constructions and creations: idealism, materialism and disability theory' (1998) 13 Disability and Society 1, 75–94.

95 Information received from participants to the Ad Hoc Committee which negotiated the Convention.

line with the Convention, it is necessary to consider whether ratification of the Convention will require the Community to take further action, in areas beyond employment, to combat disability discrimination. This paper has already revealed that the Community certainly has the competence to address discrimination in many non-employment related areas, such as access to goods and services, healthcare, education and social security.

Furthermore, it has been established that Article 9 of the Convention, requires that people with disabilities enjoy, on an equal basis with others, access to the physical environment, to transportation, to information and communications, including information and communications technologies and systems, and to other facilities and services open or provided to the public. Article 24, meanwhile, refers to the right, without discrimination, of persons with disabilities to education, Article 25 refers to a right to enjoy the highest standard of health without discrimination, whilst Article 28 establishes the right to enjoy social protection without discrimination.

Given the already demonstrated wide potential for the adoption of Community measures to combat discrimination provided by Article 13 EC, it seems clear that ratification of the Convention will impose an obligation on the Community to adopt broad disability non-discrimination legislation covering, at a minimum, the fields already addressed in Race and Gender legislation, including access to goods and services, social security, education and healthcare. The Commission has, until recently, resisted calls for the proposal and adoption of such legislation, arguing time was needed for the bedding in of the complicated requirements of the Employment Equality Directive, and further research was required in order the establish whether there was a need for additional Article 13 EC instruments.[96] In 2007 the Commission organised a public consultation on the future of Community non-discrimination legislation and in its Work Programme for 2008[97] the Commission finally announced that it would propose an Article 13 EC Directive to implement the principle of equal treatment outside employment.[98] In the spring of 2008 the Commission announced that the directive which it

[96] That research resulted in the publication of the Mapping study on existing national legislative measures and their impact in tackling discrimination – outside the field of employment and occupation – on the grounds of sex, religion or belief, disability, age and sexual orientation <http://ec.europa.eu/employment_social/fundamental_rights/public/pubst_en.htm#stud> accessed 16 November 2007.

[97] Commission (EC) 'Communication from the Commission to the Council, the European Parliament, the European Economic and Social Committee and the Committee of the Regions, Commission Legislative and Work Programme 2008', (Communication) COM (2007) 640 final, 23 October 2007.

[98] *Ibid.*, 25.

intended to propose would only address disability discrimination.[99] This met with strident opposition from many members of the European Parliament, who called for a 'horizontal' directive addressing a variety of grounds. At the time of writing, it was not clear how the Commission will respond to these calls, what the material scope of the new instrument will be and, in particular, whether it would cover all the fields which currently fall under the Racial Equality Directive. It is submitted that the consequences of EC ratification of the UN Convention should influence the Commission's decision as to what fields should be covered under the new proposal in the context of disability.

4.2 *Other Fields – The Internal Market, Transport and Beyond*

4.2.1 *The Convention*

The Convention contains a wealth of Articles reflecting substantive rights, and it is not possible to consider all of them here. However, given the established Community competences with regard to the internal market and transportation, Article 9, dealing with accessibility to the physical environment, transportation, information and communications and other facilities and services open to the public, is significant.

Article 9(1) requires States Parties to identify and eliminate obstacles and barriers to accessibility with regard to, inter alia, buildings, roads, transportation and other indoor and outdoor facilities, and information, communication and other services. Moreover, Article 9(2)(a) requires States Parties to develop, promulgate and monitor the implementation of minimum standards and guidelines for the accessibility of facilities and services open or provided to the public.

4.2.2 *Existing Instruments*

It seems to have become established Community policy to consider the needs of disabled travelers whenever adopting legislative measures in the area of transportation. Whilst this is an extremely positive trend, it is questionable if even this will be sufficient in light of the Convention which establishes clear accessibility requirements relating to transport in Article 9. Given the Community competence to legislate on the common transport policy, which covers international and intra-Community transport, it is submitted that ratification of the Convention will require a review of the existing instruments to identify still existing barriers and obstacles to travel experienced by disabled people, and, where these exist, further (disability specific) Community instruments to address these impediments. These instruments could, in time, result in a set of EU wide accessibility standards covering all areas of transport which fall within the scope

---

[99] See: <http://www.europeanvoice.com/Article/60504.aspx> accessed 17 May 2008.

of Community law. Moreover, the potential for such standards to become a model at the global level should not be under estimated.

Secondly, whilst the Employment Equality Directive might meet the Convention's standards in terms of addressing employment discrimination, Article 27 of the Convention might also require further attention be paid to stimulating the employment and training of people with disabilities in the European employment guidelines and related NRPs. People with disabilities in Europe, as elsewhere in the world, are proportionately more likely to be unemployed than their non-disabled compatriots, and the EES creates the infrastructure and monitoring system for further attention to be paid to addressing this problem.

Thirdly, it has already been noted that the Regulations on the Structural Funds now allow some room for the consideration of measures to prevent disability discrimination and ensure disability accessibility. In light of the many kind of activities supported by European funding, and the requirements imposed on States Parties by the Convention in areas such as cultural life, recreation, leisure and sport,[100] as well as those already considered with regard to accessibility and employment, it seems likely that a detailed review of Community funding will be required in order to ensure that EC funding is being used to support the achievement of the standards set out in the Convention to the full within the Member States. The obligations which the Convention brings with it should prevent the huge amount of Community funding being used to create new barriers for persons with disabilities, and may also ensure that funding is used to remove existing barriers. It is likely that the Convention will imply a need for a similar reflection on, and a review of, the Community's vast development aid programme, with the possible incorporation of suitable provisions within the many international agreements and legal instruments behind unilateral initiatives in the future. This seems all the more necessary given the current lack of (publicly available) information on how EU development aid is being used in relation to disability.

4.2.3 *New Instruments*

It has already been noted that Article 95 EC empowers the Community to adopt instruments contributing to the creation of the internal market, and that a number of these instruments have made specific mention of the need to ensure access of disabled consumers. There seems a clear link, in terms of the standardization requirement, between the establishment of harmonized standards to serve the internal market, and the requirements of Article 9(2)(a) of the Convention, which relates to minimum standards to ensure accessibility of facilities and services provided to the public for persons with disabilities. It is doubtful whether Article

[100] Article 30.

95 EC, with its internal market aim, can provide the legal basis for instruments which have the sole aim of ensuring disability accessibility, and which have only a tenuous link to the internal market. However, where the requirements of the internal market necessitate the development of harmonized standards, as was the case with Directive 2001/85 on the construction of vehicles carrying more than eight passengers, it seems that the Convention will require that disability accessibility standards are incorporated within any Community rules. Therefore, whilst the Convention may not require the Community to adopt accessibility standards with regard to all aspects of the physical environment, information and communication, and access to facilities and services open to the public, it does oblige the Community to establish such accessibility standards where the demands of the internal market require that the Community intervenes in one of these areas.

4.3 *Monitoring the implementation of the Convention and the Involvement of Civil Society*

By virtue of Article 33 of the Convention, States Parties are obliged to designate one or more independent mechanisms to 'promote, protect and monitor implementation' of the Convention. The question arises as to which body within the EU should take on this role. The most obvious choice in this respect would be the newly established Fundamental Rights Agency.[101] The Agency has a strong commitment to combating discrimination although, in line with its earlier incarnation as the European Monitoring Centre on Racism and Xenophobia, much of this work has thus far concentrated on discrimination on the grounds of ethnic and racial origin, including roma origin, and islamophobia and anti-semitism.

The Convention also requires that civil society, 'in particular persons with disabilities and their representative organisations, shall be involved and participate fully in the monitoring process'.[102] A similar requirement is reflected in Article 4(3) of the Convention, which requires States Parties to 'closely consult with and actively involve persons with disabilities... through their representative organsations' when implementing the Convention. These requirements embed the principle of 'nothing about us without us' within the Convention, and were reflected in the opportunities which disabled peoples' organisations had to influence the negotiating process in New York. The EC has already demonstrated a considerable willingness to consult disabiled peoples' organisations, such as the European Disability Forum, and the impairment and sector specific organisa-

[101] See <http://fra.europa.eu/fra/index.php> accessed 17 May 2008.

[102] Article 33(3).

tions which are active on the European stage. However, the obligation to allow such organisations to be 'activively involve[d]' in implementing the Convention and 'involved and participate fully' in the monitoring thereof seems to imply an even greater level of cooperation than has thusfar been the case.

5 *Conclusion*

The negotiating, signing and likely ratification of the UN Convention on the Rights of Persons with Disabilities takes the European Community into new territory. It is clear that the Convention will impose new obligations on the Community, as it will do for all States Parties, however the exact scope and limit of those new obligations is still uncertain. Most immediately, it seems that the Community will be under an obligation to significantly extend its action to combat disability discrimination, and to make much wider use of the potential offered by Article 13 EC than it has done thus far. A revision of the personal scope of the Employment Equality Directive, in terms of making explicit use of the social model of disability in defining who is entitled to claim protection from discrimination would also seem to be a priority.

One is engaging in greater speculation in discussing further consequences of the Convention for the Community. It has been argued here that the Convention, and particularly Article 9 on accessibility, will require the Community to incorporate disability accessibility standards into harmonizing instruments based on Article 95 EC. For this reason it seems that both Articles 13 and 95 EC should provide the legal basis for the Council Decision to ratify the Convention.[103]

However, even if that Decision only refers to Articles 13 and 95 EC, it is likely that the Community will be obliged to act in other fields as well. Transport has been highlighted as one such area where further initiatives will probably be required, given the already demonstrated Community competences with regard to accessible and safe transport for persons with disabilities. Furthermore EC funding, with its large resources and therefore potential for change, must probably also be fine-tuned to meet the requirements of the Convention and can provide a huge catalyst for change. It is likely that further reflection will reveal that other Community competences and obligations are likely to be engaged by the Convention. We are watching a legal experiment that will hopefully lead to many positive results.

---

[103] However, this should certainly not exclude references to other Treaty Articles being included in the Decision.

Postscript

Since this paper was completed, two important developments have occurred.

The Commission has published a proposal for a Council Decision concerning the conclusion, by the European Community, of the United Nations Convention on the Rights of Persons with Disabilities.[104] The proposed Decision makes reference to a significant number of EC Treaty articles, namely: 13, 26, 47(2), 55, 71(1), 80(2), 89, 93, 95 and 285.

Secondly, the Commission has published a proposal for a new Article 13 EC non-discrimination directive implementing the principle of equal treatment between persons irrespective of religion or belief, disability, age or sexual orientation.[105] As is clear from the title, this is not a disability-specific proposal, but is instead covers all the grounds already addressed in the Employment Equality Directive. The material scope of the proposal is similar to that of the Racial Equality Directive. The proposal contains a disability-specific article (Article 4), which establishes an anticipatory duty to provide "effective non-discriminatory access" as well as a duty to provide reasonable accommodations to individuals. It is anticipated that the negotiation and adoption of the new directive will be a drawn out process.

104 2008/0170 (CNS).

105 2008/0140 (CNS).

The Protection of the Rights of Persons with Disabilities in the Case Law of the European Court of Human Rights

*Davíð Þór Björgvinsson**

1 *Introduction*

This Chapter aims at reflecting upon the status of persons with disabilities within the legal framework of the European Convention of Human Rights and in the case law of the European Court of Human Rights.[1]

It is well known that the Convention primarily aims at protecting those human rights which are usually labelled as civil and political rights as opposed to social and cultural rights.

Traditionally the rights of people with disabilities have first and foremost been seen as falling within the category of social rights. On the international, as well as on the domestic level, advancement of the rights of persons with disabilities has taken the form of political pressure being put on the authorities to take specific positive measures (in form of constitutional provisions, legislation or other) to improve the living conditions and quality of life of people with disabilities, while at the same time it is assumed that they should enjoy civil and political rights on the same footing as any other person. These claims can take different forms, such as direct financial support from state funds, special facilities for the disabled in the field of health services, daily care, rehabilitation, training, employment and education. All these claims are clearly cost related. They are, accordingly, traditionally not approached as absolute rights in the same way as the classical civil and political rights, but rather rights which are, at least to some degree, dependent on available resources and their level of protection varies greatly from one country to another, to a large extent based on economic

* Judge of the European Court of Human Rights and Professor, Reykjavik University School of Law.

1 Hereinafter referred to as the Convention and the Court, respectively.

factors. The classical rights are to a much lesser degree qualified by reference to costs, although their fulfilment, in reality, usually involves some costs.

Experience has also shown us that claims arising from constitutional provisions and legislation in the field of social rights do not lend themselves to be easily adjudicated in a court of law, mainly because of the cost element. The classical response of courts in most countries is to give the legislator and the authorities a margin of appreciation, wide or narrow as the case may be, to decide how and to what extent such claims are met.

This distinction between civil and political rights and social rights is however not as clear as many of us would like to believe. First it should be mentioned that on the political platform as well as on the academic, more emphasis is now laid on defining the rights of the disabled within in the conceptual framework of classical civil and political rights. Traditionally decision makers have tended to explain the disadvantageous situation of disabled people as a result of their specific impairments, physical or mental, rather than being a result of discrimination or other inadequate respect for human rights.[2] There is in other words, a shift from the social policy approach to an emphasis on approaching the issue in terms of equal rights. Whether this change of approach will in the long run yield better results for the benefit for disabled persons remains to be seen.

Secondly the distinction between social rights and civil rights is, from a theoretical and practical point of view, not always clear. Social elements are as a matter of fact in some situations unavoidable components in many civil rights. This means that conditions must be provided for in order for some individuals, including disabled persons, to be able to fully enjoy civil rights. This would seem to be obvious.

2 *Legal Framework*

The Council of Europe has taken many steps aiming at protecting and promoting human rights of people with disabilities, although they are not directly addressed by the Convention itself. One should mention: The European Social Charter from 1961 (revised in 1996), Convention for the Prevention of Torture and Inhuman and Degrading Treatment or Punishment from 1989, Partial Agreement in the Social and Public Health Field 1997, Recommendation Rec(96)6 on a coherent policy for people with disabilities, Recommendation Rec(99)4 on principles concerning the legal protection of incapable adults, Recommendation Rec(2004)10 concerning the protection of human rights and dignity of persons

2 Lisa Waddington: Evolving Disability Policies. From Social-Welfare to Human Rights. An International Trend from a European Perspective. Netherlands Quarterly of Human Rights, Vol. 19 No. 2 (pp. 141–165), pp. 141–142.

with mental disorders and Recommendation Rec(2006)5 on the Council of Europe Action Plan to promote the rights and full participation of people with disability in society.[3]

As stated above the Convention aims first and foremost at protecting what has been termed civil and political rights. In fact it does not in explicit terms refer to any specific rights of persons with disabilities or directly address such issues, except maybe in Article 5 (1) e, which refers to persons of *unsound mind*. Having said that, it however protects the rights provided for, of all individuals, falling under the jurisdiction of the Contracting Parties, including of course persons with disabilities. This is also clear *i.a.* from Article 14, which prohibits discrimination against disabled persons. Of significance in this respect is also Protocol 12 to the Convention which contains general prohibition of discrimination.[4]

It is not disputed that people with disabilities should enjoy civil and political rights on the same footing as any other person. The question however still remains if all persons with disabilities can enjoy these rights in full without having regard to their vulnerable situation. This is related to the question as to whether the Convention, in particular Article 14 in conjunction with some of the other rights, can be considered violated when States without an objective and reasonable justification fail to treat differently persons with disabilities in order for them to fully enjoy the Convention rights. This issue will be further discussed in relation to Article 14 of the Convention in sub-chapter 3.5.[5]

3 *Status of Persons with Disabilities in the Case Law of the Court*

3.1 *Definition of Disability*

Issues concerning definitions and classification of disabilities from a medical point of view will not be addressed here.[6] For the purpose of a discussion of the kind offered in this Chapter a broad definition is sometimes used, such as including

[3] See further on the work of the Council of Europe in this field: Manuel Lezertua: The Council of Europe and the protection and the promotion of the human rights of people with disabilities. *Human Rights – Disability – Children. Conference Proceedings*. Council of Europe, December 2005, pp. 29–37. Also in the same collection Regis Brillat: The rights of persons with disabilites under the European Social Charter and Peter Barlett, Oliver Lewis and Oliver Thorold: *Mental Disability and the European Convention on Human Rights*. Martinus Nijhoff Publishers 2007, pp. 23–26.

[4] See on Protocol 12 for example Loukis G. Loucaides: The Prohibition of Discrimination under Protocol 12 of the European Convention on Human Rights. *The European Convention on Human Rights. Collected Essays*. Martinus Nijhoff Publishers 2007, pp. 55–72.

[5] See in particular *Thlimmenos v. Greece* (application no. 34369/97) of 6 April 2000, para. 44.

[6] For further information on this topic see: http://www.who.int/classifications/icf/site/icftemplate.cfm.

people with different long term diseases, for example people infected by HIV or suffering from AIDS, as well as infirmity, due to old age.[7] In some other contexts a narrower definition is more appropriate. In paragraph 2 of Article 1 of the UN Convention on the Rights of Persons with Disabilities a narrower definition is used, where it says that persons with disabilities include those who have long term-term physical, mental, intellectual or sensory impairments which in interaction with various barriers may hinder their full and effective participation in society on equal basis with others.[8]

In this Chapter the broader approach is used in order to accommodate in general individuals in need of special attention or care due to their physical or mental impairment and thereby to cover different situations that have arisen in relation to the Convention. This is of course questionable and can lead to oversimplifications, since indeed some attention to the factual details of the individual case is often necessary to draw reasonable conclusions from individual judgments or decisions. The situation of individuals and their needs vary greatly to say the least, and their impairments are of a very different degree and nature, as well as in terms of their effects on their capabilities to participate in work and social life in general. In any case, it would seem justifiable to say that the specific considerations the Court has given to all persons falling under the wider definition would as for the most part also be applicable for those falling under the narrower one.

As stated earlier the Convention does not contain provisions specifically aiming at advancing or protecting the rights of disabled persons. This does not of course prevent such individuals from bringing their case to the Court just as any other person who claims to be a victim of a violation of his rights as protected by the Convention. In many of these cases their disability is a matter of particular concern. In principle this can happen in relation to all the rights protected by the Convention, although they are of specific concern in relation to some of them. Therefore the main focus in this Chapter is on Articles 3, 5 and 8. Issues concerning disabled people have also been dealt with under other Convention

---

7 See for example Manuel Lezertua, *supra* note 3, p. 33. A detailed account of related problems in relation to mental disability in particular see Peter Barlett and others, *supra* note 3, pp. 2–9.

8 United Nations Convention on the Rights of Persons with Disabilities from 6 December 2006. On the historical background and the negotiations leading to the adoption of the Convention, see for example: Holger Kallehauge: The genesis of a new human rights convention. – A convention on the Rights of Persons with Disabilities. *Implementing Human Rights. Essays in Honour of Morten Kjærum.* Eds. Rikke Frank Jørgensen and Klaus Slavensky. Danish Institute for Human Rights, Copenhagen 2007, pp. 337–348. Also Arnt Holte: The UN draft comprehensive and integral international convention on the protection and promotion of the rights and dignity of persons with disabilities. *Human Rights – Disability – Children,* see *supra* note 3, pp. 59–61, and in the same collection Carlos Salzar: Comments on the UN Disability Convention, pp. 61–68.

Articles. They are also discussed in a separate sub-chapter. In this Chapter only a few examples are mentioned. It does therefore not offer anything close to full coverage of this complex issue.[9]

3.2 *Article 3 – Prohibition of Torture and Degrading or Inhuman Treatment or Punishment*

Article 3 of the Convention prohibits in absolute terms any form of torture and degrading or inhuman treatment or punishment. The special situation of disabled persons comes into play in relation to Article 3 in mainly two kinds of situations. Firstly, in cases concerning conditions of detention or imprisonment and secondly in cases concerning expulsion of aliens. Certain investigative methods or techniques or conditions of detention or imprisonment may be accepted as compatible with Article 3 under normal circumstances. However, the case law shows that they may amount to inhuman or degrading treatment or punishment if applied to disabled persons.[10] The same is true when it comes to the expulsion of aliens. Expulsion of a person with disabilities may amount to inhuman or degrading treatment while in other situations it does not.

3.2.1 *Conditions of Detention or Imprisonment*

It is well settled case law that when assessing the appropriateness of a treatment of a person held in detention under Article 3, regards should be had the to the person's characteristics, such as age, sex, state of health, etc.[11] If a person has any disabilities this is a factor that must be taken into account. One of the best examples of this in the case law of the Court is *Price v. the United Kingdom.*[12]

> All four limbs of the applicant were foreshortened as a result of Thalidomide. She also suffered from problems with her kidneys. She was bound to a wheelchair. In January 1995, in the course of civil proceedings for recovery of a judgment debt, she refused to answer questions put to her concerning her financial position and

[9] For further reading see for example: Loukis G. Loucaides: The European Convention of Human Rights and the Rights of Persons with Disabilities, *supra* note 4, pp. 95–106; Bertrand Favreau: Les droits de la personne handicapée et la Cour européenne des droits de l'homme. *Handicap et protection du droit européen et communautaire.* Eds. Christophe Petiti and Bertrand Favreau. Bruylant 2006, pp. 3–35. Peter Barlett and others, *supra* note 3.

[10] See also further Manfred Novak and Walter Suntinger: The right of disabled persons not to be subjected to torture or inhuman or degrading treatment of punishment. *Human Rights and Disabled Persons. Essays and Relevant Human Rights Instruments. International Studies in Human Rights.* Eds. Theresia Degener and Yolan Koster-Dreese, Martinus Nijhoff 1995, pp. 117–118.

[11] See in for example *Ireland v. the United Kingdom* (application no. 5310/71) of 18 January 1978.

[12] *Price v. the United Kingdom* (application no. 33394/96) of 10 July 2001.

was committed to prison for seven days for contempt of court. For the first night she was put in a cell in a police station. After the first night she was moved to a prison. She made many complaints concerning inadequate facilities having in mind her disabilities, both in the police cell and in the prison. First the Court noted that in accordance with English law and practice, the sentencing judge did not take any steps, before committing the applicant to immediate imprisonment – a sentence the Court found particularly harsh in the circumstances of the case – to ascertain where she would be detained or to ensure that it would be possible to provide facilities adequate to cope with her severe level of disability. As it turned out, the Court found that the facilities offered to the applicants were found to be completely inadequate. The Court states i.a. at para. 30: "There is no evidence in this case of any positive intention to humiliate or debase the applicant. However, the Court considers that to detain a severely disabled person in conditions where she is dangerously cold, risks developing sores because her bed is too hard or unreachable, and is unable to go to the toilet or keep clean without the greatest of difficulty, constitutes degrading treatment contrary to Article 3 of the Convention. It therefore finds a violation of this provision in the present case."

Another case of relevance in this context is the case of *Farbtuhs v. Latvia.*[13]

The applicant was born in 1916 (86 years old when the application was made). In September 1999, when he was 83 years old, he was found guilty of crimes against humanity and genocide for his role in the deportation and deaths of Latvian citizens during the period of Stalinist repression in 1940 and 1941. In the judgment it was noted that the applicant was 84 years old when he was sent to prison, paraplegic and disabled to the point of being unable to attend to most daily tasks unaided. He was in addition suffering from a number of serious illnesses, the majority of which were chronic and incurable. In particular, he was unable to get up, sit down, move, get dressed or wash without assistance. The Court considered that when national authorities decided to imprison him, they had to be particularly careful to ensure that the conditions of detention were consistent with the specific needs arising out of the prisoner's infirmity. The Court also noted that the applicant had contracted other diseases while in custody. The Court found that the new illnesses constituted an additional indication that a prolonged spell in prison was inappropriate. In spite of his condition the applicant had remained in prison throughout the period of more than one year. Having regard to the circumstances of the case, the Court found that, in view of his age, infirmity and condition, the applicant's continued detention was not appropriate. The situation in which he had been put was bound to cause him permanent anxiety and a sense of inferiority and humiliation so acute as to amount to degrading treatment within the meaning of Article 3.[14]

---

[13] *Farbtuhs v. Latvia.* (application no. 4672/02) of 2 December 2004.

[14] See also *Keenan v. the United Kingdom* (application no. 27229/95) of 3 April 2001. In para. 116 the Court states: "The lack of effective monitoring of Mark Keenan's condition and the lack of informed psychiatric input into his assessment and treatment disclose significant defects in the medical care provided to a mentally ill person known to be a suicide risk. The belated imposition on him in those circumstances of a serious disciplinary punishment – seven days' segregation in the punishment block and an additional twenty-eight days to his sentence imposed

From these judgments it is clear that disabled persons may, as any other person, be put in detention for investigative purposes or punished by imprisonment. Furthermore Article 3 should not be construed as laying down an obligation to release detainees on health grounds or due to their disabilities. It rather imposes an obligation on the State to protect the physical and mental well-being of persons deprived of their liberty.[15] It follows that when disabled persons are detained some extra steps must be taken, if necessary, to protect them. Under such circumstances the state may have an *obligation* to adopt *positive measures* that take account of a person's special and vulnerable situation. If this is not done, his or her treatment or punishment may be found to be inhuman or degrading, although under other normal circumstances this would not be the case.

3.2.2 *Expulsion and Deportation of Aliens*

The Convention does not as a matter principle limit the rights of the Contracting States to control the entry, residence and expulsion of aliens. It is however well established case law by the Court that in exercising their right to extradition, expulsion or deportation of aliens the expelling state must have regard to Article 3 of the Convention. In other words, expulsion of aliens can run counter to Article 3 if it is established that a person is likely to be subject to treatment or punishment in the receiving state of the kind described in Article 3.[16] This issue has come into play in relation to disabled persons or persons in otherwise vulnerable situations in a variety of situations. An example of this is the case of *D. v. the United Kingdom.*[17]

> The applicant, national of St. Kitts, had been arrested at Heathrow airport for drug trafficking and sentenced to prison. While he was in prison it was revealed that he suffered form AIDS. In prison he underwent treatment. When the prison term ended he was faced with an expulsion from the UK to St. Kitts. He was then considered to be in the final stage of his illness. He claimed that his proposed removal to

two weeks after the event and only nine days before his expected date of release – which may well have threatened his physical and moral resistance, is not compatible with the standard of treatment required in respect of a mentally ill person. It must be regarded as constituting inhuman and degrading treatment and punishment within the meaning of Article 3 of the Convention. /Accordingly, the Court finds a violation of this provision." See also in this context: *Herczegfalvy v. Austria* (application no. 10533/83) of 24 September 1992, *Peers v. Greece* (application no. 28524/95) of 19 April 2001, *Khudobin v. Russia* (application no. 59696/00) of 26 October 2006, *Sarban v. Moldova* (application 3456/05) of 4 October 2005, *Boicenco v. Moldova* (application no. 41088/05) of 11 July 2006 and *Holomiov v. Moldova* (application no. 30649/05) of 7 November 2006.

15 See for example *Testa v. Croatia* (application no. 20877/04) of 12 July 2007 (para. 46).

16 See for example *Ahmed v. Austria* (application no. 25964/94) of 17 December 1996 and *Chahal v. the United Kingdom* (application 22414/93) of 15 November 1996.

17 *D. v. the United Kingdom* (application no. 30240/96) of 2 May 1997.

> St. Kitts would be in violation of *i.a.* Article 3 of the Convention, the reason being the lack of appropriate health services in St. Kitts. The judgment *i.a.* states the following in para. 51–53: "The Court notes that the applicant is in the advanced stages of a terminal and incurable illness. At the date of the hearing, it was observed that there had been a marked decline in his condition and he had to be transferred to a hospital. His condition was giving rise to concern [...]. The limited quality of life he now enjoys results from the availability of sophisticated treatment and medication in the United Kingdom and the care and kindness administered by a charitable organisation. He has been counselled on how to approach death and has formed bonds with his carers. [...] / 52. The abrupt withdrawal of these facilities will entail the most dramatic consequences for him. It is not disputed that his removal will hasten his death. There is a serious danger that the conditions of adversity which await him in St. Kitts will further reduce his already limited life expectancy and subject him to acute mental and physical suffering. Any medical treatment which he might hope to receive there could not contend with the infections which he may possibly contract on account of his lack of shelter and of a proper diet as well as exposure to the health and sanitation problems which beset the population of St Kitts [...]. ... There is no evidence of any other form of moral or social support. Nor has it been shown whether the applicant would be guaranteed a bed in either of the hospitals on the island which, according to the Government, care for AIDS patients [...] / 53. In view of these exceptional circumstances and bearing in mind the critical stage now reached in the applicant's fatal illness, the implementation of the decision to remove him to St Kitts would amount to inhuman treatment by the respondent State in violation of Article 3 (art. 3)."[18]

It should be emphasised that the Court refers to "exceptional circumstances". This indicates that this approach of the Court should be construed narrowly. This is confirmed in the Court's recent judgment *N. v. the United Kingdom,* in which the Court did not find a violation.[19] Indeed the case of *D. v. the United*

[18] See also *Nasri v. France* (application 19465/92) of 13 July 1995. The applicant was deaf-mute and had lived since childhood in France and all his family lived there. After having served a prison sentence for rape he faced deportation from France. The Commission found that his deportation would amount to a violation of Article 3. The Court however dealt with the case under Article 8 (see further chapter 3.4). The case of *Bensaid v. the United Kingdom* (application no. 44599/98) of 6 February 2001. The applicant suffered from schizophrenia and was undergoing treatment for schizophrenia, complained that his proposed expulsion to Algeria would leave him without adequate medical treatment, threatening his physical and moral integrity. The Court found that the risk of damage to the applicant's health from his return to Algeria was based on largely hypothetical factors and that it was not substantiated that he would suffer inhuman and degrading treatment. Nor had it been established that his moral integrity would be substantially affected to a degree falling within the scope of Article 8 (right to respect for family life) of the Convention.

[19] *N. v. the United Kingdom* (application no. 26565/05) of 27 May 2008. The applicant, suffering from AIDS, was a Ugandan national who was born in 1974 and lived in London. The case concerned N's allegation that her return to Uganda would cause her suffering and lead to her early death, because of her illness. In a dissenting opinion the minority of the Court held that there had been a violation. See in particular para. 42 of the judgment which states: "In the

Kingdom is exceptional. Numerous other judgments strongly indicate that the Court will be very cautious in this regard.

3.3 *Article 5 – Right to Liberty and Security*

Article 5 of the Convention protects the right to liberty and security. Above we have seen the relevance of Article 5 in relation to Article 3 when it comes to the conditions of detention of persons with disabilities. This case law shows that states may be obliged to take positive steps in order to improve conditions of detention to avoid Article 3 being violated.

According to Article 5, paragraph 1, different reasons can justify the deprivation of a person's liberty. Of particular interest in the context of this Chapter are points d and e of paragraph 1. It is important to notice that points d and e refer to certain reasons for the detention of persons related to their characteristics and the purposes of detention. Point d refers to detention of minors for *i.a.* educational supervision and point e refers to persons that may spread infectious diseases, persons of unsound mind, alcoholics or drug addicts or vagrants. Importantly though, the focus of these provisions is the deprivation of liberty and protection of civil rights in such circumstances. The social protection, special care or living conditions of these individuals were certainly not in the forefront when they were drafted. In the following only the provision in 5(1) e will be considered.

The most important aspects of Article 5(1) e, in the context of Article 5 as a whole, are twofold. Firstly, if the conditions are met it may justify a deprivation of an individual's liberty and secondly it offers certain procedural guarantees, both when deprivation takes first place and in deciding upon continuing detention.[20] However there is more to it. If a person is for example detained on the grounds of point e it would seem that requirements should be made as to the consistency between the reasons for depriving a person of his/her liberty and the conditions of detention and treatment received. The Court's case law demands a relationship between the ground for detention and the placement, at least as to the institutional framework a person is subjected to. Therefore, if a minor is locked up in an institution for treatment or educational purposes, some treatment and educational facilities will have to be provided for the detention to be lawful onward. The same goes for a person who is deprived of his or her liberty for the reasons referred to in point e. For example a person of unsound mind

D. case the very exceptional circumstances were that the applicant was critically ill and appeared to be close to death, could not be guaranteed any nursing or medical care in his country of origin and had no family there willing or able to care for him or provide him with even a basic level of food, shelter or social support."

20 See for example *H.L. v. the United Kingdom* (application no. 45508/99) of 5 October 2004.

must therefore be held in an appropriate institution where some relevant treatment should be provided. In other words, seen from this point of view, it may be said that certain social elements are inherent in Article 5 (1) points d and e.[21] An example of this is *Ashingdane v. the United Kingdom*.[22]

> The applicant had been convicted for dangerous driving and four offences of unlawful possession of firearms. Medical evidence was submitted to the effect that he was suffering from mental illness (paranoid schizophrenia) and his mental disorder was of a nature or degree which warranted his detention in a psychiatric hospital. The applicant accepted that his detention was "in accordance with a *procedure* prescribed by law" and that there was evidence on which the authorities could properly conclude that he was a "person of unsound mind". He, however, submitted on a number of grounds that his detention was not "lawful" for the purposes of sub-paragraph (e) of paragraph 1 of Article 5 (art. 5–1-e). The judgment *i.a.* states in para. 44: In principle, the "detention" of a person as a mental health patient will only be "lawful" for the purposes of sub-paragraph (e) of paragraph 1 (art. 5–1-e) if effected in a hospital, clinic or other appropriate institution authorised for that purpose. However, subject to the foregoing, Article 5 para. 1 (e) (art. 5–1-e) is not in principle concerned with suitable treatment or conditions (see the above-mentioned Winterwerp judgment, p. 21, para. 51)". The Court goes on in para. 48: "Furthermore, at all times the purpose of Mr. Ashingdane's detention related to his mental illness. This was so even though the immediate cause of the delay in his transfer from the special security hospital to his local hospital was industrial rather than therapeutic, a circumstance which the Commission described as 'deplorable' (see paragraph 79 of the report). It is clear, however, that the delay was not in conscious disregard of Mr. Ashingdane's mental welfare. Efforts were made to find a solution as soon as possible (see paragraphs 15 in fine and 21 above). The evidence before the Court suggests that any course other than that adopted by the responsible authorities would probably have been impracticable. In any event, the Court is satisfied that the applicant's continued detention was not arbitrary or effected for an ulterior purpose, contrary to Article 5 para. 1 (e) read in conjunction with Article 18 (art. 18+5–1-e)."

Although the Court did not find a violation in this case it is important to note that the Court emphasized that at all times the purpose of the applicant's detention had to be related to his mental illness.[23] Furthermore the validity of continued confinement depends upon the persistence of such disorders.[24]

---

[21] As to whether a person is of "unsound mind" the Court is very hesitant to find differently form the national authorities, see for example *Winterwerp v. the Netherlands* (application no. 6301/73) of 24 October 1979.

[22] *Ashingdane v. the United Kingdom* (application no. 8225/78) of 28 May 1985.

[23] See also *Winterwerp v. the Netherlands* (application no. 6301/73) of 24 October 1979, *Herczegfalvy v. Austria* (application no. 10533/83) of 24 September 1992.

[24] See in particular on this point for example *Winterwerp v. the Netherlands* (application no. 6301/73) of 24 October 1979.

Another case in this category is *Shtukaturov v. Russia.*[25]

> The applicant alleged that he was deprived of his legal capacity without his knowledge. He further alleged that he was unlawfully confined to a psychiatric hospital where he was unable to obtain a review of his status or meet his lawyer and where he received medical treatment against his will. He relied i.a. on Article 5, Article 6 § 1 and Article 8. The Court found a violation of Article 5 § 1 (e) since it had not been "reliably shown" that the applicant's mental condition had necessitated his confinement and concluded that his hospitalisation for a certain period had not been "lawful". Furthermore, the Court found that the applicant's inability to obtain judicial review of his detention had amounted to a violation of Article 5 § 4.

Seen from this point of view Article 5 does not only offer procedural protection, it also offers to a certain degree substantive protection against inappropriate or insufficiently grounded decisions subjecting a person to an institution, as well as to the institutional framework an individual is subjected to.[26] The case law, however, indicates that the Court gives the defending State a relatively wide margin of appreciation when it comes to decisions concerning the exact placement, and the extent and nature of the treatment to be received. Therefore it would seem that it has less to offer when it comes to the assessment of such conditions and the appropriateness of the treatment itself. While Article 5 may be of little help in relations to complaints concerning inappropriate conditions or lack of treatment in the relevant institution they may however run contrary to other Articles of the Convention, *i.a.* Article 3 and 8 (for example if institutional regimes are too strict).

3.4 *Article 8 – Right to Respect for Private and Family Life*

Questions concerning disabled persons and respect for their private and family life can arise in various situations. The case of *Nasri v. France* (cited above, see note 18) is a good example.

> The applicant was an Algerian national, born 'deaf and dumb' in Algeria in 1960 (aged 34 when the judgment was rendered). He was the fourth of ten siblings, six of whom are French nationals. He was found guilty of rape and after serving his term in prison he faced deportation to Algeria. In the judgment the Court stated in para. 46: "In view of this accumulation of special circumstances, notably his situation as a deaf and dumb person, capable of achieving a minimum psychological and social equilibrium only within his family, the majority of whose members are French nationals with no close ties with Algeria, the decision to deport the applicant, if executed, would not be proportionate to the legitimate aim pursued.

---

[25] *Shtukaturov v. Russia* (application no. 44009/05) of 27 March 2008.

[26] See also *Aerts v. Belgium* (Application 25357/94) of 30 July 1998. For more detailed account of these issues, see in particular Peter Bartlett and others, *supra* note 3, pp. 31–74.

> It would infringe the right to respect for family life and therefore constitute a breach of Article 8 (art. 8)."

This case relates to what has been termed the negative aspect of Article 8, namely the duty of the Contracting States to refrain from interferences unless it is objectively justified on one of the grounds listed in Article 8, paragraph 2. Deportation of the applicant is seen, in the circumstances of the case and having in mind his disabilities, as a disproportionate interference into his private and family life. When assessing proportionality the vulnerable situation of the applicant as a disabled person is taken into consideration.

In other cases the focus is more on positive measures that the state may be obliged to adopt. Sometimes positive measures are deemed necessary to take due note of the special situation of the disabled. Lack of positive measures has prompted the Court to find breaches of Article 8. The most notable example is the case of *X and Y v. Netherlands.*[27]

> Mr. X and his daughter Y were born in 1929 and 1961 respectively. The daughter, who was mentally impaired, had been living since 1970 in a privately-run home for mentally impaired children. One night in December 1977, Miss Y was woken up by a certain Mr. B, the son-in-law of the directress; he lived with his wife on the premises of the institution although he was not employed there. Mr. B forced the girl to follow him to his room, to undress and to have sexual intercourse with him. Mr. X went to the local police station to file a complaint and to ask for criminal proceedings to be instituted. The police authorities rejected to open criminal investigation into the incident due to the fact that Y was unable to sign the complaint on her own, and that her father could not do that on her behalf. The applicant held that the impossibility of having criminal proceedings instituted against Mr. B violated Article 8 of the Convention. This the Court accepted, taking account of the nature of the wrongdoing in question, that she was the victim of a violation of Article 8 (art. 8) of the Convention.

These judgments show that both the negative and positive aspect of Article 8 is relevant in respect for the private life of disabled persons. However as regards the positive aspect, there are limits to how far the Court can (or is willing) to go into this direction. The Case of *Botta v. Italy* illustrates this point.[28]

> The applicant, living in Italy, was physically disabled. In August 1990 he went on holiday to the seaside resort in his country, with a friend, who also was physically disabled. There he discovered that the bathing establishments were not equipped with the certain facilities needed to enable disabled people to gain access to the beach and the sea. It was not disputed that this was in breach of Italian legislation at the relevant time. He made complaints under i.a. Article 8 of the Convention. In relation to Article 8 the Court stated in para. 35: "In the instant case, however,

[27] *X and Y v. the Netherlands* (application no. 8978/80) of 26 March 1985.

[28] *Botta v. Italy* (application no. 21439/93) of 24 February 1998.

> the right asserted by Mr Botta, namely the right to gain access to the beach and the sea at a place distant from his normal place of residence during his holidays, concerns interpersonal relations of such broad and indeterminate scope that there can be no conceivable direct link between the measures the State was urged to take in order to make good the omissions of the private bathing establishments and the applicant's private life. Accordingly, Article 8 is not applicable."

The judgment indicates that disabled persons may have difficulty in claiming violations of Article 8 for the failure of the authorities to take general measures to facilitate the mobility of disabled persons, although domestic law requires them to do so. It must be established that there is a direct link between the omission and the private life of the individual.[29] Another interesting example is *Shtukaturov v. Russia* referred to above.[30]

> In relation to an alleged breach of Article 8 the Court noted that the interference with the applicant's private life had been very serious: it had resulted in him having become fully dependant on his official guardian in almost all areas of his life for an indefinite period. Also, that interference could not be challenged unless through his guardian, who had opposed any attempts to discontinue the measure. The Court recalled that it had already found the proceedings to deprive the applicant of his legal capacity as procedurally flawed (see sub-chapter 3.3 above). Furthermore, the district court's reasoning had also been inadequate. In addition the Russian legislation only made a distinction between full capacity and full incapacity of mentally ill persons. It made no allowances for borderline situations. The Court referred, in particular, to a Recommendation issued by the Council of Europe's Committee of Ministers which outlined a set of principles for the legal protection of incapable adults in which it recommended that legislation be more flexible by providing a "tailor-made" response to each individual case.[31] The Court therefore concluded that the interference with the applicant's private life had been disproportionate to the legitimate aim pursued by the Russian Government of protecting the interests and health of others, in violation of Article 8.

Of particular interest in this case is the reference to "tailor-made" response to each individual case as provided for in the Recommendation referred to. From the judgment it is possible to conclude that deprivation of legal capacity in its entirety, where less drastic or more "tailor-made" remedies might seem more appropriate, may result in a breach of Article 8.

---

[29] See also related issue in *Marzari v. Italy* (application no. 36448/97). Decision of 4 May 1999 and *Zehnalová and Zehnal v. the Czech Republic* (application no. 38621/97). Decision of 14 May 2002.

[30] *Shtukaturov v. Russia*, see *supra* note 25.

[31] See Recommendation Rec(99)4 on principles concerning the legal protection of incapable adults.

Article 8 can come into play in other situations as well. In the case of *Pretty v. the United Kingdom*[32] fundamental questions arose concerning the right to die under Articles 2 and 8.

> The applicant was a United Kingdom national, born in 1958. She was dying of motor neurone disease, a degenerative disease affecting the muscles, for which there was no cure. When the case was brought the disease was at an advanced stage and the applicant was paralysed from the neck downwards and her life expectancy was very poor. However, her intellect and capacity to make decisions were unimpaired. Given that the final stages of the disease were distressing and undignified, she wished to be able to control how and when she died and be spared that suffering and indignity. The applicant was prevented by her disease from taking such a step without assistance. It was however a crime under English law to assist another to commit suicide. The applicant wished to be assisted by her husband in committing suicide, but the Director of Public Prosecutions (DPP) had refused her request to guarantee her husband freedom from prosecution if he did so. Her appeals against that decision were unsuccessful. The applicant complained of violation of Article 2 (right to life) and Article 8. As regards Article 2 the question arose whether Article also included the negative aspect, namely the right to die, as well as the duty of the State to protect life. The Court held that Article 2 could not, without a distortion of language, be interpreted as including the right to die; nor could it create a right to self-determination in the sense of conferring on an individual the entitlement to choose death rather than life. The Court accordingly found that no right to die, whether at the hands of a third person or with the assistance of a public authority, could be derived from Article 2. There had therefore been no violation of that provision. As concerns Article 8, the Court found that States were entitled to regulate through criminal law certain activities which were detrimental to the life and safety of other individuals and did not consider that the blanket nature of the ban on assisted suicide was disproportionate. It did not appear to be arbitrary for the law to reflect the importance of the right to life, by prohibiting assisted suicide while providing for a system of enforcement and adjudication which allowed due regard to be given in each particular case to the public interest in bringing a prosecution, as well as to the fair and proper requirements of retribution and deterrence. Nor in the circumstances was there anything disproportionate in the refusal of the DPP to give an advance undertaking that no prosecution would be brought against the applicant's husband. Strong arguments based on the rule of law could be raised against any claim by the executive to exempt individuals or classes of individuals from the operation of the law. In any event, the seriousness of the act for which immunity was claimed was such that the decision of the DPP to refuse the undertaking sought could not be said to be arbitrary or unreasonable. The Court concluded that the interference could be justified as "necessary in a democratic society" for the protection of the rights of others and found no violation of Article 8.[33]

---

[32] *Pretty v. the United Kingdom* (application no. 2346/02) of 29 April 2002.

[33] See also *Glass v. the United Kingdom* (application no. 61827/00) of 9 March 2004. The second applicant was the mother of the first applicant – a severely disabled child – and acted as the latter's legal proxy. In that capacity, the second applicant had the authority to act on his behalf

Disabilities are also a relevant factor in child-protection cases, where either the parents or the children are disabled. Such situations are obviously relevant when the authorities decide to interfere. Also, if disabled children are taken away from their parents the authorities are required to provide them with necessary services and care, a lack of which was the reason for taking them away from their parents.[34]

3.5 *Other Rights*

As stated earlier the special situation of the disabled can come into play in relation to all of the substantive rights provided for in the Convention. In addition to those already mentioned one should draw attention to the following.

3.5.1 *Article 6 – Right to a Fair Trial*

Rights under Article 6 should also of course be enjoyed in full by disabled persons. This implies that certain facilities might be necessary for en effective conduct of court proceedings for those who have certain impairments that hinder their possibilities to participate effectively in the proceedings. Thus for example for blind or deaf-mute persons must be provided with the necessary assistance by state.[35] Absence of the appropriate assistance may result in a breach of Article 6. This statement is not directly supported by reference to case law, but is inherent in the spirit of Article 6 as a whole, and paragraph 3 (c) in particular.[36] The *Shtukaturov v. Russia* judgment is also of interest in this regard.[37] The Court reiterated that in cases concerning compulsory confinement, a person of unsound mind should be heard either in person or, where necessary, through some form of representation. However, the applicant, who appeared to have been a relatively autonomous person despite his illness, had not been given any opportunity to participate in

|and to defend his interests, including in the area of medical treatment. A dispute arose as regards the appropriate medical care, namely a in this case to stop treatment and revert to the administration of diamorphine. The Court stated *i.a.* in para. 83: "The Court considers that, having regard to the circumstances of the case, the decision of the authorities to override the second applicant's objection to the proposed treatment in the absence of authorisation by a court resulted in a breach of Article 8 of the Convention…."

[34] See in particular in this context *Olsson v. Sweden* (application no. 10465/83) of 24 March 1988 and *Kutzner v. Germany* (application no. 46544/99) of 26 February 2002.

[35] See also Loukis G. Loucaides, *supra* note 4, p. 98.

[36] An indirect support for this can be found in *S.C. v. the United Kingdom* (application no. 60958/00) of 15 June 2004. In this case the Court found a breach of Article 6 because it was not convinced that an eleven year old boy charged with attempted robbery was capable of participating effectively in the proceedings due to his young age and limited intellectual capacity.

[37] *Shtukaturov v. Russia*, see *supra* note 25.

the proceedings concerning his legal capacity. The proceedings were held to be in breach of the principle of adversarial proceedings enshrined in Article 6 § 1. See also *H. v. Austria*.[38] An employer in Austria complained that a special tax on certain employers who did not employ disabled persons amounted to a criminal sanction under Article 6. The Commission dismissed the case.

3.5.2 *Article 10 – Freedom of Expression*

Issues of concern to disabled persons arose in *Sunday Times v. the United Kingdom*.[39] One of the issues in the case was the publishing of certain material relating to court proceedings concerning the marketing of the medicine thalidomide, which had caused hundreds of individuals to be born severely impaired. In balancing the different interests under Article 10 the Court laid specific emphasis on the interests of the victims to gain information. In paragraph 66 of the judgment it says:

> The thalidomide disaster was a matter of undisputed public concern. It posed the question whether the powerful company which had marketed the drug bore legal or moral responsibility towards hundreds of individuals experiencing an appalling personal tragedy or whether the victims could demand or hope for indemnification only from the community as a whole; fundamental issues concerning protection against and compensation for injuries resulting from scientific developments were raised and many facets of the existing law on these subjects were called in question.

It is difficult to assess the importance of the fact that the subject matter concerned seriously disabled people. The overriding importance should be laid on the fact that the matter was of great public concern, which seems to be the most relevant factor.

3.5.3 *Article 14 and Protocol 12 – Non-discrimination*

Article 14 provides that states must secure the enjoyment of all Convention rights without discrimination on any of the grounds listed. This list is not exhaustive, and there can not be any doubt that Article 14 prohibits discrimination on the basis of disabilities. Furthermore, the Court has also ruled that Article 14 is not confined to cases where similar situations are treated differently. It also requires that states treat differently persons whose situation is significantly different, a principle that could well be relied on by persons with disabilities.[40] The importance of this for persons with disabilities is of course limited by the fact that Article 14 only applies if the facts of the case bring it within the scope

---

[38] *H. v. Austria* (application no. 17819/91).Commission decision of 3 September 1991.

[39] *Sunday Times v. the United Kingdom* (application no. 6538/74) of 26 April 1979.

[40] See *Thlimmenos v. Greece, supra* note 5.

of the other rights protected by the Convention. It does therefore not contain an autonomous or general ban against discrimination, like Protocol 12. Also, in situations where the facts of the case would bring it within the scope of Article 14, the case law indicates that the Court will be very cautious in reading into Article 14 an obligation to take specific positive measures for the advantage of certain groups.[41]

There is limited case law under Article 14 which casts light on how these provisions operate in relation to people with disabilities in particular. One judgment of interest is *Koua Poirrez v. France*.[42] At issue in the case was the applicant's entitlement to special allowance for disabled adults. In finding violation of Article 14 on the basis of nationality the Court attached weight to the fact that the case concerned disability entitlements.[43] However, the relevance of this case in relation to persons with disabilities is marginal since the basis of discrimination was nationality, rather than disabilities.

3.5.4 *Article 1 of Protocol 1 – Protection of Property*

Questions concerning Article 1 of Protocol 1 arise in particular in relation to contributory and non-contributory benefits that a disabled person may have a right to under domestic legislation. Obviously this is a field where states are normally left with wide margin of appreciation. Still the case law shows that such rights in principle enjoy protection under Article 1 of Protocol 1.[44] Among the most important cases in this regard are *Draon v. France* and *Maurice v. France*.[45] In these cases a legislation in France, entitling parents to certain amounts of compensation for the special burdens arising form their children's disability throughout their life, had been abolished, a disability that the medical authorities did not detect due to medical negligence. The problem was that the legislation abolishing such rights was adopted while the judicial proceedings were pending. The Court considered this amounting to a breach of Article 1 of Protocol 1. However, the problem did not so much concern the disability of the children as such, but rather the retroactive nature of the legislation.

---

[41] For further reading on this issue see for example Oddný Mjöll Arnardóttir: *Equality and Non-Discrimination under the European Convention on Human Rights*. Martinus Nijhof Publishers 2003, pp. 95–122.

[42] *Koua Poirrez v. France* (application no. 40892/98) of 30 September 2003.

[43] See further Loukis G. Loucaides, *supra* note 4, p. 101.

[44] See for example *Willis v. the United Kingdom* (application 36042/97) of 11 June 2002, *Kjartan Ásmundsson v. Iceland* (application no. 60669/00) of 12 October 2004 and *Koua Poirrez v. France* (application no. 40892/98) of 30 September 2003.

[45] *Draon v. France* (application no. 1513/03) of 6 October 2005 and *Maurice v. France* (application no. 11810/03) of 6 October 2005.

3.5.5 *Article 2 of Protocol 1 – Right to Education*

Questions have arisen as regards the rights of disabled children to inclusive schooling. See in this regard in particular *Graeme v. the United Kingdom.*[46] In this case the parents of a severely disabled boy argued that he was, in line with their conviction, entitled to receive education in the ordinary school system rather then in specialised institutions. The Commission took note of the fact that according to domestic legislation children with disabilities were in principle granted this right to the extent possible. At the same time it was noted that in some circumstances this might be practically difficult to such a degree that more specialised education might be necessary. Thus, the authorities where not under all circumstances obliged to abide by the wishes of the parents in this regard. Of interest in this regard is also *D.H. and Others v. the Czech Republic.*[47]

> The applicants alleged that, as a result of their Roma origin, they were assigned to special schools for children with learning difficulties who were unable to follow the ordinary school curriculum. The applicants complained that, on account of their Roma origin, they had suffered discrimination in the enjoyment of their right to education under Article 14 in conjunction with Article 2, Protocol 1. Although accepting that the system in the Czech Republic aimed at addressing special problems relating to schooling of children of Roma origin due to their special situation, the Court found that indirect discrimination was inherent in the Czech system because of the high proportion of Roma children in the special schools. It then went on to assess whether it could be justified. It came to the conclusion that it could not and that there was a violation of Article 14 in conjunction with Article 2 of Protocol 1.

Although the Roma children concerned were not mentally impaired the case is interesting in this regard for at least two reasons. Firstly, because it shows that special arrangements for a certain group of children can be considered to constitute a difference in treatment falling under Article 14. This issue can of course be transposed to the wider problem of placing children with disabilities in special schools rather than in the ordinary school system. The presumption would seem to be that children should be put in the ordinary school system, unless there are valid reasons for not doing so. Secondly, the case may also raise interesting questions since putting these children in special schools for children with "mental deficiencies" was considered a violation, although the non-impaired children for different reasons had many problems with coping with the normal school system. Despite their difficulties with the ordinary school system, the placement of these children in these special schools is seen as a disadvantage of its own kind.

---

[46] *Graeme v. the United Kingdom* (application no. 13887/88). Commission decision of 5 February 1990.

[47] *D.H. and Others v. the Czech Republic* (application no. 57325/00) of 13 November 2007.

4 *Summary and Conclusions*

It must be emphasised that the discussion above does not contain an exhaustive list of relevant cases, nor does it cover all the variety of situations the Court has dealt with, when faced with the rights of disabled persons. The judgments and decisions referred to are only a few examples intended to cast some light on the way and under what circumstances persons with disabilities may take advantage of the Convention provisions. However, it should be enough to draw certain conclusions.

Without doubt, the European Convention on Human Rights was never meant to advance the rights of persons with disabilities in particular, nor is it the most suitable instrument for this purpose. It is not disputed that the Convention protects the rights of persons with disabilities on the same footing as any other persons and that under Article 14, as well as Protocol 12, all discrimination against them is prohibited. At the same time it is clear that the Convention, as a civil rights instrument first and foremost, is not a particularly effective instrument to address the specific needs of persons with disabilities. It is only within the framework of civil rights, as opposed to social rights, that this can be offered.

On the other hand it has been shown above that the Court has been fairly responsive to the special needs and vulnerable situation of the disabled within the narrow framework the Convention offers for this purpose. This is particularly true as regards Articles 3 and 5, and to some extent Article 8, of the Convention. In relation to other rights the cases are few and the contribution of the Court has been marginal. In addition the direct relevance of these cases for persons with disabilities is unclear, although disabled persons have been involved in the proceedings.

There is however another aspect to this. Although the Court is primarily involved in the application and interpretation of the Convention it is well known that the Court has repeatedly referred to other international instruments in its case law. Despite the regional nature of the Convention as a European instrument and the strong emphasis the Court has laid on autonomous interpretation of the Convention terminology and provisions, the Court is unavoidably often engaged in assessing the relevance of other international instruments, especially in the field of human rights, for the interpretation and application of the Convention. Numerous cases can be referred to in support of this and ample legal literature exists on the topic.[48] As concerns Article 3, which has also

[48] See for example Lucius Caflisch: "The Protection of Human Rights in Europe and the General Rules of International Law", in *Liber amicorum Cançado Trindade*. Eds. Renato Zerbini *et al.* Porto Alegre: Fabris 2005, pp. 537–558 and by the same author "Le Droit International et

shown to be relevant in relation to Article 5, the Court has frequently utilized other international instruments on this and related topics, as well as decisions of international bodies and regional tribunals, in its determination of the contents and limits of Article 3.[49] This is also true as regards Article 8, where the UN Convention on the Rights of the Child and the Hague Convention on the Civil Aspects of International Child Abduction ("the Hague Convention") have had a noticeable effect.[50]

The references made in the earlier paragraph are only but a few examples of the relevance of other international instruments when interpreting and applying the European Convention on Human Rights. This raises questions as to the possible future implications of the new UN Convention on the Rights of Persons with Disabilities for the application of the Convention in cases concerning persons with disabilities. This can in principle happen in relation to all the Convention rights. By a way of examples one could mention the possible relevance of Article 9 (accessibility) and Article 20 (mobility) of the UN Disability Convention to the interpretation of Article 8 of the Convention.[51] One could also mention Article 21 (freedom of expression and access to information) of the UN Disablity Convention providing i.a. that State Parties shall take appropriate measures to ensure that persons with disabilities can exercise their freedom of expression and opinion.[52] This could possibly have an effect on the interpretation and application of Article 10 of the Convention and lead to a positive obligation for states to adopt special measures in order to enable disabled persons to enjoy the rights under Article 10 fully. Further, Article 24 (education) of the UN Disability Convention may also have a relevance for the future application of Article 2, Protocol 1 of the Convention.

La Cour européenne des Droits de l'Homme", in *Dialogue entre juges*, Cour européenne des Droits de l'Homme, Conseil de l'Europe 2007, pp. 23–40. Christos L. Rozakis: "The European Convention of Human Rights as an International Treaty", in *Mélanges en l'honneur de Nicolas Valticos: droit et justice*. Ed. Dupuy, R.-J. Paris: Pedone 1999, pp. 497–508.

[49] See for example: *Soering v. the United Kingdom* (application no. 14038/88) of 7 July 1989, *Chahal v. the United Kingdom* (application no. 22414/93) of 15 November 1996, *Selmouni v. France* (application no. 25803/94) of 28 July 1999, *Al-Adsani v. the United Kingdom* (application no. 35763/97) of 21 November 2001.

[50] As concerns the International Convention on the Rights of the Child from 20 November 1989, see for example *Siliadin v. France* (application no. 73316/01) of 26 July 2005. As concerns the Hague Convention of 25 October 1980 on the civil aspects of international child abduction see for example *Iosub Caras v. Romanina* (application no. 7198/04) of 27 July 2006.

[51] See here *Botta v. Italy, supra* note 28. See also Article 30 of the UN Disability Convention (Particicpation in cultural life, recreation, lesure and sport).

[52] See also Article 29 of the UN Disability Convention (participation in political and public life).

At this stage this is of course unclear, both with regard to if and to what extent the UN Disability Convention will have relevance for the interpretation of the Convention. This will depend *i.a.* on how many of the Contracting Parties to the Convention will in the end ratify the UN Disability Convention and the reference of applicants, or their representatives, to it in their submissions to the Court. Based on past experiences it should in any case not be excluded that the UN Convention will in the future find its way into the case law of the Court. In that way it may help in further strengthening the rights of individuals with disabilities within the relatively narrow framework the Convention offers for such protection, and help in further specifying the obligations of the Contracting States.

Extracting Protection for the Rights of Persons with Disabilities from Human Rights Frameworks: Established Limits and New Possibilities

*Colm O'Cinneide**

1 *Introduction: What Makes the UN Convention on the Rights of Persons With Disabilities Special?*

The UN Convention on the Rights of Persons with Disabilities (hereafter 'the UN Convention')[1] is a major development in international human right law for two different reasons. Firstly, the Convention marks the point at which the dynamic growth of human rights law since 1945 begins to take disability rights seriously. Rowena Daw has commented that '[D]isability was, until very recently, the forgotten dimension of human rights and unacknowledged as a subject for a right to equality.'[2] The UN Convention transforms this situation by giving disability rights a firm and fixed place within the constellation of international human rights.[3] Secondly, the Convention is also notable for how it articulates

---

* Senior Lecturer in Law, University College London; member of the European Committee of Social Rights.

1 For the text of the UN Convention and an invaluable archive of the negotiations that lead up to the final text, see http://www.un.org/disabilities/.

2 See Rowena Daw, *The Impact of the Human Rights Act on Disabled People* (London: Disability Rights Commission, 2003).

3 The Convention has adopted key elements of the 'social model' and 'universal design' approaches to questions of disability, incorporating these within a rights framework. For analysis of the 'social model' of disability, see C. Barnes, 'A Working Social Model? Disability, Work and Disability Politics in the Twenty-First Century' (2000) 20 *Critical Social Policy* 441; C. Barnes, G. Mercer, T. Shakespeare, *Exploring Disability: A Sociological Introduction* (Malden, MA: Polity Press, 1999); B. Hughes and K. Paterson, 'The Social Model of Disability and the Disappearing Body: Towards a Sociology of Impairment' (1997) 12 *Disability and Society* 325–340; M. Priestley, 'Constructions and Creations: Idealism, Materialism and Disability Theory' (1998) 13 *Disability & Society* 75. For analysis of the 'universal design' approach, see J.E. Bickenbach, S. Charrerji, E.M. Badley and T.B. Ustun, 'Models of Disablement, Universalism and the International Classification of Impairments, Disabilities and Handicaps' (1999) 48 *Social Science &*

and gives effect to a distinctive vision of the rights of the individual within society. This differs in important respects from how the relationship between individual rights and an individual's place within society is often understood when other human rights instruments are being interpreted and applied. As such, the Convention's importance extends beyond its impact in the specific area of disability rights: it represents a significant new development in international human rights law in general.

What is this distinctive vision which the Convention embodies? Its text imposes various positive obligations upon ratifying states to ensure that persons with disabilities are provided with the minimum level of state support and assistance that will enable them to maintain a dignified existence. For example, Article 9 requires states to take 'appropriate measures' to ensure persons with disabilities can access, on an equal basis with others, the physical environment, transport, communications and other forms of facilities and services open to or provided to the public.[4] The Convention therefore adopts a particular conceptual view of the state's role in securing individual human rights as involving more than simple abstinence from the abuse of individual civil and political rights. Instead, the state is expected to play an active role in creating the social conditions necessary for individuals to be treated with dignity. The vision of rights embodied in the Convention is thus based upon the recognition that individuals with disabilities are not self-sufficient monist entities, but rather depend upon collective social action to make provision for their basic rights.

The Convention therefore articulates a very different vision of rights from that embedded in the US Constitution, for example, where individual rights are primarily conceived as imposing negative constraints upon the state in order to maximise individual autonomy.[5] However, important differences also exist between the view taken of the purpose of individual rights in the Convention, and how the role of individual rights is conceptualised within the major international and regional civil and political rights instruments, such as the European Convention on Human Rights (ECHR) and equivalent national rights instruments, such as the Canadian Charter of Fundamental Rights and Freedoms.

Medicine, 1173–1187; I.K. Zola, 'Towards the necessary universalising of a disability policy' (1989) 67 (Supp. 2, Pt. 2) *Millbank Quarterly* 401.

[4] See also e.g. the 'general obligations' upon states parties set out in Article 4, and the rehabilitation provisions in Article 26 of the Convention.

[5] For criticism of the reluctance of the US constitutional system to embrace the idea of positive rights, see S. Brandes, 'The Negative Constitution: A Critique' (1990) 88 *Mich. L. Rev.* 2271. For a defence of the 'negative constitution', see F. Cross, 'The Error of Positive Rights' (2001) 48 *UCLA Law Review* 857.

These rights instruments dominate discussion of human rights and tend to represent the 'mainstream' of rights ideology.[6] Unlike the US Constitution, these 'mainstream' rights instruments usually recognise that states may be subject to positive obligations to take particular steps to ensure respect for individual rights. However, within this 'mainstream', positive obligations are treated as useful but limited supplementary tools, only applicable when necessary to remove obstacles which prevent self-sufficient individuals from freely exercising their personal autonomy.[7] These rights instruments conceptualise the individual in essentially liberal terms as an autonomous being capable of operating in isolation from the state: civil and political rights are designed to protect this individual from unjustified state interference, and the state is only placed under a positive obligation to assist this independent individual in certain very specific contexts. Positive obligations are very much the exception to the standard negative form of rights protection.

In contrast, the Convention recognises that not all individuals are self-sufficient, inherently autonomous agents. Many persons of disabilities must rely upon the state to provide them with the essentials of a meaningful and dignified life.[8] The Convention confers legally enforceable rights upon individuals in such situations: it requires a focus on individual entitlement rather than just a general

[6] Following the Vienna Declaration of 1993 which recognised the indivisibility and interdependence of human rights, objections could be made to describing the civil and political rights instruments as the 'mainstream' of rights ideology. However, the reality is that the international and regional civil and political rights frameworks, such as the ECHR, tend to dominate popular understanding of rights. They are also the most developed, most effective and most successful rights instruments, both at international and at national level. The Vienna Declaration's grand rhetoric is largely aspirational.

[7] For the growing development of the concept of positive obligations in international human rights law, see the excellent selection of papers in S. Borelli and D. Geer (eds.), *Positive Obligations of States and the Protection of Human Rights*, 15(4) *Interights Bulletin* August 2006, available at http://www.interights.org/view-document/index.htm?id=248 (last accessed 4th February 2008). For the development of positive obligations in the ECHR case-law, see A. Mowbray, *The Development of Positive Obligations Under the European Convention on Human Rights by the European Court of Human Rights* (Oxford: Hart, 2004). For an argument that the recognition of positive obligations constitutes a radical shift in human rights law and theory, see S. Fredman, 'Human Rights Transformed: Positive Duties and Positive Rights' (2006) *Public Law* 498–520.

[8] Please note that the argument is *not* being made here that persons with disabilities lack individual autonomy or the capacity to act autonomously: as analysed by 'social model' approaches to disability, persons with disabilities face structural social obstacles to exercising their inherent autonomy and thus are therefore dependant on state action to protect their individual rights, in the same way that all disadvantaged groups and indeed all persons in one way or another are also dependent upon state action to provide for at least some of their basic needs.

group-based welfare approach,[9] and conceptualises this entitlement as a matter of individual right rather than as a question of the state exercising benevolence through social welfare provision.[10] In contrast, most mainstream human rights instruments make little or no provision for legally enforceable rights to apply in such relationships of dependence: as their concern is with protecting the autonomous individual, they lack focus when it comes to individuals who are dependant on others, tending to treat the well-being of such individuals as subsumed within the utilitarian process of collective provision through social welfare mechanisms, or at best as a matter for vague and usually unenforceable socio-economic rights protection.

Therefore, the UN Convention embodies a distinct and different vision of the rights that individuals may claim from the state. Persons with disabilities are seen as entitled to claim the essential support that will enable them to live a dignified life and to maximise their autonomy as a matter of positive right. Michael Stein has argued that the Convention therefore gives textual shape to what he describes as the 'disability human rights paradigm'.[11] This paradigm '[recalibrates] the aim of human rights discourse as a response to individual need', directed towards developing the 'capacity of all individuals on the basis of their inherent worth and potential'.[12]

Stein argues that the great strength of this disability rights paradigm as reflected in the Convention lies in how it emphasises the entitlement of all individuals to full social, political and economic participation in society, thus bridging the current intellectually unsustainable gap between 'first-generation' civil and

---

9 Regarding persons with disabilities as a generic class who constitute passive recipients of state welfare has been described as the historical 'welfare model' of disability. When used to shape policy, this welfare model has had a very questionable historical record: all too often, its application in practice has been characterised by broad-brush utilitarian decision-making, the denial of active agency to disabled individuals and a readiness to base policy and resource allocation upon implicit assumptions about the dependency and passivity of persons with disabilities. See the discussion in L. Waddington, 'Evolving Disability Policies: From Social Welfare to Human Rights: An international trend from a European perspective' (2001) 19 *Netherlands Quarterly of Human Rights* 141.

10 Martti Koskenniemi has described with his customary eloquence the shift in impact that comes with making an individual rights claim, as distinct from relying passively upon welfare allowances or charity: 'To claim a right is different from claiming a benefit or appealing to charity. It is to invoke that which applies to all, against the violence that the particular act is. To be able to say that . . . the deprivation one suffers is a "human rights violation" is to lift a private grievance to the level of public law violation, of concern not only to the victim but to the community.' See M. Koskenniemi, 'Between Empire and Legal Formalism', paper delivered at Recife, Brazil, 18 May 2003, available at http://www.helsinki.fi/eci/Publications/MRecife.pdf (last accessed 4th February 2008.

11 See Michael A. Stein, 'Disability Human Rights' (2007) 95 *California L. Rev.* 75–122.

12 *Ibid.*

political rights and 'second-generation' socio-economic rights which continues to plague human rights discourse. This paradigm also concentrates attention upon the needs of the specific individual and the active role of the state.[13] This is why Stein sees the disability rights paradigm as capable of opening up fresh and dynamic new directions in human rights law and policy.[14]

The Convention is not wholly alone in this respect. The UN Convention on the Rights of the Child contains similar positive obligations which establish individual rights in relationships of dependency. Also, the UN Covenant on Economic, Social and Cultural Rights is based upon the recognition of the interdependence of the individual and the state. The often neglected and overlooked European Social Charter, the social rights instrument that is the counterpart to the ECHR, also translates the interdependency of the individual and society into the language of rights. However, the Convention in its detail, range and precision goes further than these other instruments.

To understand how the Convention, and, to a lesser extent, the Social Charter and other instruments depart from much of the 'mainstream' of human rights law, it is necessary first of all to examine the limitations of some of the major rights instruments that form this mainstream. This will be done by considering the extent to which such instruments, and in particular the ECHR, provide protection for persons with disabilities.[15] This can be seen as an acid test of the functioning of rights instruments: persons with disabilities are among the most disadvantaged and marginalised in contemporary society, both in terms of the denial of social rights but also civil and political rights, so well-functioning rights

---

[13] In contrast, the UN Convention on the Elimination of Racial Discrimination (CERD) and the Convention on the Elimination of Discrimination Against Women (CEDAW) are more concerned with preventing discrimination against particular groups than establishing individual entitlements for members of those groups. The disability rights theorist, Tom Shakespeare, has suggested that adopting similar group and identity-focussed approaches for disability as is done to promote race and gender equality may be questionable on that basis that analogy between disability and gender/race/sexuality can be misleading. See T. Shakespeare, 'Disability, Identity And Difference', in C. Barnes and G. Mercer, *Exploring The Divide* (Leeds: The Disability Press, 1996): see also the discussion in P. Alldridge, 'Locating Disability Law' (2006) 59 *Current Legal Problems* 289–318, at n. 74.

[14] Sandra Fredman has made a similar argument that disability discrimination legislation similar to that contained in the US Americans With Disabilities Act 1990, the UK Discrimination Act 1995 and the European Union Framework Equality Directive 2000/78/EC can and should show the way forward for the development of stronger and more effective anti-discrimination legislation across the various equality grounds in general. See S. Fredman, 'Disability Equality: A Challenge to the Existing Anti-Discrimination Paradigm?, in A. Lawson and C. Gooding (eds.) *Disability Rights in Europe: From Theory to Practice* (Oxford: Hart, 2005), 199–218.

[15] The ECHR is selected for special attention because it this stage it is the most developed transnational rights framework in the world and is also without doubt the most successful such framework.

systems should be able to address their claims. However, as discussed below, it appears that mainstream human rights frameworks often only provide meaningful protection for persons with disabilities whose claims are more or less analogous to other well-established rights claims and can be analysed in terms of protecting pre-existing individual autonomy, or who are demanding *equal* treatment.

In contrast, mainstream rights frameworks do not yield much useful protection for persons with disabilities who must make claims for *exceptional* treatment, or positive provision as part of a relationship of partial dependence upon the state. Instruments such as the Convention, by acknowledging the interdependence of all individuals with social and state structures, make it easier to bring a rights-based perspective to bear in such cases. This is why they offer an invaluable new perspective based around a modified concept of the place of the individual within society, which may over time influence the mainstream and generate ground-breaking new paths in the terrain of human rights.

2 *The Limits of the 'Mainstream' Civil and Political Rights Frameworks*

Human rights frameworks are like any other legal system: their content is influenced by the historical circumstances of their birth, growth and development, as well as by the nature of the institutions that interpret and apply them, the political and social context in which they exist, and the (often inchoate and uncertain) normative values that are supposed to underpin them. The major international and regional human rights frameworks grew out of the experience of the Second World War and the Cold War, and subsequently apartheid and the civil rights movement. As a result, these rights frameworks were heavily influenced in their development by the inevitable concern with the civil and political rights of the individual and with securing what Isaiah Berlin described as 'negative liberty', i.e. the protection of individual autonomy in the face of totalitarian worldviews who denied the importance or necessity of personal autonomy.[16]

The 'positive liberties' of the individual, as such freedom from want, were initially recognised in the Universal Declaration of Human Rights, where their presence probably owed much to the rhetoric of the New Deal in the United States and Roosevelt's acknowledgement of the 'Four Freedoms'. Subsequently,

[16] I. Berlin, 'Two Concepts of Liberty', in I. Berlin, *Four Essays on Liberty* (Oxford: Oxford University Press, 1969). Berlin's analysis is often excessively simplified by commentators: in particular, his acceptance of the potential importance of welfare and equality principles as counterweights to negative liberty is often overlooked. For a useful analysis of the extensive debate on negative and positive liberty, see I. Carter, 'Negative and Positive Liberty', *Stanford Encyclopedia of Philosophy*, last revised 8th October 2007, available at http://plato.stanford.edu/entries/liberty-positive-negative/ (last accessed 5th February 2008).

these positive liberties were given formal legal status in the International Covenant on Economic, Social and Cultural Rights (ICESCR) and the European Social Charter. They were also protected via the development of the Western European and Canadian welfare states and the (more fragmented) social protection systems introduced in the USA and other states.

State welfare provision was built around the idea of the mutual interdependence of all individuals within society: it was not opposed to the idea of individual autonomy, but rather saw individual autonomy as best secured through collective provision. However, there was widespread consensus that the emerging social welfare systems were an unsuitable area for judicial intervention to protect individual rights. For example, in the UK, the views of Jennings and others to the effect that the state should be given a free hand when it chose to intervene in social and economic matters was (and still is in certain quarters) highly influential.[17] Similarly, in the USA, the discrediting of the *Lochner*-era jurisprudence of the US Supreme Court, with its readiness to interfere with state regulation in the interests of preserving individual autonomy (in the form of a right to contractual freedom), resulted in a broad consensus that rights-based individual legal remedies should not be applied in the socio-economic sphere.[18]

This concern that state intervention should not be impeded by legal constraints became linked with the perception that international rights mechanisms should be primarily concerned with securing 'negative liberty' in the form of the core civil and political rights rather than its positive counterpart. Negative liberty was easier to define and involved intervention to restrain the power of the state, a task that legal mechanisms were seen as capable of performing. In contrast, protecting positive liberty was seen (and often still is) as an inherently more problematic task, involving serious questions about how to define the scope of individual rights to positive provision, and what a state should be expected to do or not to do in ensuring enjoyment of such rights.

As a result, the task of defining the scope of the state's role in securing positive liberty was left to political processes and a dichotomy was introduced into both national law and the emerging international human rights framework. Individual autonomy was increasingly protected via legally enforceable civil and political rights instruments which protected negative liberty, while the broader question of what rights could individuals claim as mutually interdependent members of society was either classified as a contested political matter or addressed through

---

[17] See the analysis of 'green light' approaches to judicial review in C. Harlow and R. Rawlings, *Law and Administration* (London: Butterworths, 1997), Ch. 3.

[18] See the excellent discussion of this shift in H.J. Abraham and B.A. Perry, *Freedom and the Court: Civil Rights and Liberties in the United States* (7th ed.) (New York: Oxford University Press, 1998), Ch. 2.

lower-profile rights instruments such as the ICESCR and the European Social Charter. Indeed, neither of these instruments initially made any provision for an individual complaints process, again reflecting the idea that questions of positive provision by the state were matters of collective policy rather than of individual right.

However, as legal protection under civil and political human rights instruments expanded, the emerging case-law generated by the relevant enforcement bodies began to recognise that some positive provision by the state may often be necessary to secure fundamental liberties. For example, the European Court of Human Rights has imposed positive obligations upon states to take appropriate steps to protect the rights to fair trial,[19] privacy, home and family life,[20] non-discrimination[21] and life[22] amongst others.

This shift towards accepting that respect for core civil and political rights may require positive action on the part of the state is very important in many ways. It recognises that protecting individual autonomy, and the associated value of human dignity, may require positive measures on the part of the state. It also demonstrates the artificiality of the dichotomies that have been presumed to exist in the area of human rights between intervention and non-intervention, negative liberty and positive liberty, 'negative' protection against state interference as opposed to 'positive' state intervention.

However, the civil and political rights framework is still constructed around the archetype of the autonomous, free-standing individual, and directed at ensuring that this individual can enjoy the particular entitlements associated with independent and active participation in society – freedom of thought, expression and association, liberty, privacy and so on. Where positive provision is required, it is conceptualised as enabling autonomous individuals to be free to enjoy these specific rights. This means that most legal rights frameworks do not cope well with rights claims that seek to define what an individual is entitled to as part of their interdependent relationship with the state and society at large, as distinct from what they can claim to be necessary to enable them to maintain their autonomous freedom of action.

As a result, rights claims that are not predicated upon assumptions of individual self-sufficiency often face difficulties in finding a foothold within 'mainstream' civil and political rights instruments. Also, civil and political rights instruments often lack clear methods of assessing the validity of resource allocation or bureaucratic-expert decisions in contested areas of social policy. This is because

---

[19] See e.g. *Airey v. Ireland* (1979) 2 EHRR 305.

[20] See e.g. *X and Y v. Netherlands* (1985) 8 EHRR 235.

[21] See e.g. *Nachova v. Bulgaria* (2006) 42 EHRR 43, Grand Chamber.

[22] See e.g. *Jordan v. United Kingdom* (2001) 37 EHRR 52.

that such decisions require courts and rights enforcement bodies to define what constitutes an appropriate level of state support in a particular context for an individual dependant upon the state, which again is a relatively alien task for a rights framework designed to address questions as to whether interference with an individual's autonomy is justified or not.

3 *The Marginalisation of Disability within National and International Human Rights Frameworks*

These built-in limitations within mainstream rights frameworks mean that many disability rights claims will not readily fit within their conceptual structure. Claims by persons with disabilities that they should be entitled to a certain level of special support or accommodation will often constitute 'abnormal' claims for positive provision that cannot be readily assimilated within a framework designed to protect the self-sufficient autonomous individual. The exclusion of disability from the 'normal' construction and assumptions of social life is therefore often replicated even within legal and political rights discourse. Putting it in another way, the mainstream legal vocabulary of human rights struggles to cope with the articulation of disability rights claims.

Two additional factors also play a role in marginalising disability rights claims within the mainstream of legal enforcement of human rights. Firstly, to litigate a rights claim, individuals need to be willing and able to bring a legal action. However, many persons with disabilities are unable to initiate a human rights case, and the advocacy bodies that could act on their behalf are often over-stretched, under-funded and have other priorities than using uncertain and potentially costly legal routes. The difficulty with integrating disability rights claims within existing human rights frameworks also has a deterrent effect: in a Catch-22 cycle, claims are not brought because the potential for success is not clear in the absence of other successful claims, which in turn ensures a continuing absence of useful precedent and developed case-law.

Secondly, the marginalisation of disability rights is also reflected in the text and interpretation of international human rights legal instruments.[23] Prior to UN approval of the Convention, none of the major existing international human rights instruments included disability as one of the suspect forms of classification that are explicitly listed in their non-discrimination and equality clauses. For example, as with the major UN human rights treaties, Article 14 of the ECHR

---

[23] See G. Quinn, T. Degener *et al.*, *Human Rights and Disability: The Current Use and Future Potential of United Nations Human Rights Instruments in the Context of Disability* (Geneva, UN High Commissioner for Human Rights, 2002).

does not explicitly prohibit unjustified discrimination on grounds of disability. Nor do most of these instruments make any express provision for disability rights within their text, with the partial exception of the Convention on the Rights of the Child (CRC), which uniquely contains a specific article requiring States Parties to recognize the rights of children with disabilities to enjoy "full and decent" lives and to participate in their communities, which however is hedged in with qualifiers.[24] Only the European Social Charter contains express provisions for the rights of all persons with disabilities: it is no coincidence that a rights instrument that emerged from the process of establishing the European welfare states and which is predicated upon the interdependent relationship of the individual and the state does recognise disability rights, even if it initially only did so in a limited manner.

Of course, the 'generalist' UN human rights instruments are perfectly capable of being interpreted to accommodate disability rights claims.[25] The UN Committee for Economic, Social and Cultural Rights, in their General Comment 5 on the ICESCR, have indicated that both the UN Covenants should be interpreted as treating discrimination on grounds of disability as coming within the 'other status' grounds of the anti-discrimination and equality clauses.[26] However, the lack of clarity and definition when it came to the specific needs of persons with disabilities and their relationship to the international human rights structures is precisely why it has been necessary to introduce the new UN Convention.[27] This

[24] See Art. 23(1) CRC.

[25] See e.g. G. Quinn, 'The International Covenant on Civil and Political Rights and Disability: A Conceptual Framework', in T. Degener & Y. Koster-Dreese (eds.) *Human Rights and Disabled Persons: Essays and Relevant Human Rights Instruments* (Doredrecht, Martinus Nijhoff, 1995) 69. See also in the same book, P. Alston, 'Disability and the International Covenant on Economic, Social, and Cultural Rights', in *id.*, at 94; M. Nowak & W. Suntinger, 'The Right of Disabled People Not to be Subjected to Torture, Inhuman and Degrading Treatment or Punishment', in *id.*, at 117; T. Hammarberg, 'The Rights of Disabled Children: The UN Convention on the Rights of the Child', in *id.*, at 147.

[26] General Comment No. 5, *Persons With Disabilities*, (Eleventh Session, 1994), U.N. Doc E/1995/22. Paragraph 15 of the General Comment defines disability-based discrimination under the ICESCR as including 'any distinction, exclusion, restriction or preference, or denial of reasonable accommodation based on disability which has the effect of nullifying or impairing the recognition, enjoyment or exercise of economic, social or cultural rights.' The General Comment suggests the adoption of anti-discrimination legislation: 'in order to remedy past and present discrimination, and to deter future discrimination, comprehensive anti-discrimination legislation in relation to disability would seem to be indispensable in virtually all states parties.'

[27] In a 1993 report, a UN Special Rapporteur cautioned that human rights abuses against disabled persons would likely continue without redress or sufficient attention in the absence of any specific treaty protection for disability rights. See L. Despouy, *Report on Human Rights and Disabled Persons* (Geneva: United Nations, 1993), paras. 280–81.

lack of explicit protection taken with all the other factors discussed above explains the marginalisation of disability rights within the human rights mainstream.

This means that individual litigants, campaigning organisations, disability rights activists and human rights lawyers need to engage in a process of 'extraction', whereby they try to extract protection for the rights of persons with disabilities from the language and established case-law of these human rights frameworks. This is not an impossible task: protection of other types of rights claims has gradually been 'extracted' over the years by determined litigants, notwithstanding express textual provisions.[28] Some success has been obtained: the terrain of established human rights frameworks has not been completely fruitless from a disability rights perspective.[29]

However, disability rights claims cannot usually rely upon the development of good standards in particular jurisdictions to serve as a model: unlike the case for other rights claims, few if any jurisdictions have evolved a comprehensive system of protecting disability rights via legal rights frameworks. Therefore, this process of extraction has to proceed without the ability to rely on what commentators have described as the 'transnational conversation' of constitutional and human rights courts, or the emerging 'common law' of human rights.[30] Experience has also shown that 'extraction' of disability claims will often only succeed if these claims are essentially similar or analogous to well-established types of claims rooted in the mainstream of civil-political rights analysis. As discussed above, rights claims that depart from this standard model into the uncertain landscape of resource allocation, social policy and compensation for the lack of free-standing individual autonomy will rarely succeed. Therefore, the process of extracting rights protection for persons with disabilities from human rights frameworks can be very difficult.

This can be seen at UN level. From 1994 to 2004, seventeen disability-related individual complaints were made to UN human rights monitoring committees, of which thirteen were declared inadmissible.[31] In general, the case-law of the UN monitoring bodies has yielded little tangible benefits for persons

[28] See Charles R. Epp, *The Rights Revolution: Lawyers, Activists, and Supreme Courts in Comparative Perspective* (Chicago: University of Chicago Press, 1998) for an account of the role of activist groups and lawyers in expanding the scope of constitutional rights instruments.

[29] See Rowena Daw, n. 2 above.

[30] See C. McCrudden, 'A Common Law of Human Rights?' (2000) 20(4) *OJLS* 499–532. See also B. Ackerman, 'The Rise of World Constitutionalism' (1997) 83 *Virginia Law Review* 771; D. Barak-Erez, 'The international law of human rights and constitutional law: a case study of an expanding dialogue' (2004) 4 *International Journal of Constitutional Law* 611; B. Markesinis and J. Fedtke, 'The Judge as Comparativist' (2005) 80 *Tulane Law Review* 11 and the responses to their article in the same issue.

[31] See Stein, above at n. 11.

with disabilities, with the exception of the odd decision such as *Hamilton v. Jamaica*, where allegations of poor prison conditions which had a disproportionate effect on the applicant due to his disability were not contested by the Jamaican government.[32]

A similar pattern exists at national level. The US Bill of Rights has not been a particularly happy hunting-ground for disability rights activism, dating back to Oliver Wendell Holmes's justification of state-imposed sterilisation requirements in *Buck v. Bell* on the ground that '[t]hree generations of imbeciles are enough'.[33] For example, in *City of Cleburne v. Cleburne Living Centre, Inc.*,[34] the US Supreme Court decided that the standard non-intrusive level of 'rational' review under the Equal Protection Clause was sufficient where distinctions were made on the basis of mental disability, as distinct from the much more demanding 'intermediate scrutiny' or 'strict scrutiny' tests applied where decisions using gender or race classifications were challenged. While the decision on its facts was positive, with the Supreme Court striking down the particular planning decision at issue on the basis that it was the product of irrational prejudice against persons with mental disabilities, the *Cleburne* judgment established that distinctions made on the grounds of mental disability did not constitute a suspect category in US constitutional law.

This decision in *Cleburne* demonstrates perfectly how disability rights claims struggle to fit within existing rights frameworks. In its equal protection case-law, the Supreme Court draws relatively rigid demarcation lines between different methods of classification and different levels of review. This meant that the Court in *Cleburne* was faced with a stark choice as a result of its jurisprudence developed in other contexts: it had to determine whether classifications based upon mental disability were inherently suspect (thus deserving of strict scrutiny) or inherently acceptable (thus only requiring rational scrutiny). Confronted by this choice, fearing perhaps that strict scrutiny would be simply unworkable in the context of mental disability, and concerned as to how the US constitutional rights framework could set about the task of defining standards of appropriate state treatment of persons with mental disabilities, the Court applied its diluted rational review standard.[35] In other words, the disability rights claim in *Cleburne*

---

32 *Hamilton v. Jamaica,* communication No. 616/1995, Views adopted by the Committee on 28 July 1999 (CCPR/C/66/D/616/1995); see also *Francis v. Jamaica,* Communication No. 606/1994, Views adopted by the Committee on 3 August 1995 (CCPR/C/54/D/606/1994), para. 9.2.

33 274 U.S. 200, 207 (1927).

34 473 U.S. 432 (1985).

35 Alternative proposals have been put forward as to how the Supreme Court could have adopted a more nuanced form of 'intermediate' review and thereby evaded the stark choice it appeared compelled to make in *Cleburne.* Taking her cue from Marshall J.'s partial dissent in *Cleburne,*

did not fit into the standard equality rights paradigm, and as a consequence was granted a limited form of protection.[36]

This approach was confirmed in *Board of Trustees of the University of Alabama v. Garrett*,[37] where the majority of the Supreme Court confirmed that the 'rational review' standard of scrutiny should be applied to disability cases. The Court also went further and struck down the decision by the US Congress to permit individual litigants to sue the ordinarily immune sovereign federal states for failure to make reasonable accommodation in accordance with the requirements of the Americans with Disabilities Act 1990, on the basis that this level of protection was excessive when compared to the limited nature of the wrong sought to be remedied (the wrong being a failure to make reasonable accommodation, which in the view of the majority would often be capable of rational justification.)[38] This extraordinary decision perhaps reflects the discomfort frequently expressed by the US courts about what they at times perceive as the redistributive nature of reasonable accommodation requirements, which is linked to a broader discomfort with positive provision in general, reflecting the strong emphasis on negative liberty in US constitutional discourse.[39]

Martha Minow has argued for an approach that recognises group difference and the historical subordination of persons with mental disabilities: see M. Minow, 'When Difference Has Its Home: Group Homes for the Mentally Retarded, Equal Protection and the Legal Treatment of Difference' (1987) 22 *Harv. C.R.-C.L. L. Rev.* 111, 120–31. Silvers and Stein, in contrast, have argued for an approach that critically and skeptically examines assertions of meaningful difference between persons with disabilities and those without: see A. Silvers and M. Stein, 'Disability, Equal Protection, And The Supreme Court: Standing At The Crossroads Of Progressive And Retrogressive Logic In Constitutional Classification' (2002) 35(1&2) *University of Michigan Journal of Law Reform* 1–55.

[36] Note that in *Cleburne*, no issue about how to accommodate positive provision within the US constitutional framework with its strong 'negative rights' orientation arose, as the case concerned the denial of planning permission to applicants who wished to provide special accommodation for the disabled persons in question. This makes the Court's caution all the more striking.

[37] 531 U.S. 356 (2001).

[38] For a critique of *Garrett*, see J. Pirko, 'The Erosion of Separation of Powers Under The "Congruence And Proportionality" Test: From Religions Freedom To The ADA' (2001) 53 *Hastings Law Journal* 519.

[39] For discussion of the reluctance of US constitutional law to develop the concept of positive rights, see n. 5 above. For analysis of the judicial perception that reasonable accommodation is redistributionist in nature, see S.F. Befort and T. Holmes Donesky, 'Reassignment Under the Americans with Disabilities Act: Reasonable Accommodation, Affirmative Action, or Both?' (2000) 57 *Wash. & Lee Law Review* 1045; A. Silvers, 'Protection or Privilege? Reasonable Accommodation, Reverse Discrimination, and the Fair Costs of Repairing Recognition for Disabled People in the Workforce' (2005) 8 *Journal of Gender, Race and Justice* 561; M. Stein, 'Same Struggle, Different Difference: ADA Accommodations as Antidiscrimination' (2004) 153 *U. Pa. L. Rev.* 579.

4 *The Relationship between Canadian Substantive Equality Approaches and Disability Rights*

The Canadian experience has arguably been more positive. The original text of the section 15 of the Canadian Charter of Fundamental Rights and Freedoms, which protected the right to equal treatment, included no equality rights guarantee for persons with disabilities. The subsequent decision to include protection for persons with disabilities in s. 15 was taken only after considerable debate.[40] It has yielded some substantive results, but the impact of an equality analysis under s. 15 is inevitably limited by the usual factors that inhibit the protection of disability rights within mainstream legal rights frameworks.

In the Canadian Supreme Court decision in *Eaton v. Brant (County) Board of Education*,[41] there was an important recognition of both the importance of reasonable accommodation of the special needs of persons with disabilities as a method of ensuring participation in society, and of the essential validity of the social model of disability. However, the Court rejected the argument that s. 15 could be read as establishing a presumption in favour of integrated education for children with disabilities: the Court was unwilling to inquire in depth into a complex area of educational policy, again evidencing the reluctance of courts charged with the protection of civil and political rights to venture too far into the terrain of what constitutes appropriate positive provision.

However, in *Eldridge v. British Columbia (Attorney General)*,[42] the Supreme Court held that it constituted unequal treatment contrary to s. 15 of the Charter to refuse to fund sign-language interpretation that was necessary for person with hearing disabilities to access medical services. The Court stressed that the entrance of disabled persons 'into the social mainstream has been conditional upon their emulation of able-bodied norms…', and emphasised that 'the appellants…ask only for equal access to services that are available to all'.[43] This decision in many ways represents the high-water mark thus far in how disability rights claims are handled within national human rights frameworks. The Court interpreted the Charter as requiring the accommodation by the state of the special needs of hearing impaired individuals, thereby showing a willingness to intervene in resource allocation decisions and to find that a denial of funding constituted unequal treatment.

---

[40] See the historical overview in A.H. Neufeldt, 'Disability in Canada: An Historical Perspective', in H. Enns and A.H. Neufeldt (eds.), *In Pursuit of Equal Participation: Canada and Disability at Home and Abroad* (Concord, Ontario: Captus, 2003), 22–80.

[41] [1997] 1 S.C.R. 241.

[42] [1997] 3 S.C.R. 624.

[43] *Ibid.*, para. 92.

Nevertheless, *Eldridge* could be seen as marking perhaps the furthest point to which mainstream rights frameworks can be stretched to accommodate disability rights claims. In *Eldridge*, the resource allocation necessary to enable the hearing impaired individuals to access these services was comparatively minor. The positive provision required by the state was therefore a question of reasonable accommodation to enable individuals to access, on an equal basis, services which were open to all. No large-scale special provision was required, nor did the claim seek the provision of special medical or social services that were only required by persons with disabilities. In other words, *Eldridge* was a decision that turned on whether to remove discriminatory barriers that obscured access to health services by autonomous individuals: it was clearly analogous to situations where the Canadian courts had granted relief in non-disability cases.[44]

This is not to downplay the importance of *Eldridge*. It shows how disability rights claims can succeed within mainstream rights frameworks. It demonstrates that equality arguments can be useful in opening up equal access for persons with disabilities to common social goods. In the wake of *Eldridge*, a strong readiness to scrutinise social norms for unjustified limitations which prevent equal treatment for disabled persons has been consistently present in the Canadian Supreme Court's case-law.[45] However, attempts to stretch *Eldridge* into new terrain have met with mixed success. The Canadian courts have been less eager to scrutinise a failure to provide special treatment for persons with disabilities seeking special treatment.[46] Canadian legal protection against discrimination on

---

[44] This point is well made in I. Grant & J. Mosoff, 'Hearing Claims of Inequality: *Eldridge v. British Columbia (A.G.)*' (1998) 10 C.J.W.L. 229.

[45] See e.g. in *R. v. Pearson* (1994) 36 CR (4th) 343 (British Columbia CA), where the British Columbia Court of Appeal affirmed a lower court's extension of a hearsay admissibility rule to an alleged sexual assault victim whose disability precluded him from giving a full, articulate account of the assault. In *British Columbia (Superintendent of Motor Vehicles) v. British Columbia (Council of Human Rights)* [1999] 3 S.C.R. 868 (known as '*Grismer Estate*'), the appellant's eyesight was impaired by a stroke, and the Superintendent of Motor Vehicles assumed, without any individual testing, that this made him sufficiently visually impaired so to disqualify him from holding a driver's licence. The Court held that under the relevant anti-discrimination legislation, the appellant was entitled to an individual test to determine whether the impairment did in fact exist to the degree alleged. For a useful discussion of the approach adopted by the Canadian courts, see M. David Lepofsky, 'The Charter's Guarantee of Equality to People with Disabilities – How Well is it Working?' (1998) 16 *Windsor Yearbook of Access to Justice* 155.

[46] In *Granovsky v. Minister for Employment and Immigration* [2000] 1 S.C.R. 703, a social model analysis was applied again by the Supreme Court in finding that it was open for the federal government to relax a pension contribution requirement for permanently disabled persons, but not for temporarily disabled persons. The Court considered that the differential treatment in question served to ameliorate the position of those with severe and permanent disabilities, while the failure to grant a similar waiver to those with temporary disabilities did not involve an attack on their dignity. In many ways, this approach was admirable, but the decision can

the basis of disability is certainly strong: however, even post-*Eldridge*, this rights jurisprudence is coming up against some of the constraints that appear to limit what can be achieved within conventional rights instruments based around the centrality of the concept of individual autonomy.[47]

5 *The Marginalisation of Disability Within the ECHR Jurisprudence*

A similar pattern of modestly successful extraction of rights protection for persons with disabilities ultimately running up against inherent limits can be seen in the disability rights case-law of the ECHR. Disability discrimination can clearly come within the somewhat stunted non-discrimination provision of the ECHR, Article 14, as it can clearly be deemed to constitute a 'personal status', thereby satisfying the litmus test for protection under the 'other status' limb of Article 14.[48] However, the European Court of Human Rights has yet to find a violation on this basis, and in general has heard very few cases where disability was an issue at all.[49] The principal area of exception to this general rule has been applications by patients involuntarily detained in psychiatric wards, as such patients are required (by the Convention jurisprudence) to have legal representation. In contrast, other categories of disabled persons may have great

be criticised for accepting without real analysis the federal government's case that those with temporary disabilities did not require special treatment: the absence of positive provision was accepted without substantial scrutiny, with the Court happier applying standard equality analysis than venturing into unfamiliar terrain.

47 Judith Mosoff has argued that the Canadian legislative human rights/anti-discrimination framework has persistently failed to provide remedies for severely disabled applicants: despite the useful steer given by the Supreme Court, the less the degree to which a disability complaint resembles other kinds of discrimination, the less likely a decision-maker is to accept the existence of discrimination. See J. Mosoff, 'Is the Human Rights Paradigm "Able" to Include Disability: Who's In? Who Wins? What? Why?' (2000) 26 *Queen's L.J.* 225–276.

48 The European Court of Human Rights appeared to accept that discrimination on the grounds of disability would constitute an 'other status' ground under Article 14 in *Botta v. Italy* (1998) 26 EHRR 241.

49 In his analysis of how the ECHR may affect the rights of disabled persons, Luke Clements notes that the Strasbourg Court has experienced a 'general dearth of complaints by disabled people.' See L. Clements and J. Read, 'The Dog That Didn't Bark: The Issue of Access to Rights under the European Convention on Human Rights', in A. Lawson and C. Gooding, *Disability Rights in Europe: From Theory to Practice* (Oxford: Hart, 2005): see also by the same authors, *Disabled People And European Human Rights: A Review Of The Implications Of The 1998 Human Rights Act For Disabled Children and Adults In The* UK (Bristol: Policy Press, 2003).

difficulty in obtaining legal advice and may have to overcome a range of financial, cultural and access impediments to actually bring an action.[50]

This is all the more striking in that the European Court of Human Rights has been to the forefront amongst national and international courts in recognising that respect for fundamental rights must entail some degree of positive provision on the part of the state.[51] However, the scope of these positive obligations remains limited and uncertain.[52] In the disability context, they appear to be confined in scope to where positive obligation is essential to protect the core of a civil-political right protected under the Convention, or an entitlement that has a 'direct and immediate link' to the enjoyment of these rights. Also, in framing the scope and extent of such positive obligations, the Court is slow to venture into the deep waters of resource allocation. Once again, the rule of thumb appears to be that disability rights claims that are similar or analogous to the conventional type of civil-political claim adjudication by the Court will have a chance of success: however, claims that go beyond this will rarely if ever succeed. The Convention protects the dignity of the autonomous individual: as a general rule, it does not extend to protect the semi-autonomous individual denied equality of social entitlement. As with the Canadian case-law, it appears that the more disabled a person is, and the greater their disability separates them from the model of the self-sufficient autonomous individual, the less existing rights frameworks can benefit them.

The Court has recognised that the failure to make special accommodation for a disabled person within state institutions, and in particular prisons, may give rise to an Article 3 breach, even where similar treatment of non-disabled persons would not. A person with a disability is entitled to the same minimal level of treatment and freedom from degradation that any other person is within state incarceration: this may require positive provision on the part of the state to prevent a fundamental denial of dignity. As with *Eldridge*, the emphasis is on ensuring equality of treatment and status. Therefore, in *Price v. the United Kingdom*,[53] Ms Price, a woman with a physical disability who used a wheelchair

---

[50] See A. Dimopoulos (2008) 71(1) *Modern Law Review* 145–158, reviewing P. Bartlett, O. Lewis and O. Thorold, *Mental Disability and the ECHR* (Leiden: Martinus Nijhoof, 2006): 'this book's careful analysis of the case-law may provoke the sobering realisation of how few cases brought by mentally disabled applicants have reached the ECHR...'

[51] It is notable that the key decision of *X and Y v. Netherlands* (1985) 8 EHHR 235, which saw the Court for the first time recognise that a state may be under a positive obligation to take action to protect core personal rights against abuses by third parties, involved an individual with learning difficulties.

[52] For the scope of positive obligations under the ECHR in general, see Mowbray, at n. 7 above.

[53] (2002) 34 EHRR 1285.

and was described by the ECtHR as 'four-limb deficient', was imprisoned on contempt charges for seven days in a cell without any modifications to accommodate a disabled person. She was forced to sleep in her wheelchair, with emergency buttons and light switches out of her reach and an inaccessible toilet: when finally given access to a toilet, she was left there for hours and undressed in front of male guards. The ECtHR found that this treatment constituted degrading treatment in violation of Article 3, even in the absence of intent to degrade, due to the nature of the treatment to which Ms Price was subject to in custody, and, in particular, the failure to treat her differently from others in order to prevent her suffering this treatment. A similar approach may be detected in *Keenan v. United Kingdom*,[54] where the Court held that a failure to provide appropriate medical care to a person diagnosed with acute schizophrenia and a known suicide risk constituted a breach of Article 3.

Respect for the dignity of disabled persons may therefore require positive provision that departs from standard norms of treatment but which is required to prevent them from being exposed to degrading treatment.[55] This principle is now well-established in the Strasbourg jurisprudence. However, the Court has been criticised for its reluctance to find a violation of Article 3 when authorities fail to provide adequate medical treatment, in particular psychiatric care.[56] Mowbray suggests that this may reflect the poor level of such care throughout Europe, and the unwillingness of the Court to demand radical shifts in the standard of care provided.[57] This perhaps reflects an unwillingness to demand substantial resource allocation of a nature that goes beyond accommodating isolated cases where persons with disabilities would be exposed to degrading treatment due to clear instances of state inattention or neglect. Palmer considers that *Price* and *Keenan* may mark a shift in this approach.[58] That remains to be seen: the *extent* to which states must provide special assistance to persons with disabilities, and in particular mental disabilities remains uncertain.

The *scope* of this requirement to make positive provision to prevent persons with disabilities being reduced to degradation is also unclear. All of the Court's Article 3 decisions have concerned a failure to accommodate basic needs while disabled persons are in confinement or in some way subject to the coercive power of the state. The Strasbourg court has not as yet recognised a right to have the basic needs of a disabled person accommodated *in general*, i.e outside

54 (2001) 33 EHRR 913.

55 See also Application No. 23636/94, *PM v. Hungary*, Decision of 21 May 1997, ECommHR.

56 See E. Palmer, *Judicial Review, Socio-economic Rights and the Human Rights Act* (Oxford: Hart, 2007), pp. 72–3. See in particular the judgment in *Aerts v. Belgium* (2000) 29 EHRR 50, which Palmer describes as 'unduly lenient'.

57 See Mowbray, at n. 7 above, 54.

58 See Palmer, at n. 56 above, 72–73.

of the scope of immediate state control. It is not at all clear whether there is a positive obligation to prevent persons with disabilities from becoming exposed to degradation due to a lack of welfare support or community support. This would considerably extend the scope of Article 3, perhaps stretching it beyond its established function and purpose and fundamentally altering the nature of the Article 3 right.[59] Therefore, the Court's Article 3 jurisprudence appears to view special provision for persons with disabilities as required when necessary to ensure an adequate level of treatment when that treatment is directly inflicted or controlled by the state. The Court has remained thus far within the established parameters of its civil-political role: the self-sufficient, autonomous individual is to be protected against degradation at the hands of the state, but this right has not become a free-floating entitlement to dignity or to be provided with the essentials of a dignified life in every aspect of life.

In applying the Article 8 right to private life, home life and family life, the Court has interpreted this right as protecting an extended notion of private life. In so doing, the Court has been prepared to accept that special provision for persons with disabilities may be required to vindicate their right to private life, home life and family life, and this may require positive provision over and above what would be ordinarily required from the state. This is again potentially very important. However, several disability cases that have attempted to use this Article 8 route have floundered, even as the Court has used them to affirm the *potential* availability of positive obligations under Article 8. The Court has again been unwilling to extend the scope of protection offered by Article 8 to include access to general social amenities, and even has also refused to find that access to social amenities even came within the general ambit of Article 8, so as to trigger the application of the equality provisions of Article 14.

In *Botta v. Italy*,[60] the disabled applicant was unable to gain access to the beach and the sea at a private bathing establishment due to its failure to provide the disabled facilities required by Italian law. The applicant claimed that the failure by the Italian State to take measures to remedy the omission by the private resort breached his right to a private life and the development of his personality under Article 8, as well as constituting discrimination contrary to Article 14. However, the Court held that the right asserted, namely the right to gain access to the beach and the sea at a place distant from his normal place of residence

[59] It should also be noted that the threshold of denial of dignity required to 'trigger' Article 3 is very high. See the definition of 'inhuman and degrading treatment' in *Pretty v. UK* (2002) 35 EHRR 245, para. 52: 'Where treatment humiliates or debases an individual showing lack of respect for, or diminishing, his or her human dignity or arouses feelings of fear, anguish or inferiority capable of breaking an individual's moral and physical resistance, it may be characterised as degrading and also fall within the prohibition of Article 3.'

[60] (1998) 26 EHRR 241.

during holidays, did not fall within the scope of Article 8, or even within its general ambit so as to engage Article 14. There was an insufficient 'direct and immediate link' between the entitlement claimed and the right asserted: access to general amenities was not directly linked to the enjoyment of the core right. Similarly, in *Zehnalová and Zehnal v. Czech Republic*,[61] the applicants alleged an infringement of their Article 8 and Article 14 rights on the basis that many public buildings were not equipped with access facilities for the disabled in violation of Czech law. The Court again held that the entitlement claimed did not come within the scope of Article 8 or of its general ambit, so neither Article 8 nor Article 14 was engaged.

Therefore, positive provision under Article 8 appears only to be available when necessary to permit individuals to enjoy the core essence of the Article 8 right: there must be a denial of positive provision that goes to the heart of private life, home life or family life, and therefore constitutes a 'direct and immediate link' to enjoyment of the right. *Botta* is important in that the Court indicated a willingness to recognise that a denial of positive support in a disability context could result in a violation: however, as yet, the 'direct and immediate link' has proved very difficult to satisfy.

Even where this link is satisfied, other considerations may limit the impact of this jurisprudence. In *Marzari v. Italy*,[62] the applicant suffered from a rare disease that at times required him to use a wheelchair. He complained that his Article 8 rights had been infringed, in that he had been evicted and that the alternative accommodation offered to him was not suitable, having regard to his special needs. The Court was prepared to contemplate that a direct and immediate link could be established in this case, but refused to review the decisions taken by the local authorities as to the adequacy of the accommodation offered to the applicant, observing that the authorities had offered to carry out further works to make the accommodation suitable. In these circumstances, the Court held that the local authorities could be considered to have discharged their positive obligations in respect of the applicant's right to respect for private life.

In *Sentges v. Netherlands*,[63] the applicant argued that the failure of the state to provide him with a robotic arm to enable him to compensate for his progressive muscular disorder was a violation of Article 8. The evidence was that the provision of this relatively expensive equipment would greatly improve his quality of life. However, the Court was again unwilling to review the resource allocation issues involved:

[61] Application No. 38621/97, Decision of 14th February 2002, ECtHR.
[62] (1999) 28 EHRR CD175.
[63] Application No. 27677/02, Decision of 18 July 2003, ECtHR.

> The Court has held that Article 8 may impose such positive obligations on a State where there is a direct and immediate link between the measures sought by an applicant and the latter's private life (see *Botta v. Italy*, cited above, § 34). However, Article 8 does not apply to situations concerning interpersonal relations of such broad and indeterminate scope that there can be no conceivable link between the measures the State is urged to take and an individual's private life each time an individual's everyday life is disrupted, but only in the exceptional cases where the State's failure to adopt measures interferes with that individual's right to personal development and his or her right to establish and maintain relations with other human beings and the outside world. It is incumbent on the individual concerned to demonstrate the existence of a special link between the situation complained of and the particular needs of his or her private life (*see Zehnalovà and Zehnal v. the Czech Republic* (dec. no. 38621/97, ECHR 2002-V).
>
> Even assuming that in the present case such a special link indeed exists... regard must be had to the fair balance that has to be struck between the competing interests of the individual and of the community as a whole and to the wide margin of appreciation enjoyed by States in this respect in determining the steps to be taken to ensure compliance with the Convention (see *Zehnalovà and Zehnal*, cited above). The margin of appreciation is even wider when, as in the present case, the issues involve an assessment of the priorities in the context of the allocation of limited State resources... In view of their familiarity with the demands made on the health care system as well as with the funds available to meet those demands, the national authorities are in a better position to carry out this assessment than an international court...

De Schutter distinguishes *Marzari* and *Sentges* from *Botta* and *Zehnalová*, on the basis that the former two cases involved personalised accommodations of considerable importance to the individuals concerned where the 'direct and immediate link' sought in *Botta* could hypothetically exist, whereas the latter two cases involved 'general measures for the benefit of an ill-defined community'.[64] However, while leaving the possibility of a successful claim open, the Court in both sets of cases was unwilling to provide a remedy. De Schutter identifies several key concerns that may underlie the Court's reluctance to grant a remedy in such Article 8 disability cases: in particular, he highlights the 'binary, all or nothing' nature of positive obligations, whereby the Court has to determine either that a positive provision is either required by the Convention or else that no entitlement exists, and the 'polycentric' nature of resource allocation decisions, whereby the interests of multiple parties may come into tension. He suggests that these concerns lie behind the Court's reluctance to intervene in resource allocation, and also explain the restrictive interpretation of the concept of 'direct

---

[64] O. De Schutter, 'Reasonable Accommodation and Positive Obligations in the European Convention on Human Rights', in A. Lawson and C. Gooding (eds.), *Disability Rights in Europe* (Oxford: Hart, 2005) 35–63, at 40.

and immediate link' adopted in *Botta*, which he regards as a 'domestication' of positive obligations.[65]

The rights to positive provision that persons with disabilities can 'extract' from Article 8 do appear very limited, in particular due to the narrow manner in which the 'direct and immediate link' test was applied in *Botta* and *Zehnalová*. The Court seems to presume that private life is not manifested in a sufficiently direct or immediate manner via participation in certain public spheres and facilities, such as the amenities at issue in *Botta*. The narrowness of this approach can be seen in the Court's unwillingness even to recognise that the denial of access in these cases touched upon the 'ambit' of Article 8, which would have triggered an equality analysis under Article 14.

In this respect, a very interesting contrast exists with the Court's decision in *Sidabras v. Lithuania*, where a ban on the employment of former members of the KGB in particular professions was held to violate Article 14 of the Convention. In this case, the Court was willing to find that the scope of these restrictions as to what the claimants could do in the public sphere of employment was so extensive as to impact upon their family and private lives, and therefore to come sufficiently within the ambit of Article 8 so as to trigger Article 14.[66] However, the extent of the exclusion from core social amenities involved in *Zehnalová* in particular could be said to be of a similar order as that at issue in *Siadabras*. Therefore, the scope of private life recognised in *Sidabras* appears to be out of step with *Botta* and *Zehnalová*. The concerns identified by De Schutter above seem to be resulting a very narrow interpretation of Article 8's scope in these key disability cases.

A good argument can be made that there are no sharp distinctions in kind between a successful Article 8 claim such as *Lopez Ostra v. Spain*,[67] where Article 8 was unjustifiably violated by a failure to take positive action to combat noise pollution, and *Sentges* or *Botta*. Both types of case involve claims for positive provision by the state to uphold the Article 8 'bundle' of privacy rights, which have been interpreted as protecting the 'space' necessary for the private development of the person. Securing access to key social facilities (the issue at stake in *Botta*), or treatment to provide social interaction (*Sentges*), could be argued to be almost as essential in the contemporary context to personal development as having a quiet home environment. However, claims such as *Sentges* or *Botta* either involve a widening of the concept of privacy and the linked idea of securing personal development, or require the Court to push further into areas

[65] *Ibid.*, 40–45.

[66] For an excellent analysis of this decision, see V. Mantouvalou, 'Work and Private Life: *Sidabras and Dziautas v. Lithuania*' (2005) 30(4) *ELR* 573, 581–82.

[67] (1994) 20 EHRR 277.

of resource allocation decision-making that are traditionally left in the hands of nation states. This is why they do not fit readily within the development of the jurisprudence.

The historical orientation of the Convention towards securing civil and political rights and the protection of the autonomous individual may again ultimately lie at the heart of the Court's reluctance to extend the scope of the Article 8 positive obligations in these cases. The case-law shows a clear preference for imposing positive obligations on a state to prevent activity which impedes upon a self-sufficient individual's enjoyment of their home (*Lopez Ostra*) than for requiring special provision involving substantial financial costs to expand the range of opportunities for a person with a disability to participate in society. Once again, disability rights claims that go beyond protection against discrimination or a failure to make basic accommodation struggle to find a place in the case-law generated by mainstream rights instruments such as the ECHR.

6 *The Potential for Extracting Greater Rights Protection for Persons with Disabilities from the ECHR*

However, within these limits, it is worth noting that the potential does exist for the ECHR case-law to accommodate a wider range of disability rights claims. The ground-breaking Article 14 decision of the Grand Chamber of the Court in *DH v. Czech Republic*,[68] may also see new terrain opened up for disability rights claims. In *D.H.*, the Grand Chamber reversed the earlier decision of the first instance Chamber which had considered that there was no evidence that Roma children had been actively discriminated against in the allocation of school places in the Czech system. On appeal, the Grand Chamber took the view that the statistical evidence presented by the applicants as to the extent of Roma segregation in the special schooling system placed the onus on the Czech government to justify the educational policies which had produced this outcome, which it failed to discharge. While the impact of the *D.H.* decision remains to be seen, it could yet come to be recognised as equivalent to the famous *Brown v. Board of Education of Topeka* decision of the US Supreme Court,[69] on the basis that it may signal a new readiness on the part of the Strasbourg Court to examine the substantive impact of apparently unobjectionable differences in treatment, to apply the objective justification test with rigour in equality cases and to shift the burden of roof where required. This may open up new possibilities for *Eldridge*-style substantive equality claims to be brought under the Convention.

---

[68] Application No. 57325/00, Judgment of 13th November 2007, Grand Chamber ECtHR.
[69] 347 U.S. 483 (1954).

There is also potential scope for further development in the Convention jurisprudence under Articles 3 and 8, especially given the Court's readiness to recognise the existence of positive obligations. De Schutter analyses various ways in which the Court might develop its case-law so as to enable it to scrutinise resource allocation decisions in this context. He suggests that the Court could find violations of Article 8 or 14 where a failure to make positive provision was not in compliance with the state's own domestic legal requirements, or violated international standards, or resulted from inadequate safeguards in decision-making or discriminatory policies. However, as he also notes, many of these factors were present in *Botta* and *Zehnalova* and did not generate a finding of a violation.[70]

More promisingly, De Schutter also suggests that the Article 3 requirement not to expose persons to inhuman and degrading treatment may be developed to ensure some protection for persons with disabilities against state neglect.[71] There is force in this argument. For example, *Price* and *Keenan* could readily be extended to require states not to expose persons with disabilities who are dependant upon state provision to degrading treatment. Individuals dependant upon state welfare provision may often have a mental or physical disability or be subject to the impact of extreme poverty, such as homelessness: in such cases, their situation is analogous to prisoners, as they are dependant on state provision, and therefore a failure in provision that results in degradation could readily be construed as violating Article 3.

There is also some equivalent scope for stretching the current case-law under Article 8. Protection under this Article could be applied in situations where a denial of positive provision was directly impacting upon a disabled person's enjoyment of home or family life, and where the resource allocation necessary to remedy that interference with Article 8 was capable of finite or specific delineation. This approach to the interpretation of Article 8 would be compatible with the *Botta* and *Sentges* decisions, and represent a modest extension of the Court's jurisprudence. It could also be seen as justified on the basis that the ECHR rights of individuals should be interpreted and applied against the background of the existence of state welfare provision throughout Europe.[72]

The potential of Articles 3 and 8 as tools to push for greater rights for disabled people in this manner can be seen in a series of recent English and Irish decisions, which have applied the ECHR jurisprudence in a similar manner as indicated above. In the English case of *R (Bernard) v. London Borough of Enfield*,[73] the

---

70 See De Schutter, at n. 64 above, 45–53.

71 *Ibid.*

72 See the dissenting opinion of Lord Bingham in *YL v. Birmingham City Council* [2007] UKHL 27, where this point is made strongly.

73 [2002] EWHC Admin 2282.

claimants were husband and wife, who had six children. The wife was severely disabled and confined to a wheelchair. The defendant local authority had provided the family with completely inadequate accommodation. The consequences for the family and for the mother in particular, were severe, with the mother living in very poor conditions. The claimants sought damages for breaches of Articles 3 and 8 of the Convention. With some hesitation, Sullivan J. concluded that the degree of severity of the claimants' predicament did not breach the Article 3 threshold. He held, however, that there was a clear breach of Article 8:

> I accept the defendant's submission that not every breach of duty under section 21 of the 1948 Act will result in a breach of Article 8. Respect for private and family life does not require the State to provide every one of its citizens with a house... However, those entitled to care under Section 21 [the relevant legislation, which requires special accommodation for severely disabled persons] are a particularly vulnerable group. Positive measures have to be taken (by way of community care facilities) to enable them to enjoy, so far as possible, a normal private and family life... Suitably adapted accommodation would not merely have facilitated the normal incidents of family life... It would also have secured her physical and psychological integrity. She would no longer have been housebound, confined to a shower chair for most of the day, lacking privacy in the most undignified of circumstances, but would have been able to operate as part of her family and as a person in her own right, rather than being a burden, wholly dependent upon the rest of her family. In short, it would have restored her dignity as a human being... The Council's failure to act on the September 2000 assessments showed a singular lack of respect for the claimant's private and family life. It condemned the claimants to living conditions which made it virtually impossible for them to have any meaningful private or family life for the purposes of Article 8.[74]

Sullivan J. awarded a considerable sum of damages to the claimants.[75] However, the Court of Appeal in *Anufrijeva v. Southwark*[76] adopted a more cautious approach to Article 8. It considered that the European Court of Human Rights' approach in *Botta* and *Marzari* had established that there were some circumstances in which a public authority was required to devote resources to make it possible for individuals to enjoy the right to privacy, family life and home life under Article 8. The Court went on to approve Sullivan J.'s decision in *Bernard*, but however indicated that Article 8 claims would have to fall within or come very close to the definition of inhuman and degrading treatment before a violation of the Convention could be established.[77] However, in the Irish case of *O'Donnell*

---

[74] *Ibid.*, at paras. 32–33.

[75] Sullivan J. assessed damages at £10,000 sterling, £8000 to the mother and £2000 to the father.

[76] [2003] EWCA Civ 1406.

[77] *Ibid.*, para. 43.

v. South Dublin County Council,[78] Laffoy J. adopted a similar approach to the interpretation of Article 8 as had Sullivan J. in *Bernard*, awarding relief to a elderly disabled couple who had again been provided with very inadequate living conditions. In these decisions, the 'direct and immediate link' required by *Botta* was satisfied: the failure of adequate state provision in these cases had violated the right of the persons in question to the enjoyment of their home and family life, and the necessary resources that should have been allocated were clearly definable and specific to the individual circumstances.

Note also the English case of *A v. East Sussex County Council*,[79] where two disabled persons were living in appalling conditions as a result of health and safety restrictions imposed by East Sussex County Council, which considerably restricted the ability of their state-supplied carers to engage in any form of manual lifting activities. Munby J. in his judgment considered that the limits on when these individuals could be lifted had produced a situation where their living conditions could be described as verging on 'degrading treatment' contrary to Article 3. He found that the local authority had to factor in due consideration for the human dignity of the claimants in setting out its health and safety policies, and ordered it to reassess its guidelines. This judgment gave disability rights campaigners a useful tool to push for better treatment for severely disabled persons.[80]

Therefore, it appears that at times that the ECHR may be capable of being interpreted so as to require positive provision where necessary to prevent degrading treatment caused by inadequate state support to individuals dependant upon this support, or where required to give effect to the Article 8 bundle of rights, if the resource allocation in question is distinct, clearly delineated and required in a specific individual case.[81] However, the extent to which the ECHR can be applied in this way is uncertain.[82] National courts may be more willing to stretch the Convention jurisprudence than the Strasbourg Court itself, given the concerns about its ever-escalating case-load. In addition, the common problem with mainstream rights frameworks needs ultimately to be faced. As with most other legally enforceable rights instruments, the ECHR's central focus remains

---

78 Unreported, Laffoy J., High Court, 22 May 2007.

79 [2003] EWCA Admin 167.

80 The Disability Rights Commission (DRC) in Britain used the *East Sussex* judgment as a lever to push for change in how severely disabled persons were treated by carers. For the use of the ECHR in general by the DRC, see Palmer, at n. 56 above, at pp. 298–300.

81 See also A. Lawson, 'Disability, Degradation and Dignity: the Role of Article 3 of the European Convention on Human Rights' (2006) 56(4) *Northern Ireland Legal Quarterly* 462.

82 In *R (BG) v. Medway Council* [2005] EWHC 1932, a very cautious approach was adopted to the application of the ECHR in this context. See also the Irish case of *Doherty v. South Dublin County Council* [2007] IEHC 4, where a similarly cautious approach was adopted to the application of Article 8 ECHR in the context of social housing.

securing the rights of the autonomous self-sufficient individual. There are strong arguments for suggesting that the Convention should be capable of ensuring that persons with disabilities who do not necessarily conform to this model are nevertheless entitled to positive provision to rescue them from degradation and the denial of core elements of their private lives. But this will require the Strasbourg Court to move beyond the narrow confines of the standard civil and political rights model.

Both the Canadian jurisprudence and the ECHR case-law contain the ingredients of a more developed approach: in Canada, this potential is to be found in the equality jurisprudence of the Supreme Court, and in the ECHR it is to be found in the potential scope of protection under Articles 3 and 8. Both systems have travelled some way down the path of recognizing positive obligations (unlike the case with the US for the most part). However, both systems are perhaps baulking on the threshold of going further. The UN Convention may yet give them a gentle prod over that threshold: however, disability rights at present remain marginalised in both systems, as they are throughout the mainstream of international and national human rights law.

7 *Giving Substance to the UN Convention on the Rights of Persons with Disabilities – Applying 'Minimum Core' and 'Progressive Realisation' Analysis in the Context of Disability*

As noted at the outset, the potential of the new UN Convention lies precisely in how it may combat this marginalisation of disability within the existing rights frameworks, by i) providing for explicit legal recognition of the disability rights paradigm, ii) encouraging the gradual shift towards a greater recognition of the need for states to play a more role in making positive provision, and iii) by developing a language of rights that is capable of articulating the needs and entitlements of more individuals than just those who form to the liberal archetype of the autonomous, self-sufficient individual.

But what will count as a breach of the UN Convention? This question goes right to the heart of the conceptual issues thrown up by the UN Convention's emphasis on positive provision and its re-conceptualisation of the relationship between individual rights and dependency upon the state. Defining when a state has failed to make adequate positive provision is a complex question, depending as it does upon the national context in question, the resources available and the impact of the denial of positive provision upon individual persons with disabilities. The 'mainstream' rights instruments have as discussed above by and large failed to develop a meaningful approach in this area. That means it is necessary to look outside the mainstream of human rights law to find indicators of how the Convention may be applied in years to come.

It certainly appears possible to make use of the two approaches that the UN Committee on Economic, Social and Cultural Rights adopts in interpreting the obligations of states under the ICESCR: 'minimum core' analysis, whereby the Committee assesses whether states are making provision for the core socio-economic entitlements necessary to ensure the basic dignity of individuals, and the 'progressive realisation' approach, whereby the Committee assesses whether states are taking reasonable steps to ensure that socio-economic rights are progressively being realised.[83] Combining these two approaches in the context of disability could form the basis of a coherent approach to assessing whether states are meeting their obligations to make positive provision under the new UN Convention.

8 *Protecting the Rights of Persons with Disabilities in Practice – The Experience of the European Committee on Social Rights*

However, what would such an approach look like in practice? The approach adopted by the UN Committee on Economic, Social and Cultural Rights may supply the broad parameters of such an approach, but the Committee's jurisprudence lacks substantial engagement with issues of disability. To illustrate what standards may be generated from the text of the Convention, it may be worth taking a close look instead at the jurisprudence of the European Committee on Social Rights (the ECSR), and in particular what it has to say about the rights

[83] For the UN Committee on Economic, Social and Cultural Rights's approach, see para. 2 of the Committee's General Comment 3, 'The Nature of States Parties Obligations', 14 December 1990, U.N. Doc. E/1991/23. See also H. Shue, *Basic Rights* (Princeton, NJ: Princeton University Press, 1980); E.W. Vierdag, 'The Legal Nature of the Rights Granted by the International Covenant on Economic, Social and Cultural Rights' (1978) 9 *Netherlands Yearbook of International Law* 69; M. Craven, *The International Covenant on Economic, Social and Cultural Rights: A Perspective on its Development* (Oxford: Clarendon Press, 1995); A. Eide, C. Krause and A. Rosas (eds.) *Economic, Social and Cultural Rights: A Textbook* (Dordrecht: Martinus Nijhoff, 1994); P. Hunt, *Reclaiming Social Rights: International and Comparative Perspectives* (Dartmouth, Aldershot, 1998); P. Alston and G. Quinn, 'The Nature and Scope of States Parties' Obligations under the International Covenant on Economic, Social and Cultural Rights' (1987) 9 *Human Rights Quarterly* 156; S. Leckie, 'Another Step Towards Indivisibility: Identifying the Key Features of Violations of Economic, Social and Cultural Rights' (1998) 20 *Human Rights Quarterly* 81; and Chapman, A., 'A "Violations Approach" for Monitoring the International Covenant on Economic, Social and Cultural Rights' (1996) 18 *Human Rights Quarterly* 23. See also the Limburg Principles on the Implementation of the International Covenant on Economic, Social and Cultural Rights, UN Doc.E/CN.4/1987/17, Annex, reprinted in (1987) 9 *Human Rights Quarterly* 122; also the Maastricht Guidelines on Violations of Economic, Social and Cultural Rights, set out in (1998) 20 *Human Rights Quarterly* 691.

of persons with disabilities to certain forms of positive provision and reasonable accommodation.[84]

The ECSR interprets the provisions of the original European Social Charter and now also performs the same task in respect of the revised Social Charter, which is an updated and modernised 'upgrade' of the original Charter which most of the states who initially ratified the original Charter have now also signed and ratified.[85] Whether states which have ratified either of the two Charters are acting in compliance with their provisions is assessed by the ECSR through a national reporting mechanism similar to that in place for the UN Conventions. The ECSR also can hear 'collective complaints' from states which have signed and ratified the 1995 Additional Protocol to the original Charter (now also attached to the revised Charter).[86] This form of rights adjudication permits employers' organisations, employees' organisations and transnational NGOs registered with the Council of Europe, as well as national NGOs if the state in question has consented to their involvement, to bring a 'collective complaint' to the Committee alleged that that state is not complying with a Charter provision. These complaints are to be 'collective' in nature, i.e. they are to relate to a systemic failure to adhere to the Charter standards, not to specific individual cases.

This emphasis on collective action and systemic issues of compliance fits with the overall structure and contents of the European Social Charter, which does not for the most part create individually enforceable rights *per se* but rather requires States Parties to adhere to collective or general norms which when implemented secure the realisation of individual social rights, such as the right to fair remuneration, the right to collective bargaining or to right of children to social, economic and legal protection.[87] States which ratify the original Charter

---

[84] The following remarks should not be construed as representing the views of the European Committee on Social Rights, or as anything other than the opinion of the author.

[85] See R. Brillat, 'The Supervisory Machinery of the European Social Charter: Recent Developments and Their Impact', in G. de Búrca, B. de Witte and L. Ogertschnig, *Social Rights in Europe* (Oxford: OUP, 2005), 31–44.

[86] Note that Article 1(1) of the Optional Protocol to the UN Convention enables the UN Committee on the Rights of Persons with Disabilities to receive and consider communications from both 'individuals and groups of individuals who claim to be victims of a violation' by a State Party which has signed and ratified the Protocol. This enables groups to bring cases to the Committee but they must be 'victims' of a violation, whereas NGOs bringing collective complaints to the ECSR need not claim victim status. However, individuals cannot bring complaints to the ESCR.

[87] Part A of the Charter sets out a range of individual social rights, which State Parties undertake to respect: Part B then requires State Parties to commit themselves to adhering to a certain number of collective norms, which create the conditions necessary for the realisation of the individual rights described in Part B.

or its revised new incarnation must agree to respect and give effect to a certain minimum number of these socio-economic and labour rights. As with the ICESCR and the UN Convention, the Social Charter is therefore built around the recognition that positive provision by the state is essential to securing certain basic rights in contemporary conditions.

In its conclusions on state national reports and in its collective complaint case-law, the ECSR has tended to interpret the Charter as requiring states to adopt two general categories of measures to give effect to the Charter rights. Firstly, states must introduce and maintain in place the minimum range of measures that are necessary to ensure enjoyment of the core elements of each of the Charter rights which states have committed themselves to upholding. Secondly, states have to demonstrate that they are taking reasonable steps to give effect to and secure the gradual realisation of these rights.[88] In other words, the ECSR has adopted a roughly parallel approach to the UN Committee on Economic, Social and Cultural Rights use of the 'minimum core'/'progressive realisation' twin-track analysis. This has meant that the ECSR has been able to develop a 'minimum core'/'progressive realisation' jurisprudence in the context of disability, something almost unknown in the other human rights frameworks.

Gerard Quinn, a former member of the ESCR and the architect of much of the ECSR's jurisprudence on disability rights, has described the Charter as serving as a 'gravitational field' in the context of disability.[89] As Quinn has argued, the Charter acts as a mechanism for expositing common European social values and how they should be applied to disability issues, emphasises the interconnectedness of equality and social rights (a connection which as he notes can often be neglected or forgotten when it comes to disability), and exerts some influence on the development of EU and ECJHR jurisprudence through the standards established in the case-law of the ECSR.

Under Article 15 of the original Charter, persons with disabilities were recognised as having a right to vocational training, rehabilitation and social resettlement. This relatively constrained right reflected the narrow view of disability rights and entitlements that prevailed even in the glory years of the European welfare states in the post-war *Trentes Glorieuses*. However, in its conclusions in respect of national reports, the Committee has tended to take a reasonably broad and purposive interpretation of this right, which has been amplified and developed in recent years. The 'original' Article 15 has been interpreted as requiring states

---

[88] See the analysis of the jurisprudence of the ECSR in L. Samuel, *Fundamental Social Rights: Case Law of the European Social Charter* (2nd ed.) (Strasbourg: Council of Europe, 2002).

[89] G. Quinn, 'The European Social Charter and EU Anti-discrimination law in the Field of Disability: Two Gravitational Fields with One Common Purpose', in G. de Búrca, B. de Witte and L. Ogertschnig, *Social Rights in Europe* (Oxford: OUP, 2005), 279–304.

to provide a minimal level of vocational training opportunities, social provision, employment protection and support for integration within the mainstream of the workforce, as well as to take reasonable steps to enhance, widen and broaden existing positive provision.

In addition, the scope of Article 15 in the revised Charter has been considerably widened and deepened, in one of the most significant alterations to the original text. Its provisions are as follows:

> *Article 15 – The right of persons with disabilities to independence, social integration and participation in the life of the community*
>
> With a view to ensuring to persons with disabilities, irrespective of age and the nature and origin of their disabilities, the effective exercise of the right to independence, social integration and participation in the life of the community, the Parties undertake, in particular:
>
> 1. To take the necessary measures to provide persons with disabilities with guidance, education and vocational training in the framework of general schemes wherever possible or, where this is not possible, through specialised bodies, public or private;
> 2. With a view to ensuring to persons with disabilities, irrespective of age and the nature and origin of their disabilities, the effective exercise of the right to independence, social integration and participation in the life of the community, the Parties undertake, in particular: to promote their access to employment through all measures tending to encourage employers to hire and keep in employment persons with disabilities in the ordinary working environment and to adjust the working conditions to the needs of the disabled or, where this is not possible by reason of the disability, by arranging for or creating sheltered employment according to the level of disability. In certain cases, such measures may require recourse to specialised placement and support services;
> 3. With a view to ensuring to persons with disabilities, irrespective of age and the nature and origin of their disabilities, the effective exercise of the right to independence, social integration and participation in the life of the community, the Parties undertake, in particular: to promote their full social integration and participation in the life of the community in particular through measures, including technical aids, aiming to overcome barriers to communication and mobility and enabling access to transport, housing, cultural activities and leisure.

The Committee has interpreted the underlying idea behind Article 15 as being that persons with disabilities must enjoy full *de facto* citizenship, taken to mean 'independence, social integration and participation in the life of the community': barriers to this enjoyment of *de facto* citizenship must be removed. The first two paragraphs of Article 15 deal with the 'classic' integration issues: education and employment. The third paragraph is wider in scope and is based upon the idea that equal treatment in employment and education cannot be separated from equal treatment in other areas of community life.

The ECSR has adopted a 'social model' of analysis in developing its interpretative approach to Article 15, which has combined elements of the 'minimum core' and 'progressive realisation' approaches.[90] In its conclusions in respect of national reports, the Committee has expressed the view that according to Article 15(1), all persons with disabilities have a right to general education, basic compulsory education and further education as well as vocational training in the traditional sense.[91] Persons with disabilities should be integrated where possible into mainstream facilities, and positive provision should be made for those with special needs.[92] Legislation should prohibit discrimination on the basis of disability in the field of education and should, as a minimum core requirement, require compelling justification for special or segregated educational systems and confer an effective remedy on those who have been unlawfully excluded, segregated or otherwise denied an effective right to education.[93] Article 15(2) requires states to promote access to employment on the open labour market for persons with disabilities, *inter alia*, by adjusting working conditions to the needs of persons with disabilities. Legislation must prohibit discrimination on the basis of disability in employment. Sheltered employment facilities with appropriate labour rights safeguards should be provided for those unable to participate in the mainstream workforce.[94]

Article 15(3) has been interpreted as requiring that barriers to communication and mobility be removed in order to enable access by persons with disabilities to transport, housing, cultural activities and leisure.[95] States should adopt a coherent and co-ordinated policy in the disability context to ensure that persons with disability have this ability to participate in society, and make positive provision and reasonable accommodation where required after consultation with persons with disabilities.[96] Certain accessibility requirements should be legally guaranteed, legislation should prohibit discrimination in accessing goods, facilities and services and the needs of persons with disabilities should be taken into account in the development housing, telecommunications and transport policies.[97]

These normative standards that the ECSR views as implicit in the language and conceptual framework of Article 15 are broad and far-reaching, as well as involving extensive positive provision. The Committee however in interpreting Article 15 can not alone rely upon a relatively detailed text in the Charter itself,

---

[90] See Quinn, *ibid.*, for a comprehensive account of the standards established by the Charter supervision process.

[91] Conclusions 2003, Statement of Interpretation on Article 15, p. 10§5.

[92] See the decision in the collective complaint of *Autism Europe v. France*, Complaint No. 13/2002, Decision on the Merits of 4 November 2003, para. 48.

[93] Conclusions 2005, Cyprus, p. 96.

[94] Conclusions XVII–2, Czech Republic, pp. 145–146.

[95] Conclusions 2005, Norway, p. 558.

[96] Conclusions 2003, Italy, p. 297; Conclusions 2003, France, p. 170.

[97] Conclusions 2003, Italy, p. 299.

it can also take cognisance of the general European context within which the Charter applies. This means that the ECSR can with justification require a relatively broad range of positive provision, and can also specify that much of this positive provision should take the form of 'minimum core' provisions. However, there is also a 'progressive realisation' dimension to these standards: state action that unreasonably erodes or denies realisation of the Article 15 standards may be found by the ECSR not to be in conformity with the Charter, as may state failure to make positive provision for the minimum core measures that Article 15 requires.

Thus far, in its conclusions in respect of national reports, the Committee has tended to make findings of non-conformity only in respect of state failures to introduce comprehensive disability discrimination legislation or to develop any policy structure for enhancing the social participation of persons with disabilities. The ECSR is still putting substantive flesh on its interpretation of the 'new' Article 15 and is at the first stages of specifying what will constitute a violation of the Charter in this area. However, its decision in the collective complaint of *Autism Europe v. France*[98] shows how the 'minimum core'/'progressive realisation' twin-track approach can be applied with great effect in the disability context.

In this complaint, Autism Europe asked the Committee to find that France was failing to satisfactorily apply its obligations under *inter alia* Article 15(1) of the revised European Social Charter because children and adults with autism were not able to exercise effectively their rights to education in mainstream schooling or through adequately supported placements in specialised educational institutions. In essence, the NGO was arguing that France was failing to provide the necessary 'minimum core' of positive educational provision required under Article 15(1), and was also failing to progressively realise the educational rights of persons with autism by unreasonably failing to allocate sufficient resources. The ECSR agreed.

The Committee began its analysis by emphasising that it viewed Article 15 of the Revised Charter as 'both reflecting and advancing a profound shift of values in all European countries over the past decade away from treating them as objects of pity and towards respecting them as equal citizens'.[99] Securing a right to education for children and others with disabilities played an obviously important role in advancing these citizenship rights, which in turn explained why education is now specifically mentioned in the revised Article 15 and why the Committee placed emphasis on the provision of education for disabled persons within 'the framework of general schemes, wherever possible'. Article

[98] *Autism Europe v. France*, Complaint No. 13/2002, Decision on the Merits of 4 November 2003.

[99] *Ibid.*, para. 48.

17 (the right of children to social support) and Article E (the equality provision of the Charter) were also seen as relevant to the analysis, with the decision of the European Court on Human Rights in *Thlimmenos v. Greece*[100] being cited in support of the conclusion that 'human difference in a democratic society should not only be viewed positively but should be responded to with discernment in order to ensure real and effective equality.'[101]

The Committee then referred to its case-law on collective complaints and national reports, which has emphasised that the implementation of the Charter required State Parties to take practical action to give full effect to the rights recognised in the Charter. It went on to clarify that '[w]hen the achievement of one of the rights in question is exceptionally complex and particularly expensive to resolve, a State Party must take measures that allow it to achieve the objectives of the Charter within a reasonable time, with measurable progress and to an extent consistent with the maximum use of available resources. States Parties must be particularly mindful of the impact that their choices will have for groups with heightened vulnerabilities as well as for others persons affected…'[102] The ECSR therefore emphasised that state could both be required to introduce a basic level of positive provision, but also even in a resource-stretched context could be required to show its policies were reasonably compatible with the obligation to give progressive realisation to the Charter rights.

Applying this approach, the Committee noted that France had made little progress in securing the participation of autistic persons in mainstream education or in providing adequate resources to meet their special educational needs; that use was still being made of a more restrictive definition of autism in educational policy than that adopted by the World Heath Organisation; and that there were insufficient official statistics with which to rationally measure progress. These deficiencies in French policy taken together as a whole ensured that France was not meeting its Charter obligations: it could not discharge the requirement to show that it was taking reasonable steps towards progressive realisation of Article 15 and the other Charter rights at issue.[103]

---

100 (2001) 31 EHRR 411.

101 *Ibid.*, paras. 49–52. The ECSR also commented that 'indirect discrimination may arise by failing to take due and positive account of all relevant differences or by failing to take adequate steps to ensure that the rights and collective advantages that are open to all are generally accessible to all.' See para. 52.

102 *Ibid.,* para. 53.

103 *Ibid.*, para. 54.

9 *The Emergence of a Coherent Disability Rights Jurisprudence*

In *Autism Europe*, there were two elements present in the decision-making process which are usually absent from decision-making in other human rights frameworks such as the ECHR or the Canadian Charter or the US Bill of Rights. Firstly, Article 15 recognises in explicit terms that persons with disabilities have particular and distinct forms of rights entitlement: this opened the door for the NGO in question to bring a collective complaint, and for the ECSR to interpret these disability rights as requiring more than just equality of access to the usual entitlements available to autonomous quasi-citizens. Therefore, the express recognition of the special nature of disability rights in Article 15 opened up avenues for challenging resource allocation decisions by the French government which would usually not be contested within existing rights frameworks.

Secondly, the fact that the entire scheme of the Social Charter is built around the acknowledgement that states must make positive provision to secure basic rights means that the ECSR can adopt a 'minimum core'/'progressive realisation' form of analysis. This in turn meant that the ECSR in *Autism Europe* could go beyond the usual limits that restrict the scope of disability rights claims within most existing rights frameworks. The ECSR was able to assess whether a state was taking reasonable steps to address the special and particular needs of a particular category of persons with disabilities, instead of just being able to question whether equality of access to 'normal' entitlements was available (as in *Eldridge*) or whether the special needs of individuals wholly dependant upon the state were being met (*Botta* and *Bernard*).[104]

The manner in which the express disability rights guaranteed in Article 15 of the Charter were applied in *Autism Europe* perhaps offers some guidance for how the UN Committee on the Rights of Persons with Disabilities may approach its task of interpreting and applying the UN Convention. It certainly shows what could be done within the parameters of an express recognition of the disability rights paradigm, as also provided by the UN Convention. The UN Committee may be also able to develop its approach to the Convention further than is possible for the ECSR: Article 1 of the Optional Protocol permits both individuals and groups of individuals to bring complaints to the Committee, which should opens the door to a wider range of cases than is possible under the Charter's collective complaint mechanism. This will in all probability permit the Committee to carve out its own unique niche in the human rights eco-system.

It will be interesting to see how the disability rights jurisprudence that emerges from both the Social Charter Process and the Convention will impact upon

---

[104] Note that similar issues are at stake in a more recent collective complaint before the ECSR, *Mental Disability Advocacy Center v. Bulgaria*, Complaint No. 41/2007.

the interpretation and application of the 'mainstream' rights instruments. The Charter jurisprudence periodically finds its way into the case-law of the European Court of Human Rights: given an increasing pan-European interest in social rights and the new focus provided by the Convention, it will be interesting to see of cases such as *Autism Europe* prove to have an important influence in perhaps encouraging the ECHR case-law to gradually move beyond its current limits. Similarly, the Convention jurisprudence as it emerges will in all probability come to exert a steady influence on different international and national legal frameworks. Both the Charter and the Convention are at present the only sources of guidance on the shape and content of a human rights approach to disability: therefore, both instruments will inevitably set the pace for some time in the disability context.

10 *Conclusion*

Any coherent disability rights approach has to a) push for the removal of barriers to the equal participation of persons with disabilities in employment, occupation and social activities in general; b) emphasise the transformation of existing social practices and norms to ensure that they are open to and can accommodate all who wish to participate; c) provide positive support for those persons with disability who require special assistance to access social structures, but also d) provide positive provision for those who may not be able to benefit from enhanced accessibility or who otherwise depend wholly on the state to protect their dignity.[105] The Convention recognises this in its provisions, as does the European Social Charter in a less comprehensive manner. Both instruments share a conceptual view of the relationship between the individual and the state and how individual rights interact with this relationship. Human rights law must do more than just protect the self-sufficient autonomous individual against state interference: there is also a need to recognise the reality that every individual exists in a relationship of interdependence upon the state, and that individuals have positive rights to the provision of essential social goods. This vision underlies both the Social Charter and the Convention, and perhaps it will not be too long before these instruments, and in particular the Convention, begin to move this conceptual approach to rights from the margins into the mainstream of rights discourse.

---

[105] For an excellent discussion of this, see D. Mabbett, 'Some Are More Equal Than Others: Definitions of Disability in Social Policy and Discrimination Law in Europe' (2005) 34(2) *Journal of Social Policy* 215–233.

Part III

Bringing the Treaty Home

General Themes Relevant to the Implementation of the UN Disability Convention into Domestic Law: Who is Responsible for the Implementation and how should it be Performed?

*Holger Kallehauge**

Thus have I politically begun my reign, and 'tis my hope to end successfully. . .[1]

A common problem facing all international conventions is how to transform international law into domestic law. It can be carried through by a variety of methods, though not all conventions or treaties have the same need to be transformed. This chapter will not deal with the general question of interaction between national and international law but concentrate on the general themes that will require special consideration when the UN Convention on the Rights of Persons with Disabilities of December 13th 2006 has to be transposed into domestic law.

A transposition is clearly necessary because the rules of the Convention will not only be applied by governments and civil servants; they will also be invoked by individual citizens. The Convention embodies rights for persons with disabilities, which have to be known to the bearers of these rights if they are to be of any use. Of course, organisations of and for persons with disabilities will play an important role in making the rules and the implications of the rules known to their members. In principle, however, it is each and every individual with a disability who is the bearer of the human rights and fundamental freedoms confirmed by the Convention. They are the group of people that the Convention is meant for. The transposition into domestic law will have them, primarily, as the target group. Secondarily, the Convention refers to governments, their civil servants and administrative bodies and to private enterprises, companies and firms, their managers and employees and all other members of society. Thus,

---

* Retired High Court Judge, President of PTU (The Danish Society of Polio and Accident Victims).

[1] William Shakespeare, The Taming of The Shrew, Act four, 1.

the Convention has a very broad perspective This must be taken into due consideration when the implementation is discussed and evaluated.

The implementation of the Convention is the process that will lead to the fulfilment of all the obligations which a ratifying government has undertaken by this act. This process is a long-term project and not just a few practical measures. No government can ratify the Convention claiming with a clear conscience that in their country they already fulfil all that is demanded by the Convention. Therefore, all of the more than 137 UN member states that have now signed the Convention and thus declared that they also intend to ratify it have committed themselves to the implementation process. What does that mean? The signing of a convention is a government promise to work for its ratification.

The process of implementation should be divided into different phases, such as the initial measures, the first substantial issues, the ratification, the implementation of the national reporting system and the follow-up measures. Other distinctions might be chosen, but if a true picture of the essence of implementation has to be presented, the above mentioned elements cannot be left out.

1 *Initial Measures*

The first step is to make it known to the public that the government has signed the Convention and is now preparing for ratification. Nothing is more compelling or binding for ministers and other politicians than going public and disclosing what the government intends to do. That gives the media and all interested groups an open invitation and prompts them to come back, asking when the government's plans are going to materialize. To ensure that ratification will not become delusive or a mirage it is imperative not to give government too much of a free hand. Even if the preparatory work towards ratification is not simple and certainly requires time, it is important that it is not unduly delayed because the Convention cannot enter into force until ratification has taken place. According to article 45 the Convention enters into force on the thirtieth day after the deposit of the twentieth instrument of ratification. This goal was achieved on April 3rd 2008 which means that the Convention enters into force internationally on May 3rd 2008. The following ratifications are going to enlarge the area covered by the Convention.[2] More than 137 signatures within 18 months from the opening ceremony on March 30th 2007 is very promising for a human rights convention. Ratifications are not that speedy but the number of signatures

[2] The ratification process is reported on the UN enable website, see http://www.un.org/disabilities/countries.asp?navid=12&pid=166.

bears witness to the substantial interest in supporting the Convention, which will hopefully also be sustained to ratification.

Even if the official UN languages cover a great number of UN member states and also a large portion of the global population, many countries need translation into one or several national languages. When it comes to interpretation of the rules, a translation is needed or at least preferable in most countries. The EU member states may await an EU translation into the national languages or make their own national translation. Whether one approach is better than the other is difficult to say. A national translation has the advantage, however, that special national legal, social, medical and other relevant concepts are not misunderstood. If a country has more than one national translations it is very important that they do not differ and are harmonized and that one of them is made the official one. It sounds very banal, but in the light of the difficulties involved in translating the UN Standard Rules on the Equalization of Opportunities for Persons with Disabilities[3] into Spanish, for example, this problem is worth mentioning and should not be overlooked.[4]

2 *The First Substantive Issues*

No ratification can take place until government has a clear picture of the changes required in national law to avoid conflicts between the Convention and domestic law. Adaptation can go both ways: New legal rules may be adopted or existing acts of Parliament may be repealed. In article 4.1 (a) and (b) it is stipulated that all appropriate legislative measures for the implementation of the rights recognized in the Convention shall be adopted either as new legislation or as modifications or abolishing of existing laws.

Legal experts in the administration have to scrutinise all national rules to make sure that none are discriminatory towards persons with disabilities, directly or indirectly, and the review must include not only statutory law but also legal custom and practice.

During the negotiation of the Convention an EU-text proposal mentioning both direct and indirect discrimination was not accepted. Instead the Convention in article 2 (4) defines discrimination as "any distinction, exclusion or restriction on the basis of disability which has the purpose or effect of impairing or

---

[3] A/Res/48/96, 20 December 1993.

[4] The translation of the concept handicap/disability from English to Spanish gave rise to serious linguistic problems which delayed translation of the UN Standard Rules for more than a year. Similar problems might occur with tanslation of other concepts and definitions contained in the Convention.

nullifying" the human rights of persons with disability. Direct discrimination is characterized by having the goal, aim and purpose to treat persons with disabilities less positive than their nondisabled fellowmen, often by mentioning persons with disabilities openly in the text. Direct discrimination is without any doubt covered by the wording of article 2 (4). Indirect discrimination can be taken to occur when an apparently neutral provision, criterion or practice would put persons with disabilities at a particular disadvantage compared with other (nondisabled) persons. This is how indirect discrimination is defined in article 2.2. (b) of EU Council Directive 2000/78/EC of November 27th establishing a general framework for equal treatment in employment and occupation.[5] The essential part in the concept of indirect discrimination is that an in itself neutral criterion has a discriminatory effect towards a certain group of persons which should be protected against discrimination. As the Convention mentions purpose as well as *effect* one must draw the conclusion that both direct and indirect discrimination are encompassed by article 2.4. even if neither the words direct or indirect are explicitly used.

How international rules are transposed into domestic law depends, of course, upon national law, doctrine and tradition. The translation of the Convention may be incorporated directly, making this text an Act of Parliament, or a new national legal text may be drafted, covering the content of the rules of the Convention. Both methods may be adopted, preferably combined with a provision stating that any prior legislation that is not consistent will be abolished. It is an easy way to ensure that no conflicting legal provisions are still in existence. However, if a thorough scanning of national law has not been carried out beforehand, no one knows exactly what has been nullified. A combination of these two approaches should probably be recommended. A third way of transposing a convention into domestic law is making specific changes here and there in existing legislation. This bits and pieces approach is typical for common law countries.

The Convention's Article 4 paragraph 2 contains an important distinction between civil and political rights in contrast to economic, social and cultural rights. While the last mentioned rights are subject to progressive realisation, the civil and political rights are immediately applicable after ratification. The implementation of the Convention has to respect this principle, and the scanning of national law must focus special attention on all national regulations that deal with civil and political rights. When the ratification takes place, at least these rights must be in total harmony with the Convention.

It is a problem in this context that civil and political rights may not always be easy to distinguish from economic, social and cultural rights, and the two sets of rights are at times mixed up in the same articles of the Convention.

---

[5] [2000] OJ L303/16.

Examples of civil and political rights are Art. 5 about equality and non-discrimination, Art. 10 about the right to life, Art. 11 and Art. 12 about equal recognition before the law, Art. 13 about access to justice, Art. 14 about liberty and security of the person, Art. 15 about freedom from torture or cruel, inhuman or degrading treatment or punishment, Art. 16 about freedom from exploitation, violence and abuse, Art. 17 about protecting the integrity of the person, Art. 18 about liberty of movement and nationality, Art. 22 about privacy, Art. 23. about respect for home and the family and Art. 29 about participation in political and public life.

All the mentioned rules deal with civil and political rights, though some of them also include elements that may be of a different nature. One example is reasonable accommodation in the non-discrimination rule in Art. 5, paragraph 3. Other examples are the rule concerned with training of police and prison staff in Art. 13, paragraph 2, and information, education and independent monitoring in Art. 16. Thus, a careful analysis of all the articles of the Convention is required to distinguish civil and political rights from economic, social and cultural rights in order to know when an article or a part of it is subject to immediate or progressive realisation.

3 *Specific Obligations of the Convention*

Many specific obligations are emanating from the operative rules in Art. 3–33 of the Convention. This chapter will not enumerate or describe them all. Instead, only a few examples of the multiple duties the states parties have to fulfil during their implementing process will be mentioned.

Some duties are negative, presenting what states parties must abstain from doing, like using torture, cruel, inhuman or degrading treatment or punishment, exploitation, violence and abuse. However, also rules like Art. 15, 16, 17, 22 and 23 call for certain activities, like training and education of personnel dealing with persons with disabilities, respect for privacy, the home and the family, good care, understanding and due respect for the integrity of persons with disabilities and their dignity as human beings.

Other rules are far more action oriented like Art. 9 about accessibility, Art. 13 and 14 about access to justice, Art. 24 about education and Art. 27 about work and employment. Each of these and several other rules of the Convention describe quite specific actions that governments have to take if these obligations are not totally fulfilled already, like access on an equal basis with others to the physical environment, transportation, information and communications, access to support in exercising legal capacity, accommodations in legal proceedings, appropriate training for those working in the field of administration of justice, inclusive education at all levels, opportunity to gain a living by work freely chosen in an open labour market and a work environment that is inclusive and accessible.

Many other rules could be mentioned and even if only some main duties have been cited, it is obvious that the states parties will not run out of work within a few years, not even if they implement progressively with the maximum of their available resources.

4 *Mapping the Country*

When ratification has taken place the next step is to prepare the first national report to the monitoring body. The government has two years to do this, which may seem to be ample time. In reality, it can be expected that it will prove not to be.

The first government report will be the basic national report covering all aspects of the Convention, describing point zero from which all future progress must be measured.

The basic report must give a comprehensive and accurate picture of the national degree of fulfilment of all obligations under the Convention. Some rules may be fulfilled already. If so, that is fine and no more reporting will be needed about the articles concerned. However, for many countries they will not be numerous. All the civil and political rights should fall into this category. The rest, i.e. the economic, social and cultural rights, should prove to give sufficient work, first at the national level and thereafter to the monitoring body.

In respect of Art. 9 about accessibility, it is obvious that no government can write a fair national report on this subject at a desk in a government office in the capital. Local reports are definitely required. Accessibility must encompass not only access to the physical environment, like buildings and all means of transportation, but also access to information and communication.

How detailed should the report be, and how precise should estimates be? A careful effort should be made to avoid guessing. At a later stage, in follow-up reports, ill-founded prior statements will no doubt reveal themselves, leaving the government with a credibility problem.

If an assertion is not based on factual knowledge, it is better to say so and explain why, stating the reasons for doubt about figures and numbers and not giving a false impression of exactness.

A true and fair picture of the disability situation should be the aim – not too rosy, not too bleak, but realistic even if it is not pretty.

Without local reports to build on, governments will have nothing but nationwide reports and statistics to rely on, and they might be incomplete or even unavailable and hardly sufficient. In most countries, therefore, some sort of questionnaire will have to be used. Available and reliable information about persons with disabilities, their living conditions, dwellings, transportation, jobs, education, rehabilitation and cultural or recreational life is hard to procure without involving local authorities, organisations of persons with disabilities and persons with disabilities themselves. In most countries national surveys of this sort may produce documentation that is also useful for purposes other than reporting to the monitoring body.

Local reports should be collected not only from authorities but also from local disability councils and branches of national organisations of persons with disabilities. Also here, the Disabled People's International (DPI) slogan "Nothing about us, without us" makes good sense, even if it is in a slightly different connection than usual. Persons with disabilities do not give hearsay evidence. They are eyewitnesses and can provide very exact information not only about their own lives but also about the community to which they belong.

If a national report is founded on a combination of such local reports, national surveys and available national statistical data and scientific studies, it will stand a reasonable chance of misleading neither the monitoring commission nor those who drafted it.

Organizations of persons with disabilities have of course to be consulted by government during the implementation of the Convention. This is both natural as disabled persons organizations have a special knowledge and expertise in the field of disability and is also an obligation according to the Convention. This is expressively stated in Art. 4.3 and Art. 33.3 about implementation and monitoring, but not in Art. 35 about reports by states parties. Here it is up to governments to decide if they want to involve organizations of persons with disabilities. Considering the close cooperation which is prescribed for the implementation and monitoring process it is easy to imagine that governments might also invite organizations of persons with disabilities to be partners or to have a consultative role when it comes to elaboration of the comprehensive national report described in Art. 35. Such a cooperation between a government and the national organizations of persons with disabilities has certain advantages for both parties and should therefore also be considered carefully.

Depending on the way in which the government has involved organisations of persons with disabilities in the reporting exercise in accordance with Art. 35, and how the organisations have responded to an invitation to join a national committee charged with writing a national report, there will be two different models.

Either a committee consisting solely of civil servants and other government staff or such a committee combined with representatives from civil society, human rights institutes, universities and organisations of and for persons with disabilities. Where a national disability council exists, such a council may also be a good partner in the writing of the national report.

If representatives from the disability movement are to be members of a government reporting committee, they have to feel strong and capable enough to write dissenting opinions when they disagree with the majority. Otherwise, they are just taken on board as hostages. This risk should never be underestimated when the flattering offer to join a government committee is received.

The advantage to be gained by the disability movement from staying out of a government committee is the chance to write a shadow report, focusing exclusively on the weak points presented in the government report.

The advantage of being part of the government committee is, of course, direct influence on the entire process and its outcome.

What is best cannot be said generally. It is a question that all national organisations of persons with disabilities have to answer to themselves based on their experience in the country where they live and work. One thing is sure, however. If the disability movement, perhaps in cooperation with representatives from civil society like National Human Rights Institutes, the Parliamentary Ombudsman, the Bar Association, University Faculties of Law and similar influential groups, writes a shadow report, this is sure to be studied carefully by the monitoring committee. All the claims in the government report that are not disputed will be taken as read, of course, but the disputed texts will be studied with special interest and give rise to many questions. When points are argued by two opposing parties, as in a case before the court, it often gives the best illustration of a problem. Cross-examination is a very effective method of investigation.

5 *The Substantive Implementation*

When a government has translated the Convention, adapted its national legislation in conformity with the Convention, passed the ratification resolution and written its basic national report, then it will face the real work of implementing the rights. All the mentioned steps are just preliminary.

Incorporation of the Convention is a possibility but might not be as effective as implementation by means of national legislation. A convention is always a bit more of a foreign source of law than an Act of Parliament. Even if they have the same legal status they are not always equally easily accessible and do not have the same vocabulary and style which might influence the understanding and interpretation of the text.

Governments have to develop plans for some years ahead, year by year, with clearly stipulated goals to be reached within certain time limits. Such plans also have to be followed up by the allocation of sufficient resources when budgets are adopted every year. If ministers believe that a polished speech in Parliament with promises of progress is enough, they shall be disappointed. Consistent with the practice of other treaty monitoring bodies, the committee will have to go beyond simple public pronouncements on policy such as speeches in parliament.

Nothing less than detailed plans covering the whole country, all the regions and local councils will do.

This does not mean that a government cannot decide how to prioritize – on the contrary. Priorities are definitely necessary. If some may believe that the Convention has to be implemented on a broad front, with equal force at the same time in all areas, I think they are mistaken. I even doubt that it would be effective. Spreading the resources available has never been proved to be good management.

With all civil and political rights fulfilled and in place there is a solid foundation to build on, ensuring that non-discrimination is the leading principle in all areas of society along with the seven other leading principles in Art. 3 of the Convention. However, the non-discrimination policy cannot stand alone. It must always be followed up by affirmative measures, enhancing independent living, inclusive education and employment on the regular labour market.

For persons with disabilities as for all other citizens, three main issues will override all others when it comes to inclusion in modern society:

- Schooling and education,
- Work and employment and
- Health

Equal opportunities in these three sectors are absolutely essential.

For persons with disabilities the following three preconditions for inclusion are equally important:

- Habilitation and rehabilitation,
- Accessibility and
- Personal mobility.

National plans should not leave out any of the six key requirements. Other demands may be added with perfectly good reason, but the basic issues must be the above-mentioned six.

National plans designed to run for two, four or five years should continue to concentrate on the six questions but gradually open up and include other areas of importance. Giving priority to one right and not another does not mean that the latter is of no importance, of course, only that the available resources have to be administered in a focused way.

6 *Progressive Realisation*

Art. 4, paragraph 2 is the rule about implementation of economic, social and cultural rights. Ratifying governments must take measures to the maximum of their available resources to achieve progressively the full realisation of these rights.

What does progressive realization mean, and how much is the maximum of a country's available resources? Both concepts are vague but were deliberately chosen to be so. If the Convention had been sharp and unambiguous on these and other important points no country would dare to ratify. But also an unclear rule has to be interpreted, and even vague provisions have their limits.

Art. 4, paragraph 2 is very distinct in describing its scope. It covers economic, social and cultural rights exclusively, which leads to the *a contrario* conclusion that civil and political rights come into force from the very day the ratification is effective in accordance with Art. 45, meaning on the thirtieth day after the deposit of the national ratification instrument.

But what does progressive realisation mean? No doubt that if a government declares that it will take no further steps towards full realisation of an economic, social or cultural right, which is not yet fully realised, it will be a contravention or clear breach of Art. 4. Ensuring progress cannot lawfully be abandoned. A government has to continue its work towards full realisation. But steps leading to fulfilment can be great or small; as long as they are taken without stopping, however, the government is driving a process that is progressive. Whether a step is sufficient depends not only on the resources available but also an evaluation of the maximum of resources in a national context. Much more will be demanded of the rich western industrial countries, of course, than of the developing countries and countries in economic transition. But precisely how much cannot be said. It cannot be defined as a certain percentage of the gross national product. The result is up to a concrete assessment made by the monitoring commission in each case. Many parameters may be relevant in this connection, like national debt, the rate of unemployment, living costs in the country and the average daily income, defence budgets and many more economic and social factors. But most relevant of all is the priority that a government gives to this issue.

7 *Reasonable Accommodation*

The concept of reasonable accommodation is well known in Anglo-Saxon law but less so in continental and other legal systems. In Art. 2, this concept is defined. It means, on the one hand, the necessary and appropriate modifications and adjustments required in a particular case to ensure the enjoyment or exercise of a right for a person with a disability, but it does not, on the other hand, impose a disproportionate or undue burden on the party who is obliged to fulfil the obligation.

It is a question of balancing the right of persons with disabilities to enjoy and exercise a certain human right on an equal footing with others against the amount of resources that the needed adjustment will cost for those responsible for securing the right in question.

Whether a burden is disproportionate or undue depends on whose duty it is to fulfil the obligation. If it is a duty of a government or public authority or a major private company, the burden will have to be extremely heavy before it can be considered disproportionate or undue. Perhaps it cannot ever be so. But if the duty rests upon an individual or a small firm or organisation, the scales will be tipped down much more easily and the burden may deserve to be seen as disproportionate or undue. The question must always be answered based on a concrete assessment in each case, compared to previous cases of a similar nature.

Reasonable accommodation will probably become the most important legal concept of the Convention and the most crucial instrument whenever a case of implementation has to be decided.

8 *A Global Index for the Convention*

Implementing the Convention will be hard work for all States Parties, and depend on political will and commitment as well as resources. Progressive realisation is a demanding process in which the momentum has to be sustained. Such a process is at a constant risk of running out of energy. This has to be neutralized – but how?

Competition is a strong motivating factor in most spheres of life and this is equally true when it comes to governments. Any government wants to compare favourably with some of its neighbouring countries, and probably all states parties have one or two countries they want to outperform.

How could we make the degree of fulfilment of the Convention comparable between countries? Comparing national reports with differences in structure and system will not be an easy job, but if a global index is developed such comparisons become much simpler. An index should in no way make the national reports superfluous but serve as an international yardstick by which results can be measured and compared.

To be operational, such an index must be quite simple, consisting for instance of 10 parameters, carrying a value of 1 to 10 marks. The maximum then becomes 100 or 100 per cent for full implementation of the Convention, while all lower scores indicate a lower degree of fulfilment.

The 10 parameters to be chosen could be non-discrimination, education, employment, accessibility, habilitation and rehabilitation, health, standard of living, privacy, home and the family, participation in public and political life and legal capacity and access to justice.

Each state party should conduct a self-evaluation as a conclusion to each national report to the monitoring body. It is then up to the commission to accept or correct the self-evaluation as the final evaluation of the submitted national report. Thus, the result which the score of the index signifies will end up as an official figure.

This proposed model of an index is a very simple one. More parameters may be included and more sophisticated models elaborated. The idea is merely to demonstrate the possible advantages of using a global index as an international yardstick to measure the fulfilment of the Convention by each ratifying government.

9 *National Implementation and Monitoring*

The Convention includes only one article that deals with national implementation and monitoring, i.e. Art. 33, but it does not leave the slightest doubt as to who is responsible for the task. It is the ratifying states parties that are obliged to implement the Convention and put mechanisms for independent, monitoring in place. The article consists of just three short paragraphs, which leave it to the states parties to handle the implementation in accordance with their own national administrative systems. They must designate one or more fora within government to take care of and coordinate the implementation, and they must involve civil society, Human Rights Institutes and especially persons with disabilities and their representative organisations in the implementation and monitoring under the Convention.

It is obvious that the UN have no wish to interfere with the implementation and the way it is carried out as long as it is effective and progressive. The international supervision is left to the monitoring committee to be established in accordance with Art. 34, working on the basis of the reports from states parties.

Conflict between a country's national law and international obligations is a problem that may arise, even when governments do their best to avoid it. A rule of presumption of no conflict might be a highly useful and preventive instrument. Such a rule should state that unless otherwise expressed clearly and directly by government or Parliament, it should be presumed that national law respects all international obligations undertaken by the government.

Countries where such a rule of interpretation is not already in force as it is in Denmark may consider introducing it. We live in a period in which international law, especially multilateral conventions, plays an ever increasing role as an instrument that enhances legal globalization. This augments the risk of conflicts between national and international law and makes prevention more urgent than ever.

A presumption of no conflict allows the courts to give effect to State obligations under international law. This will avoid breaches of international law, which will, for one thing, be embarrassing and, for another, give rise to payment of damages as well as legislative initiatives aimed to bring national law in harmony with the international obligations of the country.

10 *Conclusion*

The Convention is an instrument to be used by many different actors, some of whom have been mentioned above. The disability movement no doubt feels that the Convention belongs to them and their members, which is only fair. Imagine if it were not so. Any lack of feeling of ownership would have been a sign of dissatisfaction with the outcome of the negotiations and therefore a disaster.

Of course, the Convention also belongs to the states parties. They may not love every bit of it but hopefully so much that they do not hesitate to ratify the document.

It is a fine international instrument we have obtained. Much better than we sometimes believed it possible to achieve during the negotiations. If the text will be ratified and implemented nationally with as much good will and enthusiasm as was demonstrated during and especially towards the end of the negotiations, persons with disabilities around the world have a much brighter future to look forward to than they would ever have had without the Convention. There is no need for me to repeat what others have so eloquently expressed about the paradigm shift that the Convention represents. The realization of the eight leading principles enumerated in Art. 3 will mean a total revolution in the lives of most persons with disabilities. What we had before the Convention was where it was best a social policy model of disability which was based on the good will of the majority both among our citizens and in Parliament. No minority can obtain progress without such good will, but it usually takes long time before good will is turned into actions of any importance and sometimes such actions never seem to materialize. The rights based approach which is the foundation of the Convention grants us rights we can demand to be fulfilled. The difference is that before the Convention persons with disabilities and their organizations had to beg to be heard. After the Convention they can point to their rights and ask the politicians when are you going to satisfy our requirements.

It has taken a long time to come this far – too long, more than twenty-five years, but the Convention has also been worth waiting for.

Are we heading towards Utopia? No, we are not, at least not within a foreseeable future and, probably, we will never get there, primarily because there is no Utopia in this world and, secondarily, because persons with disabilities are a minority and will forever be so.

Even if the Convention grants us all the same human rights and fundamental freedoms as the rest of mankind, which is an enormous step forward, we are still a minority and all minorities have to fight for their rights by making themselves visible and heard. Each generation of persons with disabilities to come must continue to fight for this, but in the future on the basis and by means of the fine instrument that the disability Convention is. There are no free meals, neither for us nor for our fellow citizens. The Convention paints a beautiful picture of the promised land of equal opportunities, which we have all been dreaming of. Now, we are looking forward to seeing its progressive realisation.

Resisting the 'Temptation of Elegance': Can the Convention on the Rights of Persons with Disabilities Socialise States to Right Behaviour?

*Gerard Quinn**

Ratification is not the 'magic moment' of acceptance of human rights norms. Rather, ratification is a point in the broader process of incorporation...[1]

1 *Introduction*

Will the Convention on the Rights of Persons with Disabilities (CRPD) make a difference in the 'small places' where people actually live as was famously suggested by Eleanor Roosevelt?[2] Normatively speaking, the obligations of the States Parties are clear – or at least much clearer than hitherto. And of course the clarification of existing international human rights law – and not the creation of new law – was one of the main purposes of the Convention.[3] So at that level the Convention is already a success.

And what about the new framework of reference in disability – justice and rights? What are its prospects? The principles contained in Article 3 (dignity, autonomy, equality of opportunity, etc.) are both inspiring and elegant. They are the 'legacy values' of human rights theory and law. As such they are not

---

* This paper is dedicated to my wife Anne Motherway whose love is a constant source of solace and support.

[1] Goodman R. and Jinks D., 'Measuring the Effects of Human Rights Treaties' (2003) 14 EJIL 171, at 173.

[2] See Glendon, M.A., A World Made New: Eleanor Roosevelt and the Universal Declaration of Human Rights, (Random House, 2001).

[3] Confirming and tailoring existing human rights law in the specific context of disability was one of the core arguments made in favour of crafting a new thematic treaty: see Quinn G., and Degener T., *et al.*, Human Rights and Disability: The current use and future potential of United Nations human rights instruments in the context of disability, (Office of the UN High Commissioner for Human Rights, 2002).

revolutionary. But of course, their application in the context of disability *is* revolutionary. If one could pour 'cynical acid' over the text to see if any thing essential remains – as Oliver Wendell Holmes would have counselled[4] – then there is indeed a profound message in the Convention. It is that persons with disabilities are not 'objects' to be managed or cared for, but human 'subjects' enjoying human rights on an equal basis with others.[5] The nature of this revolution should not be underestimated. It brings into play a different way of seeing the reality of the lives of persons with disabilities, a different set of values with which to judge existing social arrangements and wholly new policy prescriptions to bring about improvements.

So the war of ideas is over. But in many ways that was the easy part. Success at this level does not automatically translate into real success on the ground. One must resist the 'temptation of elegance' or the easy assumption that words alone will bring about the kind of change needed. After all, it is quite easy for persons – and States – to agree to language without necessarily thinking through its implications. There is no guarantee that the new values (really old values but novel in their application to disability) that are embedded in the text of the Convention will be internalised and then operationalised. There will be push-back especially where the required changes bump up against entrenched ways of doing things. This may give rise to a certain level of contradiction – even cognitive dissonance[6] – especially when the grip of the old worldview (welfare and the objectification of persons with disabilities) is tenacious and almost impervious to rational critique. This will be particularly so where whole social systems have been geared up to maintain the *status quo* and have acquired an almost irresistible momentum of their own. And social systems – like persons – can quite easily live with and rationalise contradiction since to abandon them means migrating away from a known comfort zone into a new and potentially unmanageable (or so it seems) nirvana.

Indeed, and at the risk of belabouring the point, the Convention itself would appear to allow windows through which States might rationalise – and even reconcile – existing exclusionary practices. That is to say, States might even convince themselves that their exclusionary practices are indeed reconcilable (if not even required!) by the Convention. For example, most of the rights of the Convention are said to be secured 'on an equal basis with others.' Much will turn on how this phrase is interpreted by the incoming treaty monitoring body – the Com-

---

4 Holmes O.W., 'The Path of the Law' 110 Harvard L.Rev 991 (1897), at 995.

5 See McKay D., 'The Convention on the Rights of Persons with Disabilities, A Benchmark for Action', (2007) 56 Int. Rehabilitation R. 1, 2.

6 Cognitive dissonance has been described as "the feeling of uncomfortable tension which comes from holding two conflicting thoughts in the mind at the same time." See www.changingminds.org.

mittee on the Rights of Persons with Disabilities. And the battle over how to interpret this concept could well become the lightening rod of the Convention. At one level it requires an acknowledgement of reckonable differences between persons with disabilities and others. And, invoking the Aristotelian conception of equality, this would furthermore require 'equals to be treated equally and unequals to be treated unequally.'[7] It doesn't take much imagination to see how this acknowledgment about objective inequality would be used (really abused) to rationalise separate treatment and to continue as before without making any fundamental adjustments to accumulated laws and practices – and thus defeat the purpose of the Convention. This issue – how to appropriately conceptualise the demands of equality in the specific context of disability – are expertly dealt with elsewhere in this volume by Professor Arnardóttir. Her analysis of equality theory and its many phases deserves to be read carefully. My point though, is that the text alone does not guarantee that its values will be transposed into the worldview of policy and law-makers and that there will always be textual toeholds to be found in the Convention – in any convention – that can potentially allow States to temporise about the profound reforms that its underlying philosophy demands. This is no more than what the Legal Realists have taught us several decades ago.[8]

So the main challenge in the period ahead is to translate the 'majestic generalities' of the Convention into practice. In considering how this might be done it is wise to keep uppermost in mind that the Convention was necessary primarily because of repeated failures to consider the just claims of persons with disabilities as – well – just claims. There are, of course, other more formalistic answers as to why a new thematic Convention was needed. For example, persons with disabilities were absent on the face of existing international human rights instruments (with the notable exception of Article 23.1 of the Convention on the Rights of the Child) and this needed to be rectified from a formal point of view. And this textual invisibility was not ameliorated by any conscious effort on behalf of the relevant treaty monitoring bodies (at least in the past) to raise the profile of the rights of persons with disabilities through, for example, General Comments.[9] These were real deficiencies that needed a response.

---

7 See the discussion of this conundrum in Quinn G., Ch. 8, '*Disability discrimination law in the European Union*', in Meenan H., (Ed.), Equality Law for an Enlarged Union: Understanding the Article 13 Directives, (Cambridge University Press, 2007).

8 See generally, Fisher, W., Horwitz M. and Reed T., (Eds.), American Legal Realism, (Oxford University Press, 1993).

9 The notable exception for a long time was General Comment 4 of the Committee on Economic, Social and Cultural Rights, 'Persons with Disabilities' (1994). The Committee on the Rights of the Child is the latest treaty monitoring body to adopt a specific General Comment on disability: General Comment 9 'The Rights of Children with Disabilities' (2006).

However, it is submitted that this kind of textual and normative invisibility was secondary. It reflected and rested on a deeper invisibility in the political process. Persons with disabilities were – and are – apt to spend most of their time simply surviving. They typically encounter high opportunity costs to political participation. And that is assuming they live in a country that is responsive to the wishes of its people as expressed through a free and open democratic process. And so the typical welfare response (which is in fact a parody of the true goals of welfare as Beveridge would have understood it)[10] of maintaining rather than empowering persons with disabilities has been relatively immune from pressure to change.

It is suggested that the true test of the Convention will not be whether it generates nice, but essentially self-referencing jurisprudence within, the pure ether of international law. Instead the true test will be whether it can help reshape 'normal' politics to the point that a consideration of the just claims and the rights of persons will become a natural reflex rather than an after-thought – a question of justice rather than a question of welfare. If it can be used to leverage a new politics of disability – a new natural reflex of justice and rights and a new kind of partnership between Government and civil society – then we may be able to say that it is a success.

The insights of the Legal Realists notwithstanding, expectations run high that the Convention will become a 'magic bullet'. These expectations are natural given the long neglect of the field and the euphoria of civil society at securing such a high level instrument. Some may expect that the Convention will in some way 'coerce' recalcitrant States to do what the otherwise would not do.[11] This is unlikely as international law rarely has that effect and usually only where there is a court to make authoritative and binding pronouncements. Even then, such a court would need time to build its institutional legitimacy.

Others may expect that the Convention will have 'persuasive' value. That is to say, some will expect that the Convention's values will become internalised and therefore 'belong' to the various States Parties.[12] If one may hazard a guess, this is probably already true of a minority of States including some that have ratified, some that have signed and not yet ratified and even-perhaps especially one (the

---

[10] Sir William Beveridge laid the foundation of the welfare state in the UK and best known for his 1942 Report entitled, Social Insurance and Allied Services.

[11] For an extremely insightful analysis of the uses – and limits – of test case strategies see, Strategic litigation of race discrimination in Europe; from principles to practice. A manual on the theory and practice of strategic litigation with particular reference to the EC Race Directive, (European Roma Rights Centre, Interights, MPG, London, 2004).

[12] See generally Goodman R. and Jinks D., 'How to Influence States: Socialization and International Human Rights Law' (2004) 54 Duke L.J. 621.

United States) that has neither signed nor ratified.[13] This is no surprise since often such instruments which purport to reflect the conscience of humanity emanate from policy advances in particular States anxious to gain political capital on a global stage. But perhaps the majority of States (even those that have signed) have yet to be truly 'persuaded' in the sense that they have yet to internalise its values and engage in their own spontaneous law reform programmes. In other words, if the Convention continues to be seen as an externality – with the added bureaucratic 'cost' of having to produce a periodic paper mountain – then we can expect to see only marginal change. So the intriguing question becomes 'how can we accelerate this process of internalising the values of the Convention and how can we best configure the implementation/monitoring provision of the Convention to facilitate this'? Note, the question is not whether an exogenous force – a treaty monitoring body – can 'force' change. The question is how can international monitoring play a catalytic role in ensuring that domestic policy and political narratives[14] adjust to the values of the Convention and bring about local solutions acceptable to the universal norms of the Convention.

Commentators point to a third way that international law can bring about a transformed domestic policy environment. It is said the socialisation and acculturation can also nudge meaningful change. Goodman and Jenks have usefully defined this thus:

> By acculturation we mean the general process by which actors adopt the beliefs and behavioural patterns of the surrounding culture. This mechanism induces behavioural changes through pressures to assimilate – some imposed by other actors and some imposed by the self. Acculturation encompasses a number of microprocesses including mimicry, identification and status maximization.[15]

In other words, States – or a least actors within States such as senior policy makers and especially those conscious of their country's international reputation – could become socialised to align policy with the cosmopolitan norms and thus bring about meaningful change.

If a critical mass of key policy makers can be persuaded – either through 'persuasion' or 'socialisation' – to tackle a core impediment (especially one that might have huge symbolic value such as outdated conceptions of legal capacity) then change can happen. And of course the really interesting thing about such policy breakthroughs is that even when there is significant domestic pushback

---

[13] See Hathaway O., 'Do Human Rights Treaties Make a Difference?' (2002) 111 Yale L.J. 1935. For a cogent response to Hathaway's skepticism see Goodman and Jinks, *supra* note 1.

[14] An especially insightful account of how narrow policy narratives deflect policy changes (even when the arguments for change are wholly incontrovertible) see, Sutton R., The Policy Process: An Overview – Working Paper 118, (Overseas Development Institute, London, 1999).

[15] Goodman and Jinks, *supra* note 11, at 626.

this resistance tends to fade through time and the momentous change becomes simply part of the (new) orthodoxy – thus making further change easier. But how can we ensure 'persuasion' and 'socialisation'? One should not rely exclusively on the fact that many diplomats were in fact 'persuaded' or 'socialised' during the negotiations (which they clearly were). Such delegates must also become 'normative entrepreneurs' within their own administrations upon their return home or inspire others to initiate change. Since diplomats do not often rotate home, a new set of institutional champions who are strongly motivated to reshape domestic law and policy in line with the Convention will have to emerge.

This essay explores the implementation and monitoring process put in place by the disability Convention. It is predicated on the vital need to gain traction between international monitoring and implementation to facilitate 'persuasion' and 'socialisation' to occur. It begins by briefly exploring how and why political failure occurs in the disability context. This gives an indication of the enormity of the tasks ahead. It then reflects on how and why traditional methods of international monitoring have not proven wholly satisfactory in getting a political dynamic of reform going and were themselves in need of reform by the time the disability Convention was being drafted. This factor tended to immensely complicate the debate over whether and what monitoring mechanism should apply in the disability Convention. Next the essay touches on the thorny issue of reservations to the Convention which, unless adequately policed, could delay forever the introduction of a positive dynamic of change at the domestic level. Apart from stymieing needed changes in the political process, such reservations could also undercut the core principles of the Convention and allow a patchwork quilt of normative understandings to develop and thus undermine its universal claims. It impossible to 'persuade' or 'socialise' Stats to right behaviour if the relevant core obligations have already been deflected! Finally, using the preceding analysis as a vantage point, this chapter analyses the implementation and monitoring regime of the disability Convention and concludes by assessing its potential to trigger real political change where it matters most – within the States Parties themselves.

A few caveats are needed at the outset. First, as lawyers we are naturally compelled to assume that the provisions in a legal instrument such as a Convention bear a solid, stable and autonomous meaning. And indeed as advocates for change we are naturally attracted to the view that the relevant norms are solid – especially when they support our own predilections. However, this assumption may not always hold true since ambiguity is never completely avoidable in a legal text. This is especially true as we depart the peremptory norms of international law (e.g., prohibition against torture or slavery) and enter more fluid realms. And States may sometimes even choose not to challenge certain language (even though they may in fact take exception to it) in order to avoid being portrayed as blocking progress. They will often do so on an assumption that their own preferred view is the correct one and will ultimately prevail.[16] Even if such issues do not give rise to formal reservations or 'interpretive declarations', they will rumble beneath the surface and bubble up at some point to confront the relevant treaty monitoring body with difficult interpretive challenges.

Secondly, even when there is a complete meeting of minds (which is rare) the language of rights may not always give a definitive answer to acute problems and especially where rights conflict. That is to say, adopting a new framework of reference may sometimes have the effect of re-stating difficult issues without necessarily resolving them. True, the issues are now re-stated at the level of principle which is itself a big gain. However, that does not obviate the need for hard interpretive choices.

At such points – creative ambiguity in the text or indeterminate norms that do not in themselves supply clear answers – it is normal for the adjudicatory body in question to plumb the deep intellectual structure of a text to divine its essence and decide accordingly. All of which only serves to underscore the need for a treaty monitoring body that fully understands the nature of the paradigm shift in the disability field away from welfare and towards rights.

Just as important, such open-textured obligations create a certain margin of appreciation of States to adopt local solutions consistent with the Convention. This is bound to fail unless a new practice of disability politics emerges that engages all stakeholders in a common search for solutions that work and are acceptable. But first, why has traditional disability politics failed?

2 *Identifying 'Democratic Failure' and the Curative Potential of the Convention*

Why is disability – considered as an issue of justice and rights – generally absent in the political process of most countries? And what difference will the Convention make in correcting for this deficiency?

Viewing democracy as an open-ended marketplace through which interest groups vie for resources (unmediated by any fixed anchorage points) impacts on all vulnerable groups.[17] But it tends to have a heightened effect on persons with disabilities who, because of their disability, encounter extremely high opportunity costs in engaging in 'normal' political agitation for change. Most persons with disabilities (and their families) are consumed with mere survival. And their plight

[16] For a fascinating study on the impact of legal diversity on the negotiation and interpretation of treaties (especially reservations) see, e.g., Bunn-Livingstone S., Juricultural Pluralism vis-à-vis Treaty Law, (Martinus Nijhoff, 2002).

[17] See generally Held D., Models of Democracy, (Stanford University Press, 2006).

tends to be experienced in isolation which makes the formation of effective civil society groups difficult especially in poorer countries. Furthermore, powerful blocking forces can potentially exercise either a veto over change, or slow the process of change, or perhaps worse yet, co-opt the language of change to rationalise continuing as before. These forces can exert much political influence especially in developed countries where the disability service sector is relatively large.[18] In the absence of sufficient political clout to effectuate change, the lack of enforceable rights is likely to leave intact and unquestioned social programmes that isolate and segregate people with disabilities.

The political marketplace – being a marketplace – tends to favour those with most voice – or whose issues connect with either the passing priorities of the day or with the permanent priority of maintaining the economic viability of the nation. But what of those whose voice is feeble? What of those whose issues do not connect up with the permanent priority of economic viability or with other passing policy priorities? They lack purchase power in the political marketplace. They have demands but there is little supply to meet those demands.

In his regard it is instructive to recall the 1938 decision of the US Supreme Court in the famous *United States v. Carolene Products* case. In that case the Supreme Court – under pressure from President Roosevelt who had previously threatened to pack the court with justices who could out-vote those who were finding aspects of the New Deal unconstitutional – announced a new theory of judicial review.[19] It foreswore reliance on ethereal and extra-textual concepts of natural law as being fundamentally undemocratic. Henceforth it pledged to rely exclusively on the text of the Constitution and its fair entailments. However, footnote 4 of the judgment pointed to the possibility of increased judicial scrutiny (i.e., going beyond purely textual grounds) in cases where a 'discrete and insular minority' could not safely rely on the 'normal' political process to adequately address their interests. At that point in time the Court had in mind racial minorities who were still effectively excluded from political participation by a variety of laws in the Southern States.

John Hart Ely famously used footnote 4 to expound his conception of 'representation reinforcement' as a legitimate judicial goal. That is, he uses it to develop a theory of when courts can and should intervene even in the absence of firm textual moorings in the interest of reinforcing the political influence

[18] This is not to deny that the service sector cannot itself also be a proactive agent for change. A remarkable example is the commitment of the European level service providers to bring about change based on the United Nations Convention on the Rights of Persons with Disabilities and in the interests of their clients. Visit the European Association of Service Providers for Persons with Disabilities (EASPD) at: www.easpd.eu.

[19] *United States v. Carolene Products*, 304 US 144 (1938). See generally, White G.E., The Constitution and the New Deal, (Harvard University Press, 2002).

that group might otherwise be expected to wield.[20] Building on the logic of footnote 4, others have even tried to portray different marginalized groups as similarly 'insular and discrete' thus warranting heighten judicial scrutiny with limited success.[21]

On occasion, the US Congress will itself deem a particular group to be a 'discrete and insular minority' especially when justifying using its power to enforce the 14th Amendment guarantee of equality by enacting far-reaching civil rights statutes. The intention is to get the courts to defer to Congressional findings and thus allow somewhat more room for experimental legislation. Indeed, the US Congress explicitly named persons with disabilities to constitute a 'discrete and insular minority' under the Americans with Disabilities Act. It states:

> (7) individuals with disabilities are a discrete and insular minority who have been faced with restrictions and limitations, subjected to a history of purposeful unequal treatment, and relegated to a position of political powerlessness in our society, based on characteristics that are beyond the control of such individuals and resulting from stereotypic assumptions not truly indicative of the individual ability of such individuals to participate in, and contribute to, society…
> [Section 2 (a)(7)].

If the intention was to prod increased deference on the part of the courts to the legislation it has not worked. In fact, the US Supreme Court has even struck down part of the ADA as unconstitutional.[22] To be precise, the Court held that Congress exceeded its powers under Section 5 of the 14th Amendment (which confers authority to enforce the 14th Amendment though civil rights legislation) and violated the 11th Amendment guaranteeing State sovereign immunity.

However, just because the current US Supreme Court is deaf to the argument does not mean that it lacks merit.

In reflecting on the substance of the footnote 4 insight in the disability context it is instructive to take on board the insights of Bruce Ackerman.[23] Ackerman takes issue with footnote 4's conflation of discreteness (meaning the group can be easily and readily identified among others) and insularity (meaning that the group has a deep collective life of its own) with the lack of political influence.

---

[20] Ely J.H., Democracy and Distrust, (Harvard University Press, 1975).

[21] See e.g., Michelman F., 'Foreword: On Protecting the Poor Through the Fourteenth Amendment' (1969) 83 Harvard L. Rev. 7.

[22] See, *Board of Trustees of the University of Alabama v. Garrett*, 530 US 356 (2001). For analysis see, Pirko J., 'The Erosion of the Separation of Powers under the 'Congruence and Proportionality Test' – From Religious Freedom to the ADA' (2001–2002) 53 Hastings L.J. 519. See also, Silvers A. and Stein M., 'From *Plessy* (1896) and *Goesart* (1948) to *Cleburne* (1985) and *Garrett* (2001)', in Krieger L.H., (Ed.), Backlash Against the ADA – Reinterpreting Disability Rights, (U. Michigan Press, 2003).

[23] See, Ackerman B., 'Beyond Carolene Products' (1985) 98 Harv. L. Rev. 713.

He does not abandon the key insight behind footnote 4 which is that courts should be more solicitous to groups that lack effective political influence. Rather he suggests the classic formulation should be re-stated to focus on groups who are anonymous (such as the gay community) and geographically thinly spread and not in possession of a rich communal life. It is these groups who – in his view – lack effective political clout and therefore deserve increased judicial attention.

It is suggested that something similar could be said in the context of disability. Disability is a classic case of an anonymous group (not always easily identifiable) and diffuse (thinly spread). There are genuinely high opportunity costs to political participation. For example, in addition to the daily struggle for existence, persons with disabilities must constantly bear in mind that open agitation against services might well lead to a reduction or a diversion of services or other forms of retaliation. And, perhaps most significantly, left to its own devices, the political system may easily revert to type within the disability sector. That is to say, it is much easier to fall back on social programmes that perpetuate helplessness than it is to consciously craft social systems that liberate individuals. Without the prod provided by some modicum of enforceable rights to test the design and implementation of such programmes they are likely to persist.

There is then a standing danger that high principle will be subtly but effectively discounted in the context of disability and that political market failure will substantially disadvantage persons with disabilities. Putting the person back in the frame is crucial to correcting these historic tendencies. This is why it is imperative to correct for the tendency of the political marketplace to either ignore or marginalise the just claims of persons with disabilities. So the core question then becomes 'can the Convention do this'? It is of course one thing to use rights – and the Convention – to challenge outcomes of a skewed political process. Yet that would have limited impact if the process itself is left unchanged. So the real test will be whether the Convention can help bring about a transformation in the process – one that would enable the idea that disability issues are issues of justice and rights to be the normal reflex rather than an annoying add-on.

3 *Why Monitor – A Catalyst for 'Persuasion' and 'Socialisation'*

In theory at least, the ostensible purpose of international treaty monitoring processes is to precisely bring about 'persuasion' and 'acculturation' to the point that the relevant universal norms become embedded as a natural default within the States Parties.

Those States that were present during the negotiations challenged civil society as well as National Human Rights Institutions to come up with an innovative system for ensuring that the Convention gained real traction in the domestic reform process. Ironically enough, even though some innovate ideas were produced and especially by civil society groups and National Human Rights Institutions (NHRIs), the drafters reverted to a fairly typical international monitoring model. There are, however, some notable innovations in the Convention with respect to implementation and monitoring. The question remains whether the process envisaged by the Convention – both for domestic implementation and for international monitoring – will be sufficiently robust and innovative to embed a self-sustaining dynamic of change. Such a dynamic and momentum for change is clearly needed in a convention of this sort where many (though not all) of the obligations are programmatic in character and where the process of change is almost as important as the changes themselves.

The classic understanding of the role of a treaty monitoring body was that it was secondary and designed primarily to engender a constructive and open dialogue with States Parties. Toward that end a system of considering State Reports submitted periodically to a Committee elected by States Parties but sitting in their personal capacities became the default setting.[24] And the practice of issuing General Comments to clarify the rights and legal obligations of States Parties contained in the various treaties became in time a useful tool to aid this process. As if to underscore this, the process for enabling the relevant treaty monitoring body to consider individual complaints or petitions was considered optional – depending entirely on making a declaration to be bound or ratifying an Optional Protocol to that effect.[25]

In order to determine the potential of the disability Convention in this regard, it is important to be clear as to the ideal image we have of a successful implementation and monitoring mechanism. The purposes of monitoring are succinctly set out by the Office of the High Commissioner for Human Rights (OHCHR) as follows:

> Current treaty monitoring mechanisms aim to achieve several objectives.
>
> The process of reporting provides an *opportunity for an individual State party to conduct a comprehensive review* of the measures it has taken to bring its national law and policy into line with the provisions of the treaties to which it is a party.
>
> The preparation of reports provides a *platform for national dialogue* on human rights amongst the various stakeholders in a State party.

---

[24] See generally Alston P., (Ed.), The United Nations and Human Rights – a Critical Appraisal, (Oxford University Press, 1992); and Alston P. and Crawford J., (Eds.), The Future of UN Human Rights Treaty Monitoring, (Cambridge University Press, 2000).

[25] See, Alfredsson G., Grimheden J., Ramcharan B. and de Zayas A., (Eds.), International Human Rights Monitoring Mechanisms, (Martinus Nijhoff, 2001). See also, Manual on Human Rights Reporting – Under Six Major International Human Rights Instruments, (Office of the UN High Commissioner for Human Rights, Geneva, 1997): see especially Ch. 2, Alston P., 'The Purposes of Reporting', 19–24.

> The report itself provides the Government and others, including civil society, with *a baseline for the elaboration of clearly stated and targeted policies, which include priorities consistent with the provisions of the treaties.*
> The process of reporting also *encourages and facilitates public scrutiny at the national level of Government approaches to implementation* and stimulates *constructive discussion with civil society* of ways to advance the enjoyment by all of the rights laid down in the various conventions.
> Consideration of the reports by the Committees, through constructive dialogue with States parties, allows individual States and States as a whole to *exchange experience on the problems faced in implementation of the instruments, and good practices that facilitate enhanced implementation.*
> It also allows for international scrutiny, which *underlines States' responsibility and accountability* for human rights protection.[26]
> [Italics added].

It is quite clear from this account that, optimally, monitoring should trigger a domestic reform process that should become self-sustaining. Even with respect to complaints – the closest one comes to a quasi-judicial procedure within the UN human rights treaty monitoring system – the Office of the High Commissioner defines its main functions thus:

> The complaints procedures provide an opportunity for treaty bodies with the competence to receive complaints to identify steps that States should take to comply with their international legal obligations in the context of concrete individual situations. The procedures offer individual relief to victims of human rights violations and should stimulate general legal, policy and programme change.[27]

Again, what is significant is the emphasis placed on using the complaint not as an end in itself (though it clearly is) but also a means to another end which is to stimulate a process of reform. And, in the same vein, the OHCHR states that the main function of inquiries is "to address the structural causes of systematic violations and make recommendations relating to a broad range of issues."[28]

Commentators generally agree with the above account. Forsyth, for example, argues that the main function of international human rights law is to socialise states toward right behaviour.[29] Another author puts this point more graphically:

> Why Monitor? The simple, short and popular answer to this query is: to be able to detect treaty violators so as to sanction them. This answer is [...] essentially wrong. A more accurate reply is: the process of monitoring is designed to improve

[26] Concept Paper on the High Commissioner's Proposal for a Unified Standing Treaty Body-Report by the Secretariat, HRI/MC/2006/2, 22 March 2006, at para. 8: available at http://www2.ohchr.org/english/bodies/icm-mc/docs/HRI.MC.2006.2.pdf.

[27] *Id.* at para. 9.

[28] *Id.*

[29] Forsythe D., The Internationalization of Human Rights, (Lexington Books, 1991).

> and enhance compliance with treaty obligations. But the methods of accomplishing this are more complicated, subtle and varied than the crime and punishment model popular with those who would analogize international legal models with to over-simplified domestic ones".[30]

That is the theory – a theory that fits eminently well with the core task of transposing the values of the disability Convention into the domestic policy mix. But the cloud hanging over the negotiations of the disability Convention was the reality that treaty practice often fell far short of the ideal.

The drafters of the disability Convention were mindful of the perceived 'failures' of the existing system of international monitoring. So much so that at many points during the drafting process it was unclear whether there would be a monitoring process at all or, if so, whether it would simply be engrafted onto the existing treaty monitoring bodies with one composite Amending Protocol.[31] The idea of this Amending Protocol was that, if ratified it would confer competence on the existing treaty monitoring bodies to which a State Party was subject to, to consider compliance under the disability Convention. There was, in short, little appetite among the drafting parties for a new international monitoring system – given the perceived failures of the existing monitoring process.[32]

These acknowledged failures had to do with widespread failure on the part of States Parties to meet their periodic reporting obligations. This had led to predictable backlogs. The situation was compounded by the part-time character of the treaty monitoring bodies which impeded their ability to handle the existing volume of work. A Report by the Secretary General in 2002, for example, stated that:

> The existing treaty bodies and human rights mechanisms and procedures constitute a large and intricate network. The growing complexity of the human rights machinery and the corresponding burden of reporting obligations strain the resources of Member States and the Secretariat. As a result, the benefits of the current system are not always clear.[33]

The Report went on to recommend two measures that might "help alleviate the shortcomings of the current system". First it recommended that the various treaty monitoring bodies coordinate their activities more and standardise

---

[30] Szasz P., Ch. 1, 'Introduction', in Szasz P., (Ed.), Administrative and Expert Monitoring of International Treaties, (Transnational Publishers, 1999).

[31] It is, of course, difficult if not impossible to see how this could work in practice without fragmenting the system even further.

[32] These failures were amply – and exhaustively – set out in Bayefsky A., (Ed.) The UN Human Rights Treaty System in the 21st Century, (Kluwer, 2000).

[33] Report of the Secretary General, Strengthening the United Nations: An Agenda for Further Change, A/57/387, 9 September 2002, at para. 52: available at http://daccessdds.un.org/doc/UNDOC/GEN/N02/583/26/PDF/N0258326.pdf?OpenElement.

their reporting requirements. Second, it recommended that each State should be allowed to produce a single report "summarising its adherence to the full range of international human rights treaties". An important seminar convened by Liechtenstein in 2003 came to much the same conclusion. It involved a broad range of stakeholders including members of the treaty monitoring bodies, NGOs, Governments and others.[34]

The Office of the High Commissioner presented Guidelines on an Expanded Core Document and harmonised guidelines on reporting at the request of the second inter-committee meeting of the treaty bodies in June 2004 and revised in 2005.[35] Harmonised Guidelines on reporting under the UN human rights treaties were adopted by the fifth inter-committee meeting of the UN human rights treaty monitoring bodies in June 2006.[36] This means that the new Committee on the Rights of Persons with Disabilities will have to work in harmony with the other more established bodies. This is no bad thing since this way of harmonising the work of the treaty monitoring bodies makes it more likely that the jurisprudential insights that it will hopefully develop will have a natural bridge into the working – *and thinking* – of the more established treaty monitoring bodies.

Oliver Wendell Holmes also once said that the "life of the law has not been logic: it has been experience."[37] Logic would, of course, point not merely to harmonised working methods but also to a full merger of the part-time treaty monitoring bodies into a merged full-time and well resourced body. Indeed, the 2005 Plan of Action by the High Commissioner contained a pledge to come forward with practical proposals with respect to such a merged body.[38] And the Office of the UN High Commissioner for Human Right produced a concept paper in 2006 that provided a practical blueprint for such an eventuality.[39] This has not happened – at least as of yet. But the fact that it was even being thought

[34] The so-called Malbun Report (named after the town of Malbun in Liechtenstein where the seminar took place): Report of a Meeting on Reform of the Human Rights Treaty Body System, A/58/123, 8 July 2003: available at http://daccessdds.un.org/doc/UNDOC/GEN/N03/423/25/PDF/N0342325.pdf?OpenElement.

[35] See, Harmonized Guidelines on Reporting under the International Human Rights Treaties, Including Guidelines on a Common Core Document and Treaty-Specific Targeted Documents, HRI/MC/2005/3, 1 June 2005: available at, http://daccessdds.un.org/doc/UNDOC/GEN/G05/422/26/PDF/G0542226.pdf?OpenElement.

[36] See generally, Report of the Working Methods on the Human Rights Treaty Bodies Relating to the State Party Reporting Process – Note by the Secretariat, HRI/MC/2008/4, 5 June 2008: available at, http://www2.ohchr.org/english/bodies/icm-mc/documents.htm.

[37] Holmes O.W., The Common Law, (Dover Publications 1991), Ch. 1, 'Lecture 1: Early Forms of Liability', p. 1.

[38] The Plan of Action is contained in A/59/2005/Add.3, 26 May 2005, at para. 147: available at, http://www2.ohchr.org/english/docs/A.59.2005.Add.3.pdf.

[39] *Supra*, note 25.

about had a (unintended but real) chilling effect over the negotiations of the disability Convention since it was argued – with some logic – that the monitoring provisions of the disability Convention could and should wait until a merged body had finally emerged (with the associated assumption that an Amending Protocol could be added later). To counteract that argument, in part, both civil society groups and National Human Rights Institutions came forward with creative proposals that would not mimic the existing system but which would genuinely innovate and perhaps even inform the shape of any future merged treaty monitoring body. The irony is that they were not accepted. This then, was the atmosphere in which the negotiations on implementation and international monitoring took place with respect to the disability Convention.

But before examining the arrangement finally agreed upon with respect to implementation and monitoring a short detour is necessary into the complex and murky world of treaty reservations. This is important since even the very best of implementation and monitoring mechanisms will have no impact whatsoever if States Parties are allowed a completely free hand to select which portions of the Convention they will accept and which they will repudiate. The temptation could well be to deflect obligations that best exemplify the core message of the Convention that persons with disabilities should be treated as subjects and not as objects. If this is allowed to happen then it is hard to see how the values of the Convention (Article 3) can have the transformative effect intended by the drafters. No amount of 'persuasion' or 'acculturation' can work if the relevant provisions can be easily side-tracked by unrestricted reservations and 'interpretive declarations' that, regardless of how they are phrased, function as 'disguised reservations'.

4 *The Need to Police Reservations that Deflect the Process of Change*

It must be emphasised that international law is predicated on the assumption of State sovereignty and that States cannot be held to accountable to treaty regimes unless and until they have specifically consented to the same. On occasion States may agree to be bound but only on the basis of certain conditions expressed as reservations. Logically at least, if the reservation in question is deemed essential to enable a State to ratify then any invalidation of the reservation should lead to a withdrawal by that State from the particular treaty regime. It might be crudely said that this resembles the 'will theory of contract' so prevalent in the nineteenth century at the international level.[40] The reservation might be analogised to an

[40] For modern restatement of the 'will theory' of contract see Fried C., Contract as Promise, (Harvard University Press, 2006).

'offer' that is 'subject to acceptance' and, if rejected, the offer (to join the treaty regime) is withdrawn.

Most of the obligations created under traditional treaty law were quite specific (generating a web of mutual obligations). An example would be a treaty that opens a named port to trade under certain conditions. Modern treaty law – especially modern human rights treaty law – is different in the sense that it transcends the normal web of mutual obligations to create a new corpus of generally applicable law (so-called 'law giving' treaties). An example would be a treaty that does not mandate specific conduct but contains general benchmarks against which conduct can be evaluated. Within traditional treaty regimes, and as befits the 'will theory of contract,' the policing of reservations could be safely left to the contracting parties. If a reservation disadvantaged any particular State then it could be counted on to protect its own interests and object. This would not affect the overall status of a multilateral treaty but it could suspend the relevant provisions of the treaty at least as between the reserving and the objecting State (at the election of the objecting state).

Modern treaty law still reflects this paradigm. And this is a problem when it comes to law-giving treaties such as human rights treaties since States are unlikely to be motivated to raise objections to reservations – even reservations that cut deep. Their own national interests are not as directly implicated as they would be under, for example, a trade agreement. Silence in the face of such reservations is in fact normal practice. This point was well put by the International Court of Justice in its 1951 Advisory Opinion on the Genocide Convention:

> In such a convention [as the Genocide Convention] the contracting States do not have any interests of their own; they merely have, one and all, a common interest, namely, the accomplishment of those high purposes which are the *raison d'être* of the convention. Consequently, in a convention of this type one cannot speak of individual advantages or disadvantages to States, or of the maintenance of a perfect contractual balance between rights and duties.[41]

But if the States don't object, then who can, on what basis and with what legal effect? To what extent can one transcend modern treaty law (which is not in fact modern and which still reflects a nineteenth century world view of international legal obligations)?

And modern international human rights law aspires to be universal. This creates contradictory pulls. On the one hand, a possibility for reservations must be made in a 'juricultural world' to enable near universal ratification.[42] On the other hand, and in order to preserve the integrity of the universal norms, there is a countervailing pressure to control at least those reservations that seem to

---

[41] Reservations to the Convention on Cenocide, Advisory opinion: [1951] ICJ Rep. 15, at. 23.

[42] See, Bunn-Livingstone, *supra* note 15.

undercut the very essence or integrity of the treaty in question. International law has somehow to mediate between these two universalisms – an impulse for universal ratification (with flexibility toward reservations) and the need for normative universality (which would seek to cabin reservations).

In point of fact, a possibility is expressly allowed for reservations under Article 46 of the disability Convention provided they are 'not incompatible with the object and purpose' of the Convention. This merely reflects current international law under Article 19 of the Vienna Convention on the Law of Treaties (VCLT) which essentially codifies customary international law with respect to treaties.[43]

Parenthetically, another treaty governs the law with respect to treaties ratified by international organisations: the Vienna Convention on the Law of Treaties between States and International Organisations or between International Organisations (1986).[44] This is relevant since the European Union has signed the disability Convention with a view to its ratification (explicit allowance was made for the accession of the EU under Article 44 CRPD). The relevant provision governing reservations is contained in Article 19 of the 1986 Convention and are in terms exactly similar to the VCLT. And indeed the 1986 Convention largely tailors (and does not materially alter) the terms of the VCLT to international organisations. However, the fact that two different conventions apply depending on the status of the ratifying entity should be borne in mind if any future issues should arise with respect to the obligations assumed by the 'regional integration organisations' (the EU) provided for under Article 44 of the CRPD.

Article 44 would not on its face appear to contemplate accession by the Council of Europe. To clear a path for Council of Europe accession one would have to make the argument that States had transferred some of their competence to the Council of Europe with respect to matters covered under the Convention (*cf.* Article 44.1). The fact that the Member States have ratified the various Council of Europe conventions such as the European Convention on Human Rights and the European Social Charter would probably not be held to pass the relevant test. Strictly speaking, States can withdraw from these conventions at any time. And the mere existence of the Council of Europe ten year action

---

[43] Convention on the Law of Treaties, 8 ILM 679 (1969). See however, The Status of International Treaties on Human Rights – Science and Technique of Democracy No. 42, (Venice Commission, Council of Europe, 2006). See generally, Craven M. and Fitzmaurice M., (Eds.), Interrogating the Treaty – Essays in the Contemporary Law of Treaties, (Wolf Legal Publishers, 2005) and especially, Ch. 10, Redgwell C., 'Reservations, Non-Compliance Procedures and the 'Policing' Role of Treaty Institutions', 195–208.

[44] Vienna Convention on the Law of Treaties between States and International Organisations or between International Organisations, 25 ILM 543 (1986).

plan on disability would not overcome this hurdle.[45] Still, it would be interesting to see if any creative arguments to the contrary emerge. It would certainly be useful to have both pan-European bodies as Parties to the disability Convention. Of course another option would be for the Council of Europe to draft its own convention on the rights of persons with disabilities taking the CRPD as its cue and matching the advances made within the Organization of American States (OAS).

Article 2.1.d of the Vienna Convention on the Law of Treaties defines a reservation as

> a unilateral statement, however phrased or named, made by a State, when signing, ratifying, accepting, approving or acceding to a treaty, whereby it purports to exclude or modify the legal effect of certain provisions of the treaty in their application to that State.

Reservations are less likely in bilateral treaties since the issue in contention is likely to form the basis of the negotiations leading to the conclusion of the treaty. And they are in any event to be distinguished from 'derogations' which may be specifically provided for in the text of a treaty allowing for the contraction of obligations (or not, as the case may be) under certain circumstances (typically a national emergency).

Article 19 VCLT allows for reservations unless:

(a) the reservation is prohibited by the treaty;
(b) the treaty provides that only specified reservations, which do not include the reservation in question, may be made; or
(c) in cases not falling under subparagraphs (a) and (b), the reservation is incompatible with the object ad purpose of the treaty.

Sub paragraph (c) above is traceable back to the aforementioned Advisory Opinion of the International Court of Justice in the *Reservations to the Convention on the Prevention and Punishment of the Crime of Genocide* in 1951.[46] In that case the Court announced a new rule of international law; namely,

> The object and purpose of the Convention thus limit both the freedom of making reservations and that of objecting to them. It follows that it is the compatibility of a reservation with the object and purpose of the Convention that must furnish the

[45] Recommendation (2006) 5 of the Committee of Ministers to Member States, on the Council of Europe Action Plan to Promote the Rights and Full Participation of People with Disabilities in Society: Improving the Quality of Life of People with Disabilities in Europe, 5 April 2006; available at, http://www.coe.int/t/e/social_cohesion/soc%2Dsp/Rec_2006_5%20Disability%20Action%20Plan.pdf.

[46] *Supra* note 40.

> criterion for the attitude of a State in making the reservation on accession as well as for the appraisal by a State in objecting to the reservation. Such is the rule of conduct which must guide every State in the appraisal which it must make, individually and from its own standpoint, of the admissibility of any reservation.[47]

However, the ICJ judgment did not specify who (or which entity) could determine compatibility.

The disability Convention neither prohibits certain reservations (as *per* 19 (a) VCLT above) nor does it allow specific reservations (as *per* 19 (b) VCLT above). So the default test for reservations falls to Article 19 (c) VCLT. Indeed, Article 46 of the disability Convention effectively repeats Article 19 (c) of the VCLT. It states:

1. Reservations incompatible with the object and purpose of the present Convention shall not be permitted.
2. Reservations may be withdrawn at any time.

So, the disability Convention neither specifically restricts reservations to certain provisions nor does it prohibit specific reservations. Effectively then, the validity of reservations depends on how their incompatibility or otherwise with the 'object and purpose of the Convention' is determined. Recourse might be had at a very general level to the purpose of the Convention as stated in Article 1 which is "to promote, protect and ensure the full and equal enjoyment of all human rights and fundamental freedoms by all persons with disabilities, and to promote respect for their inherent dignity". However, in close cases this general statement probably lacks the legal determinacy required to be able to make clear judgments about compatibility.

Before proceeding it is necessary to make a clear distinction between a 'reservation' and a 'declaration'. An 'interpretive declaration', according to Anthony Aust is:

> A unilateral declaration, however phrased or named, made by a State whereby it purports to clarify the meaning or scope attributed to the treaty or certain of its provisions.[48]

To put the matter another way, while a reservation means that a State does not feel bound by a particular provision, an 'interpretive declaration' means that a State consents to be bound but puts forward a meaning it wishes to ascribe to one or other provisions in a treaty. Such declarations may become an element –

---

[47] *Id.* at 24.

[48] Aust A., Modern Treaty Law and Practice, (Cambridge University Press, 2nd Ed., 2007), at 127.

among others – in the subsequent interpretation of the treaty. Depending on the circumstances (which would include the *travaux*) the remaining States may be tacitly held to the meaning put forward in the relevant declaration if they do not object to it or fail to make conflicting declarations. Like reservations, declarations can be easily revised or withdrawn.

An elusive point may arise whereby a 'declaration' may actually amount to a 'disguised reservation'. If in fact it does – and this begs a lot of questions about the process by which this is to be determined – then its validity is of course subject to the 'compatibility test' propounded by Article 19 (c) VCLT as reflected in Article 46.1 of the disability Convention.

In point of fact, the declarations and reservations lodged thus far are quite interesting.[49] Four States have lodged reservations. El Salvador lodged a reservation to the effect that the provisions of the Convention do "not prejudice or violate the provisions of any of the precepts, principles and norms enshrined in the Constitution of the Republic of El Salvador…" This is strange not just because it reverses the normal lexical ordering (conventions deemed superior to national law) but also because it bumps up against Article 27 VCLT which expressly states that a "party may not invoke the provisions of its internal law as justification for its failure to perform a treaty."

Malta entered a reservation with respect to the bundle of rights contained in Article 29 that are aimed at ensuring effective political participation. While expressing itself as being fully committed to Article 29, Malta nevertheless reserves the right to apply the relevant national law. Mauritius entered a reservation to Article 11 which deals with the rights of persons with disabilities in situations of risk and humanitarian emergencies. The reservation is to the effect that it does not consider itself bound unless domestic legislation expressly provides for the taking of the relevant measures. Again this makes the applicability of the international rule depend on local law – something which skates close to the prohibition in Article 27 VCLT. And Poland made a reservation to Articles 23.1 (b) and 25 (a) whereby it expressed the understanding that these provisions "shall not be interpreted in a way conferring an individual right to abortion or mandating state party to provide access thereto." Curiously enough, and notwithstanding the fact that it is styled a 'reservation', it seems to function as an 'interpretive declaration' since it attempts to put an interpretive gloss on the relevant provisions. It will be remembered however, that Article 2.1 (d) of the VCLT states that a reservation remains a reservation 'however phrased' by a State. So it would still be open to the treaty monitoring body to treat it as a reservation despite the fact that it seems phrased as a declaration. This of

[49] The text of the various reservations and declarations made thus far have been gathered together and are available at: http://www.un.org/disabilities/default.asp?id=475.

course begs a question whether the relevant treaty monitoring body has the legal capacity to pronounce.

Several States have made 'interpretive declarations'. Again, it will become an interesting issue to what extent some of these amount to 'disguised reservations.' Australia made three declarations. The first was to legal capacity (effectively Article 12) and expressed its understanding that it permitted substitute decision-making as a last resort and subject to safeguards. The second was to the right to physical and psychic integrity (effectively Article 17) and expressed its understanding that compulsory assistance or treatment is allowable when necessary, as a last resort and subject to safeguards. The third was to liberty of movement and associated rights (effectively Article 18) and expressed its understanding that liberty of movement does not create a right for a person to enter or remain in a country of which s/he is not a national nor impact on Australian health requirements when based on legitimate, objective and reasonable criteria. The interesting thing about the Australian declarations is that they did not specifically mention any particular Articles in the Convention. That maximizes its impact since it can ripple out to other provisions if those other provisions are subsequently given an expansive interpretation by the new Committee. On the other hand, by failing to cite specific Articles there is room to argue that their generality adds to vagueness which, in itself, might be viewed by some as a separate ground for 'incompatibility'.

Belgium entered a declaration that the provisions of the Convention are equally binding on the various regional and other entities of the Belgian State. To a certain extent this is curious since Article 4.5 of the Convention makes it plain that it extends to all parts of federal states without limits or exceptions. However, it was probably deemed necessary to put beyond doubt the reach of the Convention into the many complicated layers of the Belgian State apparatus.

Egypt lodged an 'interpretive declaration' to Article 12 (the right to legal capacity) expressing its understanding that the concept of legal capacity in Article 12 applies to the capacity to hold rights and not the capacity to exercise them. This distinction appears in Egyptian law (and apparently in the laws of some other States). This creates an interesting interpretive challenge for the Committee. Could this declaration be viewed as a 'disguised reservation' to Article 12 – triggering an inquiry as to its compatibility with the 'object and purpose' of the Convention? Why the reference back to Egyptian law? Could this be viewed as an attempt to elevate Egyptian law over the law of the Convention – thus triggering separate concerns under Article 27 VCLT?

Mexico also lodged an 'interpretive declaration' to Article 12 which will keep connoisseurs of treaty law busy for some time to come. It is to the effect that, in cases of conflict between Article 12.2 (assuring a right to legal capacity) and Mexican law, then the provision that contains the 'greater level of protection' will prevail. Assuming, *arguendo*, that a higher level is provided under Mexican law, then the declaration would appear surplusage since Article 4.4 of the Convention is already to the effect that the Convention does not prejudice any national "provisions which are more conducive to the realization of the rights" contained in the Convention. In any event, who is to say whether Mexican law provides superior protection and in accordance with what criteria? A trickier question might well be 'is this a disguised reservation' triggering an inquiry about 'compatibility' under Article 19 (c) of the VCLT? This will not be easy to untangle.

And Malta entered a declaration to the effect that the term "sexual and reproductive health" in Article 25 (a) does not create any new right to abortion. This is plain from the *travaux*. So the declaration was probably made to put the matter beyond doubt and to stake out ground for internal political purposes.

In sum, there already is an interesting kaleidoscope of reservations and declarations to the disability Convention. This brings to the fore a series of connected questions all centered on the process for determining their validity. Customary international law used to be to the effect that *all* other contracting Parties would have to accept a reservation before it became valid. That of course was not suited to the great growth of multilateral treaties from the 1900s onwards. The 'new' practice – now codified in the VCLT – is that unanimous acceptance of a reservation is not necessary for it to have effect. Silence – on the part of the other States Parties – can be taken as acceptance of a reservation at the conclusion of twelve months following the communication of the reservation (Article 20.5 VCLT). And

> an objection by another contracting State to a reservation does not preclude the entry into force of the treaty as between the objecting and reserving States unless a contrary intention is definitely expressed by the objecting State.[50]

So an objection need not have a legal effect unless *explicitly* stated to have one by the objecting State.

Interestingly, Article 20.2 of the VCT states:

When it appears from the limited number of the negotiating States and the object and purpose

> of a treaty that the application of the treaty in its entirety between all the parties is an essential condition of the consent of each one to be bound by the treaty, a reservation requires acceptance by all the parties.

However, that is not the case with the disability Convention since the very insertion of Article 46 contemplates reservations.

So treaty law – as exemplified by the VCLT – remains predicated on a vision of sovereign States as unconnected atoms contracting in and out of mutual

[50] Article 20.4 (b) VCLT.

obligations on the basis of consent – whether full or conditional. The situation is well summed up by one commentator thus:

> In the absence of [an explicit] treaty mechanism or control [i.e., for adjudicating on the compatibility of reservations], and under the default rules of the VCLT, it is for the other States party to the treaty to respond – if at all – to reservations made, and within a twelve month period of the communication of the reservation.[51]

Indeed, just as there is no obligation to object, there is also no limitation as the grounds of an objection. And, it bears repeating that it is for the objecting State to state what the legal effects (if any) of the objection would be as between the two States in question.

As previously mentioned the normal practice of States in the face of reservations is one of silence. The issue might well manifest itself in litigation when an individual may challenge the validity of a reservation that, if deemed valid, might block a hearing of his/her case on the merits (assuming that the existence of an organ to render binding adjudication is in fact specified by the treaty in question). The problem was well put by Professor Redgwell as follows:

> The difficulty arises in overlaying this horizontal, voluntary and bilateral system with a criterion of validity in the absence of a collective or institutional mechanism for determination of validity.[52]

So, who (or what) can make authoritative determinations as to 'compatibility' and what are the legal effects of such determinations? Before dealing with this crucial issue (assuming the text of the relevant treaty is silent on the matter) there would appear to be three options following upon an authoritative declaration of incompatibility.[53]

The first option – which reflects the reality that international legal regulations arise primarily from the freely given consent of sovereign states – would hold that the State remains a Party to the treaty and that the reservation would take effect notwithstanding its invalidity. This reaction comes from the view that no matter how distasteful a reservation is, it must be allowed to stand in deference to the sovereignty of the States Parties. To a certain extent this makes a mockery of Article 19 (c).

The second option would be to fix on the incompatible reservation as a reason for vitiating the consent of a State Party and holding that the entirety of the treaty does not apply. This has the merit of highlighting the importance of core

---

[51] Redgwell, *supra* note 42, at 199.

[52] *Id.* at 200.

[53] See Moloney R., 'Incompatible Reservations to Human Right Treaties: Severability and the Problem of State Consent', [2004] Melb. J.I.L. 6.

provisions and punishing States that purport to ratify but then undermine this by refusing to be bound by these core obligations.

The last option is allow the offending State the benefit of being a Party but to sever the offending reservation and to proceed as if it had not been made. In a way, this option is not faithful to the foundation of international law which rests exclusively on the express consent of the Parties. To put it another way, it prioritises one form of univeralism (the normative integrity of a treaty) over another (manufacturing space for universal ratification by allowing maximum space for reservations) and is inherently problematic for that reason.

One author suggests that there ought to be a presumption that an invalid reservation is not an essential condition of a State's decision to ratify unless clear evidence to the contrary is provided.[54] Contrariwise, if the relevant State has stated (or it can reasonably be inferred) that without the reservation in question it would not have ratified then the reservation should be left standing (in deference to State sovereignty). On the other hand, if no such evidence is forthcoming – whether on the face of the reservation or otherwise – then the relevant adjudicatory body should feel free to sever the reservation and treat the State Party as having ratified all provisions disregarding the reservation.

What does contemporary practice tell us about how international law is adjusting to 'law giving' treaties like the disability Convention? The answer is clearer at regional level than it is at the global level. The European Court of Human Rights has, on two separate occasions, asserted its inherent jurisdiction to pronounce on the validity of reservations. It is to be noted that Article 64 of the European Convention on Human Rights (original numbering) specifically allows for certain (narrowly defined) reservations. It reads:

1. Any State may, when signing this Convention or when depositing its instrument of ratification, make a reservation in respect of any particular provision of the Convention to the extent that any law then in force in its territory is not in conformity with the provision. Reservations of a general character shall not be permitted under this article.
2. Any reservation made under this article shall contain a brief statement of the law concerned.

This covers the eventuality set out in Article 19 (b) of the VCLT (allowance made for certain types of reservations – but not others). In *Belilos v. Switzer-*

54 See Goodman R., 'Human Rights Treaties, Invalid Reservations and State Consent' (2002) 96 A.J.I.L. 531.

land[55] (1988) the respondent State had made an 'interpretive declaration' to Article 6 of the ECHR (right to fair trial) which had the effect of excluding judicial proceedings in the Cantons from review. When defending itself in the instant case Switzerland argued that the 'interpretive declaration' was in fact a reservation – the implication being that the case at bar should be dismissed by the European Court. In holding that the 'interpretive declaration' was indeed a reservation the Court reasoned that it had to look beyond its title and focus on its substance.[56] But this was not the end of the matter. The Court then asserted its jurisdiction to pronounce on the validity of the reservation under Article 64. It fortified its conclusion by reference to Articles 45 (jurisdiction of the Court extends to all cases "concerning the interpretation and application" of the Convention) and 49 which helpfully stated that in the event of a dispute as to whether the Court has jurisdiction, the matter shall be settled by the decision of the Court.[57] It also alluded to the establishment of the Court itself (article 19). From these combined textual moorings, it followed, in the opinion of the Court, that it had the jurisdiction to ascertain whether the relevant declaration (in fact a reservation) satisfied the requirements of Article 64.

On a close reading of the relevant text of the declaration (really a disguised 'reservation') – which was deemed ambiguous – the Court came to the conclusion that it violated the prohibition in Article 64.1 against 'reservations of a general character.' The Court also proceeded to find a separate violation of Article 64.2. (failure to communicate a brief statement of the domestic law implicated). The Court found that two violations of Article 64 had occurred and that as a result, the relevant 'reservation' was invalid.

It will be remembered that the default setting of the VCLT is that it is for another contracting State to object and to pronounce on the legal effect (if any) of the objection as between it and the reserving State. Notwithstanding this, the European Court of Human Rights not only took it upon itself to pronounce on the validity of the 'reservation' but also went on to specify its legal effects. It effectively severed the offending 'reservation' from Switzerland's ratification of the Convention. It stated "it is beyond doubt that Switzerland is, and regards itself as, bound by the Convention irrespective of the validity of the declaration."[58]

It is to be noted that the decision in *Belilos* as to invalidity was not taken on the basis that the offending 'disguised reservation' was 'incompatible with the object and purpose of the treaty' (*cf.* Article 19 (c) VCLT). Rather, the European

[55] *Belilos v. Switzerland*, Judgment of the Court, Series A., No. 132, Application No. 10328/83, 29 April 1988.
[56] *Id.* at para. 49.
[57] Subsequently renumbered as Article 32, 1. & 2.
[58] *Supra* note 54, at para. 60.

Court adjudicated on the validity of the 'disguised reservation' on the basis that it went beyond what was *specifically allowed* under Article 64.1 ECHR. So it looks very much like an adjudication under Article 19 (b) of the VCLT (prohibition against going beyond what a treaty specifically allows with respect to reservations). Still, it was an exercise of adjudicatory power that is not expressly contemplated by the VCLT.

If *Belilos* can be explained away by reference to the text of the ECHR which seems, at least on one reading, to explicitly confer the relevant authority on the Court (and so can be rationalised as an exercise in giving effect to the will of the States Parties in ratifying the Convention) then the decision of the Court *Loizidou v. Turkey*[59] (1995) goes much further by emphasising the qualitatively distinct character of multilateral human rights treaties as an added reason to slip the mooring of the VCLT.

At issue in *Loizidou* was a 'declaration' made by Turkey that effectively purported to put beyond the jurisdiction of the European Commission on Human Rights (as it then was) any matter arising from Turkish occupied Cyprus. The declaration was attached to Article 25 (as originally numbered) which created the possibility that contracting States could, by declaration, accept the jurisdiction of the Commission to receive individual petitions.

The instant case involved a property claim by a Greek Cypriot relating to property in Northern Cyprus. The relevant 'declaration' was indeed circulated to the other States Parties by the Secretary General of the Council of Europe with his own comments (a practice not followed by the UN Secretary General since the 1951 ruling of the ICJ). And indeed, many contracting Parties did repeatedly respond (i.e., object) as the declaration was successively renewed by Turkey.

The Court held that the term 'jurisdiction' in Article 1 of the ECHR could engage Turkish State responsibility with respect to Northern Cyprus. The core question then became whether the 'declaration' was a valid restriction of its responsibilities. The Court reasoned that

> the object and purpose of the Convention as an instrument for the protection of individual human beings requires that its provisions be interpreted and applied *so as to make its safeguards practical and effective*...[60]
> [Italics added].

The Court effectively held that the choice of a State Party to opt-in to the jurisdiction of the Commission (as it then was) was on an all-or-nothing basis. It rested its conclusion both on a textual analysis of the relevant provisions allowing for an opt-in as well as on Article 64. But perhaps uppermost in its

---

[59] *Loizidou v. Turkey*, Series A, No. 310, Application No., 15318/89, 23 March 1995.

[60] *Id.* at para. 72.

mind was the damage that a patchwork quilt of varying territorial commitments would have wrought on the special 'constitutional' character of the Convention. Even if the original opt-in could once have been considered open-ended (and therefore subject to cutting reservations) it could not longer be so since both the substantive and procedural dimensions of the ECHR formed part of the same 'living instrument'. It was then a short jump to the conclusion that the relevant reservation would:

> not only seriously weaken the role of the Commission and Court in the discharge of their functions but would also diminish the effectiveness of the Convention as a constitutional instrument of European public order...[61]

Turkey next argued that if the relevant declarations (really a reservation) were invalid then its opt-in to the jurisdiction of the Commission and the Court should be itself treated as invalid and it should no longer be subjected to the jurisdiction of the Court. It is at least a logical argument. The permanent representative of Turkey to the Council of Europe had stated on the record that the declaration was so essential to the Turkish opt-in that if invalidated then the opt-in would itself fall. The question was, in light of the special character of the Convention "whether the impugned restrictions can be severed from the instruments of acceptance [of jurisdiction] or whether they form an integral and inseparable part of them."[62] It is interesting that the question was framed thus by the Court. The Court *appeared* to be allowing room for an argument that *but for* the reservation in question a State would not have ratified and that in those circumstances the ratification in its entirely could not stand. However, this was not in fact the case in *Liozidou* according to the Court. The Court concluded that the impugned restrictions could be 'severed' from the Turkish opt-in which left the opt-in standing (without the restrictions).

So, at least at European regional level, the European Court of Human Rights has asserted a jurisdiction to pronounce on the compatibility of reservations on the basis of the explicit language in the Convention which appeared to grant it this authority but also on an understanding of the special object and purpose of the ECHR to establish a new multilateral set of 'constitutional' norms and to embed a 'effective' means of supervision. This was a plausible move at regional level where legal diversity is not so pronounced. What of the global level? To what extent can the new UN Committee on the Rights of Persons with disabilities exercise a similar jurisdiction?

There is some useful precedent. The treaty monitoring body under the International Covenant on Civil and Political Rights (ICCPR) – the UN Human Rights

[61] *Id.* at para. 75.
[62] *Id.* at para. 97.

Committee (HRC) – issued General Comment 24 in 1994 on '*Issues relating to reservations made upon ratification or accession to the Covenant or the Optional Protocols thereto, or in relation to declarations under Article 41 of the Covenant*'.[63] This is a fascinating document and deserves to be read by all incoming members of the new disability treaty monitoring body. It is to be noted that there is no provision in the ICCPR equivalent to Article 46 in the CRPD. That is to say, the ICCPR does not on its face either specifically allow for certain reservations nor specifically prohibit others. Article 19 (c) of the VCLT is therefore the natural default setting (the 'compatibility' test).

General Comment 24 opens by distinguishing law-giving human rights treaties – which establish universal rules to be applied for the benefit of all human beings within the jurisdiction of the States Parties – from traditional treaties which set out rules of behavior of States *inter se*. The main theme of the General Comment is that the practice of allowing States themselves to control reservations (through the lodging of formal objections together with a statement of legal effect) is wholly inappropriate in the context of more universal instruments.

It stated that the VCLT (which speaks only on the role of objecting States and not of the legal authority of multilateral *fora* such as treaty monitoring bodies in the context of reservations) is itself inappropriate in the context of human rights treaties. It concluded that it:

> necessarily falls to the Committee to determine whether a specific reservation is compatible with the object and purpose of the Covenant. This is in part because [...] it is an inappropriate task for States parties in relation to human rights treaties, and in part because it is a task that the Committee cannot avoid in the performance of its functions.[64]

The Committee went on to identify several types of reservations that it considered to be incompatible with the object and purpose of the ICCPR. For example, reservations to the peremptory norms of customary international law (as expressed in many Articles of the Covenant) would not be countenanced. These included freedom from slavery, the right to life, the prohibition against torture, inhuman or degrading treatment, etc. Reservations to the prohibition against non-discrimination were deemed by the Committee to be incompatible with the objects and purpose of the Convention to create legally binding standards for human rights. Likewise, reservations that undermined the efficacy of the supervisory mechanism and which foreclose effective domestic remedies or which sought to give lexical priority to domestic law over the ICCPR were also

---

[63] Available at: http://www.unhchr.ch/tbs/doc.nsf/(Symbol)/69c55b086f72957ec12563ed004ecf7a?Opendocument.

[64] *Id.* at para. 18.

deemed incompatible. To a certain degree, the Committee was only drawing on exactly the same kind of logic used by the European Court of Human Rights and indeed anticipated the reasoning that emerged shortly afterwards in *Loizidou* – but with the difference that it was not a regional Court.

With respect to the question concerning the legal effects of an invalid reservation the Committee asserted that:

> The normal consequence of an unacceptable reservation is not that the Covenant will not be in effect at all for the reserving party. Rather, such a reservation will generally be severable, in the sense that the Covenant will be operative for the reserving party without benefit of the reservation.[65]

In practice, however, the Committee has stopped short of pronouncing on certain reservations as a matter of law. Certainly the US responded negatively to General Comment 24. It responded:

> The reservations contained in the United States instrument of ratification [to the ICCPR] are integral parts of its consent to be bound by the Covenant and are not severable. If it were to be determined that any one or more of them were ineffective, the ratification as a whole would thereby be nullified.[66]

All of which creates conundrums for the incoming Committee on the Rights of Persons with Disabilities.

I set out above the various 'declarations' and 'reservations' already entered – not with a view to adjudicating upon them but with a view of giving a flavour of their diversity and intricacy. Granted some reservations may be 'essential' to enable some States to ratify. Interestingly, none of the reserving States to the disability Convention have, so far, made this point (and would on that score be more amenable to severability). Equally interestingly, no State had lodged a formal 'objection' to a reservation.[67]

Assuming that the United States will, for example sign and ratify at some point, reservations may be necessary. It is hard to see the United States ratifying the relevant provisions on the right to health care unless major substantive changes are made at the domestic level. It might therefore be tempted to ratify with reservations on the basis that, *but for these reservations*, it would not feel bound. But it is equally obvious that the incoming Committee should develop its own sense of the object and purpose of the Convention with a view to enabling it to determine which reservations (including 'disguised reservations') are compatible.

---

[65] *Id.* at para. 18.

[66] Cited by Redgwell, *supra* note 42, at 202.

[67] The twelve month rule within which to make a formal objection provided for by Article 20.5 VCLT may not yet have expired on all of the reservations – depending on when the reservation in question was lodged and notified.

For the moment, it appears that the Committee would only have the authority to make 'recommendations' that such reservations would be withdrawn. But this is a fluid field and it is not beyond imagination that it might assert a more robust jurisdiction. In all likelihood, the incoming Committee will need to draft a General Comment along the lines of General Comment 24 of the HRC. The debate is contentious – but it is vital that the incoming Committee becomes alive to the dangers of unduly intrusive reservations.

It should be noted that the International Law Commission (ILC) is presently studying the issue of reservations and the continued appropriateness of the regime under the VCLT.[68] In 1997 the ILC adopted a resolution on 'reservations to normative multilateral treaties including human rights treaties'.[69] While it reiterated the primacy of the VCLT regime, it also acknowledged that the establishment of treaty monitoring bodies gave rise to legal issues that were not envisaged at the time of the drafting of the relevant treaties especially dealing with the compatibility of reservations. It went so far as to agree that treaty monitoring bodies are at least entitled to make recommendations as to compatibility – stopping short of making definitive legal pronouncements. It even suggested that consideration be given to adopting amending protocols to the relevant treaties to confer explicit authority on the treaty monitoring bodies to make definitive pronouncements on reservations. And it called on States to give due consideration to the (non-binding) recommendations of treaty monitoring bodies with respect to reservations.

One document that should also form essential reading for the incoming Committee is a paper by the 20th Meeting of Chairpersons of the Human Rights Treaty Bodies and 7th Inter-Committee Meeting published in June 2008 which gathers together the existing jurisprudence of the various UN human rights treaty monitoring bodies on reservations.[70] It recounts, for example, all of the instances in which the treaty monitoring bodies have called for reservations to be withdrawn – and its effects. And it contains a useful table of objections to reservations and the subsequent withdrawal of reservations.

And it should also be remembered that under Article 46.2 of the disability Convention a reservation can be withdrawn 'at any time'. Thus, depending on the weight of public opinion brought to bear by civil society, States should be encouraged to see even valid reservations as temporary in character to be

---

68 The ILC Special Rapporteur on reservations is M Pellet. For information on the work of the ILC with respect to treaty reservations see http://www.un.org/law/ilc/.

69 See A/CN.4/L.540, 4 July 1997: available at, http://daccessdds.un.org/doc/UNDOC/LTD/G97/624/80/PDF/G9762480.pdf?OpenElement.

70 Report on Reservations, HRI/MC/2008/5, 29 May, 2008: available at, http://www2.ohchr.org/english/bodies/icm-mc/documents.htm.

removed as soon as possible in order to uphold the normative integrity of the disability Convention.

5 *Innovative Monitoring Proposals on the Table*

In order to gauge how far the text innovates with respect to implementation and monitoring it proves important to get a flavour of how radical and innovative some of the proposals were during the negotiations.

Prior to the first session of the *Ad Hoc Committee* in August 2002, Mexico hosted an international seminar on the topic. The participants discussed a draft text produced by Mexico. Mexico then tabled this amended draft text before the Ad Hoc Committee.[71] Article 20 of the Mexican draft text proposed to establish a Committee of Experts on the Rights of Persons with Disabilities whose functions would be to (a) evaluate national periodic reports, (b) make recommendations of a general nature to the States Parties and to (c) engage with Specialised Agencies. Mexico also proposed the creation of a Conference of States Parties (Article 19) to promote international cooperation in the field, to consider the recommendations of the Committee of Experts and to elaborate reports on agreements it reaches with its members. Interestingly, the Mexican draft contained a provision that would prohibit reservations incompatible with the object and purpose of the Convention (Article 26.2) and it contained a provision to the effect that any dispute over interpretation could be submitted to arbitration and, failing that, to the International Court of Justice (Article 27).

During the proceedings of the Working Group in January 2004 the Chair of the *Ad Hoc Committee* presented 'Draft Elements of a Comprehensive and Integral International Convention on Protection and Promotion of the Rights and Dignity of Persons with Disabilities'. It was accompanied by 'Draft Elements on Implementation: Application, Implementation and Monitoring of the Convention.'[72] The Chair's proposal contained two models. Model A would have obliged the States Parties:

> to establish national human rights institutions (or use existing ones) to monitor the implementation of the Convention, and monitor implementation through a national reporting process; (b) that the United Nations establish the office of United Nations Disability Ombudsman; and (c) that States undertake to report

---

[71] Comprehensive and integral international convention to promote and protect the rights and dignity of persons with disabilities, A/AC/265/WP.1. Text available at: http://www.un.org/esa/socdev/enable/rights/adhocmeetaac265w1e.htm.

[72] Draft Elements on Implementation: Application, Implementation and Monitoring of the Convention, 24 December 2003. Text is available at: http://www.un.org/esa/socdev/enable/rights/wgcontrib-chair2.htm.

on disability issues in their reports submitted under the existing United Nations human rights treaties.

A novel element in Model A would have been the requirement to set up or use National Human Rights Institutions. It also proposed the creation of a United Nations Disability Ombudsman with the power to promote the Convention and also to receive communications alleging violations and to represent the persons before State authorities or before the relevant UN human rights treaty monitoring body.

Model B envisioned the setting up of a national implementation framework with a traditional treaty monitoring body with powers to consider periodic reports from the States Parties, an individual communications procedure and an inquiry procedure. For the moment these proposals were set to one side because the more substantive articles took centre stage during the negotiations and because of the clear insistence of many States that something much more innovative than the existing model of treaty monitoring was required. The mood at the early sessions of the Ad Hoc Committee leaned heavily against international monitoring at least of the traditional sort.

The issue came back during the 6th Session of the *Ad Hoc Committee* in August 2006. The International Disability Caucus (IDC) was especially alive to the importance of implementation and monitoring.[73] It produced its own draft text on monitoring and implementation. It envisaged the creation of an international treaty monitoring body. Many aspects of the IDC proposal were highly innovative. For example, the Committee was to be composed of members who were all persons with disabilities (IDC draft Article 2 (a)). Each State Party was to nominate two persons for election to be chosen from a list of individuals *proposed by organisations of persons with disabilities within the relevant State* (IDC draft Article 3). It was proposed that the shortlisting was to be done by a joint International Disability Consortium or IDC (an amalgam of disability NGOs brought together for the specific purpose of forging common positions during the negotiations) with the International Disability Alliance or IDA[74] (which is an ongoing alliance of the worlds major disability organisations such as the World Blind Union, Rehabilitation International, etc). and State Party selection panel. The IDC draft also envisaged the drafting of National Action Plans (IDC Draft Part IV) and the establishment or designation of independent national mechanisms (IDC Draft Part V) for the protection of the rights

[73] IDC Draft Article 25: text available at,. http://www.un.org/esa/socdev/enable/rights/ahc6contngos.htm.

[74] Visit International Disability Alliance (IDA) at: http://www.internationaldisabilityalliance.org/.

of persons with disabilities at the national level. The IDC provided very useful detail with respect to procedure.

Arguably the most innovative set of proposals came from National Human Rights Institutions (NHRIs) during the Sixth Session of the Ad Hoc Committee in 2005.[75] Due to the domestic nature of their work, NHRIs are all too keenly aware of the huge gap between international law and domestic practice. Unusually, and helpfully, the NHRI monitoring proposal came in the form of draft text for the Convention. The NHRI proposal called for the crafting of a National Baseline Report (on a consultative basis with all relevant stakeholders including civil society groups) which would form the basis of national inputs to an international monitoring body. More importantly, the Baseline Report should inform the crafting of a National Action Plan which would "specify the measures to be taken to achieve the full, effective and equal enjoyment of the human right of persons with disabilities" – again on the basis of active consultation with civil society. The idea was to use the ratification of the Convention as an occasion for focusing in a sustained way on the changes needed to bring law and practice into harmony with the Convention and to create a dynamic for the implementation of the more programmatic elements of the Convention.

Interestingly, the NHRI proposal did not start with international monitoring. It started instead with domestic monitoring. Essentially, the NHRI proposal envisaged a national monitoring body to be established or designated by States Parties in conformity with the Paris Principles[76] with a remit to 'promote, protect and monitor domestic compliance' – especially with the National Action Plan. So it was to hold Government to account not merely to the majestic generalities of the Convention but also to the specific targets contained in the Government's own National Action Plan. The NHRI proposed that the national monitoring body should also be tasked to make recommendations – of its own motion – with respect to existing or draft legislation and entertain or support complaints (depending on the specific competencies allocated to it under the relevant domestic legislation). It would have been charged to liaise directly with the proposed treaty monitoring body – the Committee on the Rights of Persons with Disabilities.

The NHRI proposal also called for the creation of a Committee on the Rights of Persons with Disabilities at the international level. But it underscored its role as secondary or subsidiary to that of the domestic monitoring body. It

---

[75] The NHRI text is available at, http://www.un.org/esa/socdev/enable/rights/ahcstata34sscomments.htm#nhri.

[76] Principles relating to the Status of National Institutions (Paris Principles), General Assembly Resolution 48/134, 20 December 1993: text available at, http://www2.ohchr.org/English/law/parisprinciples.htm.

envisaged the existing UN Special Rapporteur as an *ex officio* member – really as a way of embedding the expertise of that office into the process of international monitoring. The NHRI proposal had an interesting perspective on how the members of the new Committee were to be elected. It envisaged a Committee of ten composed of five members elected by the States Parties on the basis of nominations received from States Parties and five to be elected by the States from a list prepared by the Office of the UN High Commissioner for Human Rights after due consultation with civil society groups. The intention was to ensure that genuine expertise on human rights and disability was present on the Committee and that persons with disabilities would have some say in the process. Indeed, the NHRI proposal also insisted that a majority of the members of the Committee should include members who themselves have a disability.

Perhaps the most remarkable aspect of the NHRI proposal was that it did not envisage that the primary – or even the main – task of the Committee would be to evaluate Periodic State reports. Taking a cue from the exhortation of the States (especially in earlier sessions of the *Ad Hoc Committee*) to think innovatively, the NHRI proposal envisaged a set of '*facilitative roles*' for the Committee. Essentially these 'facilitative roles' were aimed at assisting States Parties in fulfilling their obligations. Four such roles were envisaged.

The first was to clarify the obligations of States Parties by adopting General Comments. Explicit power was added to enable this to happen – and in the result boost the flimsy legal status of such documents. The second was to help States by crafting Guidelines for the crafting of National Action Plans as well as Baseline Reports. This was felt needed in order to ensure some uniformity in the approach of States which would facilitate meaningful comparative analysis as well as pertinent recommendations (as distinct from general recommendations that are not closely tailored to national circumstances). Thirdly, and this is where the NHRI proposal was most innovative, it envisaged 'thematic reporting' from States Parties on the basis of requests from States Parties (acting either individually or regionally), from NHRIs themselves, from the Global Disability Rights Advocate (see below) or on its own motion. That is to say, such reporting would not be periodic but would be triggered by genuine concerns. For example States Parties might decide that the issue of legal capacity was urgent and relatively intractable. Ideally, they should request the initiation of a thematic reporting process whereby States would be asked to report on the basis of a prepared template on that issue. The Committee would then produce a Thematic Study with a set of recommendations to overcome their difficulties which could also be directed to the UN family of Specalised Agencies if felt useful. The core idea here is that the Committee should contribute to the *search for solutions* and not confine itself to passing judgment on individual States Parties.

The only genuflection towards 'normal' reporting contained in the NHRI proposal was that the Committee would periodically assess progress in implementing

National Action Plans. The idea here is that monitoring would be a constant spur to further action rather than a set of conclusions about past performance.

The NHRI proposal envisaged that the Committee would function collaboratively with disability NGOs (non governmental organisations) and DPOs (disabled persons organisation – essentially NGOs run by disabled persons themselves), with national monitoring bodies and with other international bodies and especially the Specialised Agencies of the UN. Another innovative feature of the NHRI proposal was that the Committee should have a regional focus

> in order to ensure that [it] has the capacity to better appreciate circumstances within regions that help explain the nature of the problems experienced and especially the kinds of solutions that would produce tangible results...[77]

In order to do this the NHRI draft envisaged that the Committee could meet regionally as well as initiate and inform regional dialogues about the implementation of the Convention.

The NHRI draft also envisaged the creation of a *Global Disability Rights Advocate* (much along the same lines of the Disability Ombudsman proposed by the IDC) which would act as a focal-point to take proactive measures to ensure the effectiveness of the Convention and to complement the work of the Committee. The functions of the Global Advocate were said to be (1) to promote the Convention, (2) to highlight and facilitate the exchange of best practice, (3) to recommend areas that require Thematic Study by the Committee, (4) to help raise the capacity of civil society organisations, (5) to help raise the capacity of national monitoring bodies, (6) to help raise the capacities of national implementation bodies, (7) to assist individuals or groups of individuals in submitting suitable complaints to the Committee and (8) to take part in all UN activities related to disability. The basic idea behind this proposal was that there should exist an institutional champion for the Convention. This view was shared by the IDC.

NHRIs did envisage a complaints role of the Committee. It envisaged both an individual complaints mechanism as well as a collective complaints mechanism. The emphasis placed on collective complaints was interesting. It was loosely modelled on the Collective Complains mechanism of the European Social Charter.[78] It stemmed from the almost atavistic hostility of the States during the negotiations to allowing any complaints mechanism at least with respect to those obligations that are cost-intensive (or at least more cost-intensive than 'normal'). The fear was that the tail (individual suit) could wag the dog (difficult decisions about

[77] *Supra* note 74, draft Article 37.

[78] See, e.g., Quinn G., Ch. 14, 'The European Social Charter and EU Anti-discrimination Law in the Field of Disability: Two Gravitational Fields with One Common Purpose,' in De Burca G. and de Witte B., (Eds.), Social Rights in Europe, (Oxford University Press, 2005).

the allocation of scare resources). Logically, however, this resistance to complaints should diminish according as representative cases emerge that demonstrate gross deficiencies that any system would want to set right (even in its own interests of cost-effectiveness as well as rationality and fairness). So admitting such collective complaints could bring to light, for example, how whole groups have been neglected (usually the ones lacking strong political voice) or where the relativities either between groups or within a particular group is not objectively justifiable. As will be seen, the text finally adopted does indeed allow for a collective dimension to the complaints mechanism under the Optional Protocol to the Convention.

The remarkable thing about the NHRI proposal was that it focused less on international monitoring as an end itself and more as a stimulus to keep the domestic reform process going. It could be said that this is more faithful to the original intention of international monitoring.

As is clear from the foregoing, the *Ad Hoc Committee* was well served with creative ideas about implementation and monitoring. It also had the benefit of a useful paper from the UN High Commissioner for Human Rights explaining the existing UN human right treaty monitoring system as well as a compilation of suggestions and proposal compiled by Mexico.[79]

6 *The Implementation and Monitoring Process under the Convention – Some Innovations*

Mexico was charged with the task of crunching down the various proposals and presented a 'non-paper' on the 'Draft elements for a monitoring mechanism of the international convention on the rights of persons with disabilities.'[80] Under the heading 'general understandings' the Mexican 'non-paper' emphasised that international monitoring is essential, that it should at least be at the same level as existing instruments, that it presents an opportunity to learn from the lessons of the other treaty monitoring bodies and that it should take into account the reform process. It envisaged monitoring powers, inquiry powers and an optional complaints function. It added miscellaneous powers such as the power to issue

---

[79] Monitoring implementation of the international human rights instruments: an overview of the current treaty body system: Background conference document prepared by the Office of the United Nations High Commissioner for Human Rights, A/AC.265/2005/CRP.2, 24 January – 4 February 2005: available at, http://www.un.org/esa/socdev/enable/rights/ahc5documents.htm.

[80] This non-paper was tabled by Mexico during the 8th Session of the Ad Hoc Committee. Non-paper on monitoring: Draft elements for a monitoring mechanism of the international convention on the rights of persons with disabilities, 15 June 2006: available at, http://www.un.org/esa/socdev/enable/rights/ahc8documents.htm.

General Comments and to conduct thematic studies. With respect to nominations to the new treaty monitoring body the 'non-paper' envisaged that States Parties could nominate up to two persons (in consultation with civil society) – one of whom need not be a citizen of the State in question (provided his/her State agreed).

The Mexican 'non-paper' also provided useful ideas on the establishment of a Conference of States Parties. It asserted that "A Conference or Meeting of States Parties could have an active role in over viewing the implementation of the Convention, by using it as a forum that may review any matter related to the operation of the Convention".[81] Anticipating that the treaty reform process might delay the development of a fully developed treaty monitoring mechanism in the disability Convention, the Mexican 'non-paper' purported to confer on the Conference of States Parties the role of "defining possible reforms of the monitoring mechanism". The 'non-paper' also envisaged a detailed relationship between the new treaty monitoring body and national, international and regional actors (note the recurring theme of a regional dimension to the Convention). And the 'non-paper' drew attention to the need to carefully consider the role of any possible Ombudsman on disability (an idea put forward both by the IDC and the NHRIs). If created, it urged that it would be used for advocacy and public awareness. And it drew attention to the need to consider the role of the Ombudsman with respect to the other treaty monitoring bodies. In this light, it even urged States to consider the future role of the UN Rapporteur on Disability of the Commission for Social Development.

So the ground was more than adequately prepared for decisions as to the shape of the implementation and monitoring that would emerge from the later sessions of the *Ad Hoc Committee.*

The Convention, as finally adopted, does innovate both at the international level and also with respect to the domestic reform process which is what matters most.

It combines a traditional treaty monitoring body – the Committee on the Rights of Persons with Disabilities (Articles 34–29) with a Conference of States Parties (Article 40) at the international level. But, probably more importantly, it demands the creation of an effective institutional architecture for change at the domestic level. It requires, for example, a 'focal point' within Government for implementation (Article 33: National Implementation and Monitoring). This will be new for most States. This – linked back to Article 4.3 which calls for active consultation with persons with disabilities and their representative organisations in designing policy – should form the engine for law reform in the States Parties.

---

[81] *Id.*, at 5.

Article 33.2 requires the establishment of a national monitoring process independent of Government to 'promote, protect and monitor' implementation. It requires these bodies to consult and interact effectively with civil society. This is truly innovative as the Convention pays attention not merely to what '*ought to be done*' but also to the institutional preconditions necessary to ensure that it '*can be done*' at domestic level. It thus opens a window between pure international law and the domestic reform process. Indeed, taking its cue from Article 33.2 the International Coordination Committee (ICC) of National Human Rights Institutions is actively engaged in helping its members raise their capacity to handle the issues that befall to them under the Convention. A database on the activities of NHRIs with respect to disability is currently being prepared and thematic events planned. Indeed, the European regional grouping of NHRI recently submitted an *amicus curia* brief (its first ever) to the European Court of Human Rights in April 2008 on the issue of legal capacity.[82] And the Mexican National Commission on Human Rights recently convened a meeting of Latin American NHRIs and produced a useful book in 2008 (in Spanish, French and English) entitled 'National Monitoring Mechanisms of the Convention on the Rights of Persons with Disabilities'.[83] It must be emphasised that Article 33.3 (mirroring Article 4.3) requires that persons with disabilities and their representative organisations should be "involved and participate fully" in the national monitoring process.

Parenthetically, interesting issues will arise under Article 33.2 when the European Union ratifies. Which entity will perform the functions of Article 33.2? Logically it should be the new EU Fundamental Right Agency. It is interesting that the Agency's work programme for 2008 announces a research project to develop a 'feasibility study on indicators measuring the protection, respect and promotion of the rights of the disabled.'[84] Though such work it may well indeed be developing its capacity to assume responsibilities under Article 33.2 with respect to the Institutions of the EU. It should be noted that Article 33.3 (consultation with civil society) would apply with equal force to the Fundamental Rights Agency if indeed it will be the designated body.

Article 34 deals with the new treaty monitoring body (Committee on the Rights of Persons with Disabilities). In many ways it will be a conventional treaty monitoring body. Although states had warned civil society to think innovatively about monitoring, they in fact reverted to a very traditional model. The

---

[82] Written Comments by the European Group of National Institutions, *D.D. v. Lithuania*, Application No. 13469/06, 11 April 2008.

[83] The Mexican National Human Rights Commission Book is available online at: http://www.cndh.org.mx/publica/libreria/libdigi.htm.

[84] Annual Work Programme 2008, Fundamental Rights Agency, April 2008, p. 6: available at: http://fra.europa.eu/fra/index.php?fuseaction=content.dsp_cat_content&catid=4836ecaa7c919.

relevant Committee (composed initially of 12 members but with a possibility of increasing its size as additional States ratify) will be elected by the States Parties within six months of the coming into operation of the Convention, that is by 3 November 2008. The States Parties are confined to nominating candidates from among their own nationals (despite a proposal to the contrary contained in the Mexican 'non-paper').

Each State Party is then obliged to submit an initial comprehensive report on measures taken and progress achieved to implement the Convention. Thereafter, States Parties are obliged to submit periodic reports at least every four years and "further when the Committee so requests" (Article 35.2). The Committee, after evaluating the reports, is empowered to make "such suggestions and general recommendations" as it considers appropriate (Article 36.1). It may also transmit the reports to the Specialized Agencies and other funds within the UN system in order to address a request or indicate a need for further technical assistance or advice. The Committee is enjoined to work co-operatively with the Specialized Agencies as well as with the other treaty monitoring bodies of the UN (Article 38).

The Committee is entitled to receive individual or group complaints under the Optional Protocol (OP). These complaints can be submitted 'by or on behalf' of individuals or groups. The text does not make clear that prior authorisation is needed. It could certainly be open to the Committee to dispense with prior authorisation in circumstances of particular vulnerability (e.g., in certain institutional settings). Or, the Committee may initiate an examination of a situation if it 'receives reliable information indicating grave or systematic violations' (Article 6.1 of the OP). The criteria for inadmissibility are the same as obtain generally: i.e., that the petition is not anonymous, that there is no abuse of the right of petition, that the same matter is not already under examination by another forum, that internal remedies have been exhausted, that the claim is not manifestly ill-founded, that the facts do not precede entry into force of the Convention for the State Party concerned (Article 2 of the OP), etc. The process for considering such complaints is likewise similar to those that obtain generally. The Committee is specifically empowered to require urgent 'interim measures' to avoid possible irreparable harm (Article 4 of the OP). This could become quite significant especially with respect to institutions where egregious violations can occur. The deliberations of the Committee on complaints are confidential. The Committee may require the respondent State Party to include details of its response in any subsequent periodic report.

A Conference of States Parties will also be established (Article 40). Its functions will be "to consider any matter with regard to the implementation of the present Convention". It remains to be seen whether civil society groups or national institutions will have a right to be present during the deliberations of the Conference or to make interventions. It is hoped that this body will become a fruitful avenue for the sharing of information as well as know-how among the States Parties.

Article 33 on national implementation and monitoring is especially valuable. On the implementation side it requires the States Parties to establish 'one or more focal points' within Government and to give due consideration to 'the establishment or designation of a coordination mechanism' (Article 33.1). It is obviously directed toward the need for 'joined-up' Government in the disability context. This will be quite an innovation for many countries. And, if deployed correctly, it should provide a useful corrective to the tendency in all Governments to fragment disability policy depending on departmental priorities (the so-called 'silo' effect). An interesting and much neglected article was added dealing with statistics (Article 31). Rational policy rests on an accurate picture of the status of persons with disabilities. It therefore makes sense that the Convention would require the collection and analyses of such data in order to give effect to the Convention. Its place in the Convention was however questioned by one influential European country during the Working Group.

Plainly many countries will require assistance in meeting their obligations. Developed countries acceded to the argument but feared the insertion of language that might lend legal recognition to the right to development. The net effect of Article 32.1(a) is that States Parties have a duty to proof their development aid programmes from the perspective of the rights contained in the Convention. This does not necessarily mean they will have to spend more or even have an earmarked part of their development budget for disability. But at a minimum it means that aid programmes should not compound the isolation of persons with disabilities (for example, by building inaccessible schools) and should ideally create pathways to inclusion. The creation of the Global Partnership on Disability and Development (GPDD)[85] by the World Bank and hosted by the Burton Blatt Institute at Syracuse University offers a real step forward.

The development aid and broader international cooperation side to the Convention is likely to assume major significance since in many developing countries it could be quite significant in getting a dynamic of change going – as well as raising local expectations. It should be borne in mind that a specific provision is made in the Convention for approval by the European Commission representing the Institutions of the European Union and that the Commission controls the single largest development aid budget in the world (Article 4).[86] Indeed, the 2005 'EU Consensus on Development', which is a joint Commission, Parliament

---

[85] See: http://web.worldbank.org/WBSITE/EXTERNAL/TOPICS/EXTSOCIALPROTECTION/EXTDISABILITY/0,,contentMDK:21151218~ menuPK:282706~pagePK:210058~piPK:210062~theSitePK:282699,00.html.

[86] Visit DG Development at: http://ec.europa.eu/development/index_en.cfm.

and Council position paper specifically mentions persons with disabilities as a target group with respect to the reduction of poverty.[87]

7 *Conclusions – Prospects for 'Persuasion' and 'Socialisation'*

In conclusion, it is submitted that the key elements for 'persuading' and 'socialising' States are present in the Convention. The disability Convention should accelerate the trend underway in most corners of the world toward respecting and advancing the rights of persons with disabilities. At its optimum, it should reinforce reform efforts underway in many countries. It will help put in place a dynamic of reform in those countries that have yet to begin a serious reform effort.

So far, the auguries are good. The UN Human Rights Council will now consider the issue of disability every year.[88] The Office of the UN High Commissioner for Human Right has recently published a joint Handbook with the World Parliamentary Union on the Convention and is steadily ratcheting up its engagement.[89] An Inter-Service Taskforce combining the main Specialized Agencies of the UN has been formed to support implementation. And all the initial signs are that the new Conference of States Parties will initiate a genuine sharing of experience and transfer of solutions.

True, the work of the incoming Committee on the Rights of Persons with Disabilities will not be easy. Key ambiguities will have to be tackled by the incoming Committee. How, for example, are the progressive elements of the Convention to be disentangled from obligations like non-discrimination that are immediately achievable? What will the posture of the Committee be to the key concept that predicates (qualifies?) the achievement of the rights of persons with disabilities 'on an equal basis with others'? Will this be used positively or will it be used to rationalize differential treatment? How will the Committee interpret the obligation of 'reasonable accommodation'? How transferable will its insights on 'reasonable accommodation' be to an understanding of discrimination in the other UN human rights treaties? Most crucially, how will it deal with reservations and 'interpretive declarations' that border on 'disguised reservations'? And

---

[87] The 2005 'European Consensus on Development' is available at: http://ec.europa.eu/development/policies/consensus_en.cfm.

[88] See Draft Report of the Council, A/HRC/7/L.11, 28 March 2008, 7.9.15: available at: http://www2.ohchr.org/english/bodies/hrcouncil/.

[89] From Exclusion to Equality: Realizing the Rights of Persons with Disabilities, Handbook for Parliamentarians on the Convention on the Rights of Persons with Disabilities and its Optional Protocol, (Inter Parliamentary Union & Office of UN High Commissioner for Human Rights, 2007).

how will it approach and unpack Article 12 on legal capacity which probably lies at the very heart of the revolution in disability – treating people as 'subjects' and not as 'objects'.

And National Human Rights Institutions are actively preparing for the roles they will assume under Article 32. This is important since they are the main champions for importing international law into the domestic legal and policy mix. So both the normative *and* the institutional matrix for change is being steadily put into place.

The main thesis of this chapter has been that we should view the Convention less as a means for coercing States and more as a powerful tool for enabling its revolutionary insights to percolate into the political process (by 'persuasion' and 'socialisation') and hence transform the political process to the point that justice and rights for persons with disabilities is seen as the primary departure point and not as an annoying distraction. The dynamics of this process will call for the emergence of new political entrepreneurial skills on the part of civil society with respect to the multiple layers of actors at the international level and especially with respect to Governments and national institutions. It calls on civil society groups to come forward not merely with considered judgments about what is wrong but also with even more considered blueprints for change.

Whatever happens now, there is no going back. Disability has moved to the core of the UN human rights agenda in theory. We should be able to see in five years time whether a reform movement sinks deep roots as a result of this Convention. If one may hazard a guess it is that this will depend on whether a new practice of disability politics emerges.

The Implementation of the UN Convention and the Development of Economical and Social Rights as Human Rights

Brynhildur G. Flóvenz

1 *Introduction*

One of the major subjects of discussion in the field of human rights law in the 21st century has been the value and boundaries of economic, social and cultural rights and to what extent these rights are justiciable. There has been a tradition among western legal scholars to classify human rights into two main categories, civil and political rights on the one hand and economic, social and cultural rights on the other. This distinction has its roots in a decision made by the United Nations General Assembly to create two separate covenants based on the Universal Declaration of Human Rights (hereafter UDHR); the Covenant on Civil and Political Rights (hereafter ICCPR) and the Covenant on Economical, Social and Cultural Rights (hereafter ICESCR), both of which were adopted by the UN General Assembly on December 16th 1966.[1]

When the United Nations Commission on Human Rights started the work drafting a new convention on the rights set forth in the UDHR, there was no agreement as to whether the rights in question should be in one or two conventions. The Commission therefore asked for the opinion of the General Assembly on the subject and it decided that one convention including all categories of human rights should be drafted.[2] This decision of the General Assembly was controversial at that time and in a new resolution in February 1952 the General Assembly changed its former decision and decided to divide the human rights set forth in the UDHR into two separate conventions, the ICCPR and ICESCR.[3]

[1] A/RES/2200(XXI) of 16 December 1966.
[2] A/RES/421(V) of 4 December 1950.
[3] A/RES/543(VI) of 5 February 1952.

Behind the General Assembly's decision was the States Parties' different approach, ideological and political, to the nature of human rights and the role of the State in the fulfilment of those rights.[4] The assumptions were that civil and political rights were 'absolute' and 'immediate' as well as 'justiciable' and 'cost-free' whereas economic, social and cultural rights were to be realized gradually and of a more political nature and costly.[5] These two sets of rights have been described as positive and negative rights, the former (ICCPR) implying only negative State obligations not to interfere with the freedom of the citizens without any duty of action, with the result that these rights have no or insignificant financial consequences for the State. The latter set of rights (ICESCR) was on the other hand positive, meaning that those type of rights demanded some measures and financial resources on behalf of the State Parties.[6] This division has been controversial and criticized from the beginning and as the years have past the arguments for this arrangement have gradually moved aside for new ideas on the nature of human rights in legal discourse. Admittedly, there is still disagreement between lawyers and other experts on whether there is a substantive difference in the nature of the two categories of rights, that is civil and political rights on the one hand and economic, social and cultural on the other. One side of this discussion is the formulation of disability rights as human rights. Regardless of whether there exists such a difference or not between the two set of rights, the tendency has been to see and deal with the rights of persons with disabilities as a social policy or welfare issue.

Until the adoption of the new Convention on the Rights of Persons with Disabilities[7] (hereafter CRPD) the rights of this group of people were usually exclusively to be found on international level in the so called "soft-law". One of the reasons for this might be that in the discourse on the rights of persons with disabilities the emphasis has mostly been placed on the most urgent needs so to say, the right to basic healthcare and education and for a great part of the disabled; a minimum standard of living, rights which all happen generally to be categorized as social rights. It was not until the demand for equal participation in the society became strong enough and the concept of disability was revaluated

[4] See Bård-Anders Andreassen, Article 22, in Gudmundur Alfredsson and Asbjørn Eide (eds.), *The Universal Declaration of Human Rights: A Common Standard of Achievement.* (Kluwer Law International, The Hague 1999) 477–478.

[5] See Asbjørn Eide, Economic, Social and Cultural Rights as Human Rights, in Asbjørn Eide, Catarina Krause and Allan Rosas (eds.), *Economic, Social and Cultural Rights: A Textbook.* (Kluwer Law International, The Hague 2001) 10–11.

[6] *Ibid.*

[7] A/RES 61/106 of 13 December 2006. The Convention on the Rights of Persons with Disabilities and its Optional Protocol were adopted on 13 December 2006 at the United Nations Headquarters in New York, and were opened for signature on 30 March 2007.

that some changes were seen. Certainly the reasons are much more complicated than this but this is one of the explanations.

In the last two decades there has been quite an interesting paradigm shift in the field of disability. A shift has been identified from the social policy approach mentioned above to a human rights approach. This development consists, *inter alia*, in viewing people with disabilities as subjects rather than as objects.[8] In the last years the emphasis has increasingly been on the right to equality and non-discrimination, the right of persons with disabilities to participate in the society on equal terms with other citizens. Underlying this demand on equality and non-discrimination are the human rights values set forth in the Universal Declaration of Human Rights and reaffirmed in the Convention on the Rights of Persons with Disabilities. Those values are *inter alia* the universality, indivisibility and interdependence of all human rights and fundamental freedoms, among other the autonomy and dignity of every human being.

In this chapter the emphasis will be on the implementation of the CPRD into domestic law in the light of the development of economic and social rights. The focus will be on the categorization/classification of human rights. The influence of classification of rights in the human rights approach will be discussed and how the development of the framework of human rights in general affects the implementation of the new Convention. The Convention's approach to the classification will be looked at and an effort made to analyse the development of this approach during the drafting of the Convention. Finally the influence of the classification of rights on the implementation of the Convention will be discussed and examples given from the judgments of The Icelandic Supreme Court in cases concerning the rights of persons with disabilities.

2 *The CRPD's Approach to the Classification of Human Rights*

The main question in the beginning must be whether the categorization or division of human rights matters. Does it affect the implementation of the new CRPD into domestic law whether the rights of persons with disabilities are viewed as social rights, civil rights, or just human rights? Firstly, it must be noted that the Convention does not solely set out economic and social rights as such rights have been defined and described in legal writings. Like most international human rights standards adopted in recent years, the Convention does not establish a clear division between economic and social rights on the

8 See further on this development: G. Quinn and T. Degener, *Human Rights and Disability: the Current Use and Future Potential of United Nations Human Rights Instruments in the Context of Disability*, HR/PUB/02/1, United Nations, New York and Geneva, 2002.

one hand and civil and political on the other. The new Convention contains all the major rights set forth in both the Covenant on Civil and Political Rights and the Covenant on Economic, Social and Cultural Rights.

Whether the categorization of rights affects the implementation of the Convention may vary from one State Party to another. It may depend on how the States implement economic and social rights in general. Some States do not make a considerable distinction between the implementation of the different categories of rights while others seem not in reality to recognize their duty to implement economic and social rights in the same way as civil and political rights.[9] Therefore one might come to the conclusion that in those States in which economic and social rights have not been sufficiently implemented until now, there may arise some problems in implementing the Convention as a whole.

The Convention itself has some guidelines on how to establish a framework and ensure the rights set forth in it. Article 33 has the title "National implementation and monitoring" stipulates:

1. States Parties, in accordance with their system of organization, shall designate one or more focal points within government for matters relating to the implementation of the present Convention, and shall give due consideration to the establishment or designation of a coordination mechanism within government to facilitate related action in different sectors and at different levels.
2. States Parties shall, in accordance with their legal and administrative systems, maintain, strengthen, designate or establish within the State Party, a framework, including one or more independent mechanisms, as appropriate, to promote, protect and monitor implementation of present Convention, When designating or establishing such a mechanism, States Parties shall take into account the principles relating to the status and functioning of national institutions for protection and promotion of human rights.
3. Civil society, in particular persons with disabilities and their representative organizations, shall be involved and participate fully in the monitoring process.

No distinction is made on the basis of different sets of rights in Article 33. It therefore might appear at first sight, according to Article 33, that the Convention

[9] There seems to be an increasing tendency among democratic states to ensure both civil and political rights and economic and social rights in their constitutions. See on economical and social rights in constitutions: Sandra Liebenberg, The Protection of Economic and Social Rights in Domestic Legal Systems, in Asbjørn Eide, Catarina Krause and Allan Rosas (eds.), *Economic, Social and Cultural Rights: A Textbook.* (Kluwer Law International, The Hague 2001) 55–84.

does not distinguish between different types of rights or set out various ways of implementing the rights set forth in it. It must though be noted that Article 33 is a general clause and does mostly describe the framework itself. The next step would therefore be to look closer on the rights ensured in the Convention. The Convention itself provides some more guidelines on how to implement it. In Article 4 there is more "meat on the bones" than in the aforementioned Article 33. In Article 4 the States Parties' general obligations are to be found. Paragraph 1 states that:

> States Parties undertake to ensure and promote the full realization of all human rights and fundamental freedoms for all persons with disabilities without discrimination of any kind on the basis of disability. To this end, States parties undertake: (...various obligations set forth in subparagraph a–i.)

Then there is a paragraph 2 of Article 4, which runs as follows:

> With regard to economic, social and cultural rights, each State Party undertakes to take measures to the maximum of its available resources and, where needed, within the framework of international cooperation, with a view to achieving progressively the full realization of these rights, without prejudice to those obligations contained in the present Convention that are immediately applicable according to international law.

Consequently, it is clear that as to the implementation of the rights the Convention does indeed distinguish on the ground of the category of rights; economic, social and cultural rights are given less weight than civil and political rights. In the light of the recent development of human rights where scholars have invariably described how intertwined those two sets of rights are this distinction appears questionable. The trend in the scholarly debate has clearly been towards eliminating the distinction between the two categories.[10] Instead the focus has increasingly been on the values and ideas that are underlying the concept of human rights. Human dignity is a crucial concept with regard to human rights in general and in the context of persons with disability specifically. It is a decisive factor in the definition of the nature of disability, especially in the shift from medical definition to human rights definition. The human rights definition focuses on the inherent value of the human beings opposed to the medical definition. It means, *i.a.*, that the problem is not to be found within the person with a disability, but rather in the interaction between the society and the person concerned.

[10] See for instance Ida Elisabeth Koch, Economic, Social and Cultural Rights as Components in Civil and Political Rights: A Hermeneutic Perspective. *The International Journal of Human Rights, Vol. 10, No. 4. December 2006*, 405–430.

Therefore one might wonder whether Article 4, Paragaraph 2 might give the State Parties a justification so to speak to implement Convention rights which normally would be categorized as economic, social and cultural rights in a "softer" way than other rights. By ranking those rights "lower" in the Convention there is a danger that even though they will be implemented they will be more difficult for the citizens to obtain than the other one. Not to mention the problems that might arise from such a categorization, resulting in a progressive implementation of some rights which may be categorized as CPR as well as ESCR. There is a risk that rights which are of particular importance to persons with disabilities, such as the right to social security, the right to an adequate standard of living and the right to health being normally categorized as social rights, will not be the subject of proper implementation as called for in Article 4, Paragraph 2. That is certainly not consistent with the purpose of the Convention as set forth in Article 1 to promote, protect and ensure the full and equal enjoyment of all human rights and fundamental freedoms by all persons with disabilities, and to promote respect for their inherent dignity.

3 *The Preparatory Phase of the CRPD*

As described in Section 1, the framework for ensuring the rights of the UDHR was controversial almost 60 years ago, resulting in two separate covenants, the ICCPR and ICESCR. Today this disagreement still seems to be unresolved among the Member States of the United Nations.

It is therefore interesting to examine the preparatory work for the CRPD with the aim of understanding the arguments behind the different approaches to the different sets of rights.

In December 2001 the UN General Assembly, acting on a proposal by Mexico, established an Ad Hoc Committee "to consider proposals for a comprehensive and integral international convention to promote and protect the rights and dignity of persons with disabilities, based on the holistic approach in the work done in the fields of social development, human rights and non-discrimination and taking into account the recommendations of the Commission on Human Rights and the Commission for Social Development."[11]

The first Session of the Ad Hoc Committee took place in July and August 2002. Among the documents of the first session were two position papers, one submitted by the European Union, the other by China, and a working paper

[11] A/RES/56/168. Resolution adobted by the General Assembly on Comprehensive and integral international convention to promote and protect the rights and dignity of persons with disabilities. 19 December 2001.

(draft of a convention) submitted by Mexico.[12] When reading those papers it becomes obvious that there is a difference in the approach of these parties to the task of the Ad Hoc Committee. The European Union emphasized a rights-based approach to questions concerning people with disabilities and an effective monitoring mechanism.[13] China on the other hand stated that the problems of persons with disabilities are social problems as well as problems of development and that many of the rights of persons with disabilities could be implemented only through social development. Furthermore the Convention should be a programmatic document that provides broad guidance for all countries.[14] At this first session it was decided to seek views on the Convention from States Parties and various international, regional and national organizations.[15]

The second session took place in June 2003. The Ad Hoc Committee decided to establish a working group to prepare and present a draft text of a convention to form the basis for negotiations by the Member States. The instruction to the working group from the Committee mostly concerned emphasis on a broad consultation. It should be with national, region and international organs in the field of disability, governmental as well as non-government.[16]

In the second session general discussions focused on the main issues to be emphasized in the drafting work. The nature, structure and elements of the Convention and monitoring system were discussed, along with the principle of non-discrimination and equality from a disability perspective – as well as critical issues concerning special measures and disability. The Division for Social Policy and Development, Department of Economic and Social Affairs, had organized three panels for delegates and representatives of NGOs where new and emerging approaches to definitions of disability – conceptual frameworks and varying contexts of definition and implications for promotion of the rights of persons with disabilities were some of the main themes.[17]

In the second session, various documents were presented. The European Union declared its commitment to a rights-based approach to questions concerning persons with disabilities and its willingness to participate actively in the drafting

---

[12] A/AC.265/WP.2 Position Paper by the European Union (hereinafter PPEU); A/AC.265/WP.3 Position Paper by the People's Republic of China (hereinafter PPPRC); A/AC.265/WP.1, Working Paper by Mexico.

[13] A/AC.265/WP.2, PPEU, p. 2.

[14] A/AC.265/WP.3, PPPRU, para. no. 6 and 10.

[15] A/57/357 Report of the Ad Hoc Committee on a Comprehensive and Integral International Convention on Protection and Promotion of the Rights and Dignity of Persons with Disabilities (hereinafter RAHC), para. no. 10 and 11. First Session 29 July–9 August 2002.

[16] A/58/118/Corr.1, RAHC Second Session 3 July 2003, para. no. 15.

[17] Panel discussions on priority themes. Second session of the Ad Hoc Committee 16–27 June 2003. http://www.un.org/esa/socdev/enable/rights/ahc2panel.htm.

of the Convention, as did some other representatives.[18] Others were less positive. In the statement of the United States it said: "Thus we hope to participate in order to share our experiences – and to offer technical assistance if desired on key principles and elements – but given our comprehensive domestic laws protecting those with disabilities, not with the expectation that we will become party to any resulting legal instrument. This may be true also of other delegations representing States with well developed legal protections."[19]

The Working Group met in January 2004 and held 20 formal meetings. The Working Group noted that its mandate from the Ad Hoc Committee was to prepare and present draft text which would be the basis for negotiations in the Ad Hoc Committee. The group took into account all contributions submitted in advance of its meetings. The Working Group did not see its task as being a drafting committee negotiating a final text but rather as identifying possible approaches, and narrowing down the options, so as to provide a basis for further work in the Ad Hoc Committee. At its 20th meeting, on 16 January 2004, the Working Group adopted by consensus its report to the Ad Hoc Committee.[20]

Annex I of the report included Draft Articles for a Comprehensive and Integral International Convention on the Protection and Promotion of the Rights and Dignity of Persons with Disabilities. In the draft Article 4 there was no Paragraph 2 (on the progressive realization of economic, social and cultural rights) identical to the one in the final Convention. The footnotes to the draft Article 4 explained how some members of the Working Group had noted that while the International Covenant on Civil and Political Rights includes a paragraph on remedies, the International Covenant on Economic, Social and Cultural rights does not include such a provision. Consequently, it might be difficult to include such an article in a convention that elaborates the rights contained in both Covenants and the Ad Hoc Committee might wish to consider this issue further.

Furthermore, the footnotes pointed out that the issue of the progressive realisation of economic, social and cultural rights had been raised by several delegations during the Working Group's discussion. The Working Group noted that, consistent with existing international human rights law, the concept would apply to some of the rights in the Convention (the economic, social and cultural rights), but not to others (the civil and political rights). The Ad Hoc Committee

[18] A/AC.265/2003/4 and A/AC.265/2003/4/Corr.1 Views submitted by Governments, intergovernmental organizations and United Nations bodies concerning a comprehensive and integral international convention on the protection and promotion of the rights and dignity of persons with disabilities. Note by the Secretary General. Second Session of the Ad Hoc Committee 16–27 June 2003.

[19] Statement of Ralph F. Boyd, United States Assistant Attorney General for Civil Rights. http://www.un.org/esa/socdev/enable/rights/statements.htm.

[20] A/AC.265/2004/WG/1 Report of the Working Group to the Ad Hoc Committee.

would need to consider how best to incorporate this issue into the Convention, and might wish to note the precedent set in the Convention on the Rights of the Child. This debate had been raised in relation to other articles as well.[21]

The Working Group met in January 2004 where they discussed the draft element presented by the chair of the Ad Hoc Committee. In the draft the discrimination on the ground of disability was *i.a.* defined as a failure to make a reasonable accommodation, defined as " introduction of necessary and appropriate measures to enable a person with a disability fully to enjoy fundamental rights and freedoms."[22]

During the Working Group there was a discussion of the link between non-discrimination and reasonable accommodation, on whether those two concepts should be linked to one another. The question arose whether a failure to 'reasonably accommodate' should in itself constitute discrimination.[23] The question was left open for the Ad Hoc Committee.

In the fourth session of the Ad Hoc Committee the issue was addressed. When discussing draft Article 7 (now Article 5 CRPD) on non-discrimination on 2 and 3 September 2004, Thailand emphasized that the definition of discrimination should include a denial of reasonable accommodation. Otherwise discrimination will continue to be dealt with in an abstract manner. New Zealand on the other hand opposed such a definition. As did Japan and noted that it might give too much license to bring charges of discrimination, which would have serious consequences. At the end of the session the definition of reasonable accommodation, suggested by the coordinator, became "necessary and appropriate modifications and adjustments, not imposing a disproportionate burden, where needed in a particular case, to ensure to PWD the enjoyment and exercise on a basis of equality with others, of all human rights and fundamental freedoms."[24]

The difficulties in classifying the human rights, that the Convention was supposed to ensure, into civil and political rights and economic, social and cultural rights were obvious in the fourth session of the Ad Hoc Committee. The representative from Israel stated that as there was uncertainty regarding what would be considered economic, social and cultural rights, Israel reiterated its proposal from the third session to "identify those articles where the economic

---

21 A/AC.265/2004/WG/1: Report of the Working Group to the Ad Hoc Committee, Annex I, Article 4, footnotes 18–22.

22 Chair's Draft Elements of a Comprehensive and Integral International Convention on Protection and Promotion of the Rights and Dignity of Persons with Disabilities, 15 December 2003, Article 2. http://www.un.org/esa/socdev/enable/rights/wgcontrib-chair1.htm.

23 A/AC.265/2004/WG/1, Annex 1, Article 7, footnote 27.

24 Daily summary of discussions related to Article 7, Equality and Non-discrimination, in fourth session on 2 and 3 September 2004, http://www.un.org/esa/socdev/enable/rights/ahc4sumart07.htm.

implications are major" in a non-exhaustive list in Article 4, including Article 9d, 13, 15, 16, 17, and 19 to 24. This would give guidance on what rights should be subject to progressive realization.[25]

The representative from New Zealand reacted to Israel's proposals claiming he was "very unhappy" with inclusion of two civil and political rights (9d on equal recognition as a person before the law and 13 on freedom of expression and opinion and access to information) in the suggested list of articles. New Zealand acknowledged there might be economic implications in ensuring the enjoyment of civil and political rights, but this did not mean such rights should be subject to progressive realization.[26]

The representative of China noted there had always been an "argument" whether civil and political rights or economic, social and cultural rights, are more important and pressing. If refer to progressive realization of economic, social and cultural rights, the representative pointed out, the same should apply to realization of civil and political rights. Indeed, for developing countries like China, the realization of economic, social and cultural rights is more pressing. Further, he noted that China believes that non-discrimination should not be subject to progressive realization.[27]

The representative from India emphasized that a number of delegates had suggested the need to introduce the concept of the progressive realization of rights and pointed out that India's resources did not permit anything but progressive realization of the economic, social and cultural rights. The same would apply to many other developing countries.[28]

In the fourth session of the Ad Hoc Committee there was general agreement that draft Article 4 should include the wording of Article 4 of the Convention on the Rights of the Child. The precise wording of the paragraph was referred to the facilitator's group on this draft article, for further work. Furthermore draft Article 4 should include the concept of progressive realization of economic, social and cultural rights, balanced by the need to implement immediately those obligations that were capable of being immediately implemented. In addition there was general agreement that non-discrimination was not subject to the doctrine of progressive realization.[29]

The representatives of National Human Rights Institutions objected to the classification of rights in Article 4 pointing out that the caricature that only civil and political rights are immediately implementable and that economic, social

---

[25] Daily summary of discussion at the fourth session 30 August 2004, Article 4: General obligations. http://www.un.org/esa/socdev/enable/rights/ahc4sum30aug.htm.

[26] *Ibid.*

[27] *Ibid.*

[28] *Ibid.*

[29] A 59/360: Report of the Ad Hoc Committee on its fourth session, Annex IV, para. 7.

and cultural rights can only be progressively implemented, had been discredited a long time ago. They did however appreciate the effort made by the Chair to reflect a more nuanced and modern perspective based on contemporary human rights law. It was pointed out that the obligation of non-discrimination in relation to economic, social and cultural rights is in general capable of immediate implementation as well as various other economic, social and cultural rights. In their opinion most, if not all, economic, social and cultural rights have aspects capable of immediate implementation, just as they have aspects requiring progressive implementation, but draft Article 4.2 did not adequately reflect that, they concluded.[30]

At the end of the meeting of the Ad Hoc Committee in August 2005, it was decided that the Chairman of the Ad Hoc Committee would prepare text reflecting the work of the Committee to date in streamlining the draft Convention, and make suggestions as to how some of the different points of view might be bridged.[31]

In a letter, dated 7 October 2005, to all members of the Committee, the Chairman described how the recurring issue of the inclusion of language relating to the progressive realization of economic, social and cultural rights came up in the discussion of many articles. While the principle might be accepted, it could be repetitive and it was often difficult to include such language in individual articles, since many of them contained a hybrid of civil and political, and economic, social and cultural rights, including non-discrimination. The Chairman assumed that there was general agreement on including a generic provision in Article 4 to cover this matter, and this was included as paragraph 2 in his proposal. He had drawn on the language from the facilitator's group and Article 4 of the Convention on the Rights of the Child, which takes a similar approach, and also made it clear that non-discrimination was not for progressive implementation.[32]

4 *The Effect of the Classification on the Implementation*

As many scholars agree that in practice there has been some difference in the implementation of economic, social and cultural rights on the one hand and civil and political rights on the other, the key question here is which implementation

---

30 Revisions and amendments at the Seventh Session of the Ad Hoc Committee. National Human Rights Institutions. http://www.un.org/esa/socdev/enable/rights/ahc7nhri.htm.

31 A/AC.265/2006/1 Letter dated 7 October 2005 from the Chairman to all members of the Committee, para. 1.

32 *Ibid.*, para. 23.

method should be used in the implementation of the CRPD? As mentioned in section 3 the conclusion of the preparatory work was progressive implementation of economic, social and cultural rights. However, it was highlighted that non-discrimination was not to be subject of progressive implementation but of an immediate one. Are these two elements consistent with one another? Is it possible to implement non-discrimination for persons with disabilities without ensuring social rights?

Most of the rights set forth in the Convention are already to be found in various other international conventions, in particular the two covenants from 1966. One might come to the conclusion that there is no need for special implementation of those rights in the CRPD already implemented due to other conventions. But it is necessary to examine each and every right from a disability perspective to find out what needs to be done to ensure the right in question for persons with disabilities on equal terms with others.

As an example the right to freedom from torture, cruel, inhuman or degrading treatment or punishment can be examined. It is guaranteed in Article 15, Paragraph 1 of CRPD which corresponds to Article 7 of the ICCPR. Article 15 (1) stipulates:

> No one shall be subjected to torture or to cruel, inhuman or degrading treatment or punishment. In particular, no one shall be subjected without his or her free consent to medical or scientific experimentation.

In addition, Article 15 includes Paragraph 2 stating that:

> States Parties shall take all effective legislative, administrative, judicial or other measures to prevent persons with disabilities, on an equal basis with others, from being subjected to torture or cruel, inhuman or degrading treatment or punishment.

Article 15 (1) of CRPD is identical to Article 7 of ICCPR apart from the words "or her" that were added to Article 15 (1) as a part of the policy of making the language of human rights law applicable to women.

Here the subject is a right that has already been implemented in many States Parties and has in addition already been subject to judicial review both internationally and nationally and its substantive content clarified.

If a certain right, as in the aforementioned Article 7 of the ICCPR, has already been implemented and consequently has a tradition of interpretation, the question arises whether it is necessary to implement the CRPD right in question and give it a new and autonomous status or whether it is enough to ensure equality to enjoy the rights set forth in Article 7 of the ICCPR and Article 15 (1) of the CRPD. Are the rights set out in the new Convention, Article 15 (1) 1 in this case, automatically interpreted as the same as those guaranteed in Article 7 of the ICCPR or is there a duty or a possibility to give the rights a new content? The answer to this question will determine whether and to what extent implementation is required.

When examining Article 15 (1) further it is for instance necessary to find out whether there are any special disability-related sides of it that would not be sufficiently ensured just by interpreting the paragraph in accordance with Article 7 of ICCPR and, in addition, ensuring equal enjoyment of the rights. If that is the case, if there are some special disability related sides of Article 15 (1), it might be necessary to give those rights new and autonomous content and interpret Article 15 (1) in an independent way and implement them in accordance with the new understanding.[33] When examining the rights in question, the general obligations of State parties when implementing international human rights in general, must be taken into consideration. General Comments of the Committee on Economic, Social and Cultural Rights and decisions of other UN human rights bodies must be considered as well.

The Committee has stated that implementing and monitoring human rights conventions, includes an obligation of the State Parties to *respect, to protect* and *to fulfil* the rights concerned.[34] Consequently, in the context of Article 15 (1) it is necessary to examine whether there are any disability-related sides of respecting, protecting and fulfilling the rights ensured in Article 15 (1) that require a new interpretation of the paragraph.

The rights ensured in Article 15 are normally categorized among civil and political rights and would therefore be subject to immediate implementation. Concerning other rights in the Convention it would be necessary to examine the right in question to find out which set of right it belongs to. The implementing method would depend on the conclusion according to Article 4 (2) of the CRPD. In addition it will of course be necessary to implement the right to equality according to par. 2 of Article 15.

If the conclusion is that Paragraph 1 of Article 15 does not need to be implemented in a new manner and the old implementation and interpretation of Article 7 ICCPR can automatically be applied, the implementation only

---

[33] See Judgement of the European Court of Human Rights, *Price v. the United Kingdom,* 10 July 2001, Reports 2001-VII, where the Court found a violation of Article 3 of the ECHR (Article similar to Arts. 7 of the ICCPR and 15 (1) of the CRPD) when a disabled woman had to stay in detention where there were no facilities to meet her basic needs. The Court found that she had been a victim of degrading treatment. The Court did not discuss whether there was a violation of Art. 14 of the ECHR on non-discrimination. See also an interesting separate opinion of Judge Greve.

[34] E/2000/22, Committee on Economic, Social and Cultural Rights, General Comment No. 12 (1999), para. 15. UN doc. E/2000/22.

concerns the equality of enjoying the rights according to Article 15 (2). Equality and non-discrimination is indeed a connecting theme of the Convention and it is quite clear that it ensures substantive de facto equality and allows or demands specific measures to achieve this goal according to Article 5:

1. States Parties recognize that all persons are equal before and under the law and are entitled without any discrimination to the equal protection and equal benefit of the law.
2. States Parties shall prohibit all discrimination on the basis of disability and guarantee to persons with disabilities equal and effective legal protection against discrimination on all grounds.
3. In order to promote equality and eliminate discrimination, States Parties shall take all appropriate steps to ensure that reasonable accommodation is provided.
4. Specific measures which are necessary to accelerate or achieve de facto equality of persons with disabilities shall not be considered discrimination under the terms of the present Convention.

The main purpose of the Convention according to Article 1 is the *equal* enjoyment of all human rights by all persons with disabilities and to promote respect for their inherent dignity. Emphasis on equality and non-discrimination is to be found in almost every article. Accordingly, the major task will be to interpret the concept "equal enjoyment of rights" best suited to the needs of persons with disabilities.

This is the core of the tasks facing the States Parties now. How they succeed in that will determine the final results of the Convention. Obviously the way in which the concept of equality is interpreted in the various states will to some extent affect the implementation. However, the most important issue is which requirements the Convention and its monitoring bodies will make.

When examining the concept of equality in the light of the development of human rights the question arises whether there is any distinction made in the CRPD between the understanding of the concept, – equality – based on the classification of the rights into economic, social and cultural rights on one hand and civil and political on the other. Based on the category of rights no distinction seems to be made in the use of this concept. Indeed it is rather the opposite, as mentioned before, where it is repeatedly highlighted in the preparatory work that equality and non-discrimination is not subject to progressive implementation. This corresponds to the understanding of the implementation of non-discrimination as set forth in some other international conventions, i.a. ICCPR, in which Article 26 ensures equality before the law without any discrimination. Article 26 does not only apply to rights ensured in the Convention itself, but is a general equality and non-discrimination provision that covers human rights, regardless of the sets of those rights.[35] It should however be noticed that the Human Rights Committee did not adopt this interpretation until 1987.[36]

As pointed out in the preparatory work of the CRPD, it can be difficult to decide in which category each and every right of the Convention should be placed.[37] The European Court of Human Rights (ECHR) has noted that civil and political rights and economic, social and cultural rights can not be absolutely separated. In the Airey judgment the Court stated:

> Whilst the Convention sets forth what are essentially civil and political rights, many of them have implications of a social or economic nature. The Court therefore considers, like the Commission, that the mere fact that an interpretation of the Convention may extend into the sphere of social and economic rights should not be a decisive factor against such an interpretation; there is no water-tight division separating that sphere from the field covered by the Convention.[38]

If the emphasis is on equality and non-discrimination in the implementation, then the importance of whether the rights in question are categorized as civil, political, social or economic might not be considerable.

When implementing the right to equal enjoyment of rights it is important that the State Parties are well aware of the development in human rights especially the emphasis on human dignity. It is also important that knowledge of the development in understanding the concept of disability will be ensured when implementing the Convention in domestic law. There is a strong connection between the understanding of those two concepts, equality and disability. One of the conditions for ensuring equality and implementing the right to equal enjoyment of human rights is a solid understanding of the concept of disability.

5 *The Enjoyment of Human Rights of Persons with Disabilities without Discrimination in the Judgments of the Supreme Court of Iceland*

The right to equality and non-discrimination is ensured in various constitutions and international conventions. In 1995 it was added to the Icelandic

[35] Human Rights Committee's General Comment No. 18 (1989), para. 12. http://www.unhchr.ch/tbs/doc.nsf/(Symbol)/3888b0541f8501c9c12563ed004b8d0e?Opendocument.

[36] *Zwaan-de Vries v. The Netherlands*. Comm. No. 182/1984, 9 April 1987. *Broeks v. The Netherlands*. Comm. No. 172/1984, 9 April 1987.

[37] A/AC.265/2004/WG/1: Report of the Working Group to the Ad Hoc Committee, Annex I, footnotes 18–22. Daily summary of discussion at the fourth session 30 August 2004, Article 4: General obligations.

[38] *Airey v. Ireland*, 9 October 1979, Series A, No. 32, para. 26.

constitution.[39] The rights of persons with disabilities in Iceland are guaranteed in the Act on the Affairs of the Disabled no. 59/1992. Equality before the law is ensured in Article 65 of the Constitution. Iceland has ratified all the main conventions on human rights as well and signed the CRPD 30 March 2007 and is preparing the ratification now. However, it should be noted that Iceland has not signed Protocol 12 to the European Convention on Human Rights, which ensures equality and non-discrimination.

The Supreme Court of Iceland has handed down several judgments on the rights of persons with disabilities to equality and non-discrimination. These judgments concern human rights, which are generally classified as civil and political rights as well as rights generally classified as economic, social and cultural rights. Most of the judgments actually concern the latter set of rights.

The judgment of the Supreme Court of Iceland, dated 4 February 1999, dealt with the rights of persons with disabilities to education.[40]

> In 1990 a young woman, who was blind, took up studies at the Faculty of Economics and Business Administration, University of Iceland, but withdrew in 1994. She filed a suit against the University, claiming that she had been forced to withdraw since she had not received the assistance and facilities necessary because of her handicap. It turned out that no general measures had been taken to assist the woman with her studies and examinations nor was there any policy in place to deal with similar cases. Instead, she had to request a special exemption each time that she was unable to follow the general arrangement of the curriculum. This lack of measures, among other things, resulted in her not being able to complete a particular examination, and she did not receive teaching materials in time. The Court deemed that that the lack of general policy had resulted in mistakes by the Faculty in fulfilling her needs. The fact that she herself had had to chase reasonable accommodation, constituted unjust tort against her person and freedom of education. The Court referred to Article 2 of Protocol no. 1 to The European Convention on Human Rights, which states: "No person shall be denied the right to education." Reference was also made to Article 14 on equal enjoyment of the rights set forth in the Convention. Furthermore, the Court referred to Article 65 of the Icelandic Constitution on the equality of citizens before the law and found that the University of Iceland had not fulfilled its obligations to ensure equality to persons with disabilities.

This judgment was a milestone in the affairs of disabled persons in Iceland. It removes all ambiguity as to whether disabled persons should enjoy full equality regarding education with respect to people who are not disabled, and constitutes the relevant school's responsibility to formulate a comprehensive policy on these matters. Since this case involved a State school the question could be

---

[39] Constitutional Act no. 97/1995, amending the Constitution of the Republic of Iceland no. 33/1944 with subsequent amendments, Article 65.

[40] The Supreme Court of Iceland, Case no. 177/1998, 4 February 1999.

raised whether the outcome would have been the same if a private school had been involved. The judgment does not rule on this, but it does state that the University of Iceland is obligated to accept students who are disabled without reference to its status as a State school. It is unlikely that something else would apply to a private school in Iceland.

By following the approach of this judgment the same method might be used to implement immediately rights of the CRPD that otherwise would be subject of progressive implementation.

The right to education has normally been categorized among economic, social and cultural rights.[41] Some scholars have though pointed out that the right to education has strong links to '*the first generation of human rights*' which defend the liberal ideas of freedom of the educational system against interference by the state and the Church.[42] The Icelandic Supreme Court did not touch upon this in its judgment. The emphasis in the case was on the right to equality to education, not on the education itself. However, the core of the right to education is generally classified as a cultural right, which requires positive action of the state providing schools, facilities, teachers etc. According to the CRPD the right to education is ensured in Article 24. In consent with Article 4 (2) it is likely to be subject to progressive implementation. By emphasizing the non-discrimination clause the state in question would have to take positive steps aiming at ensuring the enjoyment of equality of education to persons with disabilities. As non-discrimination and equality is subject to immediate implementation, the right to education on equal terms with other citizens can in reality be immediately implemented as well.

In its judgment from 6 May 1999 the Supreme Court of Iceland dealt with the question of non-discrimination in conjunction with the right to vote, a classical civil and political right.[43]

> In 1999 The Icelandic Association of the Deaf, along with a woman with impaired hearing, filed suit against The Icelandic National Broadcasting Service (RÚV). The suit demanded that RÚV's refusal to provide simultaneous sign-language interpretation of the television speeches of candidates standing for a seat in Parliament in the elections on 8 May 1999, or to make them accessible in another way to people who are deaf, be adjudged unlawful. Acknowledgment was also demanded that RÚV was obligated to provide simultaneous sign-language interpretation of candidates' speeches on television regarding Parliamentary elections or make them accessible in another way to people who are deaf. The plaintiffs claimed that by its

[41] The right to education is guaranteed in Article 26 of the UDHR and Article 13 of the ICESCR.

[42] See for example, Nowak, Manfred, The right to Education in Asbjørn Eide et al. (eds.); *Economic, Social and Cultural Rights.* (Kluwer Law International, The Hague, 2001) pp. 245–271.

[43] The Supreme Court of Iceland, Case no. 151/1999, 6 May 1999.

refusal RÚV, as a State-run broadcasting service, had violated their human rights, especially those in the provisions of Article 65 of the Constitution of Iceland on the equality of citizens, Article 21 of the United Nations' Universal Declaration of Human Rights, and Article 14 of the European Convention on Human Rights. It should be noted that the case concerned the most important live broadcast on the night before the elections, that has a high publicity in the country.

The District Court dismissed the plaintiffs' claims against RÚV. The judgment of the Supreme Court of Iceland stated, however, that the right to vote is inseparable from the right of voters to become acquainted with candidates and issues being voted on, since the right of the individuals protected under Article 3 of Protocol 1 to the European Convention on Human Rights would lose its substantive content if candidates had no way to present their policies, or if voters were barred from acquiring such information. Nevertheless this does not oblige the State or its institutions to present individual candidates or their policies to voters.

In the Court's view such publicity must especially be based on the general freedom of expression and action assured under the human rights provisions of the Constitution and international human rights conventions to which Iceland is a party. On the other hand, if the State or its institutions undertake, to some degree, to publicize candidates and their issues to voters in the interest of freedom and democratic elections, care must be taken that this is done without any discrimination, in accordance with Article 65 of the Constitution (on equality between citizens) and Article 14 of the European Convention on Human Rights as well as the Act on broadcasting no. 68/1985 and Article 7 of the Act on the Affairs of the Disabled no. 59/1992.

The Supreme Court stated it was clear that RÚV was specifically entrusted by law with the function of being a forum for the free exchange of views on issues involving the general public. Consequently, RÚV must observe equality when performing this function. This duty pertains not only to equality between the candidates and political parties involved but also to those to whom broadcasts are directed.

The Supreme Court of Iceland deemed that the case involved important rights, and that the demand for sign-language interpretation was technically possible to implement. The Court stated that RÚV's arguments were not made sufficiently valid substantive to justify the discrimination entailed in its decision. The demands of the Association and the woman were therefore agreed to and RÚV made to provide sign-language interpretation of the televised speeches the evening before elections.[44]

The outcome of this suit substantially clarified the extent of equality of access and participation in society for persons with disabilities in Iceland. The judgment is clearly based on a substantive concept of equality. Also, these two cases recognize an obligation of the State to provide some remedies when ensuring non-discrimination whether the right in question is categorized as civil and political right or economic, social and cultural right. In both cases the State had a positive obligation to ensure the fulfilment of the rights in question. The

---

[44] The Supreme Court of Iceland, Case no. 151/1999, 6 May 1999.

Supreme Court did not make an explicit distinction between the sets of rights. In both cases there was a question of the service of a State-institute. However, the question still remains whether the conclusion would have been the same in a case regarding a private broadcasting service and a private university.

In December 2000 the Supreme Court of Iceland gave a judgment in a case raised by The Organization of Handicapped in Iceland (ÖBI) against the Icelandic state. This case shows how the Supreme Court takes a stand on the question on the justiciability of social rights.

> The case regarded an administrative regulation, which reduced the pension of people with disabilities in marriage or in cohabitation on the ground of their spouses or partners income. ÖBI claimed that the reduction was not authorised by the Social Security Act and since administrative regulations will need to be based on an Act of Parliament under Icelandic law, the reduction could not be legally introduced solely on basis of an administrative regulation.
>
> The Supreme Court confirmed that the regulation in question had lacked the necessary basis in law when it was introduced in 1994 up until 1999, when the Social Security Act was amended. More interestingly, it referred to the European Social Charter and the ICESCR, adding that according to Nordic legal traditions, domestic legislation should be interpretated in accordance with international conventions the State has ratified. In that context, the Court stated that Article 76 of the Constitution obliges the state to ensure by law every person's right to a minimum level of support in accordance with a system that is decided upon in advance on objective grounds. It also stated that while it was the task of the Parliament to decide how that system should be formulated, the system had to respect the minimum rights included in Article 76 and the conditions of Article 65 of the Constitution on equality as well as human rights in general.
>
> The Court stated that it was a main rule of Icelandic law, based on gender equality, that an individual's right to payment from public funds should be independent and regardless of their spouse's income. Nevertheless, the Court considered that there may be some objective grounds to paying a different amount to individuals depending on whether they are living alone or in cohabitation or marriage. The Court pointed out that people in cohabitation are not legally obliged to support each other. Furthermore, the Court stated, although married couples have the duty to support each other, it is not only a duty but also a right. The people concerned also have the *right* to support their families and are unable to do so with only 170 € a month which was the amount of the pension.
>
> The Court stated that Paragraph 1 of Article 76 of the Constitution had to be seen as ensuring certain minimum rights on an individual basis. Although the Parliament is generally given a margin of appreciation to decide how these minimum rights are to be implemented, the Courts cannot avoid to pronounce on whether that evaluation is in accordance with the basic principles protected by the Constitution. When considering the organization of the rights of disabled people according to the Social Security Act and its consequences for individuals, the Court found that this organization of rights did not ensure those minimum standards, which Article 76 of the Constitution requires, in a way that respected Article 65 of the constitution on equality. In reaching this conclusion the Court mentioned specifically that Article 65 of the Constitution should be interpreted in light of Article 26

> of the ICCPR and Article 9 of the ICESCR. Consequently, the Supreme Court accepted the ÖBI's demand that it was not legitimate to reduce the pension of disabled persons in marriage in the way that had been done.[45]

This judgment called for a strong reaction in Iceland. Members of the Government accused the Supreme Court of disregarding the representative Parliament and the Prime Minister appointed a committee to make a proposal for changes of the law. Three months later the Parliament adopted a new legislation, which gave full pension to those who had their pension reduced in the years 1997 and 1998, but the pension for the years 1999 and 2000 was reduced by different means.[46] One of those who got a reduced pension according to the new Act raised a case against the State which the Supreme Court ruled on in October 2003.

> The Court stated that the judgment from 2000 made clear that the reduction of the pension of disabled persons in marriage was not legitimate. Following that judgment the individuals concerned had a right to full pension until the adoption of the new Act no. 3/2001 on the change of the Act on Social Security no. 117, 20 December 2003. The Court noted that these rights were protected by Article 72 of the Constitution which protects the right to property and cannot be reduced by retroactive legislation. Although the new Act was more favorable to disabled persons than the older one, it nevertheless led to lower pension than they were entitled to according to the judgment on unreduced pensions. Therefore the Supreme Court found that the new Act was no more in accordance with the Constitution than the previous one.[47]

Those two judgments were a turning point in Icelandic understanding of law and interpretation of the Constitution. It is now clear that the Court has drawn a line, which the Government and the Parliament can not overstep to reduce the constitutional rights of the citizens to adequate standards of living. Furthermore, it is quite clear that it is the task of the courts to decide whether Parliament's evaluation of minimum standards is in accordance with the Constitution. In addition, the Court has promoted the rights of persons with disabilities and shown that it is a practical and realistic possibility to bring such a case to the courts.

---

[45] The Supreme Court of Iceland, Case no. 125/2000, 19 December 2000.

[46] Act no. 3/2001 on the change of the Act on Social Security no. 117, 20 December 1993, with amendments.

[47] The Supreme Court of Iceland, Case no. 549/2002, 16 October 2003.

6 Conclusion

In this chapter an effort has been made to examine the connection between the implementation of the CRPD and the classification of rights into civil and political on the one hand and economic, social and cultural on the other.

It is clear that the Convention distinguishes between the sets of rights in implementation, where economic, social and cultural rights are subject to progressive implementation. Nevertheless there is no guidance in the Convention as to which rights should be categorized as economic, social and cultural rights and which as civil and political.

The above mentioned judgments of the Icelandic Supreme Court exhibit that the impact of the classification of rights may not be so great if the duty of non-discrimination under Article 5 is emphasized when implementing the rights ensured by the Convention.

Although it might be possible to implement immediately all the rights of the Convention by referring to non-discrimination it is important to establish and develop a solid interpretation of the rights set forth in the Convention in the light of the needs of persons with disabilities. It is necessary to interpret each and every right from a disability perspective.

The Convention provides some measures to ensure the fulfilment of the States Parties' obligations. Those measures are both national and international. The Convention assumes that NGO's and National Human Rights Institutes play a considerable role in addition to more traditional measures, an altogether positive development. By involving those, who have the best knowledge of disability and its impact, the best results should be assured.

The UN Convention in Nordic Domestic Law – Lessons Learned from other Treaties

Ragnhildur Helgadóttir

1 *Introduction*

International treaties impact national law on a variety of levels. Firstly, and most importantly, they influence policy-making. Second, they do influence legislation – as is indeed their aim. Other papers in this collection discuss these aspects of the implementation of the U.N. Convention on the Rights of Persons with Disabilities (hereafter CRPD).[1] This article attempts to predict how that Convention will come to be viewed and applied in the domestic courts of Iceland, Norway and Denmark.[2]

The gist of the discussion concerns conventions or treaties which have been ratified but not incorporated into domestic law. This is a problem particular to those countries that have a dualist tradition towards international law, such as the Nordic countries.

In dualist traditions, international law and domestic law are, in principle, viewed as two distinct legal systems.[3] This entails that unless rules stemming

---

1 Convention on the Rights of Persons with Disabilities (adopted 13 December 2006, entered into force 03.05.2008) A/Res/61/106. According to the Convention website there are 129 signatories to the Convention as of 18 May 2008 and 26 ratifications.

2 Denmark, Iceland and Norway will be jointly designated as „Nordic" here even though the correct form is to refer to them as „West-Nordic." The term „Nordic" is normally used to designate those three states as well as Sweden and Finland. The usage here thus differs from the general one.

3 See M.N. Shaw, *International Law* (3rd edn. Grotius Publications Cambridge University Press 1991) 101–128. In British law and many jurisdictions which have been influenced by the English common law or have adopted it, a distinction is made based on whether the international law rule is a customary one or based on a treaty. See also Per Helset & Bjørn Stordrange, *Norsk statsforfatningsrett* (AdNotam Gyldendal 1998) 163–168; Ida Elisabeth Koch and others, *Menneskerettigheder og magfordeling: domstolskontrol med politiske prioriteringer* (Aarhus Universitetsforlag 2004) 11–13; Joakim Nergelius, *Konstitutionellt rättighetsskydd: Svensk rätt i ett komparativt perspektiv* (Fritzes 1996) 174–175 and 188.

from international law are expressly incorporated into domestic law, they are not viewed as an integral part of the domestic legal system and can, in principle, not be relied upon in domestic courts.[4] The Nordic tradition has been to ratify international human rights conventions but not incorporate them into domestic law.

Dualist approaches stand in contrast to monist approaches, according to which rules stemming from international law become part of the (only) legal system. Holland is often taken as an example of that, although Germany and France could also be mentioned.[5]

In theory at least, the status of an international treaty that has been duly signed and ratified poses no problem in those countries which take a monist approach: The treaty rules simply become part of the legal system. In practice, the issue may not be quite so clear, but nonetheless, it is clear why the questions raised in this paper are important primarily in those countries who tend towards a dualist view of international law.

It must be noted that irrespective of the differences between the monist and dualist traditions, it is beyond dispute that the CRPD, like other international conventions, is binding on the States Parties.[6] However, this article will consider the Convention's effect in the domestic courts, not states' obligations under international law.

Dualist systems differ. While some systems have, during certain periods of time, kept international and domestic law strictly separate, others are quite faithful to international law. One can thus envision dualist approaches as existing on a continuum, running from utter disregard of international law to being quite faithful to it, even though that adherence is not based on the same principles as it is in monist approaches. Instead, it will generally be based on interpretative approaches and rules.[7] Dualist jurisdictions will be located at different places

---

[4] This view was put quite clearly by Icelandic Supreme Court in 1987, when it stated in a case concerning the European Convention on Human Rights: "The provisions of art. 6 of the ECHR [...] have not been given the force of law in this country. They do not change the system prescribed by law...." Hrd. 1987.356, 357–8. See, for a similar treatment, the judgment of the Danish Supreme Court published in UfR 1986.898H. All translations of judgments are by the author, unless otherwise noted.

[5] See Shaw, *supra* note 3 at 124–127. The distinction between dualist and monist systems can seem somewhat artificial since jurisdictions differ and some dualist jurisdictions are quite faithful to international law, as discussed *infra*.

[6] Even while treaties have not entered into force, signatory states and states who have expressed their consent to be bound by the treaty are under the obligation not to defeat the object and purpose of the Convention prior to its entry into force. See art. 18 of the Vienna Convention on the Law of Treaties (adopted 23 May 1969, entered into force 27 January 1980) 1155 UNTS 331.

[7] Chapter II.2 describes such interpretative principles in the Nordic countries.

on the continuum, based on the context and the legal culture, as well as the methods applied when interpreting or construing the law.

An uncompromising dualist answer to the question of the Convention's effect before domestic courts would provide that even though the Convention is binding upon the states under international law, it can not be utilized in domestic courts and the citizens cannot base their rights on it, vis-a-vis the state or any private parties.[8]

But the dualist approach started shifting, in Nordic law, already in the 1970s and 1980s. The European Convention on Human Rights[9] (hereafter ECHR) was the focal point for the changes. There was substantial disagreement in the late 1980s and early 1990s on the exact status of the ECHR and that question was the seminal question in Icelandic constitutional law and legal theory at the time.[10] This was also a very important question in Norwegian and Danish law around 1990.[11] In all these countries, for various reasons, there was, to use the words of Guðrún Gauksdóttir, an increase in the "status of the convention…which finally led to its incorporation."[12] Even though the situation concerning the ECHR was resolved by the incorporation, the dualist approach of these countries was irrevocably changed. Few Nordic lawyers will, when asked about the probable impact of the CRPD in the national courts, give the uncompromising dualist

[8] Such an answer would place a jurisdiction quite close to the „disregard of international law" end of the continuum described *supra*.

[9] The European Convention for the Protection of Human Rights and Fundamental Freedoms (adopted 4 November 1950, entered into force 3 September 1953) CETS No. 5.

[10] See Guðrún Gauksdóttir, 'Iceland' in Robert Blackburn & Jörg Polakiewicz (eds.), *Fundamental Rights in Europe: The European Convention on Human Rights and its Member States 1950–2000* (Oxford University Press 2001), 399–422.

[11] See Ragnhildur Helgadóttir, *The Influence of American Theories on Judicial Review in Nordic Constitutional Law* (Martinus Nijhoff Publishers 2006) 236–244 and the sources and cases cited therein. The dualist theory of the relation between international and domestic law took a beating in these three countries. In Denmark this occurred in a couple of Supreme Court judgments (UfR 1989.928H, UfR 1990.13H and UfR 1990.181H) in which the Convention was directly applied. In Iceland this was seen in two Supreme Court judgments, Hrd. 1990.2 and Hrd. 1992.174. In the first one a parliamentary act was interpreted in a way that would not have been chosen (would have been unthinkable) were it not for the Convention. In the second one, which concerned the right to a translator during criminal proceedings, the Convention was directly applied without further ado. The issue did arguably not come to such a head in Norway, since Norwegian legislation was interpreted so as not to clash with the Convention.

[12] She attributed those changes to a judgment of the European Court of Human Rights finding Iceland in violation of the Convention; to the 1990 Icelandic Supreme Court decision previously mentioned (Hrd. 1990.2), to the deficient constitutional protection of some rights and the developments in other Nordic countries. See Gauksdóttir, *supra* note 10 at 399–400. The European Convention was incorporated into Icelandic law by Act no. 62/1994, into Danish law by Act no. 285 of 29.4.1992 and Norwegian law by Act no. 30 of 21.5.1999.

answer. That is no longer consistent with the position of the Nordic countries on the continuum described above. But the question remains: Which importance do Nordic courts accord to ratified human rights treaties?

It was mostly the European Convention on Human Rights which caused or showcased the shifting approach. For a variety of reasons, however, it is not ideal to rely mostly on the example of the ECHR before its incorporation when attempting to describe the impact of conventions which have been ratified but not incorporated. In part, that is due to the Convention being such a lightning-rod for change and coinciding with the "rise" of human rights (or at least a rise in their visibility). In part, it is also due to those changes coinciding with constitutional amendments in both Norway and Iceland and the first important judgments of the European Court of Human Rights that found the Nordic countries in violation of the Convention.

All this, as well as the ECHR's enforcement mechanism and the time that has passed since it was incorporated and therefore ceased being relevant for our purposes, make the usefulness of the ECHR as a main example questionable.

In order to examine the status of ratified treaties, the following will be considered:

a) the comments of domestic courts on the influence of such treaties;
b) some theory on the influence of such treaties;
c) the application of the ECHR before it was incorporated;
d) the application of the International Covenant on Civil and Political Rights[13] (hereafter ICCPR) and to some degree the International Covenant on Economic, Social and Cultural Rights[14] (hereafter ICESCR) and other UN human rights conventions in domestic courts;
e) and the comments of governments concerning especially the ICCPR.

A variety of theoretical factors that may impact how the CRPD fares in the courts in the next few years, will then be examined. Amongst those are worries about the democratic legitimacy of the courts and of international obligations and about the separation of powers.

Finally, factors inherent in the CRPD that may influence how domestic courts implement it will be looked at, and some conclusions drawn.

---

[13] International Covenant on Civil and Political Rights (adopted 16 December 1966, entered into force 23 March 1976) 999 UNTS 171.

[14] International Covenant on Economic, Social and Cultural Rights (adopted 16 December 1966, entered into force 3 January 1976) 993 UNTS 3.

2 *Lessons from Other Conventions and from Theory*

2.1 *The Application of U.N. Human Rights Conventions in Domestic Courts*

It was already mentioned that Norway incorporated the two international Covenants in 1999.[15] The implementation of these Covenants by the Norwegian courts in the last few years will therefore not be discussed here.[16] The Covenants have not been incorporated into either Danish or Icelandic law.

In the last 10 years, there are four mentions of the ICCPR in Danish Supreme court judgments.[17] In one of those[18] the appellant referred to the Covenant, but the case was not decided on the merits because of procedural reasons. The second judgment[19] is not to be found in its entirety in the relevant Reports but the abstract of the decision notes that "[t]here was no reason to determine that the decision of the Ministry of Justice violated a general principle of equality or encompassed a breach of the European Convention on Human Rights or the International Covenant from Dec. 16, 1966 on Civil and Political Rights." The administrative decision in question was therefore upheld.[20] In a 2006 judgment concerning the pay of those employed by the state after a period of unemployment, the parties referred to both Covenants.[21] In such cases, a "ceiling" on pay meant that the appellant was paid substantially less than co-workers doing similar jobs. The Supreme Court stated that there was "no reason to suppose that his work was forced or compulsory labor in the meaning of art. 4:2 of the ECHR and of the other Convention provisions that [he] referred to"[22] and that the difference in pay was not a violation of either the non-discrimination clauses in the conventions he mentioned, or their provisions on freedom of association. The fourth mention of the ICCPR is a mention by the parties as they argued that an administrative decision should be reviewed, in spite of an

---

15 See Lov om styrking av menneskerettighetenes stilling i norsk rett, Act no. 30 of 21.5.1999.

16 This is the case even though Norwegian judgments predating 1999, such as Rt. 1997.580, are very interesting in this context.

17 Additionally, there seems to be one High Court decision that mentions the Covenant but it is not published in UfR. In UfR 2006.2083H, which will be discussed in more detail below, the High Court (the court of second instance) discussed the Covenant but the Supreme Court did not.

18 UfR 2007.1482/2H.

19 UfR 2001.529H.

20 It concerned the Justice Ministry's refusal to allow the appellant to the Bar.

21 UfR 2006.2083H.

22 UfR 2006.2083H, 2094. This judgment will be discussed in more detail below.

Act providing for limited judicial review. The Supreme Court found no reason to review the decision.[23]

In UfR 2006.2083H, the appellant also referred to art. 6 of the ICESCR. The Supreme Court's alluding to the "Convention provisions referred to"[24] is the only reference by the court itself to the ICESCR in Danish Supreme Court judgments.

There are thus two judgments which seem to suggest that it would have impacted the Court's decision had it found that the administrative decisions in question were in violation of the ICCPR. But it is also noteworthy, that there seem to be only a handful of mentions of the two Covenants in High Court and Supreme Court judgments and some of them by parties to the cases only.

By contrast, the UN Convention on the Rights of the Child (hereafter CRC)[25] has been mentioned in two Supreme Court judgments and seven High Court judgments.[26] In one Supreme Court judgment,[27] the rules of the Convention seem to have been applied directly, albeit in conjunction with other laws.[28]

The facts of the case were that two minors, 15 and 16 years of age, were held in isolation while an armed robbery, which they confessed taking part in, was investigated. Amongst the issues still under investigation were the identity of their accomplices and the whereabouts of the stolen money. The Supreme Court stated that neither "art. 37(c) of the U.N. Convention on the Rights of the Child nor art. 3 of the ECHR prevented youth under 18 to be held in isolation"[29] but stated that it should only be done under quite extraordinary circumstances and held that such circumstances had not been present in the case.

In one of the High Court judgments,[30] a decision to forcibly bring an almost 13 year old child into his mother's custody was invalidated and remanded because the matter was not discussed with the child.[31] The High Court stated

---

23 See UfR 2006.1831H.

24 UfR 2006.2083, 2094.

25 Convention on the Rights of the Child (adopted 20 November 1989, entered into force 2 September 1990) 1577 UNTS 3.

26 The letter at the end of Danish Supreme Court citations refers to the court handing down the judgment. V in the citation thus refers to this being a judgement of the Western High Court (Vestre Landsret). Similarly Ø at the end of a citation to a Danish case refers to the Eastern High Court and H to the Supreme Court.

27 UfR 1999.1415H.

28 In the other Supreme Court case (UfR 2004.2764H) only the parties referred to the Convention.

29 UfR 1999.1415H, 1417.

30 UfR 2000.1260V.

31 In another High Court judgment, UfR 1997.1440Ø, it was briefly mentioned that the Convention on the Rights of the Child did not prevent deportation of an alien who had lived in Denmark for eight years, was married to an alien and had three young children.

that the authorities should, before a decision was made about bringing the child to his mother, "have had a discussion with [the child], cf. the principle of art. 29 [of the relevant Act] and art. 12 of the UN Convention on the Rights of the Child."[32]

Perhaps the most theoretical treatment of the CRC was in UfR 2006.2468V. At issue was the right of the children of a Danish citizen of Turkish ethnicity and a Turkish citizen to receive free Turkish lessons. The parents argued that the denial of this right violated arts. 29 and 30 of the CRC. The Ministry of Education and the municipality argued that "[t]he UN Convention on the Rights of the Child is not breached. Art. 29 does not apply since the children are born in Denmark and art. 30 is not breached since it is the choice of [the parents] to use their own language. Even if it was presumed that the Convention was breached, this would not lead to the setting aside of Danish legal rules, since the provisions do not have the clear and unconditional substance, which is necessary for direct effect."[33] The High Court rejected the parents' argument, noting simply that "[t]here is no ground for determining that it is a violation of the UN Convention on the Rights of the Child that [the] children are not offered Turkish instruction at no cost. Already for that reason the Convention cannot lead to the acceptance of the [parents'] claim."[34]

In the last 10 years, the CRC has been mentioned by the Icelandic Supreme Court itself[35] in 10 judgments, almost twice that of any other convention. There were 4 instances of the Supreme Court itself citing the ICCPR while parties had cited it in altogether 38 cases. The numbers for the ICESCR seem to be similar to that of the ICCPR.

In most such cases any mention of the two Covenants is very brief.[36] However, Icelandic court decisions – just like Danish ones – are generally written in a very concise style. One extreme example is Hrd. 1992.174, which was a criminal case. At the very end of the judgment the Supreme Court added: "Under the court proceedings, the accused has received assistance from an interpreter, since he does

---

32 UfR 2000.1260V, 1262.

33 UfR 2006.2486V, 2471.

34 UfR 2006.2486V, 2471. The other Danish High Court judgments where the CRC has been mentioned are V2000.B-1186-00, OE2004.S-0679-04, OE2002.B-2607-01 and OE 1998. B-3092-98.

35 I.e. not by parties only.

36 In a 1999 free expression case concerning alcohol advertisements, for instance, the Supreme Court described how the Icelandic Constitution and the ECHR allow limitations on the freedom of expression and noted that "Similar provisions are to be found in art. 19 of the ICCPR from 1966, to which Iceland is party, cf. official advertisement nr. 10/1979 in the Official Gazette (Stjórnartíðindi) part C. [/] It is beyond doubt that advertisements are protected by the provisions mentioned above..." Hrd. 1999.781, 783. See also Hrd. in case no. 98/2006 (unpublished).

not speak Icelandic, cf. para. 1, art. 40 of Act no. 85/1936 on Civil procedure and para. 2, art. 19 of Act no. 74/1974 on Criminal Procedure, which shall be interpreted in light of art. 6, para. 3, point e, of the European Convention on Human Rights, cf. official announcement no. 11/1954. The cost of this, before the lower court and the Supreme Court, should be paid by the state."[37] The issue of the interpretation costs had not arisen before the lower court and this was the full extent of the Court's discussion of it. So even though the Court in effect amended[38] the law of procedure, which stipulated that the accused should pay all costs when found guilty, the reasons were given in a few lines of text. Because of this tradition of very brief and concise judgments, everything that receives a mention in the text is presumed to have played a role in the outcome.

In a judgment from 2001, it was argued that the opening of parcels sent from abroad, in order to establish the contents' value for tax purposes, was unconstitutional on right to privacy grounds. The Supreme Court discussed art. 8 of the ECHR[39] and said: "It is also stated in paragraph 1 of art. 17 of the ICCPR that no one shall be subjected to arbitrary or unlawful interference with his privacy, family, home or correspondence, nor to unlawful attacks on his honour and reputation. Under paragraph 2 everyone has the right to the protection of the law against such interference and attacks. This Convention does not have the force of law in this country but it was ratified on behalf of Iceland on Aug. 22, 1979, cf. official advertisement nr. 10 in the C section of the Government Gazette 1979."[40] This is more than just a brief mention, and the provision of the Convention is clearly important even though the court notes that it does not have the force of law.

In recent years, the Icelandic Supreme Court has decided two cases concerning disability in which the ICCPR and the ICESCR were argued.

In a 1999 judgment, a blind university student sued the University of Iceland for damages because she had not received the necessary support in her studies and had had to abandon them. She referred *inter alia* to the ICCPR, the ICESCR and other conventions. The Supreme Court did not refer directly to the covenant but said: "Art. 2 of protocol 1 to the ECHR from Nov. 4, 1950, states that no

[37] Hrd. 1992.174, 175. The case is mentioned briefly in note 11, *supra*.

[38] It may be discussed whether it amended the law or set it aside for another rule. What is clear is that the rule stemming from art. 6 of the Convention was applied by the Court.

[39] The article provides that "Everyone has the right to respect for his private and family life, his home and his correspondence. [/] There shall be no interference by a public authority with the exercise of this right except such as is in accordance with the law and is necessary in a democratic society in the interests of national security, public safety or the economic well-being of the country, for the prevention of disorder or crime, for the protection of health or morals, or for the protection of the rights and freedoms of others."

[40] Hrd. 2001.1188, 1191.

person shall be denied the right to education. Art. 14 of the Convention states that the enjoyment of the rights and freedoms set forth in the Convention shall be secured without discrimination on any ground whatsoever. This must be understood so as to apply also to the right to education and to thus ensuring an equal right to education. This Convention was given force of law in Iceland by Act no. 62/1994, on the European Convention on Human Rights. Before the incorporation, it was considered correct to interpret Icelandic law so as to be in harmony with the Convention, since it is a recognized rule in Nordic law that legislation shall be construed, as far as possible, in accordance with the international conventions that have been ratified by the state."[41]

Based on this equal right to education; on statutory rules guaranteeing persons with disabilities equality and service by the same institutions and according to the same rules as others; and finally on an unwritten principle of equality, the Court "...concludes that the University of Iceland was obliged to accept the appellant, which it did, and to take the general measures necessary due to the studies of so disabled a student at the university, for her to be able to enjoy the services enjoyed by other students enrolled in the faculty she chose."[42]

The woman was awarded damages, since it was held that "...when looking at the conditions that the appellant was offered at the business faculty as a whole, the conclusion cannot be avoided, that some things went awry and the university and the faculty violated the rights enjoyed by the appellant as a disabled student. This is primarily based on the fact that no general recommendations were made concerning her studies and examinations...to which she had a legal right, in order to be, as far as possible, on an equal footing with non-disabled students."[43] This, as well as the fact that she had had to ask for and fight for "reasonable accomodation" was held to have been an illegal tort against her person and her right to education.[44]

This judgment is noteworthy for a number of reasons, including the fact that the Court seemed unperturbed by positive obligations. The judgment was based in part on the equal right to education and the concept of equality can, in some circumstances, and did here open the door to positive obligations. However, the judgment was also based on the Act on the affairs of people with disabilities, which stipulated, inter alia, in art. 7, that "People with disabilities shall be entitled to all general services provided by the State and by municipalities. It shall be endeavoured at all times to provide services for people with disabilities

[41] Hrd. 1999.390, 392.

[42] Hrd. 1999.390, 392.

[43] Hrd. 1999.390, 394–5. The Court continued: "Instead, she had to request reasonable accomodation and it has been proven that this lack of general recommendations led to mistakes being made by the faculty and to confrontations with the appellant."

[44] Hrd. 1999.390, 395.

in accordance with general laws in the field of education, health and social services." In its judgment, the Supreme Court stated that it is "...an accepted principle of Nordic law that to the extent possible Parliamentary Acts shall be interpreted so as to be consistent with international treaties that have been ratified by the state."[45] No citations were given in support of this statement, but a statement to the same effect can be found in a Norwegian Supreme Court judgment from 1984.[46]

In 2000, the Icelandic Supreme Court repeated this comment.[47] The facts were that the Organization of the Disabled in Iceland (ÖBÍ) claimed that the curtailment of income supplements based on the income of the spouse of the disabled person was unconstitutional.[48]

ÖBÍ claimed that the reduced social security payments violated the right to minimum social benefits guaranteed by art. 76, para. 1 of the Constitution, according to which "[t]he law shall guarantee for everyone the necessary assistance in case of sickness, invalidity, infirmity by reason of old age, unemployment and similar circumstances". It noted that article 76 has its roots in international human rights conventions ratified by Iceland, including articles 12 and 13 of the European Social Charter, and articles 9 and 11 of the ICESCR. ÖBÍ argued that it could not be viewed as legitimate under those provisions to exclude married individuals on the basis of the income of their spouses. ÖBÍ claimed that the curtailment also violated article 65 of the Icelandic Constitution which prohibits discrimination, in that individuals were subject to discrimination based on their marital status.[49]

The State Social Security Institute argued that the curtailment did not violate the Icelandic Constitution or international conventions on human rights to which Iceland is a party.[50]

The Supreme Court stated: "The Constitution has provided for the right to assistance from public funds for those unable to support themselves, since 1874. This right, however, was subject to his/her maintenance not resting upon others. This condition was abolished through constitutional amendment in 1995.

[45] Hrd. 1999.390, 392.

[46] Rt. 1984.1175.

[47] Hrd. 2000.4480, 4487.

[48] Hrd. 2000.4480. In effect, ÖBÍ argued that the decrease was unlawful for two reasons. First, that in the period from 1994 to 1998 there had been insufficient legal authority for curtailing income supplements by means of government regulation, and secondly, that even when enacted into legislation, it remained unconstitutional.

[49] It stated that article 65 has its roots in paragraph of article 2 of the ICESCR. Hrd. 2000.4480, 4497.

[50] This description of the facts of the case in English is based on International law in domestic courts, www.ildc.oxfordlawreports.com. The commentator was Thordis Ingadottir.

According to Paragraph 1 of Article 76 of the Constitution, [as amended], the law shall guarantee for everyone the necessary assistance in case of sickness, invalidity, infirmity by reason of old age, unemployment and similar circumstances. The commentary, attached to the Bill to Act No. 97/1995, made particular note that it was assumed that more detailed rules on social assistance of this nature would be established by law and that the provision set the condition that rules ensuring such assistance must exist. In this respect, particular attention was brought to Articles 12 and 13 of the European Social Charter, ratified by Iceland on 15 January 1976, […] and Articles 11 and 12 of the Covenant on Economic, Social and Cultural Rights, ratified by Iceland on 22 August 1979. […] Parties to the first Convention undertake to *i.a.* establish or maintain social securities or maintain them at a satisfactory level at least equal to that required for the ratification of International Labour Convention No. 102 Concerning Minimum Standards of Social Security. Article 67 of this Convention establishes the conditions that this minimum must fulfill and states that no curtailments may be made except in the case of substantial additional amounts. The second Convention involves *i.a.* that the parties to the Covenant recognize the right of everyone to an adequate standard of living for himself/herself and his/her family."[51]

The Court then reiterated that "[i]t is a recognized rule in Nordic legislation that legislation shall be construed, as far as possible, in accordance with the international conventions that the State has ratified. According to the above, Article 76 of the Constitution must be construed so as to legally ensure the right of each individual to at least some minimum maintenance pursuant to a predetermined arrangement, determined in an objective manner."[52]

---

[51] Hrd. 2000.4480, 4487.

[52] Hrd. 2000.4480, 4487. The Court continued: "According to Article 2 of the Constitution, the general legislator has the power to decide the manner in which this arrangement shall be. An arrangement, decided by the legislator, however, would have to fulfill the minimum rights provided for in Article 65 of the Icelandic Constitution. Moreover, it must fulfill the provisions of Article 65 of the Icelandic Constitution to the effect that each individual shall enjoy rights equal to others who enjoy rights, as well as common human rights. The general legislator has defined the policy with regard to these human rights, insofar as they concern the disabled, in Article 1 of Act no. 59/1992, on the affairs of people with disabilities. The stated objective of this Act is to ensure that the disabled have equal rights and enjoy comparable standards of living to other members of society and to create an environment where they can lead a normal life. The Legislature has, through the Social Security Act No. 117/1993 [now reissued as Act. No. 100/2007], met its obligations with respect to rights pursuant to Paragraph 1 of Article 76 of the Constitution as regards the disabled specifically. Other legal provisions of this nature, such as those in accordance with the Social Assistance Act No. 118/1993 and Chapter VI of the Local Authorities Social Service Act no. 40/1991, however, are enablement clauses and provide no instruction on the rights of the disabled." Hrd. 2000.4480, 4487–8.

The Court finally found that the law as challenged "cannot be seen to ensure the minimum rights inherent in the above Constitutional provision, in such a manner that [those receiving a disability pension] are able to enjoy the human rights provided in Article 65, as that provision should be understood in Icelandic law, cf. Article 26 of the International Covenant on Civil and Political Rights, ratified by Iceland on 22 August 1979...and Article 9 of the above international Covenant on Economic, Social and Cultural Rights."[53]

This judgment is fascinating, firstly, in that it sets out explicitly how the constitutional provision shall be construed in light of its drafting history and the relevant international conventions. The international instruments clearly impact the substance of the constitutional provision considerably. However, it may very well be important that the conventions referred to in the decision had also been utilized – and cited – when the constitutional article in question was drafted. The fact that the international instruments were mentioned in the *travaux préparatoires* to the constitutional amendments of 1995 provides a safe haven for courts: They can rely on international conventions when interpreting and applying constitutional provisions while arguing, quite correctly, that they are primarily looking at legislative history!

Secondly, the judgment is important because of the court's willingness to enforce constitutionally guaranteed economic and social rights. The decision was widely discussed, *i.a.* in light of separation of powers and the democratic legitimacy of the courts.[54] Those issues will be discussed further below.

What, then, can be deduced from this admittedly small number of judgments? First, Icelandic parties to cases obviously find it pertinent to refer to the Covenants for they do so frequently. Secondly, the courts refer to them as well, but often very briefly and always without elaborating and without reference to practice. Courts generally do not rely on the Covenants alone but refer to them to bolster their conclusions. However, the traditional disclaimer of the Covenants not having been incorporated into domestic law is on the wane.

2.2 *Principles Stated by the Courts and Theory*

It has already been mentioned that in Norwegian law, it was stated already in 1984 that "as far as possible" Norwegian law "must be presumed to be in

---

[53] Hrd. 2000.4480, 4491. This translation is taken in great part from International Law in Domestic Courts, www.ildc.oxfordlawreports.com.

[54] See, on the implementation of economic, social and cultural rights: Björg Thorarensen, 'Beiting ákvæða um efnahagsleg og félagsleg mannréttindi í stjórnarskrá og alþjóðasamningum' (2001) Tímarit lögfræðinga 51(2), 75–105. For a more critical discussion of the decision, see Davíð Oddsson, 'Valdheimildir löggjafans og úrskurðarvald dómstóla' (2002) Tímarit lögfræðinga 52(1), 7–14.

accordance with treaties by which Norway is bound."[55] Likewise, the Icelandic Supreme Court stated in 1999 and 2000 that "[i]t is an accepted principle of Nordic law that to the extent possible Parliamentary Acts shall be interpreted so as to be consistent with international treaties that have been ratified by the state."[56] This principle is not really in dispute. By itself, however, it says little. It has been fleshed out somewhat in theory.

In Norwegian constitutional law, the two relevant principles are named the principle of presumption[57] and the principle of effectivity.[58] The former entails that domestic law is presumed to be in harmony with international law. It is therefore interpreted, supplemented and applied in accordance with international law. This principle was clearly enunciated by the Norwegian Supreme Court in the judgment cited above.[59] The second principle entails that when national law is less than clear it is interpreted so as to render rules stemming from international law more effective.[60]

In Danish constitutional law, the labels are different but the theories, at least in very abstract form, quite similar. First of all, there is the rule of interpretation[61] which entails that if there is doubt about the interpretation of a domestic legal source, it shall be interpreted so as to be in accordance with the state's international obligations.[62] Secondly, there is the presumption principle[63] which, like its Norwegian counterpart, presumes that domestic law is not intended to breach international obligations.[64] Finally, Danish scholars have spoken of a principle of instruction, which is particularly relevant concerning administrative decision-making.[65]

---

55 See Rt. 1984.1175, 1180. See also Erik Møse, 'Norway' in Robert Blackburn & Jörg Polakiewicz (eds), *Fundamental Rights in Europe: The European Convention on Human Rights and its Member States 1950–2000* (Oxford University Press 2001) 628 and 630–634 and Ragnhildur Helgadóttir, *supra* note 11, p. 238.

56 Hrd. 1999.390, 392 and Hrd. 2000.4480, 4487.

57 In Norwegian "presumpsjonsprinsippet".

58 In Norwegian "effektivitetsprinsippet".

59 This is also a principle in Icelandic law. See Davíð Þór Björgvinsson, *Lögskýringar* (JPV 2008) 261–275.

60 See Per Helset & Bjørn Stordrange, *supra* note 3, pp. 165–167.

61 In Danish "fortolkningsreglen".

62 See Henrik Zahle, *Dansk forfatningsret 2: Regering, forvaltning og dom*, (2nd edn. Christian Ejlers' Forlag 1998) 271. He criticizes this principle as being too narrow and for not being a correct description of practice. See, as far as Icelandic law is concerned, Hrd. 1999.390 and Hrd. 2000.4480 as well as Davíð Þór Björgvinsson, *supra* note 59, pp. 261–275.

63 In Danish "formodningsreglen".

64 See Zahle, *supra* note 62, pp. 271–272. He criticizes this principle as well, for *inter alia* having a wider scope than is supported by the case-law.

65 See Zahle, *supra* note 62, pp. 273–275.

The rule of interpretation has, in Icelandic law, been held to apply not only to statutory law but also to the constitution and to administrative regulations.[66] It is not only applied so as to increase the protection of human rights but also to support statutory interpretation allowing restrictions of rights that generally can only be restricted by law.[67]

In sum, it has been argued in Nordic constitutional theory that the impact of international instruments is best described by a series of principles: It is presumed that domestic law is consistent with international obligations. Domestic law is then construed so as to be in accordance with the state's international obligations. In addition, Norwegian constitutional law accepts a principle that domestic law shall be interpreted so as to render international law more effective and Danish constitutional law may include a principle of instruction – which concerns administrative law.

Due to the acceptance of these principles in the past two or three decades, the Nordic countries have moved away from uncompromising dualist approaches and are much more faithful to international law than before.[68] Meanwhile, it is important to note that these principles are not unique to the Nordic countries. Similar principles or interpretative approaches exist in other jurisdictions, including some common law ones.[69]

2.3 *Statements of Governments Concerning Unincorporated Treaties*

Before the Human Rights Committee, the Icelandic[70] and Danish[71] governments have in essence argued that as far as the ICCPR is concerned, incorporation

---

[66] See Davíð Þór Björgvinsson, *supra* note 59, pp. 261 and 263.

[67] See Davíð Þór Björgvinsson, *supra* note 59, pp. 267–269. See also Hrd. 1999.1709, which will be discussed later.

[68] Their place on the continuum, described in part I, has thus shifted.

[69] See e.g. Shaw, *supra* note 3, at 116. The principles or methods of interpretation in different jurisdictions, and thus the position of their dualist approaches vis-a-vis that of other jurisdictions will not be discussed any further here.

[70] The Icelandic government has argued: "As far as conflicts between the Covenant and the Constitution were concerned, in many instances it had been possible to interpret Icelandic legislation in the light of the European Convention on Human Rights without any conflict. In fact, since the incorporation of the Convention in Icelandic domestic legislation, there had been no cases in which the courts had declared that Icelandic legislation should prevail over a conflicting provision of the Covenant. It was quite common for the parties involved in a case or even the courts themselves to invoke the provisions of the Covenant and other international human rights instruments." www.unhchr.ch/tbs/doc.nsf/(Symbol)/CCPR.C.SR.1704.En?Opendocument (23.08.2007).

[71] The Danish government has argued: "As the Danish Government has previously stated, any incorporation of the Covenant into domestic law would not result in better legal protection of the individual. The provisions of the Covenant are already applicable before the Danish courts

into domestic legislation would not serve to increase the legal weight of the Covenant in domestic courts, since the system now in place ensures consistency with international law.[72]

These claims before the Committee are primarily evidence that the governments view at least this particular Covenant to be influential and the rights it protects to be secured even though the Covenant has not been incorporated. So the interpretation method obviously has meaning, according to the governments, enough to guarantee respect for the rights enumerated once a convention has been ratified. The Human Rights Committee, however, has begged to differ.[73] The Committee's concluding remarks in 2000, as far as Denmark was concerned, mentioned that "The Committee is concerned about the full protection in Denmark of individual rights under the Covenant. The Committee notes that Denmark has set up a body to consider the incorporation into domestic law of several human rights treaties, including the Covenant [...] The State party should take any steps necessary to ensure that all rights under the Covenant secure full protection in Danish law. It should inform the Committee about the measures taken and the success of such measures."[74]

In UfR 2006.2083, which was mentioned earlier, it was argued, based on a doctrine of "estoppel,"[75] that the Danish state was "unable to argue...that

---

and administrative authorities, and the Danish authorities are under an obligation to apply the provisions of the Covenant in connection with the interpretation and application of Danish legislation. Obviously, the Government is aware that incorporation would be of informative value to the citizens. [/] The question of incorporation of the general human rights conventions, including the International Covenant on Civil and Political Rights, is therefore being considered. In this connection, it is being considered whether a committee should be set up to consider the issue in detail." www.unhchr.ch/tbs/doc.nsf/(Symbol)/CCPR.C.DNK.99.4.En?Opendocument (23.08.2007).

[72] See e.g. the remarks of Mr. Scheinin www.unhchr.ch/tbs/doc.nsf/(Symbol)/CCPR.C.SR.1704. En?Opendocument (12.09.2007) and the recommendation of the Committee: www.unhchr.ch/huricane/huricane.nsf/0/32F18CF885D0AB46802566A50030720F?opendocument (12.09.2007), www.unhchr.ch/tbs/doc.nsf/(Symbol)/CCPR.C.79.Add.98.En?Opendocument (12.09.2007) and www.unhchr.ch/tbs/doc.nsf/(Symbol)/0f1891e92f3eaaa6c1256ffc004903ba?Opendocument (12.09.2007).

[73] From a separation of powers standpoint, this poses certain problems, because the executive branch cannot unilaterally change domestic legislation simply by ratifying treaties. In many countries, however, the legislature has a role to play in the ratifying of treaties. In Iceland, for instance, the legislature's approval is needed if the ratification requires changes to prior legislation. That is, if the government feels that in order to ensure compliance with the treaty, it needs to change some legislative acts before ratifying, the changes are first passed and then Parliament accepts the treaty. See Gunnar G. Schram, *Stjórnskipunarréttur* (Háskólaútgáfan 1999) 380–381.

[74] www.unhchr.ch/tbs/doc.nsf/(Symbol)/CCPR.CO.70.DNK.En?Opendocument (12.09.2007).

[75] The doctrine of estoppel can, in Anglo-American law, mean a legally imposed bar resulting from one's own conduct and precluding any denial or assertion regarding a fact but it is also a doctrine that prevents someone from adopting an inconsistent position, attitude or action if

some of the conventions cited by the appellant have not been incorporated into Danish law and can therefore not be the basis of individuals' rights."[76] In this context the appellant cited the state's report to the Human Rights Committee as well as additional information given by the state's delegates "according to which there is, in practice, no difference between the status of the ECHR and e.g. the ICCPR and the [International Convention on the Elimination of All Forms of Racial Discrimination] in Danish law."[77] The appellant also cited directly the government's statement that the provisions "of the Covenant are already applicable before the Danish Courts and administrative authorities, and the Danish authorities are under an obligation to apply the provisions of the Covenant in connection with the interpretation and application of Danish legislation."[78] As already mentioned, the High Court noted that the law in question "did not contain such elements of compulsion as to make them inconsistent with international obligations, such as the ECHR's art. 4, para. 2 or the ICCPR's art. 8, para 3, as those are interpreted in the light of ILO conventions."[79] The Supreme Court, by contrast, only noted that there was "no reason to suppose that his work was forced or compulsory labor in the meaning of art. 4:2 of the ECHR and of the other convention provisions that [he] referred to."[80]

Similar considerations apply to the Icelandic government as to its Danish counterpart. It was already mentioned that some criticism was leveled at the Icelandic courts in the aftermath of the Social Security decision, not least because of the courts' use of international law. Of course, governments cannot have it both ways: You cannot argue that the implementation of international law in the courts ensures the effectivity of those treaties while also criticizing the courts when they interpret domestic law so as to be in accord with international obligations.

Is the government's faith in this method of implementing international treaties justified? It is, at least to some degree, since some Icelandic judgments concerning international treaties other than the ICCPR, point in the direction of international law having even more of an impact than indicated in the judgments concerning the ICCPR. The primary example is the the utilization of various international instruments in the social security and the disabled student cases as well as *inter alia* a case concerning environmental issues.[81]

it will result in injury to another. See e.g. the definition of estoppel in *Black's Law Dictionary* (Garner, ed.) West 1996.

[76] UfR 2006.2083H, 2089.

[77] UfR 2006.2083H, 2089.

[78] UfR 2006.2083H, 2089.

[79] UfR 2006.2083H, 2094.

[80] UfR 2006.2083H, 2094.

[81] See Hrd. 1999.1709. The decision concerned restrictions on the import of ozone-depleting substances. A statute was in force, which provided that the import of goods and services to

Before looking at factors from theory and factors concerning individual treaties that may influence courts to pay more or less attention to treaties and thus trying to gauge how the CRPD will influence court decisions, a sum-up of the main lessons to be learned from Nordic court judgments, theory, the status of the ECHR before its incorporation into domestic law and the status of the ICCPR is in order.

First of all, domestic law is interpreted and construed so as to be in accord with international obligations. The courts will not presume that there is a conflict between national and international law. This is quite clear but does not provide much of an answer. There are no examples of conflicts, pointed out by e.g. the domestic Human Rights Institutes or the Human Rights Committee, in which the ICCPR has been argued before a court but the argument has been ignored or explicitly rejected based on the primacy of domestic law. The Icelandic government says clearly there are no such examples: That there has been no conflict between domestic law and the ICCPR since the ECHR was incorporated. The Norwegian Supreme Court similarly found no conflict between domestic law and the ECHR from 1984 to 1999, when the Convention was incorporated. This may point to the courts reaching quite far in their interpretation of domestic law but it is also possible – and indeed many of the cases described above support such a claim – that the ICCPR is mainly cited along with provisions in domestic constitutions and the ECHR.

3 *Factors from Theory that may Influence how much Attention the Courts pay to International Obligations*

In the Nordic countries, the courts' relying on international law has given rise to discussions about a set of issues related to the legitimacy of international law on the one hand and the proper role of domestic courts on the other. It stands to

---

Iceland should be free unless otherwise stated in statutes or international conventions. A provision in the Act on poisons and noxious substances permitted the Minister of Environmental Affairs to enact regulations concerning the import, sale, use, safe handling and disposal of the substances covered by the Act. Under the usual rules governing the delegation of legislative power, the principle of free import would have prevented the Minister from enacting a regulation restricting the import unless the restriction was specifically permitted by law. The court construed the Act on poisons and noxious substances as permitting the Minister to restrict the import of those substances noting that "[t]his has taken into account both the aim of the legislation on noxious substances and the amendments to that legislation and the substance of the international agreements on protection against ozone-depleting substances to which Iceland is a party." Hrd. 1999.1709, 1713. While not completely unambiguous the court seems to have veered fairly far off the usual course based on international agreements.

reason that theories on these matters will influence the application of international treaties in the courts, and these issues will therefore be discussed briefly.

The issues that have been raised in Nordic theory concern, firstly, the democratic legitimacy of rules that stem from international law, whether they stem directly from international treaties or indirectly via the interpretational activities of international organs. Secondly, they concern the democratic legitimacy of the courts and concerns about them usurping legislative powers. These are traditional questions of constitutional theory. Finally, some questions have been raised concerning the separation of powers in the context of the interplay between the executive and legislative powers. Superimposed on these questions of democratic legitimacy and separation of powers is the distinction that is often still made between civil and political rights on the one hand and economic, social and cultural rights on the other.

The main question here is how the CRPD is likely to fare in the domestic courts of Denmark, Iceland and Norway. In order to make that prediction, it is necessary to look at these issues, all of which concern neither the rights of persons with disabilities nor international obligations, but the proper role and competence of courts. These are questions of justiciability and constitutional theory. These issues are also discussed in some of the other chapters in this collection. The most important points are the following:

It is questionable to which extent the considerations of separation of powers should play a role before the courts.: Such considerations provide (or may provide) a theoretical foundation for dualist approaches: It is (at least partly) because the executive power is not supposed to be able to legislate by entering into treaty obligations that rules stemming from such obligations are not immediately a part of domestic law.[82] Considerations concerning the separation of powers may therefore be more useful as an explanation of the legal situation concerning unincorporated international obligations than as a factor that needs to be taken into account when trying to predict how courts will use the CRPD.

These separation of powers considerations may suggest that the CRPD will be more likely to influence courts if it elaborates on points that are also present in national law. This may well be the case as far as many provisions of the CRC are concerned, but as mentioned earlier that Convention is more frequently cited in Nordic courts than other non-incorporated treaties.

Issues concerning the democratic legitimacy of the courts have sometimes, been resolved by the contention that democracy does not mean simple majority rule[83] – or that if it does, it is not a desirable form of government when left unchecked. The democracy that is valued and upheld is characterized by

---

[82] See, regarding English theory on this point, *e.g.* Shaw, *supra* note 3, at 114.

[83] See *e.g.* Ragnar Aðalsteinsson, 'einungis eftir lögunum' (2000) Úlfljótur 53(4) 569–600.

majority rule tempered by the inviolable rights of all, irrespective of the view of the majority. Issues concerning the democratic legitimacy of the courts[84] may, however, in conjunction with worries about the separation of powers, have an impact on the courts.

In theory and public discourse,[85] this argument has frequently been linked to considerations of civil and political rights on the one hand and economic, social and cultural rights on the other. That brings us to the discussion of those factors concerning the CRPD in particular which may affect how it will fare in the courts. In that context, it is necessary to be aware that the question is not only whether the Convention will be cited by domestic courts, but also whether the ideas that inform the Convention will impact national court judgments with or without them citing the Convention.

4 *Factors regarding the CRPD, that may Influence how the Convention will fare in Domestic Courts*

Four issues will be discussed under this heading: First the different categories of human rights; second, the shift from social policy to a rights-based approach; third, the relation of the CRPD to domestic law and fourth, the principles of the Convention.

As far as different categories of rights are concerned, Ida E. Koch and Brynhildur Flóvenz have in their contributions discussed the perceived dichotomy between civil and political rights on the one hand and economic, social and cultural rights on the other. As far as the Icelandic Supreme Court is concerned, however, it is impossible, based on the Social Security case, to argue that it holds economic and social rights to be non-justiciable. But this dichotomy exists in theory in most jurisdictions, and many lawyers are more ambivalent about the

[84] It will not be discussed in any detail here but in Denmark and Norway, and to a certain degree in Iceland, there has been criticism of international human rights. This debate has focused on the ECHR and the European Court of Human Rights, as well as the national courts' implementation of the ECHR. See e.g. Jonas Christoffersen, 'Den danske debat om den internationale menneskeret', Nordisk Tidsskrift for Menneskerettigheter 2006(2) 97–114; Inge Lorange Backer, 'Tendenser – Om Høyesteretts forhold til den Europeiske Menneskerettighetskonvensjon' Nordisk Tidsskrift for Menneskerettigheter 2005(4) 425–432 and Carsten Smith, 'Om Høyesteretts forhold til den Europeiske Menneskerettighetskonvensjon' Nordisk Tidsskrift for Menneskerettigheter 2005(4) 433–440.

[85] This was e.g. the case concerning the Icelandic Social Security judgment discussed above. It was argued in the aftermath of that case, that the courts had not only overridden the legislature on a stereotypical political question (how much money is necessary for subsistence) but that it had in fact usurped the financial power.

courts' proper role when dealing with economic, social and cultural rights than when they are dealing with civil and political rights.

In light of this dichotomy, it is noteworthy that in art. 2 of the CRPD, "discrimination on the basis of disability" means "any distinction, exclusion or restriction on the basis of disability which has the purpose or effect of impairing or nullifying the recognition, enjoyment or exercise, on an equal basis with others, of all human rights and fundamental freedoms in the political, economic, social, cultural, civil or any other field." In the field of discrimination under the Convention, there is therefore no clear boundary between economic, social and cultural rights and civil and political rights.[86] Art. 4, para. 2 of the Convention concerns economic, social and cultural rights, and states that the State Parties undertake to "take measures to the maximum of its available resources and, where needed...with a view to achieving progressively the full realization of these rights" but it is also noted specifically that this is "without prejudice to those obligations [in the Convention] that are immediately applicable according to international law." Those are e.g. the obligations regarding discrimination on the basis of disability, which includes, as just noted, economic, social and cultural rights.

In those jurisdictions where there is a gap in the justiciability and "enforcement" of economic, social and cultural rights on the one hand and civil and political rights on the other (or where it is argued that there should be such a gap) it is possible that the link forged by the CRPD between equality law and economic, social and cultural rights will entail the justiciability of these rights as well – within the orbit of the Convention. This is a "Trojan horse effect" which will serve to increase the justiciability of social and economic rights.

As to the second point, it has been rightly pointed out that the CRDP takes a rights-based approach instead of viewing the rights of people with disabilities as a matter of social policy.[87] This matters in the context of the courts. The

---

[86] For a discussion on the difficulties of drawing a boundary between preventing discrimination on the one hand and the positive obligation of promoting equality on the other see Oddný Mjöll Arnardóttir, *Equality and Non-Discrimination under the European Convention on Human Rights* (Martinus Nijhoff Publishers 2003) 113–116.

[87] Another change that has been mentioned in the context of the adoption of the CRPD is a shift in emphasis from procedural administrative law to substantive human rights. This will not be discussed in any detail here, even though the issue is fascinating. Procedural administrative law provides a minimum safeguard for those dealing with the state, including those receiving services from the state. Administrative law has thus guaranteed that decisions concerning e.g. social security as provided by law, are made after thorough consideration, based on legitimate and relevant considerations and are non-discriminatory. Of course, it does not, in and of itself guarantee human rights – since human rights are binding also on legislatures while administrative law applies only to the implementation of those Acts already passed. Also because while human rights are guaranteed vis-à-vis everyone while administrative law applies primarily to

courts are generally not supposed to make social policy. They are supposed to be very careful when they enter that realm, as it lies in the orbit of the legislature. But from the point of view of constitutional law, moving from social policy to human rights means engaging the courts in policing that rights are respected – enforcement is one part of the difference between rights and ideals. The focus on equality is the logical next step in this context, as it serves to resolve at least some of the justiciability and judicial restraint issues that are generally presumed to exist when dealing with economic and social rights.[88]

Concerning the relation of the rules in the CRPD to domestic law, it is important to note that based on the example of the CRC, it may be that this Convention will become unusually successful in domestic courts because there are similar principles in the domestic legislation of many jurisdictions.

As an example, the rule of domestic law and the CRC of the best interests of the child may be mentioned. It is clear from Icelandic court decisions that this principle gains a lot of strength by being not only a rule in national law but a rule of an international instrument as well. A similar cumulative impact of an international instrument superimposed on domestic legislation may become important in the case of the CRPD.

As a final point, it is a specific question, and an interesting one, whether the principles of the Convention will be important in the courts. They are listed in art. 3 and are:

(a) Respect for inherent dignity, individual autonomy including the freedom to make one's own choices, and independence of persons;
(b) Non-discrimination;
(c) Full and effective participation and inclusion in society;
(d) Respect for difference and acceptance of persons with disabilities as part of human diversity and humanity;
(e) Equality of opportunity;
(f) Accessibility;
(g) Equality between men and women;
(h) Respect for the evolving capacities of children with disabilities and respect for the right of children with disabilities to preserve their identities.

These principles are explicitly stated in the Convention and may therefore affect the interpretation of national law just like other rules of the Convention.

---

the state. But it is important to note that administrative law and human rights coexist. Shifting the emphasis doesn't preempt administrative law or make it moot. In many contexts, especially in countries where domestic law is largely in conformity with the Convention, administrative law can provide an important tool to guarantee that the state abides by its own laws in a non-discriminatory, legal manner.

[88] It is presumably not a coincidence that in both the blind student case and the social security case, see *supra* notes 41 and 47, equality was argued along with other rights.

However, their status as principles of the Convention adds to their impact, compared to other articles of the Convention. If that turns out to be the case they may end up being very important as principles which govern the interpretation of domestic law.

5 *Conclusions*

Based on the discussion in this chapter, what is the possible, or likely, influence of the CRPD in the domestic courts of the Nordic countries?

First of all, it is generally accepted that domestic law should be construed or interpreted so as to be in accordance with international obligations. It is also clear, that it is assumed whenever possible that international law and domestic law are not in conflict. Finally, Norwegian domestic law is interpreted so as to make international law more effective.

The Convention will thus, at the very least, affect the interpretation of domestic law and it will be assumed that domestic law is consistent with it. But the judgments concerning unincorporated treaties suggest that this description of their impact is an understatement rather than an exaggeration.[89] The very fact that international instruments are referred to at all in the reasoning of the Danish and Icelandic courts means that they did play a role in the outcome of the case and some judgments, which have been discussed, suggest that they are quite close to being directly applied.

While it is very difficult to reach a conclusion as to the importance of unincorporated treaties in general, it is easier, if only marginally, to answer this question concerning a particular Convention – here the CRPD. Three considerations are important.

Firstly, the traditional "constitutional" law defenses against applying international conventions in domestic courts may be unusually weak in the case of the CRPD. The reasons for that are firstly, the emergence of disability rights as human rights (as opposed to disability or social policy issues). Secondly, this might be due to the boundaries between equality law, social and economic rights and civil and political rights becoming blurred. That may partially resolve justiciability and separation of powers issues that might otherwise restrain the courts. This makes it more likely that the Convention will be used, for more

89 To name just three examples, all Icelandic, such a conclusion can be supported by the judgments concerning ozone-depleating substances (Hrd. 1999.1709); the case concerning the blind university student (Hrd. 1999.390); and Hrd. 1992.174, which concerned the ECHR before its incorporation.

cases will be adjudicated substantively, which entails more construing of domestic law, hopefully in accordance with the Convention.

Secondly, the Convention will increase the status of existing rules. Many of the rules in the Convention will be like the rules in the ICCPR – cited by courts when they are applying, construing or interpreting similar rules from domestic law. The ICCPR judgments, and, in particular, judgments concerning the CRC, give an inkling on how that works. The principles of the best interest of the child and the child's right to access to both parents are the most frequently cited rules of the Convention and both have sibling rules in Icelandic and Danish domestic law. Just like predicted here concerning the CRPD, these principles gain triple strength from being regular statutory domestic law, as well as an accepted human right as well as a treaty provision which shall influence the interpretation of domestic law.

Finally, it is likely that the principles of the Convention will become principles of interpretation of domestic law.

However, it must also be noted that while the CRC has been successful in the Danish and Icelandic courts, the Convention on the Elimination of All Forms of Discrimination against Women[90] (hereafter CEDAW) has never been mentioned in those courts.[91] So there exist full-fledged, ratified human rights conventions that are almost completely bypassed by Nordic courts. CEDAW and the CRC both concern particular groups of people. Both are UN treaties and both are relatively recent. There are therefore no obvious reasons for the discrepancy. Possibly, there are political reasons for the difference. Possibly, the Nordic countries think they have less need for CEDAW. Possibly, it is simply a question of children being a particularly vulnerable group. But the question is, where will the CRPD land on this scope: Will it count or will it not? It does seem likely that it will prove important in the courts, for the reasons dicussed in this Chapter, particularly the links with equality.

[90] The Convention on the Elimination of All Forms of Discrimination against Women (adopted 18 December 1979, entered into force 3 September 1981) 1249 UNTS 513.

[91] Similarly, the CRC was incorporated into Norwegian law in Menneskerettighetsloven, (Lov om styrking av menneskerettighetenes stilling i norsk rett, Act. No. 30 of 21.5.1999) while CEDAW was not. It was, however, incorporated into Norwegian law via an amendment to Act no. 45, of 9 June 1978 Lov om likestilling mellom kjønnene (likestillingsloven). See art. 1b of the Act.

Notes on Contributors

Professor Oddný Mjöll Arnardóttir

Professor Oddný Mjöll Arnardóttir, Ph.D. (University of Edinburgh) is a Professor of Law at the Reykjavik University School of Law. She was admitted to the Icelandic Bar in 1995, and was a partner in a law firm before taking up a full academic position. She served as the President of the Icelandic Women Lawyers' Association 2005–2006 and on the National Bioethics Committee 2003–2006. She is currently a member of the Board of the Icelandic Human Rights Centre and a member of the Icelandic Expert Council for Research in Social Sciences and Humanities. Her research interests mostly focus on non-discrimination law, the European Convention on Human Rights and health law. She is the author of the book Equality and Non-Discrimination under the European Convention on Human Rights (Martinus Nijhoff Publishers, 2003) and has published numerous articles on human rights law, constitutional law, equality and non-discrimination law.

Judge David Thor Björgvinsson

Davíð Þór Björgvinsson is a Judge at the European Court of Human Rights and a Professor of Law at the Reykjavík University School of Law. He studied history, philosophy and law at the University of Iceland and the Duke University School of Law (North Carolina). He was formerly a Professor of Law at the University of Iceland and has been a visiting scholar at the University of Edinburgh, Rand Afrikaans Universiteit (Now University of Johannesburg) in South Africa and Copenhagen University. He has also served as a lawyer at the EFTA Court in Geneva and Luxembourg and is the former Chairman for the Institute of Human Rights at the University of Iceland.

Colm O'Cinneide

Colm O'Cinneide is a Senior Lecturer in Law at the Faculty of Laws, University College London. He previously worked as Legal Officer to Lord Lester of Herne Hill QC (1999–2001) in the UK House of Lords (second chamber of Parliament). He has also lectured in Constitutional Law at the University of Limerick, Ireland (1998–1999), and is a member of the Irish Bar. He is a member of the European Committee of Social Rights; co-editor of the leading UK academic journal Current Legal Problems; Age Equality Co-ordinator, EU Expert Group on Mapping Anti-Discrimination Law in Areas Outside of Employment and Occupation; UK rapporteur, EU Network of Anti-Discrimination Experts; and was a member of the UK Task Force on the Establishment of a Commission for Equality and Human Rights 2003–2005. He has also published extensively on issues of human rights, constitutional law, equality and anti-discrimination law.

Brynhildur G. Flóvenz
Brynhildur G. Flóvenz is a Lecturer at the University of Iceland, Faculty of Law where her main subjects are women's law, social law and family law. She holds a Cand. Jur. degree from the University of Iceland. She is the Chairwoman of the Board of the Icelandic Human Rights Centre and Chairwoman of the Equality Committee of the University of Iceland. Previously she worked as a lawyer at the Office for Gender Equality in Iceland. She has published a book on The Rights of Persons with Disabilities in Iceland and has published numerous articles, mostly on women's rights and the rights of persons with disabilities.

Professor Ragnhildur Helgadóttir
Ragnhildur Helgadóttir is Professor of Law at the Reykjavík University School of Law. She has taught constitutional law and comparative constitutional law, as well as legal history, administrative law and social security law. She earned her doctorate in law from the University of Virginia in 2004, on a thesis documenting the direct and indirect influence of American law on Nordic constitutional law, inter alia through the European Convention on Human Rights. In addition to her thesis, published as The Influence of American Theories on Judicial Review in Nordic Constitutional Law (Martinus Nijhoff Publishers, 2006), she is co-author of a book on the Icelandic social security system. She has written numerous articles on topics in constitutional and administrative law. Her most recent articles concern the social security system and the rule of law, and article 9 of the ECHR. She is currently doing research on the history of parliamentarism in Iceland and changes in Nordic social security and compensation law systems.

Judge Holger Kallehauge
Holger Kallehauge, Deputy Ombudsman and retired High Court Judge, is a Polio survivor since 1951 and a wheelchair user. He graduated from law school at Copenhagen University in 1961, practised law in the Ministry of Justice and was admitted to the bar. He was appointed as judge in 1973 and as a High Court Judge in 1983. He served as the Vice-President of the Danish Ethical Council 1989–1993 and as Deputy Ombudsman 1994–2008. He is President of the Danish Association of Polio and Accident Victims, since 1973. He was

a member of the UN ad Hoc Committee drafting the UN Convention on the Rights of Persons with Disabilities. He has written a draft bill on internment and compulsory treatment of mentally ill persons and published articles on various subjects of law, such as marriage by proxy, legal aid, agent provocateurs, drug enforcement, law enforcement and mentally disturbed offenders, ethics, ideals and competence of judges, freedom of speech for judges, the human rights of persons with disabilities (2004) and the genesis of a new human rights convention for persons with disabilities (2007).

Dr. Ida Elisabeth Koch

Ida Elisabeth Koch is Senior Researcher, Ph.D. at The Danish Institute for Human Rights. Her primary research field is economic, social and cultural rights, division of powers and the legal content of the notion of human rights as indivisible rights. She has published monographs and articles on these and other topics and is currently writing a book with the following title: *Human Rights as Indivisible Rights – the Protection of Socioeconomic Demands under the European Convention on Human Rights.* She has carried on research at Columbia University (2001), Essex University (2004) and European Inter-University Centre (2006). Ida Elisabeth Koch is a member of ANESC (Academic Network on the European Social Charter). Previously, she worked for 13 years in the Department of Prisons and Probation, and she wrote her Ph.D-thesis on treatment as an alternative to imprisonment for drug addicts and mentally ill persons. Moreover, she has functioned as a secretary for the parliamentary committee monitoring the conditions for people who are deprived of their liberty by administrative decision.

Anna Lawson

Anna Lawson is a Senior Lecturer in Law at the University of Leeds and a member of the University's Centre for Disability Studies and its Centre for European Law and Legal Studies. She teaches a range of subjects which include an undergraduate course in Equality Law and a postgraduate course in Disability Rights and Law. Her research interests centre around disability, human rights and equality law and she has written about relevant issues at national, European and international levels. Anna worked closely with the UK's Disability Rights Commission and co-edited a book with its special advisor, Caroline Gooding. She has also acted as a disability law expert in a number of EU funded research projects and as a legal trainer in an EU project which has involved raising awareness and understanding of the disability-related aspects of the Framework Employment Directive 2000 in a number of central and eastern European countries. Anna became disabled at the age of seven and, since the age of eighteen, has played an active part in the work of various disability-related NGOs, particularly those concerned with visual impairment.

Janet E. Lord

Janet E. Lord is a founding partner of BlueLaw LLP, a service-disabled, veteran-owned international law and international development firm based in Washington, DC where she directs and implements human rights, disability & development programming. An international lawyer by training, she holds law degrees from the University of Edinburgh (LLB; LLM) and the George Washington University Law School (LLM). Janet participated in all of the negotiating sessions for the UN Disability Convention, serving as legal advisor to Disabled Peoples International and providing counsel to the Goverments of Mexico and Costa Rica. She teaches on human rights and disability at the American University School of International Service (with Katherine Guernsey) and the University of Maryland School of Law. She has published both scholarly and practitioner-oriented works on the human rights of persons with disabilities. She is the co-author of *Human Rights YES!*, a participatory human rights education manual on the rights of persons with disabilities.

Professor Gerard Quinn

Gerard Quinn is the United Nations Focal Point for Disability among National Human Rights Institutions (NHRIs) and is a member of the Human Rights Commission of Ireland. He has taught comparative disability law since the early 1990s and established a Disability Law & Policy Research Unit at his University in Ireland (National University of Ireland, Faculty of Law, Galway). He has worked in various capacities with and in the European Commission on disability law reform and recently directed its Network of Legal Experts on Disability Discrimination Law. He is a former First Vice-President of the European Committee on Social Rights (Council of Europe) as well as a former of Director of Research at the Law Reform Commission of Ireland. He was a member of the Irish Government's Commission on the Status of Persons with Disabilities. Together with Theresia Degener and others he co-wrote a 2002 Study for the Office of the UN High Commissioner on Human Rights on Disability. He served as a delegate at most of the drafting sessions for the UN Convention on the Rights of Persons with Disabilities. He led the delegation from Rehabilitation International at the Working Group on the Convention (2004). He is a Professor of Law at the National University of Ireland and a graduate of Harvard Law School. He has a child with a disability.

Professor Michael Stein
Michael Stein holds a J.D. from Harvard Law School and a Ph.D. from Cambridge University. Currently the Executive Director of the Harvard Project on Disability as well as Cabell Professor of Law at William & Mary Law School, he has taught at Harvard, New York University, and Stanford law schools. An internationally recognized disability rights expert, Professor Stein participated in the drafting of the United Nations Convention on the Rights of Persons with Disabilities, and actively consults with international governments and national human rights institutions on their disability laws and policies. He serves on several disability rights advisory boards and blue ribbon disability research panels, and conducts human rights training for persons with disabilties worldwide. Stein also acts as a legal advisor to Rehabilitation International and to the Special Olympics. He is currently an American Bar Association Commissioner on Mental and Physical Disability Law. Professor Stein is the recipient of various grants and awards and has been a fellow in both the East Asian Legal Studies Program and the Human Rights Program at Harvard Law School. Professor Stein's extensive scholarship has been published in various leading journals.

Professor Rannveig Traustadóttir
Rannveig Traustadóttir is Professor and Director of the Center for Disability Studies in the Faculty of Social and Human Sciences at the University of Iceland. Much of her research has examined the intersection of disability and gender, as well as other categories of inequality, such as social class, ethnicity, and sexuality, and how these create multiple layers of discrimination and social exclusion in disabled people's lives. Recently her research has also examined the experiences of children and youth of growing up with disability. She has been one of the leaders in developing Disability Studies as a scholarly field in the Nordic countries and was the president of NNDR, The Nordic Network on Disability Research, for seven years (2000–2007).

Professor Lisa Waddington
Professor Lisa Waddington holds the European Disability Forum Chair in European Disability Law at Maastricht University, the Netherlands. The Chair is based on a unique cooperation between the disability movement and academia, and has resulted in the first such Chair in this field. She has published widely in both the areas of disability law and European and comparative equality and non-discrimination law and has recently completed work, with a team of colleagues, on a casebook on European Non-Discrimination Law (D. Schiek, L. Waddington, M. Bell (eds.) with the collaboration of T. Choudhury, O. De Schutter, J. Gerards, A. McColgan and G. Moon, *Cases, Materials and Text on National, Supranational and International Non-Discrimination Law* (Oxford, Hart Publishing, 2007)). The Casebook includes, amongst others, an extensive

comparative analysis of the concept of reasonable accommodation in favour of disabled people. Professor Waddington is the disability coordinator for the European Network of Legal Experts in the Non-Discrimination Field and a board member of the European Academic Network of Experts on Disability (ANED). During the negotiations on the UN Convention, the European disability movement was represented by the European Disability Forum, and Prof. Waddington provided legal advice to the director of EDF.

Index

www.ingramcontent.com/pod-product-compliance
Ingram Content Group UK Ltd.
Pitfield, Milton Keynes, MK11 3LW, UK
UKHW022209051026
15624UKWH00001B/69

9 789004 169715